ESQUIRE'S GREAT MEN and MOMENTS IN SPORTS

Esquire's GREAT MEN

ILLUSTRATED

and MOMENTS in SPORTS

BY THE EDITORS OF ESQUIRE

HARPER & BROTHERS PUBLISHERS
NEW YORK

Library of Congress catalog card number: 61–10232

CONTENTS

8. GOOD SPORTS ALL

9. "SPORTS: HAIL OR FAREWELL?"

PREFACE

Great men and great moments in sports have been a particular interest of the editors of *Esquire* for nearly three decades. Nearly every great writer who put his pen to the task of capturing this in words and the artists (like John Groth) who were intent on picturing the action of sport have appeared at one time or another in the pages of *Esquire*. Often great moments have been described by men who themselves participated in them, as in this excerpt from an article by Charles W. Paddock, who had twice, in the Olympic Games of 1924 and 1928, come within inches of being a champion himself. It appeared in the first issue of *Esquire* (Autumn, 1933), describing the way great men go down.

"It is hard for the layman to understand how a champion in any sport can go to pieces all at once. Sometimes it is due to a lack of condition. But not often. The man who loses his title is generally as physically fit as his successor. But he is seldom as mentally keen. Having reached the goal, he does not possess the same eager flame of desire, and the longer he stays out of the game, the more difficult it is for him to come back again.

"We often get the impression that a star today is only a shell of himself, tomorrow. In such cases the deterioration has been so subtle and gradual that we fail to recognize it. Yet it has been going on just the same. There are no exceptions. Great athletes like Gene Tunney in boxing, Paavo Nurmi in running, Johnny Weissmuller in swimming, Jim Thorpe in football, Babe Ruth in baseball, Helen Wills Moody and Bill Tilden in tennis and Bobby Jones in golf have either retired while still at the top or have possessed the happy faculty of being able to make perennial comebacks. This has been due to extraordinary natural ability or lack of severe competition.

"Most of us in sport, however, suddenly drop from some place near the top to the bottom and stay there. It is not such a remarkable thing, when you analyze it, that a man can wake up one morning as champion in his particular sport and go to bed that night with no more athletic future than a broken-down gigolo. It happens regularly. I know.

"No finer illustration of the futility of trying to stay at the top too long can be pictured than the story of Jack Dempsey at Philadelphia. He told me after his fight with James Joseph Tunney that he knew in the eighth round of that battle that he could not win. Time and again he hit Gene with everything he had and Tunney always came back for more until Jack was sure that he could not knock Tunney out. He was also equally certain that he had been outpointed and outboxed to such an extent that even if he should win the eighth, the ninth and the tenth rounds, nevertheless he would still lose the championship of the world.

"It would have been relatively easy under those circumstances for Dempsey to have taken one of Tunney's blows a little bit harder than it actually came and to have been counted out. By doing so he felt that he might have saved himself for a return match. But the code of a championship is to fight to the finish. And Dempsey that night at Philadelphia was still a champion. He stayed on his feet.

"Physically, Dempsey was badly battered and bruised. But in time he recovered his full strength, though one eye continued to give him trouble. But Jack never again regained the same mental poise in the ring that he had possessed before he faced Tunney. It was firmly rooted in his mind that 'a champion cannot come back' and that the terrible beating he had taken from Gene had sapped his strength too much for a successful rematch.

"It was Dempsey's attitude more than his legs which whipped him at Chicago in the return bout. He could not get away from the idea that people had him pegged as a has-been and that what had happened to Jim Jeffries at Reno would happen to him. The most daring fighter of all time, who had the gameness to stay on his feet at Philadelphia on a night when he was ill, did not have the courage to conquer himself.

"Athletes, except in very rare instances, do not go to pieces overnight. Only one man has beaten them and generally if they could retain confidence in themselves, they would have a good chance to regain their championships. Certainly, they should still be able to conquer the rest of their opponents. But such is not the case.

"The defeated champion loses his belief in himself along with his crown. He is swayed by what people say and the moth-eaten tradition that 'they can't come back.' Sometimes the star is bewildered by the decisions of the officials or the roar of the crowd.

"Incentive melts away. The ex-champion says to himself: 'I have already been at the top. The best that I can do is get back there again. What's the use of going through all of the hard work and making the sacrifice which victory demands?'

"Some 'wilt inside' when they so much as see a youthful rival and lose before the contest even begins. Norman Ross, 'The Big Moose' of swimming, who was the greatest champion the game had known, went to pieces overnight. He won the Inter-Allied swimming championship for the United States singlehanded, and then came back to victory again in the 1920 Olympics.

"Soon after his return home he one day watched a long-legged youngster swimming like mad in Lake Michigan. The moment he saw him, Ross afterward told me, he some way sensed that he had met his match. He called the boy out of the water, found out that he knew nothing about the science of swimming, but was anxious to learn. So he arranged a tryout for him at the Illinois Athletic Club tank in Chicago. The youth broke the pool record the first time he swam there and within a few months shattered many of the world's best marks, winning international fame for America and several Olympic championships.

"Blissful ignorance of the history of swimming, coupled with youthful confidence, made this boy unbeatable and brought him immortal athletic fame as 'the human fish' and later screen glory as 'Tarzan' Weissmuller.

"A friend writes of Johnny: 'He couldn't swim. His father couldn't swim. His mother couldn't swim. He didn't have any yen to become a swimmer. He went into the water the same as a kid taking medicine. Yet he came out the fastest swimmer in the world and with a physique which has made him into a motion-picture idol.'

"While Weissmuller has risen into the world,

Norman Ross, 'The Big Moose,' who discovered him, has been almost entirely forgotten as an athlete. Ross lost that 'something' which made him the greatest champion of his time, during the first few minutes that he watched the Austrian boy in Lake Michigan. Norman had beaten every swimming star of his generation, but he could not conquer his own inferiority complex or overcome the knowledge that his friends were saying that Johnny was going to be faster than himself.

"As a matter of fact, there are certain distances where 'The Big Moose,' if he had only believed in himself, could always have beaten Johnny Weissmuller. He had greater strength, a cooler head and more stamina. Yet he wilted in a single day.

"This same timidity has played havoc with the swimming career of Duke Kahanamoku, the famous Hawaiian champion who won the Olympic hundred-meters title in 1912 at Stockholm and again at Antwerp in 1920. Duke finished second to Weissmuller at Paris in '24 and now that Johnny is out of amateur competition, Duke is again the best in the world, even though he has turned the corner past forty.

"No one has ever broken his world's record for fifty yards of twenty-two and three-fifths seconds, though Weissmuller tried on many occasions along with the countless other speedsters during the last twenty years. Duke has no confidence in himself. He has heard the world say that he is too old for the game and was never in a class with Johnny Weissmuller, and he has believed what he has heard.

"Bobby Jones, the only golfer ever to win the American Amateur and Open, and British Amateur and Open championships in the same year, has suffered a similar reaction. Just as soon as he retired from competition he 'let down.' His scores in exhibition and practice rounds have been far below his former standard and it is doubtful indeed if he could ever reach the top again.

"It is not a matter of condition with Bobby or the other ex-champions. They have simply lost their will to win. Most of them have in the final analysis, I believe, been dependent upon outside opinion. The grandstand has more than played its part.

"Tennis fans will recall when the graceful Mlle. Suzanne Lenglen first came to the United States to participate in our national women's championships at Forest Hills. She possessed all of the glorious confidence which comes from a long series of brilliant victories. She had been winning titles since she was seventeen and in her early twenties she was not only universally recognized as the finest feminine player in the world, but the greatest of all time. Then she faced Mrs. Molla Mallory, the United States champion whom she had beaten abroad, but who was the favorite of American tennis fans.

"The Frenchwoman sensed the confidence of her opponent, playing in her own 'back yard' with the gallery behind her. The great Lenglen, who had never been beaten, suddenly fell deathly ill. The weight of a nation seemed to beat down on her racket. Her arms grew heavy from returning Mallory's steady serves. She lost faith in herself. She thought of the responsibility of winning for France and the strain was too much. She was on the verge of collapse before the match had gone two sets and she was forced to abandon play. That was her single defeat during more than a decade of championship tennis. The grandstand was entirely responsible. She allowed the spectators to defeat her—not Molla Mallory.

"Five years later at Cannes, Suzanne Lenglen faced another great American champion who had not yet come into her own—Helen Wills. This time, the Frenchwoman had the gallery with her. She made a grand entrance, arriving from her villa at Nice in a Voisin motorcar. She darted with a springy step from her machine and threw a light kiss to the crowd. She was greeted by a mighty roar. *Vive la Suzanne! Vive la belle Suzanne!*

"An army of cameramen assaulted her. She posed and smiled for them and later stood beside Helen Wills for more pictures. Helen wore a rose-colored sweater, a middy blouse and a pleated skirt. She looked about as emotional as Buster Keaton. Suzanne was resplendent in a salmon-colored, closely knitted sweater and a short white skirt, with a salmon-colored headdress, which was almost a turban, to match. The California champion was stolid and sturdy; the girl from France was effervescent, like the champagne of the famous Rheims Valley.

They formed a great contrast—placidity versus impetuosity.

"But the ruling spirit of that battle was the grandstand itself. Suzanne had the confidence of knowing almost every spectator was cheering for her and her play became superhuman. Helen Wills fought courageously and well, but the odds were against her and she finally lost 6-3, 7-5. Yet in defeat, little 'Poker Face' had conquered.

"Suzanne Lenglen never met her again. She preferred to retire rather than face such an opponent. Lenglen later toured the United States as a professional, appearing in many exhibitions, but she was no longer the champion of former days. Those two sets at Cannes marked the zenith of her play.

"Meeting Helen Wills had much the same effect upon her as did his professional football debut on Red Grange, the galloping ghost of Illinois. Red, who had flashed to national gridiron fame as a sophomore against Michigan and who had come back to glory in his senior year against Pennsylvania, as the greatest halfback in an open field that the game has ever known, always played with the grandstand behind him in college competition. With the gallant Earl Britton to run interference and a great line to shove him into the open, Grange relied upon his genius to carry the ball. No man was ever a more brilliant master of the art of changing pace or of shaking off tacklers by a simple twist of his wriggling hips than the Illinois halfback. Behind his natural ability was the inspiration of the crowd which gave him confidence to do the impossible.

"In his first professional game, Grange found himself in an entirely different atmosphere. The crowd was cynical, skeptical and unemotional. The players were the same. Team spirit was lacking and in its place were cold hard fundamentals. Men ran interference like clockwork, but without enthusiasm. No one was ready to 'die for dear old Rutgers' that Grange might gallop to glory.

"The boy, if he made good at all, would have to do so entirely on his own. Red realized that his ability was beyond and not behind the line of scrimmage. He tried valiantly to break away. The inspiration was lacking. The crowd had paid to see Grange run and when he was smothered on almost every play, they soon lost interest. No one was more alive to their indifference than the redhead. He tried his best, but it was not good enough.

"Though Grange later remade himself into a fine all-around football player, he was never again the ghost of the gridiron. His genius deserted him overnight, just as the spark of immortality was snuffed out of Hal Chase, the greatest first baseman of all time, when he was barred from organized ball.

"Looking back at the record of our heroes of sport, it seems to me that public opinion—the grandstand—is the most important factor in victory or defeat. Men are made in striving to give their best and when they have reached the top and incentive no longer burns so brightly, and they hear and read that they are 'old men' in competition, the majority soon commence to believe it themselves, and the first good boy who happens along sends them hurtling down the hill to athletic oblivion."

"The bigger they come, the harder they fall" goes the adage, and the following pictures illustrate two big "falls." They were printed, along with the accompanying editorial comment, in the November 1947 Esquire.

"With your mind sharpened to a keen competitive pitch by all this reading, we couldn't resist bringing out the two photographs (opposite) for your speculation and debate. The first one shows Jess Willard taking the heavyweight championship from Jack Johnson. Poor old Jack is gone now, gone from the ring where they feared the terrible skill of his fists, and gone, happily, too, from the flea circus on West Forty-Second Street where he spent his last days as an exhibit for the heavy spenders in a penny arcade. But the debate over whether he took a dive for Willard is still just as hot as that tropic sun in Havana, thirty-two years ago.

"A lot of money changed hands that day. And, say the yes boys, look at the picture of Johnson down and out on his back. Yeah, 'out' while he shields his eyes from the sun and takes a ten-second rest cure, to say nothing of a satchel of cash from the fixers.

"Well, we don't know. But a few days ago we were fussing around with some pictures of the sec-

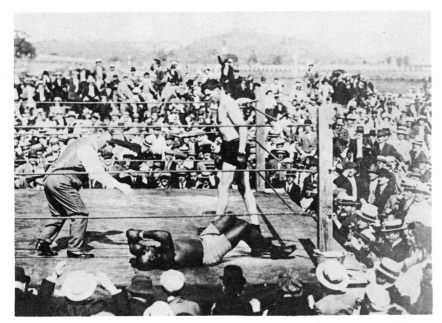

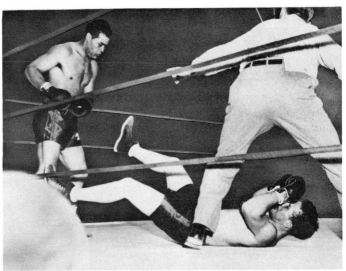

ond Louis-Conn fight and we came across the one which is shown here. To begin with, let's state that we are absolutely convinced of the honesty of that fight or any other in which Joe Louis fought, and we hasten to emphasize the truthful fact that everybody recognizes that Joe knocked Bill kicking, for good, in the eighth. With that established, let's look at the picture. Look at Conn. There wasn't any sun in his eyes that night. It was 11:42 P.M. in the Yankee Stadium. There may have been some slight starlight, but most of the stars Billy was counting at that moment were appearing by courtesy of Mr. Louis. Now look at Jack Johnson.

"Louis and Willard are also startlingly similar in stance. Joe is standing there, arms hooked for an-other haymaker in case young Mr. Conn is so ill-advised as to return to the perpendicular within ten seconds. Joe is standing, then, the way a guy does who has just flattened another guy. So is Wil-lard. Could it be, then, that Jess had just clouted Johnson on the whiskers with a real punch? Could it be that when you catch one of these, and flop on your fanny, that your arms bounce up around your eyes when you are hit? As we say, we don't know, because we weren't in Havana that day, and we have only the evidence of this picture to go by—only it looks as though you can figure the Johnson-Willard deal two ways now, if you want to."

And so we recommend a brief bout with *Es-quire's Great Men and Moments in Sports.*

1

BOXING: **THE MANLY ART**

A book about sport, like a prize fight, ought to be a "crowd pleaser" if it comes out swinging. From the dozens of articles chronicling the great men and moments of ring history which have appeared in the over quarter-century of Esquire, here are six contenders, each of which packs a wallop. Ladies and gentlemen, introducing Joe Walcott, Billy Miske, Harry Greb, Jack Dempsey, Joe Louis and Stanley Ketchel. Representative of what is to follow in other rounds, you will find in each of these champion's corner a champion of sports reporting seconding them: Red Smith, Arthur Daley, Jimmy Cannon, Paul Gallico and James R. Fair. Time was when a fight lasted until one man failed to answer the bell. Now a championship is decided in fifteen rounds. But in the long run an athlete's reputation rests not so much upon his own feats as upon how (or more pertinently if) they are remembered. The longest fight never lasted a day. The greatest champion never held his title twenty years. The memory of the crowd survives the strength, courage, stamina and reflexes of the greatest of champions. A new "tiger" always waits to take the belt from any man, because he is a man and his body is perishable. If great men and great moments have any immortality it is because of the things that are said and written about them. When the Broadway wit Wilson Mizner, who was Stanley Ketchel's companion and sometimes manager, heard of the fighter's untimely death, he said: "I don't believe it. Start counting ten over him and he'll get up." In a sense, that is what each of these authors has done for his subject. Re-creating the accomplishments and exploits of great men with admiration and excitement, they have somehow succeeded in bringing them back to life, in their prime, in the center of the ring, the crowd cheering, the lights blazing down, the cigar smoke hanging heavy in the stifling air. They begin to count ten over them, and so far not one has been counted out.

The Hungry Man Makes Good

HE CLIMBED THROUGH THE ROPES INTO the ring at Forbes Field, Pittsburgh, on Wednesday night, July 18, 1951, and the crowd of 28,272 cheered him as his balding pate poked above the canvas. He didn't feel like an old man, but he was. Some fighters make the top before they're twenty-one, but Arnold Raymond Cream was twenty-one years past his first professional fight. He'd already seen his thirty-seventh birthday, and had six kids waiting for him at home. He called himself Joe Walcott, the boxing writers called him the old pappy guy, and he was coming into the ring to fight for the big one, the heavyweight championship of the world. The bookies held it at six to one against him, and nobody wanted to bet.

He'd had four other shots at the title—two against Joe Louis, two against Ezzard Charles, who was dancing about now in the opposite corner, confident, ready. But for Joe Walcott the trail led back to a time long before the first Louis match, to the first fights in 1930 and the dismal years when boxing hadn't brought him enough money to feed his family and he'd worked as a hod carrier and a garbage collector.

Joe Walcott's first thirty years were one long hard-luck story. His father died when he was fourteen years old, and he left school to work in a soup factory, push wheelbarrows, sell newspapers and groceries. He was a tough kid, with a lot of street fighting behind him, and he began to hang around Battling Mac's Gym in his home town of Camden, New Jersey. He got his first fight when he was sixteen, and he won it with a first-round knockout. His share of the purse was $7.50.

So he built himself up as a prelim fighter, winning twelve in a row before somebody—he doesn't remember the name—knocked him over. He got married when he was a little short of eighteen, and the next year he won the light-heavyweight championship of Southern New Jersey, the only title he

ever held before the big one. Typhoid fever caught him then and he spent the next two months in bed while his family tried to live on a relief check of $9.50 a week. When he got off his back, nobody was much interested in the ex-light-heavyweight champion of Southern New Jersey. He fought for supper money in clubs so small the record books don't know about them, and sometimes he lost because he was too hungry and too weak to fight.

When he had to have cash he did odd jobs. He kept an eye out for automobiles in distress—nobody could refuse a tip to a man who fixed his flat. He won some medium-sized fights—including the main event in one of Jack Dempsey's "White Hope" tournaments—and pulled himself into the ranks of the second-rate, where Al Ettore and Abe Simon knocked him kicking.

Finally, in 1941, he stopped kidding himself, quit the ring and took a job in the Camden shipyards. But the old lure became too much for him and in the summer of 1944 he put on the gloves again. After one of his fights he met Felix Bocchicchio, a Camden promoter, who decided to boost him.

With money behind him Walcott cut his way slowly through the heavyweight class, and Joe Louis' managers signed him to fight for the title. Then they told Louis the man he was going to fight, and the champion had to admit he'd never heard of Joe Walcott.

Those days were behind Joe Walcott as he stood in the Forbes Field ring and listened to the referee's gabble, which he'd heard so many times before. Everybody knew him now, and his share of the purse for this fight alone would come to nearly $50,000. But all his life he'd prayed to win a championship, and he'd prayed hard. Nobody else had ever received five cracks at the title, and he was an old pappy guy—he wouldn't get another. He had to win it now.

out of the sky and exploded on the button, and the champion was down.

At the count of four Charles stirred for the first time, working his gloves on the canvas; at six he raised his head; at eight he got his arms loose; at ten he jerked to his knees. Referee Buck McTiernan waved that the fight was over, and Charles dropped back to the canvas, dead to the world.

In the neutral corner Joe fell to his knees in a half-faint; then his friends were storming into the ring, the ball park was screaming, and they brought over the mikes and asked him to talk to 60,000,000 people.

He'd plodded to the end of the rainbow and he'd found the silver belt. The pappy guy was champ!

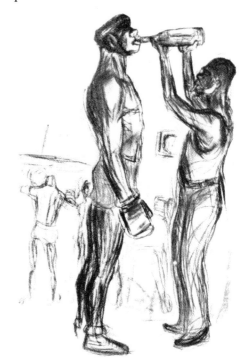

The bell rang and he came out and touched gloves with the champion, and then he waited, sparring easily, feeling Charles out to see how he wanted to fight. Charles was waiting, too, and the first round was dull and went to the champion. The second round was a repeat, with Charles landing solidly toward the end; after that, Jersey Joe was boss.

He snapped punishing hooks at Charles through the next four rounds, took the champion's counters and came out for the seventh round fresh and unhurt. They sparred for half a minute near the center of the ring. Then Joe feinted a left jab and Charles moved his head; Walcott's left hook came

Christmas Is for Giving   by RED SMITH

WHEN HE HEARD ABOUT THE MATCH, George Barton reached for the telephone and called his old friend, Jack Reddy, manager of fighters and promoter of fights.

George Barton was a Minneapolis newspaperman, perhaps the most widely respected and warmly liked sports writer in the Northwest. He was a small man, not much bigger in 1923 than when he boxed Terrible Terry McGovern, featherweight champion of the world. When he was through with fighting, George refereed bouts and later became a member of the Minnesota Athletic Commission.

When Reddy answered the phone, George said:

"Don't ever speak to me again. I never thought you were so hungry for a buck that you'd kill a friend for it."

"Hold everything," Reddy said. "Please don't write anything for ten minutes. I'm coming up to see you."

In Barton's office, Reddy said, "You know how it is with Billy, of course."

Barton said he knew how it was with Billy Miske. He had known this German-American kid since Miske started fighting out of St. Paul in the early years of the century. George had seen Miske grow up as a light-heavyweight good enough to fight the best of the big men—Jack Dempsey, Battling Levinsky, Tommy Gibbons, Harry Greb, Kid Norfolk, Charley Weinert, Gunboat Smith, Fred Fulton.

In 1918, when Dempsey was at his incomparable best, Miske had gone six rounds with him in a no-decision bout in Philadelphia. In 1920 Miske had fought Dempsey for the heavyweight title in Benton Harbor, Michigan, and Jack knocked him out in the third round.

Now it was autumn of 1923 and Miske had not fought since January. He had not fought because he couldn't. He was sick with a mortal illness; too sick, even, to go to the gymnasium for exercise. He knew he was dying. Barton knew it. Reddy knew.

For months, Billy had stayed at home with Mrs. Miske and their three children. He couldn't work

and there wasn't much money and Christmas was coming.

"So," Reddy told Barton, "a little while ago Miske came to see me." And here's the story Reddy told:

"Jack," Miske said, "get me a fight."

"You're kidding," Reddy said. "You're not serious."

"Get me a fight," Miske said.

"But, Billy—"

"Listen, Jack," Miske said. "Please listen. I'm

broke. I can't afford to buy things for the wife and kids. I haven't got long to go, Jack, you know that. I want my family around me, happy, just one more Christmas. I won't be here for another."

"I don't like to say this," Reddy told him, "but you know it's true, Bill, as well as I do. If you tried to fight now, in your condition, you could be killed. You could die in the ring."

At that, Miske's face twisted. He grinned without humor.

"Jack," he said, "wouldn't that be better than sitting in a rocking chair waiting for it?" He said, "I'm a fighter, Jack."

Reddy protested. He argued. He refused, flatly and positively.

"I'd do almost anything for you, Bill," he said. "You know that. But I won't help kill you. I'd have to face your wife and kids—"

"Jack," Billy persisted, "please. Get me a fight."

"Do one thing for me," Reddy said at last. "Go to the gym and start working out. Let's see if you can get in some sort of shape. Then we'll see about getting you a match."

But Miske was looking at him straight.

"Stop it, Jack," Billy said. "Quit kidding. You know I can't get in shape. You know I can't go to the gym. Get me a fight, Jack. I've gotta have one more Christmas."

That's the story as Reddy told it. Now he was sitting in George Barton's office and he said, "Well, what would you do, George? You know Billy. I've got him a fight."

It was because of that fight that Barton had telephoned Reddy. Jack had signed Miske to box Bill Brennan in Omaha, Nebraska.

It was a good match, a match that figured to draw. Brennan never had been a great fighter but he was big and rough and strong. He was a sort of policeman in the heavyweight ranks, a fellow whom aspiring challengers had to beat to show they were worthy of a shot at the title.

Not many had beaten the big Irishman from County Mayo. He'd been knocked out only three times, and twice it was Dempsey who stiffened him. He was, at this time, one of the two men in the world who had gone more than ten rounds with the champion. In 1920 Brennan had astonished a crowd in Madison Square Garden by whacking

Dempsey around and tearing an ear half loose before Jack knocked him out in the twelfth round.

Brennan and Miske were a cinch to draw a good gate. They had met three times in three good fights. Miske had won the first in fifteen rounds. The other two were no-decision bouts. And Miske was popular in Omaha. The only fight he'd had in 1923 had been there; he had knocked out a character named Harry Foley in the first round.

"So he's going to get himself one more payday, if he lives," Reddy told Barton. "Are you going to stop it, George?"

Barton wasn't going to write anything to stop it. What the hell, he was a friend of Miske's, too.

On November 7, 1923, Miske got into the ring with Brennan in Omaha. Billy had not been able to train. Considering how the game is administered today, it seems remarkable that he could have disguised his condition. Perhaps supervision by boxing commissions wasn't so strict then. Or maybe a doctor did look him over and declared, as doctors often declare before big bouts, that this was the finest specimen of manhood he'd ever had the privilege of poking in the gizzard.

At any rate, Miske did get into the ring. He boxed Brennan for three rounds. In the fourth he knocked him out. As it turned out, this was Brennan's last fight. Six months later he was killed by gunmen in New York.

Miske took something like $2400 out of the bout. He went home and spent it on a big Christmas for the family. On December 25 his wife and kids were around him and happy. On December 26 he called Jack Reddy.

"Come get me to a hospital, Jack," he said. "I'm dying."

Reddy got him to a hospital. On New Year's Day, Billy Miske died.

The Wildest Tiger

by JAMES R. FAIR

THE MEN WHO FOUGHT HIM WILL never forget him because it was from him that they learned about "sneak" punching, heeling, hitting on the breakaways, slapping, butting, etc. It was from him that they learned about sticking the thumb in the eye without detection by the referee, about a training regimen that was pleasant and altogether different from the accepted routine of ten miles on the road before breakfast. His roadwork consisted largely of bouncing up and down the stairs in the red-light district.

Turn back the years to 1923. The wildest tiger, or Harry Greb of Pittsburgh, was world's middleweight champion. He suddenly came up with the notion that he was only a "prophet in his own town" and decided to remove to Hollywood,

"where," he said, "the pastures are greener and the skirts swishier." He told a pal, a sports columnist, he would stand for quotes to this effect. In bold, black type the size of an egg, the columnist imparted to his readers Greb's farewell message, which stated that Greb could get along nicely if he never again set foot in Pittsburgh. Following which the only man to hold a decision over Tunney—and it was as decisive as a knockout—lit out for Hollywood.

The pastures there proved greener, indeed. Viewing Greb's work for the first time, Hollywood fans lauded him for the rare artistry displayed against Ted Moore, English middleweight champion, who with bowed head and bloody brows moped off to a rest cure. But two weeks later when

Greb played a return engagement, this time using up a native son so badly he had to be taken to the Missing Persons Bureau for identification, the pastures turned brown from the scorching of the fans, who yelled bum, thief, loafer, scoundrel and so forth.

It was all Greb needed to make him forget about being a prophet back home in Pittsburgh, where, unlike those uncomplimentary Californians, the fans merely smiled and collected their bets as Greb's victims, like sick dogs, limped off to lick

their wounds. Still, Greb had been rather severe in his chastisement of Pittsburgh only a few weeks before, and to return—and save face—he needed an excuse. A fight in the East, for instance. So he pleaded, via telegraph, with his columnist friend to put a bug in some promoter's bonnet. Slyly, the columnist suggested to Benny Franklin, a Baltimore promoter, that it would be less than difficult to secure the ring services of the middle-weight champ.

"Who," Franklin asked, "would I put on with Greb and how much would the champ work for?"

"Feed him Fay Kiser in a nontitle bout," the columnist said owlishly, "and Greb'll work for marbles. Why? Because he's already whipped Kiser eleven times before—in Pittsburgh, Youngstown, Cumberland and all around the fistic loop—but never in Baltimore."

Kiser was a Maryland boy of considerable fame. He boxed Soldier Bob Martin for the A. E. F.

heavyweight title in France and it was the concensus of everybody except the officials that Kiser won. Mustered out of the service, he fought Soldier Bob in Baltimore, but by some strange coincidence the ring lights went out every time Soldier Bob was in trouble and when they came back on he was all right again. It was under these somewhat mysterious circumstances, after being flattened at least once by Kiser, that Martin won the second fight.

But it established Kiser as a box-office draw in Baltimore. And in there with the terrific Greb he figured to break the turnstiles down. Promoter Franklin began beating vigorously on the ballyhoo tom-toms, even before offering Greb the match. Then he telegraphed him an offer of $3000 to meet Kiser in a nontitle fight. Greb was so anxious to come East that he skipped the "nontitle" angle as he would a fat old doll and volunteered to put his title on the line. Tex Rickard would have paid him that much for the privilege of introducing him from the ring. It was worth more than $3000 just so see the immortal Greb climb into the ring, bow his busted phiz around and about, then climb out without so much as tossing a punch. Yet here was Greb, as unpredictable as a feather in a cyclone, agreeing to defend his title for such chicken feed! It nearly floored the slightly apoplectic Franklin, a former featherweight now bulking 250 pounds, who hastily got out life-size posters of the principals announcing that Baltimore was to see its first championship fight since the early days of America.

Greb's journalistic benefactor was waiting on the station platform in Baltimore when the champ piled off the train three weeks later with a brace of ladies he slapdab introduced as Hollywood glamour propositions but who were something less than that.

"They're for you," Greb said, nodding to the girls.

"No, thanks," the columnist said, "I don't want to go to the sneezer on the Mann Act."

Neither did Greb, when the possibility occurred to him. Whereat he left the ladies, looking very forlorn, standing on the platform.

On the way to the hotel the columnist said:

"You damn fool, why did you sign for a title defense when Franklin offered to show you at over-the-weight?"

"I didn't," Greb said soberly.

"You did so," the columnist said. "I saw your wire and you volunteered to make 160 pounds and that automatically makes it a title defense."

"Anyhow," Greb said, dismissing the matter in the same calm manner in which he stuck his thumb into an opponent's eye, "I ain't defending my title and taking a chance on losing it on a home-town decision, or a foul, or somethin', for a measly 3000 potatoes."

The columnist withdrew for a moment. Then he asked:

"Do you know the date of the fight?"

"Sometime this week," Greb said.

"Tomorrow night," the columnist said. "You barely get in under the wire."

"I never run out on a fight yet," Greb grumbled; "I'm reliable."

"If you don't defend your title tomorrow night," the columnist warned, "the boxing commissioner may question your reliability."

Greb's jowls were beefy and he looked woefully out of shape.

"Been training hard?" the columnist asked, with implications.

"Between us," Greb said, "no; I ain't had a glove on in three weeks. But why should I worry? I've beat Kiser eleven times already."

"Then," the columnist snapped, "why are you worrying about tomorrow night for?"

Greb realized he had led with his chin and refused to answer. But he finally came out of his shell and agreed to talk with Franklin and the Chairman of the Maryland Boxing Commission. Between long periods of small talk Greb asked numerous concessions but refused to grant any himself. The boxing commissioner sought to break the monotony.

"What'cha weigh, Greb?" he asked.

"Hundred seventy-three and a half," Greb replied.

"Humph!" the commissioner said. "Thirteen and a half pounds over the middleweight limit."

Greb squirmed.

"What's Kiser weigh?" he put in.

"Hundred eighty," the commissioner said, ob-viously pulling Greb's leg, because Kiser had peeled down to 158½.

"Sonofabitch!" Greb yelled.

"What does that make you?" the commissioner chided.

It was getting late and all parties concerned were fighting off sleep. Finally, having conceded nothing, Greb fell over on the bed and went to sleep.

Came nine o'clock that evening and Greb saun-tered into his dressing room, his hat pulled down to hide his cocked right eye into which many a retaliatory thumb had been stuck. With him was Al Foss, a referee he had picked up between trains the day before in Pittsburgh.

"The best referee in the world," Greb said, by way of subtly announcing that his own private referee would be the third man in the ring.

But the commissioner saw through the thin veil.

"Charley Short," he said, "is going to handle the bout."

Greb said no.

The commissioner said yes. He harangued Greb but Greb was adamant. Exasperated, the commis-sioner asked Greb why he objected to Short as the referee. Greb said he was afraid Short would let Kiser claim the title on a foul. He said Kiser was pretty cute inside those ropes and might go down yelling "foul" and that Short would award him Greb's title.

"Is that all that's bothering you?" the commis-sioner moaned.

Greb said, "Sure."

The commissioner turned to Short and said, "If Kiser goes down count him out, regardless of the circumstances."

"Okay," Short said. "I'll count him out even if Greb kicks him on the chin."

"Does that suit you?" the commissioner asked Greb.

"No," Greb said. "I still don't trust Short."

"Okay," the commissioner said. "I'll bar you from boxing everywhere I can extend the ban. Promoter Franklin will refund the money to the fans and you may have a lawsuit on your hands."

He moved toward the door, but Greb called him back and said, "Can't we compromise?"

"What the hell," the commissioner bawled,

"have I been trying to do ever since you hit town?"

Greb then suggested that roly-poly Franklin, whose blood pressure was so high it had broken most of the Johns Hopkins pressure gauges, be permitted to referee. Franklin finally agreed and the commissioner begrudgingly consented. There was still the matter of Greb's weight, since he was thirteen and a half pounds over the middleweight limit and the customers had paid to see a championship contest. But the commissioner said he wouldn't be too technical.

As Greb hustled up the aisle to the ring wild-eyed spectators grabbed at his dressing gown in vain attempts to tear off souvenirs.

The bell rang for round one.

Greb stood in his corner waiting for Kiser to come across the ring. They clashed, with Greb holding onto the top rope with his right hand, while with his left hand, extended at full length, he proceeded to carve his initials and other fancy designs on Kiser's face as he came close. Greb wasn't in shape and was stalling. Rolls of fat bulged over his green trunks. He was easily winded. It was a messy fight.

Came, after much puffing and fumbling, the twelfth round. Kiser closed in and Greb gave him the thumb in the left eye. *Touché!* Greb was beginning to look good. He pushed Kiser's head back with a long right and as Kiser fell in and sought to hold, Greb gave him the thumb in the other eye. Kiser protested. Referee Franklin moved Greb away and inspected Kiser's eyes. Finding them still in their sockets, which was a surprise, he slapped Greb on the back, signaling him to continue. Greb leaped up in the air and flung a sweeping left hook that caught Kiser off balance and floored him.

It was just the moment Franklin, ready to drop from exhaustion, was looking for. He grabbed one of Greb's hands, without starting a count over the fallen Kiser, and held it aloft. It was a technical knockout for Greb.

Kiser, unhurt, scrambled to his feet as his belligerent handlers swarmed into the ring. Greb's men swarmed in, too. But Greb was on the *qui vive* and ushered his men out before hell could break loose. As he looped his left arm around Franklin's beefy structure and scampered across the ring, the limp arbiter looked back and yelled, "Winner, and still champion—Greb!"

Kiser's men, bearing water buckets, took after them. But the fleet Greb, still holding onto his quarry, galloped off to safety.

It is considerably less than understatement to say there was bedlam in Greb's dressing room, what with the Kiser contingent on the outside trying to break the door in and the boxing commissioner on the inside demanding an explanation for Franklin's strange actions. Franklin pulled himself together and said: "Gents, if I hadn't a took steps to end it when I did, I'd'a collapsed myself. I was plumb wore out." This explanation seemed as good as any and Franklin wobbled off to a Turkish bath to try to forget.

Greb put on his clothes and came outside. Two thugs motioned him and a handler into a cab and drove to the outskirts of Baltimore, where they opened the door and, hands moving inferentially in bulging hip pockets, said, "Git, and don't come back!"

Greb looked at his trembling handler and said, "I fought their boy and beat him and now they toss me outa town. I never seen such ingratitude."

Yet that was the Greb who, after Kid Norfolk blinded him forever in the right eye and dumped him hard on the ring floor, arose on unsteady legs, lowered his head of pain, charged and gave the Kid the pasting of his pugilistic life. A short time later an injury to the other eye left it with less than half sight.

The men he fought after that constituted a roster of the fistic greats of the time—Mike and Tommy Gibbons, Jack Dillon, Mike McTigue, Zulu Kid, Tunney and Johnny Wilson for the light-heavyweight and middleweight titles, respectively, which Greb won with the greatest of ease;

Tommy Loughran, Battling Levinsky, Billy Miske, Gunboat Smith and at least 275 others. Greb just shuffled out of his corner, yanked his trunks up, snorted, spat, charged and exploded in their faces.

And when Greb was thirty-two and so blind he couldn't see ten feet in front of him he came down from 175 pounds to defend his middleweight crown, entered the ring with a fever from weight-making and whipped the then welterweight champion, Mickey Walker, so thoroughly that twice during the closing rounds Walker stood crying, pleading with Greb not to knock him out.

Portrait of a Legend   by PAUL GALLICO

THE DEMPSEY-FIRPO HEAVYWEIGHT championship fought at the Polo Grounds in 1923 is already fading from the active memory of man and entering the limbo of legendary events. It will continue to live and grow as a legend as long as the United States remains a sports-loving nation.

The famous canvas by George Bellows caught the high point in the shortest and wildest roughhouse in the annals of heavyweight championship brawling, the moment when Luis Angel Firpo of Argentina, berserk and battle-blind, clubbed heavyweight champion Jack Dempsey out of the ring and into the press row.

The Dempsey-Firpo fight was the first heavyweight championship I saw and covered.

It lasted exactly three minutes and fifty-seven seconds. During that time Firpo was floored nine times, Dempsey twice.

When Dempsey was swatted out of the enclosure, he fell onto a sports writer by the name of Jack Lawrence, who pushed him back to the ring platform. One of the longest-winded arguments in the history of boxing was started by the claim that Dempsey should have forfeited his title because he was helped back into the ring.

Lawrence's contribution to the tons of rhetoric and *belles lettres* pursuant to the discussion of this claim was brief and to the point. He said he wasn't helping anybody. He was merely trying to get 192 pounds of muscle and sinew off his typewriter so that he could go on pounding out the head-shaking details of the Pier-Sixer.

Luis Firpo was managed by the late Jimmy De-Forest. Luis knew absolutely nothing about the manly art of self-defense. He swung his fists as the cavemen wielded their clubs. A brief attempt to teach him something about boxing before he entered the arena against Dempsey only confused him. Firpo assumed a ring stance for a few seconds after the opening bell. The first time Dempsey clipped him he abandoned sweet science and charged in, clubbing like a madman. He came within a second of becoming the rawest novice ever to win a heavyweight title.

In Dempsey's corner was Jack Kearns, the man who made him champion. The promoter was the late Tex Rickard, a fabulous figure of the Golden Decade of American Sport; the referee, Johnny Gallagher.

Dempsey's purse was $475,000. Figured on a piecework scale, it was the highest fee ever paid a professional brawler. He received approximately $100,000 per fighting minute, or $2000 per second.

Ninety thousand people saw the fight. One man died of heart failure. No two spectators agreed on how many times Firpo had been down, how long Dempsey was out of the ring and what kind of a punch turned the trick. At the first exchange, the entire crowd got to its feet and remained standing for the balance of the fight, yelling, screaming, climbing up on the benches, falling down, clawing at each other, roaring forth a wild, tumultuous cataract of sound in the greatest sustained mass audience hysteria ever witnessed in any modern arena.

Dempsey won because he hit faster and oftener. Both men were wide open and made not a single effort at defense during the entire 237 seconds of action. In three of the nine knockdowns, Firpo was flat on his face and apparently out cold. Yet each time he managed to roll over, regain his feet before the count of ten and charge Dempsey, snarling like a wounded animal.

Both men broke the rules of the ring, Firpo by charging Dempsey when he knocked him to one knee in the first round and Dempsey by standing over Firpo when he got him going, instead of retiring to a neutral corner, and pasting him as soon as he got up.

Dempsey remembered nothing of the fight after the clubbing left to the temple had swept him from the ring. Thereafter he fought entirely by instinct. Firpo was berserk and out of his mind from the first time Dempsey dropped him with a left hook to the chin early in the first round.

Altogether it was the purest exhibition of untrammeled savagery, truculence and sustained animosity in the history of glove fighting.

It was one sweet quarrel.

Joe Louis: Greatest of Champions

by JIMMY CANNON

THE CODE OF FAIR PLAY WHICH RULES most games is not apparent in the boxing racket. The bribing of referees and judges happens as often as a certain type of manager can get to them. It is not considered wrong to scream for justice and accuse honest officials of being crooks when your man has lost on the square. The reputations of honest officials are often damaged by managers even when they give a true verdict against a fighter. Most managers who do not holler consider themselves to be slackers and the shrieking of lies is supposed to signify love of your fighter.

Seconds figure ways to evade the rules. Many instruct young fighters how to jab with the thumbs, as a blind opponent is not considered to be as formidable as one who has ordinary vision. Low blows are valid in the minds of such handlers as long as a fighter is not penalized for them. Dirty fighters are those who do not draw large money.

It is only natural that the public is suspicious of fights and the journalists are forever searching for

evidence of larceny. But in all the time that Joe Louis fought I never heard one of his contests denounced as a frame-up, although many of them appeared strange due to the curious deportment of his opponents. In the days of his greatness Louis inspired his straight men with a fear which caused them to fall in clammy ecstasy as soon as the first punch grazed their chins. It was an authentic happiness and they were eager to get out of his way before his cobblestone fists damaged them beyond reconstruction. Many of them resigned with joyous cowardice after being slapped a cuff which would not disturb the senses of a high-school girl. They ran from him in disgraceful retreats after panic looted them of their dignity. Some of them sweated in the dressing room as though they imagined he would use a baseball bat on them instead of his fists. There were some who began to lose weight the day they signed the contract and there were others who never pretended they were engaged as prize fighters and acted as though they were clowns

employed to make the audience laugh at their shameful tactics to avoid being struck. Great fortunes were bet on the results of these fights. But it is a tribute to Louis that the public always believed he was an honest man in a league of burglars and rewarded him with a faith which is amazing in this cynical age of the breaking atom. As Louis came to the end of his term as heavyweight champion we must consider what happened in his last fight with Jersey Joe Walcott in order to appreciate the purity of this great athlete. It was first made as an exhibition match. So mediocre was Walcott's history as a heavyweight that the promoters believed the public would not accept him as a contender. He was a cautious man with little respect for his own ability. He had resigned from the ring many times to work as a handy man because doing odd jobs paid him more than he would make with his fists. He was a fair puncher and what the fight racket calls a cutie.

His style consisted of no style at all. He would run and hide, skip and loiter, occasionally punch with a right hand, pausing timidly in his constant flight. The State Athletic Commission of New York jostled the promoters into changing the billing for the bout and when the time came it was advertised as a fight for the heavyweight championship of the world. It was considered a swindle and a humorless joke on the people who pay to watch

fights. But I can't recall a fight which blew up more action among the gamblers. Only a few bet on the result because this is what they call proposition gambling. They bet that Walcott would or wouldn't last a round and spread their money down to the fifteenth, the odds changing with the rounds selected. At the end of the fight the majority of the people in Madison Square Garden thought Walcott had won the decision. I was one of them and I scored eight rounds for the challenger, seven for Louis. The referee gave it to Walcott, but the two judges overruled him and saved Louis' title. An inspection of their score cards showed that Walcott had won the fight on points, which is a system the New York Commission installed to prevent draws, and I have not the space to go into it here. The verdict was heckled and all over the town people complained that Walcott should have won. But there was no sense of injustice among those who were steady patrons of fights in New York. They believed in the old tradition of the ring that a title can't be won by a man who runs away. They figured the judges had made an honest error and they let it go at that. If any other fighter had fallen heir to such an unexpected legacy of bad judgment the district attorney probably would have had detectives out putting the sleeve on everyone mixed up with it. But this was a Louis fight and he is a special guy. All of them believe he was never party to a crooked fight and they respected him as a good man in a business dominated by thieves. Even a decision which they considered wrong could not molest their conception of him. They were absolutely right.

It was Louis himself who acted as though prize fighting were a sacred calling and not the ugly graft it is. Not once in the time Joe was champion did he abuse the office. In all the fights I saw him make I can't recall him striking a foul blow. There were times when Joe could have used illegal tactics without any criticism. They tried everything against him, but it never agitated him out of his stately and always honorable fury. Max Baer hit him after the bell and this would have provoked the average fighter into retaliation. But Joe looked at Baer with disgust and shambled back to his corner, the contemptuous glance the only indication that he knew he had been fouled. He made

Baer quit that night and I suppose that is the classic revenge.

The commercial anger of brutality does not recommend a man anywhere outside the ring unless you are looking for a guy to break a strike or roll a lush. It must make you wary of a man because if you are a good fighter you must inflict pain on another man and the chances are you may enjoy it. But Louis was more than a prize fighter; he was a promise that the equality promised all men in the basic documents of our freedoms may be achieved by all of us.

There are those who will tell you that Louis was an ordinary heavyweight who was erroneously accused of greatness because of the ineptness of his opposition. But you don't believe them. There were few as good in any age and that goes for all of them. You can start with John L. Sullivan and come right down to Jimmy Braddock, the one before Louis. There never was a heavyweight champion who took the chances Louis did. They were all alike to him and he fought them all. He never ducked anyone. There were nights when he was slovenly and could not solve the moves of his opponents, but always he went at them and tried to compel them to fight. The only plan he ever had was to go for a guy and stick with him until he could catch him. It will be remembered when a lot of things are forgotten that Walcott knocked him down twice. But Louis was always the aggressor. He never backed up. Walcott ran and hid and Louis pursued him even when he was rickety-legged and his left eye was a blood-flecked crevice in a lump of discolored flesh. If you looked at the course of the fight you would have believed that Walcott was the one who had been injured early and was trying to protect himself from further punishment.

What happened with Walcott humiliated Joe and irritated his pride. He hid himself out in an apartment in uptown Manhattan and sat there with Manny Seamon, the trainer, dourly listening to jazz records. The telephone rang and no one bothered to answer it and the doorman in the apartment house denied there was any tenant by the name of Joe Louis. I was the first newspaperman to interview him after this fight. On a wind-cleansed day we stood at the window of his apartment and looked down at the Harlem River through the weather-stripped trees. Joe pointed to a small frame building.

"George Washington slept there," Louis said.

"He slept in a lot of joints," Seamon said.

"Sleep all the time," Joe said. "Must of had some second lieutenant run the army for him."

We discussed jazz and then he told me what he thought had made him slow and tired-looking in the Walcott fight.

"I made the fight for myself," he explained. "He didn't make it tough for me. He did so many wrong things. I saw every opening. But I couldn't go get him. It was such a lousy fight. I saw him when he made the mistakes. It's like a guy running. You can't make a sprint at the end. Your legs feel you can go, but you feel bad in the pit of your stomach."

I said this sounded like a rundown of the symptoms of old age.

"Diet and drying out," said Louis, who came in at 211 for Walcott. "I wanted to weigh '12. I should have weighed '14 for the fight. I dried it out of me. I killed myself taking off the four pounds. But that ain't no excuse. It was a real lousy fight."

The first time I ever saw him was with Primo Carnera and he was a myth already. They said he was the best to come up since Gene Tunney, but

a lot of us were careful and waited until we saw him. If you saw him that night and still doubt his claim to greatness then you are afflicted with amnesia or are a liar.

Primo Carnera was a big but harmless man. At one time he was moved around by a syndicate of gangsters and they pushed guys off the raft in dives which many thought were square fights. Primo was agile in a big-footed way, but his arms were impotent when they laced the gloves on his hands. He could not punch and what he knew had been taught to him because he had none of the instincts a fighter must have to survive. But they had protected him and some of the opponents had been bribed not to hit him and there were still some who believed this grotesque man with the picket-fence smile could take a punch. Louis had a stately manner beyond his years when he came into the ring that night. He was blank-faced and quiet as

he sat in his corner and he appeared to be a concentrated man. The first left hook Louis hit him was a solid one. It smeared Carnera's spit-wet lips and the mouth seemed to open and swallow his face as the blood spread like a grimace he could not control. The punch amazed Carnera. Never before had he been hit that hard. The terror seemed to wither his gross features because his eyes became large with astonishment. They had guarded him from beatings, but this one was on the level and the guy who was hitting him was the best puncher of his time. Louis was fast then. It was not the speed of body and feet. It was a swiftness of the arms. He would jab, hook and then suddenly the punches started and they didn't stop until you fell. He knew you were hurt before you did and that is when he commenced to let them go with a reckless accuracy that reminded you of Dempsey. In those days they were shaken up with the first punch and frappéed with the flurry that followed. There were some who were in there to stay and they did. They did not try to win, but wanted the dubious honor of going the limit. They disgraced themselves, but this made them attractions because a guy who went fifteen rounds with Louis was accused of being a hell of a fighter. They fooled him once, but never twice and the next time around he caught up with them and they finished on their backs.

When the Max Schmeling match was rigged I was a reporter on the New York *American*. There was a young fellow named Joe DiMaggio in his first year as a big-leaguer and I liked to travel with the Yankees because this was a great team and your story figured to lead the sports section every day of the baseball season. Schmeling had retired. They had run out of opponents for Louis and they sent for Schmeling because he had been heavyweight champion of the world and this would give the match the appearance of a contest. The *American*'s sports editor was the late Ed Frayne and he asked me if I wanted to hang around for the Louis-Schmeling fight or go West with the Yankees. I figured Louis would take Schmeling when he wanted to and I wanted to see what Di-Mag would do against Western pitching. So I went out of town with the Yanks. We were in Detroit when Schmeling knocked him out. So I have never seen Louis beaten. But I was there the next time they fought and that night Louis was the greatest fighter I have ever seen. I wasn't there when Dempsey knocked out Jess Willard in Toledo. But I have seen the movies of that fight and this is the only other heavyweight I would have made an even-money shot with Louis on the night he destroyed Schmeling in one round.

There is little malice in Louis. The only men he fought whom he truly hated are Schmeling and Walcott. Schmeling degraded him by declaring that Louis had quit in the first fight. Walcott insisted that he had knocked down Louis while working as his sparring partner and had been fired for

what he did. I remember sitting with Louis and talking about Schmeling on the night before the second fight.

"Why he say I quit?" Joe asked. "He looked to quit hisself in the seventh round. I hit him in the belly and I see 'quit' looking out at me. Why he say I quit?"

"He's trying to steam you up," I said.

"Who you pick?" he asked.

"You," I answered. "By a knockout."

"How many?" he asked.

"Six," I replied.

"One," Joe said. "It go one."

"Why one?" I asked.

"That's all it go," Joe said. "It go one."

The first punches Louis reached him with were jabs. They made Schmeling's neck jerk as though he had run into an invisible wire. Louis never paused after that. Schmeling screamed and turned his back to Joe, holding onto the ropes. Louis had a fury which is seldom seen in the ring. It was a calculated rage and one controlled by intelligence. If ever a fighter made a perfect fight Joe did that night.

It always has been Joe's theory that a champion does not defend his title. He puts it there for them to take. They never have to search for him. Always he comes at them and he tried to get them out of there as fast as he could. There never was any stalling to make the other guy look good. If he caught you he nailed you and his pursuit was always hurried. In the first fight with Billy Conn many thought Louis was too far behind and only a knockout saved him from defeat. On my score card it was even, although the officials had Conn out in front. The truth was deformed because it made a better story, but never in this fight was Louis in any real trouble. But if you read the memoirs of some sports observers you would think that Joe was on the border of insensibility all evening. Conn was not a powerful puncher and his skill as a boxer was exaggerated. Billy was a fast fighter. He got around with a wise nimbleness. But Conn couldn't force you out of your style with false moves as a good boxer is supposed to do. He depended on quickness and this scheme took him into the thirteenth round. It is the popular conception that Conn made the decision which got him knocked out. Some insist he broke his diagram of movement and decided to knock Louis out instead of jabbing and running. But that is not true. Conn made a mistake. Louis caught up with him. Those were the years of Louis' greatness and you were only entitled to one error. Joe stepped in and the next thing you knew a guy had smelling salts under your nose.

There have been a lot of guys who could fight better than Jimmy Braddock. But there were few who came into the ring the way he did. He approached a fight the way a clerk goes to his desk every morning. It was the job he worked at to make a living for his family and he did the best he knew how. It was his philosophy that a fighter goes as far as he can. It is the referee's job to count you out and you are supposed to get up if you can. The night Louis took the title from him Braddock fought with the calmness of a man with great pride in himself. In the first round Braddock knocked Louis down. It wasn't much of a punch, a right uppercut, and Louis ran into it. It sat Joe down, but it didn't hurt him. After that it was obvious that Braddock didn't have a chance. The people in his corner demanded that Jimmy quit. But Braddock said no and Louis took care of him and gave him a terrible beating. He lay in the ring with the blood running all over him and there were many in the ball park who believed he was fatally hurt. I was supposed to have filed a humorous story of the fight, but I asked them to let me out of it because I could locate no comedy in the butchery of a guy who was brave according to the rules of his profession. I tell you this because Braddock was better than the record in the book. I doubt if Jimmy ever considered himself a valorous man, but he was when you compare him with some of those who made more money by running and holding. So you must take his opinion of Louis seriously and appraise the champion by what he says.

"Nobody hits like Louis," Braddock said.

"What about Max Baer?" I said.

"A joke compared to that Louis," Braddock insisted. "A punch is a punch. But that Louis. Take the first jab he nails you. You know what it's like? It's like someone jammed an electric bulb in your face and busted it."

"What about the right hand?" I asked.

"It ain't like a punch," Braddock said. "It's like someone nailed you with a crowbar. I thought half my head was blowed off. I figured he caved it in. I felt it after he hit me and I couldn't even feel if it was there."

I talked with Louis about Braddock after the fight. "I like to fight old Jim again," Joe said.

"I thought you liked him," I said. "You want to murder him?"

"He make me the money," Joe said. "I like to make old Jim the money."

The second Conn fight confused the authorities. The years had begun to rot Louis, but we believed he was as good as ever. They watched him hunt

down Conn in a desperate chase. But Conn was so bad that night it was impossible to detect what time had done to Louis.

"Billy not even half the fighter he was," Joe said. "I knock him out any time after the first round. I feel him out and come back and say I can get him. But Manny Seamon say to take it easy. Manny say I punch myself out and lose him. Manny say I may have to go fifteen. Billy wasn't like a heavyweight."

The one after that was with Tami Mauriello. On the morning of the fight they weighed in at the Garden and again Louis asked me the old question.

"What you pick?" he asked because I had called the round in the second Conn fight. "How long I fighting tonight?"

"Three," I answered.

"You must be in a mood for a long fight," Joe said.

It went only one, but Joe was fortunate to get by. Tami Mauriello was never much. He is a fat man and that makes it difficult for him to train. But Tami hit him and the punch jostled Louis into the ropes. Mauriello was amazed by what had happened. He took a tourist's look at the champion hanging on the ropes and that cost him any chance he had of winning. Mauriello went down with the first hook Louis hit him and he never was able to get going again. Then came the Walcott fight and when you saw it you realized Louis had come to the end of the line. Jersey Joe is a guy who had one good night and it almost made him

champion of the world. But Louis was the greatest champion that ever held the title. No one ever fought more. Not one of them ever had his grace as a guy. When I say Joe was the best I am not defending my generation. The book will tell you how good he was and all the fights were won without the edge most fighters need to build a reputation.

EDITOR'S NOTE: *Joe Louis retired in 1949, abandoning the title. Ezzard Charles defeated Joe Walcott in that year, but only earned N.B.A. recognition. In 1950 Louis attempted a comeback but was defeated by Charles, who thus earned universal recognition. In 1951 Walcott then defeated Charles and became champion.*

June 26, 1959: Ingemar Johansson Knocks Out Floyd Patterson

Right hand aloft and clenched,
"Thunder," the fighter said.
But when the hand, unclenched, slipped toward a slim girl's waist,
the fight men grumbled, "Lover," spitting out the word
through wet cigars.

Rain leaked the night that thunder struck.
One long, straight right, then six more knockdowns
and soon the thunder hand, unclenched,
reached toward the girl again.

"How can he be a fighter and a lover both?"
the fight men asked. The fight men
who did not understand violence.

They Always Come Out Like I Say

by ARTHUR DALEY

THE SYSTEM WAS PRACTICALLY FOOL-proof. Kid Tracy, the roistering welterweight fighter in the Butte, Montana, honky-tonk, hadn't had to pay out a dime. His offer seemed generous enough—ten dollars to any man who could last four rounds with him. For a month he'd been meeting all comers on the dimly lit stage and deftly belting them into dreamland.

If any of the volunteers proved more troublesome than expected, the careful Kid maneuvered him against the curtained backdrop. Thereupon Texas Joe Halliday, proprietor of the honky-tonk, thoughtfully brought a sandbag in brisk contact with the bulge in the curtain caused by the victim's head. That was always the convincer.

The explosive hitting prowess of Tracy was the talk of the mining camps—until the blond-haired Polish bus boy from Butte's Copper Queen Saloon elected to try for the ten-spot. On the stage with Tracy, the seventeen-year-old youngster with the appealing baby face flew at his opponent so savagely that Texas Joe Halliday rushed in alarm to his sandbag station. The innocent-looking boy was a fighting fiend. He drove his rival across the ring with a two-fisted body attack and lashed so fierce a right to the jaw that Tracy's knees buckled. Desperately Tracy clinched and wrestled Ketchel toward the curtain—and the rendezvous with the sandbag.

But the youngster twisted away and hooked a

left to the chin that sent Tracy reeling against the curtain. The curtain bulged and the thankful Halliday swung the sandbag with gentle care. It caught the Invincible One on his sconce and young Stanley, entering into the spirit of the occasion with unexpected gusto, hit Tracy flush on the jaw as he fell face downward.

That May night of 1903 Kid Tracy established his only claim to ring immortality: he was the chap who officially launched the professional career of mighty Stanley Ketchel (born Stanislaus Kiecal), one of the greatest performers ever to pull on a boxing glove.

Ketchel's start was meteoric. His career was meteoric. He blazed across the fistic firmament as no man ever had before or has since: one vivid, blinding flash—and then extinction. "I'll die before I'm thirty," he once confided. But he over-estimated his life span.

Ketchel fought for just seven years. He fought during the era of the greatest middleweights our country ever has had and was the greatest of them all. He was such a tremendous hitter that he actually knocked down Jack Johnson, the heavyweight champion. He was so clever that he won a decision from that wraithlike light-heavyweight, Philadelphia Jack O'Brien. In sixty-three bouts he blasted into unconsciousness the astonishing number of forty-seven opponents.

The young Polish boy had established a reputation even before he won ring renown. He had run

away from home in Grand Rapids, Michigan, at an early age, and headed for the Wild West. While still in his teens, he was visiting a Billings, Montana, rancher friend, Jack Stagel, when one moonlight night a rifle bullet whined through the air. The rancher fell, wounded in the shoulder. Undaunted Stanley whipped out his trusty six-shooter—the true Wild West touch—and fired back. He didn't have to be told who the would-be slayer was. A half-breed Mexican, wanted for murder, had been pursued through the hills for almost a week. The price on his head was high—$1000 dead or alive.

Young Stanley could barely discern the desperado advancing cautiously from the underbrush, too far away to be reached by a revolver bullet. The murderer drew another bead with his high-powered rifle and fired. Immediately Ketchel reeled and fell on his back, arms outstretched. Edwin Booth never did a better job of acting. With complete confidence the gunman strode toward the wounded Stagel and the inert Stanley.

He glanced at the boy and stepped past his outstretched hand toward the rancher. Suddenly his ankle was caught in a viselike grip and he was violently jerked off his feet, his rifle flying from his hands. Ketchel undoubtedly should have used his six-shooter to subdue the hunted man, but he was much too fundamental for that. He made a tigerish leap atop the half-breed, ground his knees into the killer's stomach and squeezed him relentlessly by the throat. That seemed slow, however, so the youngster slugged him on the jaw. One punch was enough. The desperado lost both his desperation and his consciousness.

Young Stanley then tied his prisoner hand and foot, patched up Stagel's superficial shoulder wound and dumped the deflated bad man into a buckboard wagon for delivery to the sheriff. So great was the excitement caused by this exploit in Butte that the authorities had to hire a dance hall to accommodate all the Ketchel admirers when the youngster was formally presented with the $1000 reward for singlehandedly bringing the outlaw to justice.

The Ketchel fame as a fighter really blossomed from his first match with Joe Thomas, the feature of a Fourth of July celebration at Marysville, California. Twenty-one-year-old Stanley still had no more than a local reputation around Montana's mining camps when he went into this bout. Joe Thomas, however, was one of the cleverest middleweights of his time—a deadly two-fisted hitter of such class that he was deemed the logical successor to Tommy Ryan, the middleweight champion who'd just outgrown his division and vacated his title.

Totally unimpressed by the Thomas reputation, the cocky Ketchel sailed in in his usual wildcat style. Thomas jabbed delicately, feeling out his foe. But never had he encountered such a dynamic bundle of fighting fury as the kid from the mining camps. It took all of the Thomas ring guile to get as far as the eleventh round without being upended. But toward the end of that round Ketchel hooked savagely with his left and the champion sagged to the canvas. The bell saved him at the count of nine. One report had it that a Thomas supporter reached across the shoulder of the timekeeper and rapped smartly on the bell with his cane, thus concluding the round abruptly.

Often during the remaining nine rounds Ketchel had his foe groggy and ready for the kill. But he was so shy on ring technique that he punched himself out, unable to finish the job which was so close to consummation.

Although the referee raised the gloves of both fighters at the end, symbolic of a draw, the result electrified the sports world. The eyewitnesses knew that Ketchel had won, and everyone else was startled at the news that an unknown had held his own with the mighty Joe Thomas.

A return match was natural, of course. And for it Ketchel made an astonishing proposition: he asked for the loser's share in advance so that he could bet it all on himself to knock out Thomas.

This fight has been pretty generally hailed as one of the great fistic battles of all time. Ketchel was a demon, Thomas the cooler ring general. In the ninth Stanley lashed out a terrific left to the head. Had the blow caught Thomas on the jaw instead of the cheekbone, the fight might have ended then. Thomas went down for the count of nine, but his head was clear when he arose.

In the twenty-ninth round—the fight was scheduled to go forty-five—came two punches which did

as much as any others to establish Stanley as a great fighter. He was on the receiving end of it. As Ketchel came charging in, Thomas delivered a right-hand smash flush on his chin, every ounce of strength in his body behind it. Ketchel went down like a felled ox. It was all over—or so the crowd thought. At the count of seven, however, Stanley crawled to one knee. At nine he staggered to his feet. He was slugging toe-to-toe when the bell finally clanged.

That recovery took the heart out of Thomas. Even his best punch couldn't halt the ceaseless attack of this runaway cyclone. In the thirty-second round Ketchel hooked a ruthless left to Thomas' body and crossed with a right to the jaw. Thomas lay draped across the ropes, mouth open, eyes glazed. Ketchel had knocked him out.

Billy Papke was another who might have ranked with the all-time boxing greats if there had been no Michigan Assassin, as Ketchel came to be called in the papers. Papke was one of the two men credited with a knockout victory over the rugged gamester from Grand Rapids. Stanley was undisputed middleweight champion then. In five short months he had beaten all four of the other claimants to the title: Mike (Twin) Sullivan, Jack

(Twin) Sullivan, Papke and Hugo Kelly.

So Papke was given another chance at the title. And he won it—by trickery. As the two fighters advanced to the center of the ring for the customary handshake, Papke ignored Ketchel's friendly, outstretched glove and drove a cruel left hook to his rival's unprotected jaw. Then he crossed a sledgehammer right to the bridge of the nose that closed both of Ketchel's eyes. Still, for eleven rounds Stanley fought back blindly and by pure instinct, swinging at an opponent he could scarcely see.

In the twelfth round Papke dropped his helpless foe with a stunning right cross, and referee Jim Jaffries tolled off a count of eight before Ketchel staggered drunkenly to his feet. Immediately he was smashed to the canvas again. At nine he was struggling gamely to regain his footing when the referee motioned for Stanley's seconds to haul him to his corner. The Michigan Assassin had been knocked out for the first time.

Ketchel and Papke were rematched later, of course. This time Ketchel didn't offer to shake hands. Ringsiders insist that Stanley could have knocked out the Illinois Thunderbolt any time after the first round. But he didn't. He'd prop Papke up, steady him, then cut him to ribbons.

Papke paid heavily for those two sneak punches before Ketchel mercifully dispatched him in the eleventh.

Ketchel's most amazing fight beyond doubt was when this brashly confident youth met Jack Johnson for the heavyweight championship. The giant Negro, a clever boxer and extremely sharp hitter, was in his prime then. Historians dispute their weights: Nat Fleischer's *All-Time Ring Record Book*, boxing's bible, lists Johnson at 205½ and Ketchel at a bloated 180¼; some lesser authorities have insisted that Johnson weighed 248 and Ketchel only 154, less credible figures.

The climax to this encounter was jammed in thirty-four seconds of the twelfth round. The fighters had clinched in the center of the ring and wrestled their way to a corner. Spotting an opening, the unafraid Ketchel fired with his right at Johnson's lowered head. Providentially Jack ducked and the blow hit him behind the ear instead of on the button. So great was its force, however, that the giant champion tottered and fell.

Johnson was hurt but far from dazed. Slowly he crawled to a crouch. It was the crouch of a tiger leaping to the kill. The heavyweight champion plunged across the ring, his bludgeonlike right ready to swing from the very floor. There have not been many punches such as that one thrown in the entire history of the ring; so violent was the blow that it carried Johnson with it. It landed sickeningly on Ketchel's mouth and he fell backward with big Jack falling across him. Two of Ketchel's teeth were later found embedded in Johnson's right glove.

Thus did Ketchel sustain the second and last knockout of his career. He was obviously overmatched for that fight, just as he had been outtricked for the other.

Ketchel was a paradox in many ways. He could be cruel and sadistic, soft and tender. Once he had an opponent on the verge of a quick knockout in an exhibition match and was startled to find him sobbing on his shoulder in a clinch.

"What's the matter, kid?" he asked. "Punches hurt that much?"

"It ain't the punches, feller," whispered his foe. He said that he'd been promised $10 a round and that he wanted to win $100 in order to buy a violin for his talented little son.

"He'll get his fiddle," said Stanley grimly. And he "carried" his rival for the full ten rounds.

The next afternoon the two bitter opponents of the night before strolled arm-in-arm down the main street, charged with champagne and singing the cowboy songs Stanley loved. In the pocket of the erstwhile adversary were ten $10 bills and under Ketchel's arm was a $200 violin he'd purchased for the small boy himself.

Practical jokes were Ketchel's idea of humor at its best. He thought it a magnificent prank to order a bottle of champagne for every man in a saloon, to pay for the drinks and then to sweep every bottle off the bar while he bellowed, "Do you bums want to ruin your stomachs with that stuff? Go back to beer where you belong."

It was a gigantic jest for him when he entered a heavyweight tournament out in the mining country. Wearing an old pair of faded overalls and a battered hat, he innocently sauntered into town and introduced himself as Kid Glutz. Whereupon the disguised middleweight champion of the world knocked out six heavyweights in succession.

The confidence of the Michigan Assassin in his own abilities was monumental. As soon as he checked into his hotel, just before his bout with Philadelphia Jack O'Brien, he walked over to the telegraph desk. Nat Fleischer, a boxing reporter, aware of Stanley's limited command of the written word, volunteered to help him.

"I want to send a telegram to Pop in Detroit," said Ketchel. "Just write: 'I won the fight, Stanley.'"

"What fight?" asked Fleischer.

"The fight with O'Brien tonight," stated the champion.

"But that doesn't go on for four hours," exclaimed Fleischer.

"What's the difference?" said Ketchel with a shrug. "They always come out like I say."

Ketchel delighted to return to the little school where he had received what slight formal education he'd obtained. There he would buy ice cream, cake and candy for every youngster, and tell them

stories of a world which so few of them ever would see.

Ketchel's life outside the ring was almost as breath-taking as it was inside. In playboying from town to town, his passion was a high-powered automobile which he drove at breakneck speed. When he reached the ripe age of twenty-four, this pace began to take its toll. That's how he elected to visit the ranch of Colonel Pete Dickerson near Conway, Missouri, to rest. There he was sitting one day, his trusty six-shooter resting on his lap in habitual fashion, when for the first time he failed to follow an Old West custom: never sit with your back to a door. To this day historians don't know whether it was cupidity or Cupid, greed or jealousy, that caused Walter Dipley, a crippled stablehand, to creep up behind him and send a .22-caliber bullet cracking into Ketchel's back.

2
HUNTING AND FISHING

WHEN A BOY FEELS A NIBBLE AT THE WORM ON HIS *bent pin it's a great moment to him. Hunting and fishing are sports that are by nature solitary, participant and played somewhere beyond the cheers of a crowd. It's good to pose with your trophy but the great moment was the one when the fish struck or the buffalo charged. Those who have hooked a marlin or drawn a bead on a bull elephant testify that there is no thrill to equal it. That is why we have chosen the articles in this chapter. They are by men who have done it. Robert C. Ruark gives us the inside story of the most dangerous animal in the African jungle: a man named Harry Selby, white hunter. Reginald Wells takes you to the awe-inspiring sight of the giant tuna running in the Gulf Stream. Zane Grey, a writer known for great stories of men on horseback with drawn guns, writes of his own experience on a small boat with a fishing rod . . . at the end of which fought the biggest fish that ever took the bait. And finally Philip Wylie tells the amazing story of IGFA, the organization which keeps the records of the ones that don't get away. So for those sportsmen who, for one reason or another, can't get away this May to Cat Cay, or won't be able to make the rhino season in East Africa, we offer you this collection as the next-best thing.*

The White Hunter

by ROBERT C. RUARK

THE POPULAR CONCEPTION OF A WHITE hunter, built largely in the American mind on film portrayals by Gregory Peck and Stewart Granger, is almost as erroneous as the movie and popular-magazine accounts of African safaris. According to what you may have seen or read, the basic idea of a professional hunter is this:

He stands about six foot five, sports a full beard and is drunk (off his client's liquor) most of the time. He always makes a play for the client's beautiful wife and/or sister and always scores. He shoots lions with pistols and wrestles with snakes and buffalo for fun. When he is not out on safari, he hangs around bars in Nairobi, ogling the girls and thumbing the big cartridges he wears in the loops of his jacket. He does all the shooting for the client, while the client sits comfortably in the shooting car. He is always taciturn in a "Me Tarzan-You Jane" manner. He has a secret sorrow, which drove him to a life among the wild beasts. His business is regarded as butchery, and it takes a superhuman man to be a competent butcher.

This is about as accurate as the average movie presentation of high life in New York, or the general supposition that all Englishmen sport monocles and have no chins. In some respects the white, or professional, big-game hunter, African variety, is the toughest man in the world, and in others he is as gentle as a dead dove and as unsophisticated as Huck Finn. He is competent at his job, which is why he is alive, but you will see more rugged types on the dance floor at El Morocco. And he is the last of a breed of men who have such a genuine love for the wilds, and such a basic hatred of civilization, that they are willing literally to kill themselves with backbreaking work and daily danger, on a nine-month-per-year basis, for less pay than a good waiter in New York draws down. They forswear matrimony, generally, because no wife lasts long when the old man is off twisting the tails of leopards for most of the calendar year. They save little money, for the upkeep on their hunting cars largely outweighs their income, and they blow the rest in Nairobi in between safaris or in the rainy seasons when hunting is impossible. They are referred to as a vanishing breed because even in the early 1950's there were fewer than thirty practicing top pros in British East Africa, and soon there will be little big stuff left to practice on, so swiftly is the dangerous game disappearing.

Let us consider Harry Selby, with whom I had the good fortune to hunt in 1950-51. Selby was possibly the best of the then current bunch—certainly there was none better, and his popularity was such that he was booked up through 1954. He was not yet twenty-seven, but had been an able pro since he was twenty. He was born and raised in East Africa, on a cattle farm in Nanyuki, Kenya Colony, and killed his first elephant before he was fifteen. He looked like a public-school boy, and spoke an impeccable British English in such a gentle voice that even an occasional "damn" sounded very wicked.

Some of the other practicing top pros were younger. Tony Henley, raised on the slopes of Mt. Kenya, was an old pro at twenty-three. He was a blond youngster who looked like a substitute end on a high-school football team. Tony Dyer, at twenty-six, looked like the valedictorian in a junior-college graduation exercise. Donald Ker, a partner in Ker and Downey Safaris, Ltd., was older, a small, thin, mild-seeming man in his forties, who practically put himself through school shooting elephants for ivory when he was a 110-pound stripling. His partner, Syd Downey, looked like an ordinary businessman, was pushing fifty and still was rated one of the best in the business. Andrew Homburg, the expert on African mountain game, was a strapping, rosy-cheeked six-footer who might very well have been a junior advertising executive. And the then-retired dean of the bunch, Philip Percival, was a plump old gentle-man with stubby fat legs, who looked about as fierce as Colonel Blimp.

Yet all these men made a business of mingling daily with lions, leopards and the most dangerous trio—buffalo, elephant and rhino—and managed to stay alive, although nearly all had horn wounds and claw scars, and all had looked death squarely in the eye at distances up to one inch. They had a tremendous respect for dangerous animals, and only a bad break accounts for the occasional death or injury in their ranks. When they were hurt, 99 times out of 100 they were injured trying to pro-tect a client who had just shown arrant cowardice or complete stupidity. Yet no client is ever pub-licly branded a coward. No client is ever tagged as a kill-crazy meat hog. No lady ever misses her lion —not for the record, anyhow. The code says that the hunters don't talk, once the safari is over. That is ridiculous, of course. They talk plenty, mostly among themselves, but occasionally to customers they have come to know and respect.

The function of a professional hunter, on safari, is almost Godlike. He is responsible for the safety of the whole shebang—you, himself and the black boys who make up your *shauri*. He is the guide, over trackless wastes. He is the expert on finding game and seeing that his dude is in the best pos-sible position to shoot it. If you ask him, he will shoot it for you, but he will quietly despise you as a man, and the contempt he feels will be mirrored in fifteen or twenty black faces, from gunbearer to the kitchen Mtoto, who washes the dishes and helps the cook.

If you wound an animal, it is the hunter's re-sponsibility to go into the bush and finish it off, both out of humanitarianism and caution, since a wounded lion or buffalo is bound to kill the first luckless native who crosses his path. At all times he is the servant of the Game Department, whose laws are strict, and in whose employ are many spies. If it was known, for instance, that a hunter failed to exert all possible effort to find a wounded animal, his license would be immediately forfeit.

The hunter stands at your side to backstop you on dangerous game. His idea of the pleasant safari is one in which he was not forced to fire a gun once. But if the going gets nasty his double rifle is your insurance. White hunters seldom miss—at close range. They can't afford to.

"I don't care a damn about these people who can split a lemon at three hundred yards," old Phil Percival once remarked. "What I want to know about a man is how good is he on a charging buffalo at six feet."

My man Selby, to that specification, is excellent. The last buffalo he was *forced* to shoot was on the safari ahead of mine. The buff had gone down, and it appeared his back was broken. As Selby and the client approached, cautiously, the buff got up and charged at about fifteen yards. The client let him have one in the chest and one in the face.

"The first bullet hit him here," Selby said later, "just under the right eye. He kept coming. At about ten feet I hit him just here, over the left eye. He continued to progress."

"What did you do then?" I asked him, more or less breathlessly.

"Well," the young man said. "At about four feet I shot him again. I shot him through *the pupil*." He rummaged through some photos and showed me the dead buffalo. There was a hole under one eye, a hole above the other, and where the left eye belonged was a hole as big as an egg. The buff had died and fallen on Selby's feet.

On one occasion, I watched Selby hold his fire in the face of a lioness' charge, until the angry cat was a long broomstick away. She stopped, and we eventually drove her off. I had no chance to shoot, since I was working on the male, and I was a little angry that Bwana Selby had let her come so close.

"After all, Bob," Selby said, "she had cubs. I thought I'd give the old girl another foot or so."

The heavy work for a hunter is not so much the location of game, and the supervision of the final kill, as the camp routine. His is the super-vision of a tiny portable city—administration of loading and unloading, in exactly the right order; of pitching camp, selecting camp, looking after the water supply, supervising the skinners and trackers and gunbearers and porters and cooks and body servants. He must be an expert mechanic—he must be able to rebuild a motor car from the spare parts he carries, and improvise those parts he has not. I once saw Selby settle a ball-bearing assembly with a nail and an old piece of strap iron. Another hunter whittled a workable flywheel out of a piece of hardwood. When the hunting car and the truck broke down, as they frequently did, due to the terrific pounding they took in the field, Selby worked harder at replacing leaves in busted springs or rejiggering cantankerous carburetors than any of his crew.

The hunter is responsible for correct victualing of an expedition that may be out from town three or four months, so that he has perforce a dietitian's knowledge of supplementary canned goods and a balanced menu. He is directly responsible for providing an average of ten pounds a day, per man, of fresh meat. In most cases the ordinary day's killing will keep sufficient meat in camp, but I have seen periods when we hunted a fifty-pound Thompson gazelle harder than we hunted lions, simply because we needed meat.

As the head of a safari, the hunter finally combines the duties of a sea captain, a bodyguard, a chauffeur, a tracker, a skinner, a headwaiter, a tourist guide, a photographer, a mechanic, a stevedore, an interpreter, a game expert, a gin-rummy partner, drinking companion, social equal, technical superior, boss, employee and handy man. The difficulty of his position is magnified in that he lives in the pockets of his one or two clients for weeks, and unless he is a master of tact, nobody is speaking to anyone else when the safari pays off in Nairobi. The old-timers had a phrase to describe a safari gone sour.

"I'm still drinking their whisky," the hunter would say, meaning that all social intercourse had ceased and the safari was operating on a basis of frigid politeness, with the hunter keeping himself to himself except during shooting hours.

Of all his problems, however, the client is the No. One headache. Selby had one sport I recall, who fancied himself to be Tarzan and insisted on sleeping in trees and cavorting naked in rivers that contained crocodiles. There have been clients like the *señor* from Mexico, a colorful type who now is blacklisted by the professional hunters' association. The *señor* was fond of shooting everything that moved, female or not, and through indis-

criminate blasting managed to get three hunters severely mauled by wounded game. He also fancied shooting from the car, an unforgivable violation of game laws.

One hunter I know was terribly butchered by a buffalo, because the superbrave client panicked after wounding the buff, and threw away his gun to run. This left the hunter all by himself with the buffalo, who took about fourteen slugs up front and still kept coming. The buffalo threw the hunter twice, opening him up on each side like a slit herring.

More dangerous than an angry cow elephant with a young calf, however, is the woman on safari. She is generally rich and spoiled, old and full of complaints, or young and apt to fall a little bit in love with the hunter. In a tent community, this puts rather a strain on the young man who is accepting the husband's pay to hunt animals instead of wives. Living *à trois* can be a difficult operation, in the midst of Tanganyika, when the *memsaab* has a tendency to cast goo-goo eyes at the professional and invent ways to catch him alone. Even the best of the sporting ladies, even the most rugged of the female hunters, has a tendency to woof at the monotony of the food, the lack of toilet facilities and the prevalence of bugs, snakes and scorpions. I know of no hunter who is delighted at the prospect of setting out with a lady who may turn out to be shrew or nymphomaniac, or a combination of both.

Some of the ladies can be fun, however. Selby was out once on a more or less photographic safari with the Duchess of Grafton.

"We were taking some snaps of impala, or something tame," Selby recalls, "when we spooked an old gentleman rhino who was very cross at being woken from his nap. As we'd no license for rhino, I didn't like to shoot it, so I said to the Duchess: 'Your Grace, you'd best make for yonder tree.' The old girl took off at the speed of knots, and went up the tree like a squirrel, camera and all. Then I entered into a delaying action."

Back in Nairobi, however, the Duchess told a different story.

"I was safely ensconced on my limb," the Duchess said, "when I heard a small, polite voice below me. It was Mr. Selby, who was running round and round the tree, with the rhino's horn just behind him. The small voice said: 'If you please, Your Grace, would you mind moving up another branch? I may need the one that you're sitting on.' "

Selby denies this. He says it would never have occurred to him to address her as "Your Grace" under such trying circumstances, but he did have definite need of the branch she was occupying.

The sense of humor of these men in moments of strife is rather amazing. Some time back an old-timer, Murray Smith, dived into the bush with his client after a wounded rhino. The old rhino boiled out from behind a thorn tree, and as Smith squared away to face it, he stumbled backward into a pig hole and sprawled flat. The rhino came at him, and all Smith could do was seize its horn with both hands and hang on for dear life, with the rhino bouncing him savagely up and down. The client, no coward he, ran up and stuck his gun in the rhino's ear and saved Mr. Smith from a very sticky finish. Later, somebody asked Smith what he thought of when the rhino had him down.

"All I could think of," Murray said, "was that now I had hold of it, the horn seemed *longer* than I thought it was when I told the client to shoot."

There are clients who are too brave, who insist on shooting everything themselves and who also insist that the hunter not shoot under any circumstances. These are the people who generally get the hunters maimed, since they are prone to shoot too fast and from too great a distance, wounding the quarry and making it necessary for the professional to collect it from the thornbush.

There are the too timid who shoot wildly, run away, drop their guns and generally foul up the detail. They refuse to take advantage of the old safety axiom: "Get as close as you can, and then get ten feet closer." They bang away from afar, and gut-shoot the lion or annoy the buffalo, and the pro has to make amends in the name of the Game Department.

There is the complete phony who gets out of the city limits and says: "Look, you shoot it all, but don't tell anybody." This is a fairly simple type to handle, since a competent pro can round up the fraud's complete bag, on reasonably mediocre animals, and quickly send him back to brag in his club. But a hunter spits when he mentions a client of this sort.

From the hunter's standpoint the ideal customer is a man who is scared enough to be cautious, but brave enough to control his fear. He follows instructions, knows and is frank about his own limitations on stamina and quits when he has had enough of mountains and swamps and dust and bumps for one day. He shoots his own game, but is not averse to a little help when a buffalo or something else large and fierce needs some extra killing. An example of what I mean is the first buff I shot, in fear and trembling, 2500 pounds of heavy-horned demon who looked at me as if I owed him money.

We crawled up on this baby as close as we could, and at about forty yards Selby whispered: "You'd best get up and wallop him. We aren't going to get any closer."

I squeezed on his front section with a .470 Westley-Richards double, and by some freak both triggers loosed off. One hundred and fifty grains of cordite knocked the buffalo tail-over-tip in one direction and bowled me over in the opposite way. Selby looked at me, who was down, and the buffalo, who was down, and remarked coldly:

"Well, for Crissakes, *one* of you get up."

The buff staggered up before I did, and took off. Selby casually raised his .450 and broke its back as it entered the bush. It was dying from my bullet before we reached it—the .500 grains of my bullet had cut its jugular, shattered its heart and exploded its lungs. Selby was apologetic.

"I'm frightfully sorry I shot, Bob," he said, "but I'd no way of knowing whether you'd hit it fatally, as I'd not had time to take its temperature. He'd have been dead twenty yards inside that bush, but it's very nasty bush, and I didn't like the idea of us having to go in and pull him out. I hope you're not angry I shot?"

I said something very profane to the effect that under any similar circumstances, I would personally shoot him if he ever failed to back me up on anything that big and ugly. He was still serious.

"You know," he said, "there's hell's own amount of clients who carry on frightfully if the hunter collaborates. They won't even accept the animal, won't even let the boys skin out the head. Lot of bloody nonsense, of course, but there you are. They're the chaps who get us killed."

The true professional hunter has something of the bullfighter's philosophy, in that he has no guarantee he will see the bright lights and pretty girls of Nairobi ever again. In the final analysis he has to stand and fight. Each man I know has had a dozen slim squeaks, mostly from elephant and buffalo. When the crisis occurs, there is no place to run, no tree to climb as a rule, because the wounded animal usually starts his charge in thick bush, from a few feet, and he nearly always sees you before you see him. Some remarkable escapes from certain death have occurred.

Frank Bowman, an Australian and a very fine hunter who is now retired, once sat on the ground with a twisted ankle and no bullets for his gun while a wounded buffalo got up and staggered, sick but still furious, toward him. Bowman screamed for a gunbearer to fetch more bullets, waited until the bearer had run to the car to get them, slapped two fresh bullets in his double and shot the buff at a range of about one foot. It fell in his lap.

One of my gunbearers, a *Wa-Kamba* boy named Adam, was elevated to the aristocracy of gunbearing in the following manner: Old Philip Percival, with an empty gun, was being chased round and round the hunting car by a wounded buffalo, and all the natives in the back—save Adam—panicked and went over the side. Adam, then a porter, had the presence of mind to sort through the dozen different varieties of cartridges in the back of the car until he found a couple of slugs that fitted Percival's gun. These he handed the doughty old boy as he rounded the car for the umpteenth time, and Percival loaded his weapon in full flight. He killed the animal, and thenceforward Adam was promoted, as a reward for presence of mind.

Anyone who hunts elephant, rhino or buffalo is a candidate for catastrophe. It is occasionally necessary, in a buffalo stampede in high grass, to whack the nearest animal and *climb upon him,* so that the other great beasts can swerve aside and pass around you. Both elephant and rhino will charge, unwounded and unpredictably.

The point is that what is one client's rare thrill is routine for the pros. I imagine Murray Smith has been hurt three or four times. Selby has had six or seven scrapes with buffalo, several with elephant and a couple of dos with lions and leopards. Syd Downey has been tossed twice by buffalo, and has contracted sleeping sickness from tsetse fly bites. Nearly all East African hunters have a chronic malaria that reduces them to bone-breaking agony and pitiful shakes several times a year. Their lungs are abrazed from constant inhalation of lava dust, and their eyes are permanently bloodshot from dust and glare.

Their average day starts at 4:30 A.M., and they rarely seek the sack before 11 P.M. During the course of a day they will drive a hunting car an average 125 miles, over trackless, tough terrain. They will walk an average ten miles, over mountain and through swamps, and they will crawl from one to five miles on their bellies. If you are hunting elephant you will walk from twenty to thirty miles a day, over dry river beds that suck your shoes into the sliding softness and make every step a mighty effort. The sun smites like hammers all day long, and the nights, in most parts of huntable Africa, are bitter cold. After a full day's work they are still supposed to supervise the constant necessary repair of the hunting vehicles, see that the camp is in good order, solve the problems of from one to two dozen natives, tend the sick and still be jovial drinking, talking and card-playing companions to the paying guests. Added to the general chores is the task of explaining the same things, over and over, to a succession of clients who want to know (and rightly) what is that tree, what kind of bird is that, why do we camp here instead of there and what were the boys saying in Swahili. The hunter also must listen to all the alibis, again and again, as to why the shooter missed the *topi* at twenty-five yards from a steady rest, and must soothe the injured pride of the man who is paying $100 a day to do something he would really rather not do, such as crawling through thorns after a sick and angry leopard.

The question, then, must be: *What do they get out of it?* They don't shoot unless they have to, and mostly they take no delight in killing, but rather regard it regretfully as the logical end-point of an exciting adventure. They are the greatest of game conservationists—the strictest abiders by the rules. They'll average five or six hundred bucks a month, plus free food and whisky, but they'll spend three or four hundred fixing up the cars they wreck in their mad dashes over rocky hills and pig-hole-riddled fields. They put up with boors and bores and bitches and cowards, and braggarts and creeps and occasional homosexuals who have the eye more on the hunter than the game. They work harder than any of the blacks in their retinue. They consider death as calmly as life, even when it applies to themselves. They drink too much when they are in town, and they mostly throw their money. There is no real future in professional hunting—when you get older you get too cautious for your own safety, and your slowed reflexes make you a liability to yourself and to your party.

I believe I know, as a friend of several hunters, what they get out of it. There is a simple love of nature, and of nature's creatures, as against a hatred for the contrived living of cities, for the claustrophobic connivances of civilization, that drives a man to the vastnesses of Africa to fulfill some need of basic simplicity in himself. My friend Selby, hopelessly lost in the jungles of so small a town as Nairobi, is Moses leading his flock when all he can see is horizons and a lion or two. The complete love and trust of his blacks is testament to this.

He is happy in the dawn and in the tiny gleaming fires of the camp, and secure in his knowledge of domination of his element. He worships a

buffalo or a lion or an elephant because he knows it can kill him painfully if he is not very careful. He builds his own bridges—makes his own roads. He still has the thrill of providing his own food, and the food of his friends. He recognizes the inevitability of death as an adjunct to life.

There are no more jealous people in the world than hunters. They have an intense pride in their work. A good white hunter will work himself into a breakdown to scare up a record bag for a man he despises. Hunters criticize each other constantly, and each man has his secret ground, a territory he endeavors, as long as possible, to keep from the ken of rival hunters. That personal pride prevents him from shooting the easy animal—what he wants is "heads."

"You are not shooting an elephant," Selby told me once, over a hot Martini at the day's end. "You are shooting the symbol of his tusks. You are not shooting to kill. You are shooting to make immortal the thing you shoot. To kill just anything is a sin. To kill something that will be dead soon, but is so fine as to give you pleasure for years, is wonderful. Everything dies. You only hasten the process. But you remember we hunted rhino for three weeks, and never shot a single one we saw? That's what I mean. When you shoot a lion, you are actually shooting its mane, something that will make you proud. You are shooting for yourself, not shooting just to kill."

This was an undue burst of eloquence from a usually taciturn young man, but I think I have his point, and the point of his brothers.

Cat Cay: Big Fish, Big Men, Big Money

by REGINALD WELLS

IN THEIR THOUSANDS THEY COME: giant bluefin tuna, big as baby elephants, barreling along the Great Bahama Bank northward up the Gulf Stream. The time is May, as the annual migration gets underway. Their breeding over, the tuna (weighing 400 to 700 pounds) shoot up Tuna Alley green and sassy, voraciously feeding along the way. And to meet them the men come out in boats from the mainland: big men with big tackle and enough money and strength to take this, the toughest fighting fish, out of the sea.

There is only one way to take giant tuna—the expensive way—and the few who do are the envied elite of big-game fishing. Like the fish, they come every year to Cat Cay, a storybook, palm-studded island paradise that lies off the Florida coast like a sumptuous fishing village anchored fifty miles out to sea. For these few mad weeks while the tuna run is on, this normally quiet, privately owned, club-operated haven-in-the-sun turns into one of the most fascinating sporting spectacles of the day. For days on end—against a backdrop of lush and carefree living where the stink and sweet smell of fish bait and expensive perfume mingle in an exciting, incomprehensible aroma—the battle of men and fish goes on.

Ashore, the women wait: exquisite, beautiful and as near perfection as everything else. They wait with the children, the governesses and the household staff, all ears cocked to the crackle of portable short-wave radios bringing the catch-by-catch report of the battle being fought at sea. "*Caliban* to *Samaki* . . . *Caliban* to *Samaki* . . . fish boated": Billy Carpenter has his second aboard and it's not yet eleven o'clock. Cheers from the beach of the Carpenter house. The wives playing cards at the club deal on uninterrupted. Hearing that Carpenter caught another fish is like being told God is Good. Here on Tuna Alley when they

say B.C. they don't mean Before Christ, they mean Before Carpenter. There is none better. The others try, year after year. They fish more days and more ways; but nobody can beat Carpenter. They swear he uses a secret, potent, fish-bait oil; they try to get his crew drunk, to bribe them away; and over it all Billy Carpenter, sportsman member of the Wilmington Du Pont clan, smiles in shy embarrassment at being best.

The little more than a square mile, T-shaped Cat Cay, which was bought in 1931 by millionaire New York advertising executive Louis R. Wasey, has become one of the most fabulous island playgrounds in the world; its burgee of a frightened cat perched atop a clover-leaf key is one of the most sought-after symbols of social acceptability. It offers its members and guests in a setting of Tahitian tranquility a way of life that most men only dream of. Championship golf can be played on the island's Windsor-Downs; two skeet and trap layouts test the most practiced shot; well-tended courts invite tournament-quality tennis; there's pool swimming and ocean swimming in surfless, azure-blue water. Guests live in individual cottages of native architecture and breakfast comes delivered to the door by "bicycle express." Nights, balmy but cool with the gentle breeze of the trade winds, are filled with the sounds of dancing, dining and a continuous round of parties. A fleet of station wagons cruises the island's roads at five-minute intervals, ready to pick up and deliver anybody anywhere. There is no tipping: natives who accept tips are fired; guests who offer them are never invited back. Cat Cay even has its own coin currency (one key is worth one dollar; half a key fifty cents), and during the winter season boasts one of the only two gambling casinos in the British Empire (the other is in Nassau). It is little wonder quite a few members have built permanent homes on the island. Sportsmen like Wendell Anderson, John Olin, Fred Matthaei and Carl Badenhausen have found in this island retreat the ultimate in leisure living. Yet, contrary to popular belief, Cat Cay is not the private domain of millionaires and you don't have to be one to stay there. Double accommodations per person at the height of the season are about thirty-five dollars a day, American plan.

But it is the tuna that has really made Cat Cay. From all parts of the world big-game anglers come here to pit their skill against the giant bluefin. They come as though called by a mountain and while this isn't the biggest fish in the sea, it is the toughest, and will test a man as no other. Over the years the ritual of taking them has been refined to a tough science. The formula: a fast maneuverable boat plus a keen-eyed captain, and massive, precision-made tackle. To these elements the fisherman must add his own armor: the strength of his back and legs and the limit of his endurance. The boat, if one is not to feel second-class, must be a Rybovich sport-fisherman ($65,000 and up). From a fish tower thirty feet above the water, your boat captain (salary: $6000 to $10,000 a year) stands ready to mastermind the battle. In the stern, harnessed to a heavyweight glass rod ($200) and hunched over a 12/O Fin-Nor handmade reel ($600), the fisherman sits in a dentistlike fighting chair ($550). On the reel, tightly wound, lies 750 yards of wetted thirty-nine-thread linen line which has a breaking strain of 117 pounds, and a drag lever that can increase the pressure from zero to 120 pounds. In the bait box, the bait waits, lovingly prepared: mullet mostly (fifty cents a flown-in pound), dressed and rigged in a ritual as carefully followed as a sacrificial offering. First the backbone is broken, then the belly slit open and the entrails cleaned out. Next, a needle-sharp size 12/O hook is placed in the belly opening and then the whole fish is sewn up with a cross-stitch to keep the gills together. A one-ounce lead weight is fixed to the piano-wire leader and anchored securely underneath the mullet's lower lip. When trolled across the path of a tuna, the bait must look "alive" and swim right side up.

The fisherman is ready for his first tuna.

The boats lie waiting at Gun Cay Cut, twenty or thirty of them, their fish towers bobbing and weaving in the swell like drunken oil derricks. The starting gun ("Touchdown Tommy") booms on the committee boat *Samaki,* and in one mad surge the fishing fleet roars at top speed for the Gulf Stream. Like thoroughbreds out of the starting gate they race south to meet tuna. A shout from the tower as a school is sighted quickens and panics the pulse. Is the harness clip secure? How's the drag? Got it set at forty pounds? Brace yourself against the footplate. Wrap both hands around the rod butt. My God, it feels as thick as the wrong end of a baseball bat. The mate now clips the baited leader to your line and stands poised, ready to throw it overboard at the exact instant. Moving in a fast turn, the boat throttles back and comes up on the tuna school from ahead, pacing them obliquely, ready to cut across their path.

"Christ, look at 'em!" shouts the captain. "They're so thick you could walk on 'em." You see the huge brown shadows just under the surface, moving steadily northward. "Now!" yells the captain and overboard goes the bait. You throw the drag into free spool and let it drop back. Twenty yards . . . twenty-five yards. . . . "Okay! Hold it there. . . ." Back comes the drag lever to forty pounds, and now you wait. "He's coming up on it . . . steady." Spray explodes and, in one frightening, body-lifting jerk, fish and man are tied. "Strike! Strike! Harder! Again . . ." And you can strike no more. The reel is screaming as line burns off in the tuna's desperate first run. My God, how far is he going? The line hisses and cuts its way through the water. "Ease off on the drag . . . quick!" shouts the captain, throwing the boat into a sudden turn to iron out a dangerous belly in the line. Behind the chair the mate keeps angler, rod and line lined up with the fish. Excessive sideway pull on the rod will snap the line like cotton.

The fish stops. You start. Increase the drag pressure and start to take line. Lean the rod down and winch it up. Then with everything you've got lean back against him until the rod tip can go no higher. Forward again, greedily winding the line back on to the reel. Fighting, gut-pulling, by sheer strength the line must be taken back. Pump it up, wind it down, pump it up, wind it down. He objects and stops coming. You're beginning to feel it. Your reeling arm is ready to drop off, the harness is chafing your back raw, you are sick to your stomach with fatigue but, by God, you've got him coming. Just a few more turns; there can't be much more line out. Keep the rod tip high. Maintain the pressure. A moment's slackness in the line and he'll be off. "See him? About twenty yards out . . . about a 500-pounder," calls the captain. You double the effort. The hurts aren't hurting any more. The pumping and winding are automatic. You've been on him half an hour. He stops again and you feel him measuring his strength against yours. "Watch it . . . he's turning. . . ." And suddenly the line is screaming away again as he makes his second fantastic run, this time, alas, not on the surface, but down, down, down.

At this moment grown men have cried openly and uncontrollably. Others vomit on the spot. Enough is too much. Down, down, he goes, taking twice as much line as before. Paralyzed, helpless, you watch the wet line on the reel turn to dry and every nerve in your body cries out, "Don't make me pull that thing up again." And for another half hour the body-breaking business of pumping and winding, gaining and losing goes on. He's dead weight now—500 pounds of him—and lying deep, deep, deep. With your back and legs pump him hard, but gently, too. Give him more pressure on the drag. Will the line take it? Too much and you'll break him off. Up and down you tune the drag lever, testing his mettle by the pulsating tautness of the line. Screw down hard and make him feel it when he moves. The rod tip dips and shudders and you lean back on it. He didn't like that. Again, the whole rod and the life line that joins you to him shudders and jerks like a tugging signal for help. He's slapping his gill plates; watch it . . . ease off the pressure. O.K., screw it down again and pump and wind, pump and wind. Your back is fit to break in two. The veins in your arm stand out like bloated blue rivers and blisters are forming on your reeling hand. Minute by minute, trembling from exhaustion, wet and itching from the salt of your own sweat, you wear the monster out and bring him up. This time he's coming easier and fast. The boat backs up toward the fish, and you race to pick up line. Another few yards and the line bellies out dangerously. You're cussing now and mouthing horrible things. You want him bad, like you've never wanted anything else. He's coming good now, and you know you've got him.

You can see him again, a big silver and blue bullet, his head moving back and forth slowly with every wincing wind of the reel handle. For an hour he has fought you. Now he comes. The mate stands ready to gaff. The captain inches the boat back toward the fish. At last you can see the leader wire—the finish line.

Then, while you watch, a flashing brown torpedo dashes in from nowhere and makes a lightning pass across your fish, a whitish-yellow belly turning your heart to stone. "Sharks! Get 'im in, Goddamit. . . ." yells the captain. As if he, too, heard the warning, the fear-ridden big fish thrashes against the line in one last desperate plunge to escape. Frantically you pump him back in. Then they hit. The bastards. Those jumped-up-never-come-down, no-good stinkin' bastards waited for you to bring it up and serve it to them. They come in fast underneath and from behind and hit again and again, tearing forty-pound chunks of flesh out every time they bite. The mate is pumping bullets into them from an automatic, but it stops nothing. They're out of control now, in frenzied attack, ramming the stern of the boat, slashing and tearing in a churning, bloody foam. Right up to the rod they follow it, attacking all the way. Just the head of the bluefin remains, and a mawed-up mess with a tail. You hang limp in the harness, spent, trembling still, sick and sorry. It's all over. The mate cuts the carcass free and you watch it sink slowly, turning over and over, wide eyes big as teacups staring back with death and disbelief. Ashamed, so the captain won't hear, you mumble, "I'm sorry, big fish."

The boat guns its way to full speed. From the tower the captain, annoyed, yells, "For Christ sake, get the fish in the boat quicker next time," and then turns his eyes to the horizon to search for another school and another fish. Broken, you stagger out of the chair like falling from a rack and go in search of a jolt. Then, aching, you lie down and pray hard that your captain won't find another fish all day.

This is the stuff of taking tuna and the greats at this sport—men like Carpenter, Bob Maytag, Charlie Johnson, George Bass, Julio Sanchez and a score of others—can overpower a 700-pound bluefin in twenty minutes, do it five or six times in a day, play and celebrate all night and then get up at

dawn for more. The addiction to this punishing pastime is growing and is fast becoming an international cult. Gathering at Cat Cay every May are anglers from Australia, South Africa, Cuba, Peru, England and a dozen more countries. They come to take part in the World Series of tuna fishing— the Bahamas International Tuna Match, but more than that they come because the giant bluefin calls them.

Great Writer Versus Great Fish

by ZANE GREY

A HALF TON OF RUBBER AND STEEL *springs, hurling itself twice its length out of the bright green sea.*

That was what Zane Grey saw at the end of his line as he braced himself in the stern of his launch. If he could hang on it would be the biggest game fish ever landed with rod and reel.

For three years Grey spent the fishing seasons at Tahiti trying in vain to bring one of the giant marlin to gaff. Then came the day, May 16, 1930. Let him tell it. He has just come out of the pass this rainy morning for his last try of the year:

"As usual we put out a big bonito for bait. My heavy outfit holds 1500 yards—1000 of thirty-nine thread line with 500 yards of forty-two thread for backing. A rain squall was obscuring the white-tumbling reef and slowly moving toward us. Peter Williams, New Zealand whaler, my right-hand man in the boat, sat with me in the stern holding the rod. We were just fishing, hardly expecting anything in these few remaining hours.

"Suddenly I heard a sounding, vicious thump of water. I leaned over to press my gloved hand on the spool to keep the reel from overrunning.

Out where the bait had been was a whirling, closing hole in the boiling white-green water. I saw a wide purple mass close under the surface. I leaped to straddle the rod. It was an incredible, wonderful strike.

"In a very few seconds the fish ran out 200 yards of line, then, turning to the right, he tore off another hundred. Then a white splash, high as a tree, shot up, out of which leaped the most magnificent of all the leaping fish I had ever seen.

"Here at last at the end of my line was the great Tahitian swordfish. He looked monstrous. He was pale—shiny gray in color, with broad stripes of purple. When he hit the water he sent up a splash like the flying scud of surf on a reef. Out he blazed again, faster, higher, longer.

"I kept working like a windmill to get up the slack. The monster had circled in these two leaps. Again he burst out, a plunging leap. Next instant such a terrific jerk as I had never sustained nearly unseated me. He was away on his run.

" 'Water,' I ordered. *'Water on this reel! Quick!'*

"The white line melted, smoked, burned off the reel. I smelled the scorching. It burned through my gloves. John was quick to plunge a bucket over-board and to douse reel, rod and me with water. That saved us.

" 'After him, Pete!' I called. The engines roared and the launch danced around to rush full speed after the fish. A third of a mile from us he came up to pound and beat the water into a maelstrom.

"I pumped and reeled as never before in my life and got back 200 yards before he was off again. At the end of this race he showed like a plunging elephant and sounded. This gave me a chance to get the harness on. With the strain transferred to my shoulders I felt that I might not be torn asun-der. I got back all but a hundred yards. Close enough when he came up again. Pete tried to keep the stern toward him, but he shot ahead again so that I missed seeing two leaps directly in front of the boat. As the launch sheered around I saw the third of that unbelievably swift and savage series of plunges.

"The swordfish sped off another hundred yards of line, but we drew close and saw him leap again only 200 feet from our starboard bow. His power to leap was beyond belief. This swordfish was so huge that when he came out in dazzling swift flight my crew simply went mad. I did not need to warn Peter not to let that fish hit us. He would have made splinters of the launch.

"He curved back and to the left again. We sheered, but not quick enough; the swordfish went under the bow. For a sickening moment I was sure the line had fouled on the keel or propellers. Jimmy, the big Tahitian, was about to dive to clear it, but I ordered the men to hold him, there were sharks milling about. I plunged the tip of the rod over, deep. A second later came the scream of the reel. He was away on a tight line.

"Then came the long struggle in the rain and chill. My swordfish, with short, swift runs, took us five miles further out and then brought us back, all this without leaping. He broke water on the surface a number of times, but never sounded after that first dive. At last he slowed and took to milling, a sure sign of a rattled fish. He made one high frantic jump about 200 yards ahead of us and then threshed on the surface, sending the bloody spray high. All on board were quick to see that sign of weakening, of tragedy—blood.

"In all, he leaped fifteen times clear of the water. I kept no account of his threshings. He had leaped too often and run too swiftly to make an extremely long fight. In another hour I had him coming. The slow strokes of his tail took no more line. I saw a wide, shining mass, greenish silver, crossed by purple bars. It moved, it weaved, but I could drag it easily. Then I felt tugs at it. 'Sharks!' I yelled.

"Peter grabbed a gaff and lunged. There was an enormous roar of water and a sheeted splash. I saw a blue tail so wide I thought I was crazy. It threw a six-foot yellow shark into the air.

"I unhooked the harness and stood up. The swordfish rolled on the surface, extending from forward of the cockpit to two yards or more be-yond the stern. His barred body was as big as that of an ox. A big shark had a hold just below the anal fin. Peter sent the lance clear through its neck. Sharks came in from all directions. It was Peter with his lance who whipped them off, though all were fighting them. We made fast a towline and started for camp.

"It took a dozen men to drag him up on the sand to the tripod. His body was as symmetrical and round as that of a good big stallion. He car-ried this roundness back to his anal fin, an extra-ordinary feature for a marlin spearfish. Right there I named this species the Great Tahitian Striped Marlin. His tail had a spread of five feet two inches. His length was fourteen feet two inches. His girth was six feet nine inches and his weight 1040 pounds. Every drop of blood had been drained from his body, and this, with at least 200 pounds of flesh the sharks had torn away, would have fetched his true weight to 1250 pounds.

"Nevertheless, despite my elation as I looked up at his appalling shape as he hung, I remembered the giant marlin which Captain Mitchell had lost in 1928 from one of our boats on our first trip. We estimated that one at twenty-two or twenty-three feet. Or the twenty-foot fish I had raised at Tau-tira, or the twenty-eight-foot specimen the natives had seen repeatedly alongside their canoes. And I thought of the prodigious leaps and astounding fleetness of this one I had caught. 'My Heaven,' I breathed. 'What could a bigger one do?' "

EDITOR'S NOTE: *Zane Grey never found a bigger one. He died in 1939. On August 4, 1953 off Capo Blanco A. C. Glassel, Jr. pulled in a black marlin fourteen feet six inches long weighing 1560 pounds. In 1959 Alfred Dean of Ceduna, South Australia, landed a white shark sixteen feet ten inches long, nine and a half feet in girth, weighing more than a ton—2664 pounds.*

Big Fish and High Seas by PHILIP WYLIE

A FRIEND INVITES YOU, LET US IMAGINE, to go out in the Gulf Stream off Miami or Palm Beach for a day's trolling. You are, let us presume, an ace on the golf links and no slouch with a tennis racket, but your angling experience is limited to hauling up a few catfish from the muddy bottom of the Mississippi River. Your friend can run a boat, but he's no angler, either.

But out you two go, in your friend's brand-new and snappy motor cruiser, with some fishing tackle he "picked up" at a store in Miami and some bait bought at a public dock—mullet, let's say. Your host has had a quick lesson in "rigging" these baits and, after some failures, he finally manages to get one of them trolling smoothly. It has a hook in it, and a leader attached to the hook and a line running to the rod and reel—which *you* hold.

Now to your intense surprise, out of the sea, in pursuit of your bait, there suddenly roars a broad-headed hammer-bill. (Note: there's no such animal—this is an *illustrative* tale.) The broad-headed hammer-bill grabs your mullet and you, in turn, hook the giant. You battle him all afternoon, and at long last—the friend forgot to buy a gaff—you and he get the fish on board by using a lasso and main strength. Proudly you steam to shore. Bystanders at the dock—old fishing hands—allow this to be "the biggest doggone broad-headed hammer-bill" they ever heard of—a world record for the breed. They talk mournfully about "beginner's luck." Who wouldn't like to hold a world record for *something?*

Time was, however, when you'd have been out of luck on your record. Various institutions and publications used to keep what they called "world-record charts" of game fishes taken in the seven seas. But they were hazy lists. Some of the entries were fish that had been harpooned and shot—not fairly caught on rod and reel. Some were fish that had been dragged to boatside after sharks had torn away half their flesh—and the weights given were imaginative guesses about what the scales might have registered if the sharks hadn't been so hungry.

Certain clubs—notably in California, Florida, Australia and Great Britain—had exacting rules for sea fishing. Those old standards were often rigorous, and anglers still look with awe at the perfectionist Californians. Standing in open boats, wearing business suits, using twenty-four-thread line (which broke at a strain of seventy-two pounds)—with reel handles which *spun backward* whenever a hooked fish ran and no more "drag" than could be exerted by thumb pressure on a leather tab against the line spool—these sportsmen caught tuna, marlin, broadbill swordfish and other rugged giants of the blue waters. They came home with bloodied hands, busted knuckles, broken fingers—they always had a surgeon on duty at the club—and only occasionally with a fish. They were the purest sportsmen the world had ever seen—but there weren't many like them. The others made their own rules, with changes when changes were convenient. It was pretty unsatisfactory.

In 1939, when he was in Australia as head of an expedition for the American Museum of Natural History, Mike Lerner, one of the top sports fishermen of the world, debated these matters with the late Clive Firth, a noted Australian angler. Firth suggested that Americans should devise and administer rules. He had noticed that the British colonies and the mother country quarreled about everything—even fishing—and he thought that England, along with her colonies and dominions, would accept American judgment as sporting and impartial—and without starting another Revolutionary War. He thought all other nations would accept the lead of the U.S.A. and Britain.

Mike talked over Firth's proposal with other members of the expedition, then got in touch with leading anglers and prominent fishing clubs the world over. They were enthusiastic. Everybody wanted to be in the game—but nobody wanted to umpire.

A bit reluctantly, Mike selected a group of deep-sea fishermen known for their skill and fairness, a number of ichthyologists and other scientists, and a few chaps like Van Campen Heilner and Ernest Hemingway, who had fished about everywhere and written on the subject. Later on, this writer (who has wet an occasional line, but is still a tyro compared to others on the Association's official roster) also became an officer of the world-umpiring society now known everywhere as the International Game Fish Association or, for short, the IGFA.

Let us get back now to that gigantic "broad-headed hammer-bill" we imagined you caught while trolling with a friend. Fifteen years ago you would probably have weighed him. You might have measured his length. A local fishing editor might have published these details, along with a photograph—which you were almost sure to take. If you didn't somebody on the dock would. News of the fact that a 486-pound broad-headed hammer-bill had been "brought in" off Palm Beach—or Miami—*might* have reached one of the institutions or the top-notch sports magazines that tried, haphazardly, to keep "world records" for marine angling. And, since the largest "broadhead" hitherto

"reported" would have been a 308-pounder that had washed up on the beach at Cape May, you would hold the world record. Nothing official about it. Nothing formal. A week later a guy might hook a bigger broadhead, shoot him full of holes with a rifle, harpoon him three times, boat him with a windlass and a steel cable and take that record away from you—most unfairly.

The IGFA stopped all that.

Today the IGFA supplies, on request from anybody, printed rules for standard tackle and "fair" fishing methods. It also supplies forms to be filled in by anybody claiming a world record—forms which demand exact data on the kind of line used, the type of rod, the reel, the number of hooks (no more than two are allowed) and so on. A snapshot of the fish and the tackle is required. So is a sample of the line actually used in making the catch; and that sample, in every case, is checked by a professional testing company. "World records" are kept for lines of various strengths. There is a set of world records for fish taken on line that breaks at a strain of twelve pounds (or "twelve-pound test"), on twenty-pound test, thirty, fifty, eighty and so on—with a final "All Tackle" class which lists the biggest fish caught fairly on any size tackle.

The IGFA has been in existence for more than two decades, and its reports are recognized almost everywhere except in the U.S.S.R. Any established fishing club (the IGFA has no individual members) will be admitted upon application after an examination to make sure the club is *bona fide* and its members are genuine sports fishermen. In the angling centers of all civilized nations (and many that would be considered highly uncivilized) the IGFA has a "representative" who serves for the honor of the post and the love of the sport. He is available to give anybody and everybody IGFA information and to investigate any question about a record claim that may come up.

The IGFA itself has its offices in the Dupont Building in Miami, Florida, with Miss Anne H. Schiehl in charge. (Miss Francesca La Monte, the noted ichthyologist, who handled the office while it was housed in New York's Museum of Natural History, did not go to Miami when they moved. She recently retired from her post at the museum, and is living in New York City.) The "okay" of at least the president, a vice-president and the secretary is necessary for a claim to be accepted as a new record. Wherever the information about a catch is insufficient or confusing, the secretary asks for clarification. If it doesn't clear up, a local representative is instructed to make an on-the-scene investigation.

So, frequently, men in Cape Town and Queensland, in Tahiti and Chile, take trains and planes to some remote spot where a gigantic fish—or a fish spectacularly large for the type of tackle used—has been caught. If the "local" man fails to solve a questionable situation (Was the line really twelve-lb. test? Did the fish actually weigh seventy-six and one quarter pounds? Are the scales that said the marlin went over a thousand *accurate?* Was the fish gaffed according to IGFA rules—or is there something to the rumor it was harpooned?), an official from the home office may start a long trek to check in person.

People cheat, occasionally—but damn rarely. The IGFA relies on the integrity of the angler. It has to. It cannot have an inspector in every boat and on every dock and beach where anybody is fishing, the world over. So you *might* be able to pull a fraud—send in far lighter tackle than you actually used or get a dockmaster and a weighmaster to swear that your fish was bigger than he really was—and get away with it.

But we at IGFA believe there are no violations of even the most trifling parts of the rules among the catches listed as world records. For one thing, anglers—contrary to the legend about them—tend to be more scrupulously honest than the general run of Homo sapiens. For another, the eyes that scan the photographs and read the affidavits are very expert—the eyes of trained scientists, veteran anglers. For a third, the angler who cheats raises the hackles of *all other anglers*—and the rumor of a faked entry gets around. Somebody—some indignant angler—writes the IGFA. Investigation gets under way. And presently the malefactor is trapped or persuaded into admitting his dishonest attempt.

Anglers are funny people, and the IGFA is a sort of world crossroads for them. People drop in for advice on where to take a vacation or on what

tackle to carry to the Celebes or Patagonia. Then they drop in again on their return with marvelous tales of fish, seen, hooked, lost—and caught, mounted and ensconced above the mantel at home. Cablegrams come in from every quarter of the globe, asking for every imaginable sort of fishing information, telling every conceivable kind of tale about fishes seen or apparently seen or reported by somebody to somebody else.

A great many travelers to America know only the IGFA when they arrive here. Americans voyaging into the sixty-odd regions where IGFA has a representative or a member club, or both, have found that "I'm a fisherman" is an open sesame to new languages and new friends, and a sure means of finding new piscatorial fun. For fishermen, being philosophers, are also friendly; ninety-nine in every hundred take pride and pleasure in "hanging" a stranger on one of their local big-game beauties. The notion that anglers keep secret their "best" fishing grounds has been blown to statistical mincemeat by IGFA. Hunters may have such a selfish practice; if so, fishermen are different.

"I know," they will say (on the shores of the Red Sea or the Yellow Sea, or the coast of Wales or Africa), "a special spot where the monsters really bite!" And then they take you there.

Nowhere else is there such an association: men and women by the hundreds of thousands, familiar with fishing and the sea, fond of both and devoted to their pursuit. These people are ideally suited to collecting scientific information which may help to fill out unknown chapters of sea knowledge. One IGFA "Yearbook" shows what they can do, for it is a huge table, by months, of what fish may be caught where on this planet, with what baits—not just a superguide for sportsmen who want a new kind of fishing vacation, but a huge, scientific survey of where the fish are, and go, *when.* The problems of ichthyologists in various parts of the earth are sent to IGFA headquarters—whence they go out to appropriate clubs and persons for answers that often overwhelm the inquiring scientists with useful data.

It is apparently a law of human nature that the sea hunter will become the observer and the observer the amateur naturalist, or more. Indeed, many anglers, like many hunters, have put aside their killing equipment and replaced it with the gear of observation and study. So the IGFA hopes and expects that in the years to come it will be increasingly an organization for gathering marine data as well as a sports society.

The tab for these many enterprises is picked up by one man: Michael—or, as I've called him here, Mike—Lerner. (Pretty nearly everybody who knows him—and that includes potentates and porters in every segment of the round world's map, calls him Mike, anyhow. We might as well.) In middle life Mike was already a world-famous angler, among the world's foremost big-game hunters and a leading collector of museum specimens. He was also one of the founders of the Lerner Stores (if that doesn't ring a bell in your head, ask your wife). He decided he owed a debt to his favorite sport of ocean fishing, a debt he hadn't managed to repay by contributing many huge specimens of fishes, and in some cases whole rooms of specimens, to half a dozen of the world's leading museums.

When he founded the IGFA, he arranged to pay all expenses himself. But Mike didn't want the IGFA to be a "patriarchal" organization, a Mike-bossed affair. So it is the member clubs which make, by majority vote, all decisions on matters of principle and rules; on other matters the officers decide.

Following that law of human nature I set down earlier, Mike finally went into science. On the island of Bimini, in the Bahamas, he built the American Museum of Natural History a "field station" for research. There, in a magnificent laboratory—and a commodious adjoining residence—scientists can study the wide variety of sea habitats that occur at Bimini. Because of the value of primitive sea life in studying cell structure and basic biology, the laboratory has attracted large numbers of scientists from all parts of the world.

That's the story of IGFA. Its worth to human relations the world over cannot be exaggerated. Its value as an umpire in a great sport is deeply appreciated by many and should be understood by all. Those who serve as its officers love fishing —and they love people too.

An Australian dreamed it up. An American made it a fact, surpassing the dream. And everybody who wets a line in salt water—whatever his nationality, his bait or the fish he hopes to hang —has reason to rejoice in the result.

STERNGLASS

3

BASEBALL: THE GREAT AMERICAN GAME

PERHAPS NO SPORT DEMANDS MORE OF A MAN OVER *a sustained period of time than baseball. Day in and day out, season after season, nearly every move a player makes is recorded. The sum total of all these moves is his accomplishment. Many thrilling moments may have been consumed in the compiling, a great catch like Al Gionfriddo's of DiMaggio's sure home run in the World Series, or a great hit like Bobby Thomson's home run in the '51 play-off game with the Dodgers. But in the long run (and in baseball, that is what counts) they are only statistics, one put-out, one home run. The great men of baseball are those who deliver like the postman, "through rain and snow and in the darkest night . . ." Babe Ruth, Joe DiMaggio, Ted Williams . . . there are others equally memorable, but here are three tributes to these three which seem to capture the quality that made them champions. Then there are two pieces on teams, teams being, after all, what win ball games: the Orioles in the nineties and the early days of the Dodgers when they first moved into Ebbets Field. Speaking of Ebbets Field, which has made way for an apartment house, we have included a eulogy to the Polo Grounds which is scheduled to meet the same fate. This just about covers everything in baseball except the little mannerisms which make it colorful, and Ford Frick gives us the inside dope on that. As a bonus we bring back the Babe for an encore, in his—and maybe the game's—greatest moment, when he called his shot in the World Series and put the ball where his heart was . . . in the bleachers.*

The Real Babe Ruth

by ROGER KAHN

IN HIS TIME AND IN HIS WAY, GEORGE Herman Ruth was a holy sinner. He was a man of measureless lust, selfishness and appetites, but he was also a man undyingly faithful, in a manner, to both his public and to his game. Tradition, which always distorts, had remolded Babe Ruth almost as extensively in a decade as it had remolded Abraham Lincoln in a century. Thirteen years after Ruth's death and twenty-six years after his last disastrous season, only the image of holiness remains.

Ruth died on August 16, 1948. After the funeral service, as a great crowd stood in reverent silence, pallbearers, many of them Ruth's own teammates, carried the casket into the fierce heat of the summer day.

"Lord," whispered Joe Dugan, the Yankee third baseman during Ruth's prime, "I'd give my right arm for an ice-cold beer."

Waite Hoyt, the former pitcher, grunted under the burden of the coffin and turned slightly. "Joe," he murmured, "so would the Babe."

The middle-aged men, who spent their youth playing side by side with Ruth, remember. They remember more clearly than the writers who traveled with him or the fans who watched him; even more clearly, perhaps, than the women—the adopted daughters and the wife—who loved him most. For they knew him in the camaraderie of strong, successful men, where no man passed verdict on the other but where everyone knew "Jidge" Ruth was at once the strongest and most successful.

There is a curious derivative of Gresham's law that applies to American heroes. Just as good money drives out bad in economics, so heroic fancy drives out heroic fact and, in the case of heroes, we are often left standing in a forest of chopped-down cherry trees wondering what our man was actually like. The greater the hero, the more prevalent the fictions. Since Ruth was the most popular of all

baseball heroes, movie companies, careless writers and glib storytellers have busied themselves with the obfuscation of fact.

But to begin with, everything you have ever heard about Ruth on a baseball field is probably the truth or close to it. Ruth could hit a baseball higher, farther and more dramatically than anyone else. His record of sixty home runs in one season is unquestionably the classic of all sports standards. His career totals of 714 home runs and 2056 bases on balls are still far beyond mortal challenge. His great swing, even when he struck out, was more awesome than the stroke of a lesser man which happened to produce a home run.

He probably did, as he claimed, call his shot against the Chicago Cubs in the 1932 World Series, when with two strikes he pointed toward the bleachers, then whaled the next pitch where he had pointed. Wally Pipp, one of Ruth's old teammates, explains that whenever Ruth was sure of himself and on a spot, he held up the first two fingers of his right hand to let the pitcher know that there was still one strike left, which would be enough. But others who were there say the Chicago gesture was unmistakable, so the incident well may have transpired as Ruth told it.

He does seem always to have made the right play in the outfield. He did have superlative baseball instincts. He did bring all players' salaries up behind his own and, more assuredly than anything else, he was the savior baseball had to find after the Chicago White Sox dumped the 1919 World Series. All these are part of the legend and all ring true.

But once the stories of Ruth move off the diamond, fact fades away and dies. He liked children, but his life was not a priestly dedication to healing sick boys. He liked jokes, but his humor at best was coarse. He was devoutly religious, but only sporadically, when suddenly he felt compelled to make up for lost time in church. He may not have been an utter social boor, but he was something less than tactful, something less than gracious, something very much less than sensitive.

Once when he accidentally spiked a Yankee named Ray Morehart, he apologized profusely, then said to a veteran, "Hey, when that guy join the club? Last week?" Morehart had been with the club for months. Ruth hadn't noticed. To him everyone under thirty-five was "kid" and everyone older was "doc." He was absorbed in himself and his talent and although he was generous with audiences to fans, these were never anything more than audiences. Fans came to Ruth. Celebrities came to Ruth. The world came to Ruth. Ruth went to no one, unless summoned.

What was he like? Bennie Bengough, the old catcher, remembers that in his own rookie year of 1923, Ruth, the veteran, made a point each payday of displaying his pay check from the Yankees. "Hey, kid," he'd say to Bengough. "Hey, Barney Google. How'd you like to have this, kid?" Each two-week check was for $2000, which Bengough says was more than he earned all year. "But," Bengough adds, "he didn't show it in a boasting way. More like it was his idea of fun."

Dugan was already established as a star when the Yankees acquired him from the Boston Red Sox that season. On the day Dugan joined the club, Ruth dumped a batch of mail in his lap. "Open these for me, will ya, kid?" Ruth said. "Keep the ones with checks and the ones from broads. Throw out the others." It was just before game time and Ruth, following his custom, was late. He undressed quickly while Dugan went through one pile of mail and Whitey Witt, the centerfielder, went through another.

"Here's a wire from Ziegfield," Witt said. "He'll give you fifteen hundred bucks a week to go in a show next winter."

Ruth crumpled the wire and threw it away. "I ain't an actor," he said.

"Christ," said Mike McNally, a reserve infielder, "make it while you can. For fifteen hundred a week, learn to act."

"Yeah," Ruth said, putting on his spikes. "Yeah."

"If you go in a show," McNally said, "and I come into town to see you, can you get me a couple of Annie Oakley's?"

"If I go in a show, I'll get you guys all the broads you want."

Babe Ruth, a huge, ignorant, sentimental emperor, was the product of a childhood so bleak that it was almost no childhood at all. Then, in his early manhood, he found himself earning considerably more money and possessing far more popularity than the President of the United States. He was not humble in his change of fortune. He knew that he was the biggest name in baseball and whatever his skill brought him, he not only accepted, but demanded.

Once when he visited France, accompanied by his wife and daughter, he surprised Americans who knew him well by announcing, "Paris ain't much of a town." Parisian crowds had failed to recognize him. The American Embassy there, receiving a letter addressed to George Herman Ruth, took an advertisement in the Paris *Herald Tribune* listing Ruth's name along with many others found on unclaimed mail. "How do you like them guys?" Ruth said in anger and in pain. "Taking an ad in the paper to find out where the hell I am! That could never happen in New York."

It never could have. Ruth lived for fifty-three years, but his special time was the fifteen seasons he played for the New York Yankees. In the twenties,

the country teemed with sports figures whose names meant immediate idolatry: Tilden and Grange, Rockne and Dempsey, Ty Cobb and Bobby Jones and John McGraw. No one gathered and awed so many crowds for so many years as the man the whole nation called "the Babe."

On the field, his shape was unique. It was thick through the shoulders, prodigious at the belly and set on comically thin legs. He was pigeon-toed and he ran with delicate, mincing steps that all but concealed his speed. Off the field the man had other marks. He chewed cigars and wore camel's-hair polo coats and affected a light-brown cap. His face was broad and wide, dominated by a vast, flat nose and an overhanging brow. His voice was hoarse and loud. As he moved, center stage moved with him.

Ruth appeared on the American scene through the unlikely gateway of Baltimore, Maryland, where he was born in 1895, one of the number of children with which the union of Kate Schanberg and G. H. Ruth, Sr., was blessed. In later years, Ruth invariably claimed that his father owned a saloon and that he had been born a few flights above the bar. This is open to serious question. Photographs of Ruth's birthplace show no ground-floor saloon, only the inevitable Baltimore white stoop-front. Undoubtedly, the elder Ruth was familiar with Baltimore saloons, but whether as entrepreneur or client remains uncertain.

Like W. C. Fields, Babe Ruth never tasted liquor before he was six. He also chewed tobacco and appears to have stolen whatever loose change his parents left about the house. "I was a bad kid," Ruth himself said afterward. In 1902, when he was seven, Ruth was placed in St. Mary's Industrial School as an incorrigible. He was not, of course, an orphan, as legend insists. He was the unmanageable child of parents who were not passionately dedicated to parenthood.

St. Mary's, a pile of masonry as solemn as a prison, was fenced off from the outside world and run by the Roman Catholic Order of Xavieran Brothers. There, under the guidance of Brother Matthias, a gentle man six and a half feet tall, Ruth was taught to read and to write, schooled in the crafts of tailoring and shirtmaking and, in his spare hours, he played baseball. No one ever had

to teach him baseball. Ruth was the ultimate natural. When he was nineteen, St. Mary's released him to the Baltimore Orioles, who were then in the International League, and, staggered by a $600-a-year contract, Ruth went forth into the world. He was a babe; the nickname came quickly and logically.

Within two seasons he was starring as pitcher and pinch hitter for the Red Sox. In eight matches with Walter Johnson, the finest of modern American League pitchers, Ruth won six, three by scores of 1 to 0 and once when his homer provided the only run. In World Series competition he pitched twenty-nine consecutive scoreless innings, a record that still stands. Ruth was a superb left-hander. He chose to move into the outfield for Boston in 1919 only because his pinch hitting was so effective that he felt he could earn more playing every day.

In 1920 the Yankees, then as now owned by millionaires, purchased Ruth for $100,000. Colonel Jake Ruppert, one of the owners, had to take out a $370,000 mortgage on Fenway Park, the Red Sox's field, as the second provision of what was the biggest of all baseball deals up to that time. Dividends were prompt. In his first season with the Yankees, Ruth hit fifty-four home runs, almost double the old record and an achievement beyond belief to fans accustomed to home-run champions with totals of ten or twelve. Abruptly, Ruth was the wonder of baseball. The fans recognized it and so did Ruth.

This, then, was his stage:

An incredulous, idolizing America, gaping through the twenties, and all the while congratulating itself on its own maturity.

Here were the supporting players:

Jumping Joe Dugan, out of Holy Cross. Intelligent, quiet, gifted. Could take a drink.

Waite Hoyt, high-school graduate, who later attended a school for undertakers. Acerbic, witty, skilled. Could take a drink.

Miller Huggins, manager. Diminutive old baseball pro. Acid, tough and unamused by jokes about his size. Could take a drink, but preferred his players not to.

Bob Meusel. Tall, silent. Could take a drink.

Whitey Witt. Short, garrulous. Could take a drink.

Assorted other players, courtesans, lords, ladies and Presidents.

This is what he did:

Led the American League in homers every year but one in the decade.

Led the Yankees into seven World Series.

Drew a salary that went in rapid stages to $52,000 to $70,000 to $80,000.

Provided the gate appeal that built Yankee Stadium.

Rebuilt the game, which had been scientific, into an extension of his own slugging style.

And this is how he played his role:

One day in 1924 (forty-six homers for the Babe) Herb Pennock, a genteel pitcher, was asked to attend a party sponsored by a prominent family near Wilmington, Delaware. "Hug," Pennock said, "they want some Yankees; I need two dozen autographed balls and three players."

"You got the balls," Huggins said. "Which players?"

"Ruth, Dugan and Meusel."

"Okay," Huggins said, "but remember. We got a game in Philly tomorrow."

Ruth was the hit of the party. Yes, he said, baseball had come easy to him. The swing? Well, he'd liked the way Shoeless Joe Jackson used to swing and maybe he kinda copied Jackson's wrist action. That guy swung good. Later, after hours of drinking and baseball talk, Ruth grew bemused and set out for a brunette, who, it developed, was one of the maids.

"Babe," said a boxing promoter from Philadelphia, "you got to get outa here."

"Not without that broad," Ruth said.

"Come on," said the boxing man, "I'll get you broads in Philly better than her."

"You sure?" Ruth said.

In Philadelphia, the boxing man took Ruth to a building in which he was absolutely certain they would find girls. Hours later, as dawn came up over Eastern Philadelphia, the boxing man suggested that Ruth leave. Ruth was sitting in an easy chair, a girl on each knee. He held an open bottle of champagne upside down over his head. "I ain't gonna be leaving for a while yet," Ruth said.

At Shibe Park that afternoon, Ruth, who may not have slept, announced, "I feel real good."

"You don't look real good," said Fred Merkle, a National League veteran who was finishing his career with the Yankees.

"I'll hit one," Ruth said.

"Bet?" Merkle said.

"A hundred," Ruth said.

"Wait a minute," Merkle said. "This is an easy ball park."

"All right," Ruth said. "I'll give you two-to-one."

On his first time at bat, Ruth walloped an outside pitch into the left-field stands and won his bet. Then he lined a triple to right, crashed a triple over Al Simmons' head in center and pulled a homer over the right-field wall. He had gone four for four, with two triples and two homers, without benefit of bed rest.

One day in 1927 (sixty homers and $70,000), Ruth played golf at a course near suburban Scarsdale, New York. Ruth drove long and well, as he generally did, but his putting was terrible. After nine holes, he diagnosed the difficulty. "Them goddam squirrels running in and outa the trees," he said. "They're killing my game."

"It isn't the squirrels," Joe Dugan said.

"Kid," Ruth said to his caddie, "get me an air rifle."

"There isn't one around," the caddie said.

"Get one for the Babe," Ruth said.

Presently the caddie found a .22-caliber rifle and a handful of shells. "Now," Ruth said, "we're gonna fix 'em."

He loaded and began picking off squirrels as easily as he picked off fast balls. "Mr. Ruth, Mr. Ruth," shouted the club pro, who had come running at the sound of gunfire, "you'll have to stop that. You're endangering our members."

"Just a couple more," Ruth said, "and I'll be going."

That night in his suite at the Hotel Ansonia on Broadway, Ruth cooked a squirrel potpie. "Did you ever taste squirrel potpie?" Dugan asks. "Hell, I couldn't eat for a week."

One day in 1928 (fifty-four homers and $70,000), it came up rain at Yankee Stadium and Ruth, who had spent the morning waiting for the rain to stop, grew bored. "What are we gonna do?" he asked Hoyt. "Let's get drunk."

"Not me," Hoyt said. "I pitch tomorrow."

"Joe?" Ruth said to Dugan.

"Let's go out to the track," Dugan said.

Ruth bet $500 across the board, a total of $1500, on a steeplechase horse that had caught his fancy. The horse fell at the first jump. "You Irish son of a bitch," he roared at Dugan. "You shanty bastard. We coulda been drunk for six weeks on the dough I dropped." Before the afternoon ended, Ruth recouped. "Come on, Joe," he said. "You had a helluva idea. I'm gonna throw you a party soon as we get back."

To George Herman Ruth, women, money and liquor were equally important. They were necessities which he took for granted. In 1915, his first full year with the Red Sox, he married a Nova Scotia girl named Helen Woodring, but a few years later they separated. The first Mrs. Ruth died in a fire in 1929. Ruth then married a former actress named Claire Hodgson, whom he called Clara and to whom, despite her continual efforts to tame him, he remained deeply attached. Still Ruth was more than a two-woman man.

"Every spring," says one old Yankee, "he used to hand me a hell of a laugh. We'd play in one town after another in the South and whenever the train pulled out of the station, there'd be a half-dozen girls waving good-by to him. 'Good-by,' the big guy would say real sweet. 'See you next year, girls.'

"One year it caught up with him. He collapsed on the field, all doubled over, and the club had to put out a story that he'd eaten a dozen hot dogs and drank a couple dozen bottles of soda pop. He was real sick and it made a lot of headlines. 'The bellyache heard round the world,' the writers called it. Well, Ruth hadn't been drinking that much pop and it wasn't even a bellyache."

Until Whitey Witt left the club after the 1925 season, he roomed with Dugan and the two had a standing invitation to join Ruth in his suite early any evening. It was always the same. Cases of good bootleg liquor were piled in the bathroom and a keg of beer stood in the tub. When the phone rang, Witt was expected to answer.

"Tell her to come up," Ruth would shout. "Tell her I'm glad to see her."

By midnight, Ruth would have made his selection from the available entries. "Good night," he'd tell Dugan and Witt, who would then leave in a swirl of rejected applicants.

In the course of this existence, money was a casual thing, except during the late winter when Ruth negotiated his contract with Ruppert. Overall, Ruth earned $1,076,474 from baseball. No one, least of all Ruth, ever calculated what he earned from ghost-written articles, personal appearances and endorsements. The generally accepted figure is $1,000,000 and it must stand.

One April, when he was earning $70,000 a year, Ruth found himself without funds to pay his income-tax bill, which in those *laissez faire* days was $1500. Hoyt and Dugan each put up $750 and Ruth paid the tax.

A month later Ruth approached with a bankroll. "I wanna give you six per cent," he said. "You guys figure it out."

"Six per cent," Hoyt said, shocked.

"What the hell do you think we are," Dugan said, "taking interest from a teammate? Just what we lent you, Jidge. No more."

It was some time before the two convinced Ruth that the loan was a favor, not a business transaction. Later, on a Western trip, Dugan found himself strapped before a dinner date in Cleveland. Ruth was talking to tourists in the hotel lobby and Dugan walked up quietly and said, "Jidge, I am empty-handed."

Without looking and without interrupting his conversation, Ruth pressed a bill into Dugan's palm. Dugan pocketed it, also without looking and, when the check was presented in the restaurant, he handed the borrowed bill to the waiter.

"You kidding, mister?" said the waiter, who looked.

"What?"

"I can't change it. Come on, gimme a twenty."

Dugan examined the money. It was a $500 bill. As soon as the Yankees returned to New York, he gave Ruth a $500 check.

"What the hell is this?" Ruth asked.

"The dough you lent me in Cleveland," Dugan said.

"Christ," Ruth said, "I thought I blew it."

Ruth apparently never voted in an election until 1944 when, moved by opposition to a fourth term for Mr. Roosevelt, he registered, took a literacy test and passed. But without benefit of voting, he was actively interested in the 1928 campaign of Al Smith, who, like Ruth, was a Roman Catholic. Ruth organized a political-action group called "Yankees for Smith" which was effective in a limited way.

During the early stages of the 1928 race, Herbert Hoover, like all presidential candidates, became an ardent baseball fan. During one of his trips to Griffith Stadium, he decided a picture with Ruth might be in order. One of the Yankees overheard a Washington official discussing the plans and tipped off Ruth, who then remained in the clubhouse until game time. "I ain't gonna pose with him," Ruth said. "I'm for Smith."

Actually, Ruth had already acquired some experience not only with presidential candidates, but with Presidents. Once when Calvin Coolidge went to a ball game, the Yankees were lined up for formal introductions.

"How do you do, Mr. President," said Hoyt.

"Good day, sir," said Pennock.

Coolidge was walking slowly, shaking hands with each of the players, and Ruth, as he waited, took off his cap and wiped his forehead with a handkerchief.

"Mr. Ruth," President Coolidge said.

"Hot as hell, ain't it, prez?" Mr. Ruth said.

People were always trying to reform him. Miller Huggins tried, first gently, then severely and ultimately with a $5000 fine for breaking training. Ruth responded by holding Huggins at arm's length off the rear car of a speeding train. Christy Walsh, Ruth's agent and one of his many ghost writers, ultimately did convince Ruth that the $80,000 income would not long endure. Trust funds set up by Walsh and an attorney helped Ruth live out his years in comfort. Mrs. Claire Ruth succeeded somewhat in slowing her husband's pace, but significantly, at the end of his active baseball career, it was the old wild instinct that betrayed him.

After the 1934 season, in which Ruth's salary had dropped to $35,000, he realized that he was no longer a full-time player. Ruppert released him, and Ruth joined the Boston Braves as part-time outfielder, and full-time vice president and assistant manager. The last two titles were meaning-

less. Judge Emil Fuchs, who owned the Braves, wanted Ruth to hit home runs. When Ruth failed —he was batting .181 in June—Fuchs dropped him as a ballplayer. The other two jobs promptly disappeared.

The specific was a party in New York. "I'm slumping," Ruth told Fuchs, "and a slumping ballplayer ought to get the hell away from the ball park. I want some time off." The French liner *Normandie*, then the largest ship afloat, was docking in New York and Ruth had been invited to a welcoming brawl.

"Stay with the team," Fuchs ordered.

"I'm going to the party," Ruth said.

When Ruth went, Fuchs announced that team morale had been impaired and that Ruth, clearly, was neither managerial nor executive material.

The later years were not bright. Ruth wanted to manage in the majors and the Yankees offered him their farm team in Newark, New Jersey. "You can't take care of yourself," Ruppert said. "How can I be sure you can take care of my best players? Newark, Ruth, or nothing."

"Nothing," Ruth said.

In 1938, Larry MacPhail hired him as a Dodger coach in midseason. That winter Leo Durocher, whose only talent in Ruth's view was a sharp tongue, was appointed Brooklyn manager. Ruth resigned and was out of baseball for all time.

He lived in a large apartment on Riverside Drive, high above the Hudson River, and each year he threw a big birthday party for himself. He occupied his days with golf, fishing and watching baseball. Once he spoke at the Baseball Writers' dinner in New York. "I gave twenty-two years of my life to big-league baseball," he said, "and I'm ready to give twenty-five more." Nearly a thousand baseball men heard him. No one offered him a job.

Was it simply Ruth's intemperance that kept him out of baseball? Or was it the mass resentment of club owners against a man whose personal impact pushed baseball salaries up as his own income soared? The reason is less important than the fact. Baseball turned away from the man who, more than anyone else, made it big business.

Yet till the end, outside the game, Ruth the man and Ruth the legend grew. Anywhere he wandered he was the Babe, unique, unrivaled, unchallenged.

What made him happy was that children knew him. He loved children genuinely, as well might a man who had no childhood of his own. Nor any sons.

Cancer struck him in 1946 and he faced death, for two agonizing years, with utter disbelief. Dugan saw him when Ruth was confined to a wheel chair. "Joe," Ruth said, his voice cut to a whisper by the cancer. "Joe," he said, caught in the final horror of truth. "I'm gone, Joe. I'm gone." Dugan clutched his old friend's hand and the two men wept. A few days later Ruth was dead.

"To understand him," says Dugan, who prob- ably knew "Jidge" better than any man alive, "you had to understand this: He wasn't human. He was an animal. No human could have done the things he did and lived the way he did and been a ball- player. Cobb? Could he pitch? Speaker? The rest? I saw them. I was there. There was never anybody close. When you figure the things he did and the way he lived and the way he played, you got to figure he was more than animal even. There never was anyone like him. He was a god."

Let the memory ring true, down to the last home run, down to the last bacchanal, through a small corridor of time.

October 3, 1951: Bobby Thomson's Homer Wins the Giants a Pennant

Good ballplayer,
long striding, lean and supple,
at ease, mutely remote from greatness
until a single swing, the home run plucked
from children's dreams,
stopped time.

After that, still the good ballplayer,
still youthful,
he found each swing, each game,
each wild, reverberating cheer
was anticlimax.

Joe, The Center Fielder

by JIMMY CANNON

OF ALL THE REPORTING I HAVE DONE I enjoy baseball writing best. It is not that I am better at this than my competition or I am getting rich at it. There are other fields which offer me a better living. But I go out to the ball game on my day off and I find it to be a valid place of mass happiness. It is a man being delighted by a child's toy, but I feel no shame when I state that baseball has moved me more than music ever did. I get paid to attend ball games and I go in free. But I would be there anyway, if I worked at other chores. It is the best of all games for me. It frequently escapes from the pattern of sport and assumes the form of a virile ballet. It is purer than any dance because the actions of the players are not governed by music or crowded into a formula by a director. The movement is natural and unrehearsed and controlled only by the unexpected flight of the ball. I believe the finest sight in the game is to watch Joe DiMaggio go back for a fly that has been hit behind him. Only Ty Cobb and Tris Speaker are remembered as his superiors. They are through and gone, but their excellence can't be disputed. It is not my plan to disfigure the greatness of another generation with senseless comparison. I concede they were as good as it is possible to be. But in this time there is not a ballplayer who is DiMaggio's equal. He is a ballplayer without a flaw. There is nothing that he does not do well and no one has more style.

Club owners are men engaged in a commercial enterprise and they protect their employees' reputations with a mercenary fervor. Executives may hate a player, but they praise him publicly as long as his contract is in the office safe. But I have never heard one of them practice this evasion when DiMaggio is being discussed.

They are proud they are connected with the game at which he excels. It was Horace Stoneham, the president of the New York Giants, who delivered the most eloquent tribute. One Christmas Stoneham distributed gold tie clasps to his friends of the trade. On the back of each was inscribed the man's full name and address. But the one Stoneham gave to DiMaggio was inscribed with a flattering simplicity. It read: "Joe, the Center Fielder." It was a salute from a competitor because Stoneham is a stubborn National Leaguer and in New York his Giants are the Yankee's competitors. I never have met anyone who admires the National League more than Stoneham and he will argue this, no matter what the figures indicate. But, like all those involved in baseball, Mr. Stoneham is glib in his appreciation of DiMaggio. When Bobby Thomson came up to play center field for the Giants the majority of the journalists traveling with the Giants predicted he would be a star. They prepared singing essays which compared Thomson to the Giants who had been there before him.

I asked Mr. Stoneham one hot afternoon if he believed Thomson was going to live up to his extravagant notices.

"Sure," Stoneham was quick to tell me. "He looks more like DiMaggio than anyone I've ever seen."

Ted Williams believes diplomacy to be the coward's sanctuary. It is his philosophy that the truth should not be concealed and he ransacks other ballplayers for flaws with an honesty I have always admired. Ted discusses himself as though he were not present. Such frankness is mistaken for swelledheadedness, which it is not. Williams regards himself with an esteem that is not unfounded. But he does not challenge the statement that DiMaggio is the greatest ballplayer of his age. There were some who thought that Williams should have won the most valuable-player award in 1947, but the baseball writers picked DiMaggio and Williams agreed with them. It is unusual for Williams to concede that a sports writer realizes what is happening on a ball field. But it pleased him that he came as close as he did.

"It took DiMaggio to beat me, didn't it?" Williams replied when a reporter asked him if he was annoyed by the results of the journalists' poll.

The figures in the records do not signify DiMaggio's worth as a Yankee. The guys on his ball club boost him with an eagerness that approaches reverence.

Their confidence is not misplaced because this is a loyal member of their team and not an isolated star who shines with a selfish brilliance. Once we were sitting in a hotel lobby in Palm Beach when a she-fan from Brooklyn annoyed him with impolite references to his inability to hit Whitlow Wyatt in the Yankee-Dodger Series of 1941.

"Wyatt took good care of you," taunted the woman from Brooklyn.

"He's a pretty good pitcher," Joe said.

"Pretty good," screamed the harridan. "He had your number."

"But we won the Series," Joe protested.

"But Wyatt took good care of you," the lady screeched.

"The big thing is we won the Series," DiMaggio replied. "I wasn't playing Wyatt. The Yankees were playing the Dodgers and we beat them."

When the baseball guys sit down in the off-season the conversation always comes around to DiMaggio. They will talk about what this one did and how another guy handled a certain situation, but they always reach DiMaggio no matter what league they're in. What delights the pros of the game is the way he plays fly balls and makes difficult plays appear to be simple catches.

If you hear a complaint it is that DiMaggio has no color. What they mean is that DiMaggio is an even-tempered man who does not sulk or show his anger on a ball field. He never tries to showboat or make a play seem complicated. He is a ballplayer of exceptional purity and never exaggerates his skill by breaking the design of his lounging race to compel the stands to understand what he is doing. What happens to him on a ball field moves him deeply, but DiMaggio believes that frustration is a private matter and it is very seldom that he discusses any of his disappointments with reporters.

I remember being with him in the clubhouse after the sixth game of the '47 World Series when Al Gionfriddo stole his home run out of the bull pen with one of the most remarkable catches ever made. DiMaggio was poised and good-natured with the reporters who were nagging him with questions and he seemed undisturbed by the commotion the play had caused. He told them it was a fine catch and let it go at that. But after he was dressed he got into his car and drove aimlessly around the town, alone and depressed, his stomach churning painfully.

"I couldn't get it out of my mind," Joe told me later. "I must have driven for hours . . . and that's all I could think of. That was the ball game if he hadn't caught it."

The attitude of the gallery during the exhibition season is an indication of DiMaggio's accepted greatness. They sit back and say there's nothing like him playing ball anywhere when he gets a base hit or shags a fly ball with that swift simplicity which I have never seen duplicated on a ball field. But when he rolls out to the infield or a ball shies away from him on the hills of the bush-league parks they mock him with their laughter. They believe it is comical for him to make a wrong move. They consider themselves fortunate when he does something wrong because that seldom happens and only the unexpected is truly exciting in sports. But their rebukes are gentle and only made to inform him

they will not tolerate anything but perfection from him.

The ballplayers are the same way because he must make them all feel small and unimportant when he has a bad day because he is what most of them try to be. Up in the press box on the roof of the grandstand in St. Petersburg, Florida, Red Barrett, then a right-handed pitcher with St. Louis, unintentionally revealed the way DiMaggio awes them all. Barrett raged at the official scorer for nine innings because he did not give DiMaggio an error on a ground ball that took a slanting bounce off a pebble and jumped over his shoulder.

"No wonder this guy is great," Barrett admonished. "You guys do his fielding for him."

It was a pitcher's old beef about hitters, but it was more than that. It was as though Barrett insisted that DiMaggio be handicapped for his greatness. One of the writers answered Barrett with a question:

"What do you want—special rules for DiMaggio?"

"Yes," the pitcher answered. "Then, maybe, you could get him out once in a while."

On days when the New York sports columnist is hung-over or the run is dead there is always the fast piece about the decency of the home-town sports fan. We claim he is unprejudiced and faithful beyond the others; sweet-natured even in his dislikes and cautious with his tirades. We blow the dust off the adjectives usually held out for the obits when we come down to the groveling paragraph concerning his intelligence and courtesy. But during a Yankee-Red Sox series in '46, the behavior of a spiteful minority made these accolades the falsehoods of lazy men who fill an off day's space with lies which our critics insist is a daily occurrence. They insulted Williams and DiMaggio all through a double header with the brutality of ignorance and their monkey sounds should have banished them back to their ancestral homes in the trees. It must be admitted that Williams constantly protested to the umpires and courted the disfavor of the idiots in the seats. But DiMaggio's blank-faced patience should have been rewarded. On the Friday before, he had hit a four-run homer and broke an infielder's finger with a line drive. But, because he couldn't buy a base knock against Boston, rising above the cheers was the contemptuous sound which resembled the noises made by a herd of cows in pain. It is not my intention to make this a publicity man's handout for DiMaggio and Williams, but this was their first season out of the Army. In that crowd were guys who had tougher jobs and had done more time, but they had gone into service at the height of their careers, and they were entitled to do a little floundering. What they had then, before they were drafted, was still there, and I am only using this isolated incident to illustrate the way that both Williams and DiMaggio reacted.

"They boo me up in Boston," Williams said. "But I'm immune to that stuff now. Let them holler. Know what they are?"

"No," I said, but I suspected.

"————," said Mr. Williams. "Put that in the paper. They're a lot of ————."

It was a charge that would be difficult to refute. But across the field in the Yankee clubhouse DiMaggio sat drinking hot coffee out of a leaking container.

"They were on you today," I said.

"Yeah," Joe said. "They didn't like me."

"Does it annoy you?" I asked.

"Nobody likes it," DiMaggio answered. "But that's the way they feel and they're entitled to it. If you stop them from booing, you ought to stop them from cheering. That's part of the game."

Baseball is a game played with nine men on each side, and without the eight other guys the Yankees wouldn't have been a team in '37. But this quiet-mannered and solemn-faced guy is an inspirational athlete and there are few of them in any sport. The Yankees do as good as Joe does, and this was proved in '47. He was more than the best outfielder in baseball. He risked his future as a big-leaguer because most of the season he played with a chip-boned arm and a lame leg. But he demanded that they play him. There are many who sulk when they have been misused, but DiMaggio isn't one of these. I have watched them dogging it in agitated isolation, and they pretend they have an imaginary hurt when they get a bad deal. But DiMaggio did not lag when McPhail fined him at the beginning of the season. It was a photographer's charge that caused McPhail to bite DiMaggio a $100's worth. The camerman insisted Joe had deliberately walked away when asked to pose for a picture previously arranged. It was the first time in DiMaggio's career as a ballplayer that he had ever been reprimanded by a ball club. It troubled him, but resentment improved him. It harmed his pride and caused him to be a reckless man. It was obvious that he was a cripple because the foot dragged when he ran and he was in pain a lot of the time. But it did not tamper with his skill and despite the objections of physicians and Bucky Harris, the manager, DiMaggio was in there before the operation scar had healed. He wore a special boot most of the year, and every time he slid into a base or stopped quickly he gambled on the years to come.

The Yankees took advantage of the times in '42 to compel DiMaggio to sign at their own figure after he had a big year in '41. In that season he put a new record into the ledgers by hitting safely in fifty-six consecutive games and he turned ordinary contests into special ones with his presence, and great crowds came out to watch what is one of the shining feats of the sport. But they were drafting guys into the Army and soldiers were working for twenty-one a month and the Yankee management used that to round Joe up. But he enlisted as soon as the season was over. I see a lot of him and I have never heard him mourn for the big money he should have made in the years when the other guys were earning it.

EDITOR'S NOTE: *The year this article appeared, 1948, DiMaggio hit thirty-nine home runs to lead the American League. Ralph Kiner in the National League hit forty. DiMaggio retired in 1952.*

Ted Williams: Evangelical Swatter

by AL WESSON

REMEMBER HOW TALL, RAWBONED TED Williams became the hero of the Major League All-Star game in Detroit one year when he blasted a homer with two on, two out and two strikes on him in the last of the ninth to give the American League a 7-to-5 victory? Do you sometimes wonder what the young hero's mother was doing about that time? Ted's mother was praying. She is deeply religious, and in her conversation she refers frequently to the thirty-five years of service she has given to the Salvation Army.

During the ball game May Williams was at home in San Diego listening to the radio. Ted's team was trailing 5 to 4 with two out in the last of the ninth when he came to bat. As he took one strike and then another, his mother at home in San Diego was overcome with trembling and suddenly began to pray. "Oh Lord, help my Ted," she cried, falling on her knees before the radio. "He needs you now. Give him strength!"

About that time, Red Barber, who broadcasts the Brooklyn games during the season, let out: "Ted Williams has connected! There it goes . . . headed for deep right. It looks like it's going over. Yes . . . there it is . . . a home run!" Barber was so astounded by the sudden turn of events that he was rendered actually speechless for several moments on the air, which was broken only by the loud guffawing of some American League fan in the background.

And lanky Ted Williams loped around the paths, leaping boyishly to shake hands with himself in glee as he turned first base.

If you knew Ted Williams' zealous mother, you would have a better idea of the wonder kid of the early 1940's. She was enthusiastic, fervent, emotional. Her mission was religion. The son has all the parent's high spirit and evangelical qualities. And every bit of his own fanaticism ever since he

was old enough to hold up one end of a bat has been directed at baseball.

Ted has never wanted to be anything but a baseball player. He has never wanted to be anything but the best baseball player in history. But what he really means by the best player in history is really the best hitter in history. In Ted's book the ability to lay the wood on the apple is the only measure of a ball player.

"Gimme a bat! Lemme at that ball! Oh, that poor pitcher! He's my lamb!" That's always been Ted's single-track idea of baseball. Ted's penchant for calling all opposing pitchers "lambs" brought on himself the nickname "the Lamb."

Nobody seems to know just where Ted Williams got his burning desire to play baseball. His mother recalls that at the age of three he would pull a baseball cap many sizes too big over the side of his head, drag along a bat that seemed twice his length and stop strangers passing by his house with, "I'm gonna be a Babe Wooth."

His folks weren't particularly interested in baseball, and there wasn't much talk about it in his home town. San Diego had comparatively few baseball fans, and didn't even get a Coast League club until 1936—that team, incidentally, being Ted's first pro nine.

When Ted, as an eleven-year-old youngster, started spending most of his time at the University Heights playground near his home, daily he used to pester Rod Luscomb, the playground director, to play "big league" with him. This was a game played by a twosome on a handball court, the object being for the batter to hit an indoor baseball past the pitcher against areas on the handball wall marked off for singles, two-baggers, etc. Even then Luscomb marveled at the skinny-youngster's wonderful swing. "He had it from the very start," according to Luscomb. "It's exactly the same swing he has now. He just walked into the playground with it."

When he was back in San Diego early in the forties for an exhibition game, Ted went to see Rod and got him to bat a few. "Ted," said Luscomb, after watching some wallops, "your swing hasn't changed a bit."

"Nope," Ted replied. "Nobody ever taught me anything. I just swing."

On his way up, he had followed the advice given him on his first baseball trip with the San Diego club by Lefty O'Doul, San Francisco manager: "Don't let 'em change you, kid. Stay as sweet as you are."

Almost any entranced fan or player who has seen Williams at the plate will be glad to demonstrate for you his version of the Williams swing, but for a correct technical analysis of that swing the best source is Frank Shellenback, who managed Ted for two years in the Coast League and coached him beginning with 1940 at Boston. Shelly undertook a study of the form that made Williams the .406 hitting champion of the American League in '41.

"Ted starts with a medium stance at the plate," explains Shellenback, "with a space of about fifteen inches between his insteps. He digs his left foot in about six inches from the back of the box. When he starts his move, he takes a step of from eight to ten inches with his right foot, the toe of which is pointing toward the shortstop when the foot is planted. He follows the ball right up to the plate with his eyes and doesn't start his swing until the last possible moment. As in the case of a long hitter in golf, his club swing is preceded by a forward twist of the hips that brings the power of the legs and the big muscles of the body into the blow. He swings the bat with a tremendous snap of his wrists, co-ordinating this wrist action with his step and the twist of his hips. Before he swings he carries the bat almost perpendicularly, with his arms fully relaxed. His left elbow is a little high at the start, but comes down with the snap of his wrists."

Pictures of Williams in action at the instant of contact between the bat and the ball show him looking at a point right over the plate. Like a good golfer, he keeps his head down. Even though his eagle eye enables him to wait out the pitch, he swings with such remarkable speed that he is strictly a "pull hitter," hitting mostly to right or right center. Because he is a "pull hitter" some say he is actually pulling away from the ball at the instant of impact. The hip twist that seems to tilt back his trunk, combined with the popping of his wrists like a rattlesnake whip, is what creates this illusion. In baseball parlance he "rides the ball." Like the good golfer, he follows through with his weight. At the finish of his swing, his weight is on his right foot, somewhat over on the right side of the foot, while the left heel has been lifted well off the ground by the shift of the weight.

But while fundamentally the swing that Ted Williams carried onto the kids' playground hasn't changed, what he learned in his first years at Boston improved his batting. The principal lesson: to concentrate on the ball every inch of the way to the plate and to wait until he is sure it is going to be in the strike zone before swinging.

In Ted's first year with Boston, hurlers found that the best pitch to give him was a high, fast one. Ted loves a hot one almost letter high, and pitchers took advantage of this yen by trying to keep the ball above the letters. In his first big-league season he fanned sixty-four times and went out on a good many fly balls because he couldn't resist going after the high, fast ones. Soon he had earned the reputation of going after fewer bad balls than any hitter in the league, and as a result in two years struck out only twenty-seven times and drew 145 walks in 143 games. Ernie Stewart, the American League umpire, said: "I didn't see him strike at a bad ball all year. He doesn't mind taking a strike or two as he knows he needs only one to hit. Pitchers try to keep from delivering anything to him that's in there, but he isn't anxious and always gets a good ball to hit."

Williams started shining as a ballplayer at such an early age that in San Diego every third citizen claims to be his discoverer. If a discoverer is necessary for the lad who began starring as a pitcher and outfielder for the Padre Serra American Legion Post while still a fourteen-year-old student at Horace Mann Junior High School, the honor belongs jointly to sports writers Frank Haven and Earl Keller. While Haven was working for the San Diego *Sun* and Keller for the *Tribune*, they tipped off the late Bill Lane, owner of the San

Diego *Padres,* that the young beanpole was a sure-fire coming sensation.

As a junior at Hoover High, young Williams clouted the ball for a .586 average. Eager, agreeable and self-confident, he nevertheless had his moments of temperament. Once after he had been purposely passed four times in a game, he blew up and declared he'd never again play such a game. In those days he was already over six feet tall and when he ran the bases he was all arms and legs. He never could keep his cap on, and usually stopped to pick it up when it flew off. The first time Frank Haven saw him play he started from first to second on a ground ball, lost his cap and was thrown out by a city block at second when he ran back for it.

On days when he went to the outfield, he would spend most of his time taking practice swings with an imaginary bat. Earl Keller recalls seeing him going through this performance one day while a fly ball that should have been an easy out sailed over his head for a four-bagger. To this day Ted can't pass a mirror or his reflection in a store window without taking his stance and trying a few phantom swings.

Next to his batting, he is remembered most by his old high-school teammates for his appetite. Roy Engle, his catcher at Hoover High, remembers one day when the team was on its annual big trip to Pomona 100 miles away to play in a tournament and Ted started out with a breakfast of strawberry shortcake and malted milk. The team had two games to play that day and didn't have time for lunch. During the twin-bill, Ted consumed thirteen ice-cream bars and eleven bottles of pop. It was nothing for him to order a second dinner right after going through the first. Although Ted still consumes groceries in wholesale lots, his terrific energy uses it up and he has always been slender. Today, at six feet three inches in height, he rarely goes over 180 pounds.

During his second year at Hoover High he batted 403 and his home began to buzz with the enticements of baseball scouts. Bill Essick of the Yankees blew in one evening just after one of Ted's homers had smashed a window across the street and was at first mistaken for the irate owner. "I know what

you're here for," said Ted's mother nervously. "It's that home run."

"Yeh, wasn't it a dilly?" was Essick's reply.

Marty Krug of Detroit came, and so did Herb Benninghoven of the St. Louis Cards, and others, but in the long run it was Bill Lane who signed up the lad by arguing that he ought to start his baseball career at home. Joining up in mid-June after school, Ted made $600, or about $150 a month, his first season in the game. He was always broke at the end of the month. He loved shootin' pictures and when the team was playing night ball he would often take in two or three "horse opera" matinees in one day. He was a pigeon for a pinball game and often would go through twelve or fifteen bucks in nickels in one session. Generous and easygoing, he always wanted company in whatever he was doing and consequently he was always dragging teammates along to shows or goofy games or the corner soda fountain.

Sid Durst was handed Williams as a roommate that first season, and he describes the lad as "big, gawky, good-natured, self-confident, full of the devil, but never at any time showing a trace of meanness." On his first road trip to San Francisco, Durst was awakened at 6 A.M. in the Pickwick Hotel by an unearthly yell. There was the new rookie jumping up and down on his bed, beating his chest and giving out with "Yowee-e!" at the top of his lungs.

"What's goin' on here, son?" asked Sid in his slow Texas drawl.

"Jimminy cripes!" yelled Ted, continuing to jump around and beat his chest. "Ain't it great to be young and fulla vigor! Yowee!"

"Not at six o'clock in the mawnin'," drawled Durst.

Williams was used only as a pinch hitter at first, but kept pestering Manager Shellenback to let him pitch as he had been signed as a chucker. On the first trip to Los Angeles, three Padre pitchers were sent to the showers in one of the games and San Diego was trailing 9 to 3 at the start of the seventh. Shelly figured this was the time to try Williams. Ted got 'em out in the seventh, but in the eighth the first man up doubled. Then came a homer, another double, and another homer! That was Ted's last as well as his first turn on the mound in professional baseball. Toward the end of that first season, in 1936, he got a chance to play regularly when Chick Shivers, the left fielder, quit to take a football coaching job in Georgia. From then on Ted played in the outfield with Durst. Ted's batting average that year was only .271.

He was a wild young colt and it was hard to get him to obey orders, not because he was ornery, but because he wasn't used to discipline and couldn't see the sense of running to get in shape, throwing to the right bases, chasing flies and practicing on ground balls. From the first, he just wanted to hit. When an opposing pitcher took the mound, Ted would say, "Hot dog, there goes my lamb." With all his devil-may-care ways, he could always outfigure a pitcher, and by the end of his first season he could demonstrate the batting stance and swing of every good hitter in the league.

At the end of 1937, during which Ted hit .291, Lane sold Williams to the Red Sox for a reputed $35,000 and three players—Al Niemiec, a second baseman; Dominic Dallessandro, left fielder later with the Cubs, and outfielder Spencer Harris. A row broke out between Lane and the Williams family on the grounds that Lane had told Williams' parents that he would not be sold for three years, and that when he was put on the block the boy would get part of the sale price.

When Lane said no dough for the Williamses, Ted said he would not go to Boston. Eddie Collins, general manager of the Red Sox, flew to the coast, and eventually the boy got a check for $2500 from the Red Sox, of which Lane is believed to have had to put up a share.

Ted reported at Sarasota in 1938, but failed to stick. When manager Cronin barked an order at the gangly nineteen-year-old, Ted came back: "Okay, sport!"

"Who is this fresh punk?" yelled Cronin. "Get him back to the minors where he belongs."

Ted was heartbroken when the Red Sox pulled out and left him waiting for a train to Minneapolis. But as some of the departing gang jeered at him, he came back: "Yah-h-h, I'll be back . . . rattling them off the fences."

It was in the one hundredth year of baseball

that Ted Williams at a salary of $4500 had his first major-league season in 1939. In his first year in the big show, only his teammate Jimmy Fox, and Hank Greenberg led him in homers—Fox with thirty-five and Hank with thirty-three to Ted's thirty-one. Ted had his troubles, like all other ballplayers, during slumps, and got in bad with the baseball writers during some such flare-up. Then there was the publicity about his remark to his uncle: "I wish I was a fireman like you. No worryin'. No nothin'. You don't have to do anything but sit around all day."

But it grew mostly out of his youth, and his zeal to reach the top in his game. Disappointments throttled him momentarily, but not for long. That's the way he played ball, too.

Once when the count was three-and-two in a game in Detroit, Rudy York, then catching for the Tigers, chided him: "It's a tough spot; you won't hit here, Lamb."

"Watch me," shot back Ted, and on the next pitch socked one over the double-decked pavilion in right center.

The next time he came up, Rudy said to him: "Pretty lucky last time, Lamb. Whaddya gonna do now?"

"I'm gonna bust it outa the park again," said Ted, and hit another homer.

After his homer in the All-Star game, Ted remarked: "Those National Leaguers brought that on themselves, razzing me for striking out the time previous."

Ted's brilliant finishes, like that All-Star game and his final drive in Philadelphia in 1940 for his .406, are the result of his boundless confidence. He fears no pitcher, believing he can hit anything they choose to dish up. When he was playing his last game in the Coast League against the Missions, he wanted to top things off right. That day a terrific wind was blowing against the batters, and Wayne Osbourne, Missions pitcher, said, "If that guy thinks he can hit a homer against this gale, he's gonna have to furnish his own power."

Osbourne lobbed over a slow ball, and against that driving wind, Ted lambasted the pitch over the fence, across the street and against a high wall 425 feet from the plate. He had hit plenty of homers of 450 feet or more on the Coast, but Western fans consider this prodigious blow the most terrific ever made in the Coast League.

Ted is quick-tempered but also quick to cool off. Intensely loyal to his friends, he won't stand for any criticism of them. Because of his desire to be a good influence on youngsters, he has refused thousands of dollars to give his endorsement on cigarette and liquor ads. However, he endorsed a breakfast food for $500 and says he would have done it for nothing "because things like that are good for kids."

When Ted is tramping through the woods he continually grips his gun or fishing rod like a bat and takes practice swings. He keeps in perfect physical condition and helps develop his "Popeye"

forearms and powerful wrists by daily doing from fifty to one hundred push-ups off the floor. He can follow fifty ordinary push-ups from the hands by twenty-five more in which he pushes up from his fingertips.

Ted had one desire: to be known as the world's best baseball batter. He doesn't go for frills and once when a newspaperman asked him how he liked a special feature article he had done on him, Ted said, "Aw, never mind that stuff. Just tell 'em what I do in the ball park."

When Ted was going great guns in 1940 and booming down the stretch for his .406, a newspaperman in New York said, "Say, I never saw so much publicity for any one guy." Ted snapped back, "Yeh? And you never saw so much hitting from one guy, either." Then he cut loose with one of those laughs that carries six blocks. He thought he'd gotten off a pip.

Late in the season in Boston he clouted out a double and when he pulled up at second, Umpire Ernie Stewart, who was stationed near the bag, said to him: "Ted, you're the best hitter I ever saw."

"No foolin', Ernie, ya really mean it?" Ted replied. "Say, but that ain't nothin' to what I'm gonna be. Wait till I get stronger and bigger, about 200 pounds; I'm gonna be a lot better. When I'm twenty-five or twenty-six, say, there's no tellin' what I'll be hittin'."

EDITOR'S NOTE: *This article was written after Williams had won his first batting title in 1941, hitting .406. He went on to win the batting title in 1942; then, after three years of military service came back to win it again in '47, and '48, served again in the Korean War, and won it again in '57 and '58. He hit the most home runs in '41, '42, '47 and '49, and holds, among other records, the record for most consecutive playing years leading in runs scored and 100 or more bases on balls. He was named Most Valuable Player in the American League in '46 and '49 and lost to Joe DiMaggio by only one point in '47. He retired in 1960.*

October 8, 1956: Don Larsen Pitches a Perfect World Series Game for the Yankees

He liked comic books, he said,
and cold beer, and "So what!"
was what he wanted to know.

When his time came round
under the three-tiered shadows,
under the unrelenting shadows of autumn,
they wrote it was a month of Sundays
and that the moon turned blue.

That night strangers toasted his name
at a dollar or two dollars a drink,
and he went out to celebrate
by swilling beer.

Foxy Ned's Orioles

by TOMMY O'SHANE

AMOS RUSIE, THE OLD-TIME SPEEDBALL pitcher, was warming up. His great hulk was behind every pitch, and the ball whistled menacingly to the catcher. He was good. He felt good.

Over on the Baltimore Oriole bench, Foxy Ned Hanlon chewed on his upper lip and the lower fringes of his black mustache. Rusie had always been anything but an Oriole benefactor. Hadn't he and Jouett Meekin kept the Temple Cup from the pennant-winning Orioles in 1894? And didn't he stand calmly on the hill every time they met, deaf to the epithets and insults the Orioles used as a part of their strategy, turning back batter after batter?

Hanlon wanted the game badly. The Orioles were only a few points ahead of the Cincinnati Reds, and they needed this victory over New York and Rusie to stay on the top. Tommy Murphy, the groundkeeper, wearing his conventional black suit and plug hat, opined to Hanlon that the field was still wet from the morning rain.

Hanlon, whose abilities have often been overlooked by baseball fans when a discussion of the great managers takes place, called his charges around him. They included such standout players as Jack Doyle, Henry Reitz, Hughie Jennings, John McGraw, J. B. Donnelly, Joe Kelley, Walter Brodie, Wee Willie Keeler, Joe Quinn and Wilbert Robinson. He had such pitchers—in 1896—as Bill Clarke, Bill Hoffer, Arlie Pond, George Hemming, Charley Esper, Sadie McMahon and Joe Corbett, brother of prize fighter Jim.

"Everyone bunt," Hanlon said.

The Orioles, a mean club on the field, questioned the edict with their eyebrows, but went about as bidden. Hellcats to opponents, they were kittens to the manager. The first man up bunted. The ball zinged straight from the bat into pitcher Rusie's hands. The next man dropped one and was out easily. So was the third man.

The second and third innings were the same. Bunts went either to the pachydermic Rusie or to the third and first basemen. The fans began booing their own Orioles. "Play baseball!" was heard from all sides. Hanlon refused to switch his plans.

Then in the fourth inning, the first man up bunted safely down the first-base line. The second batter sneaked a piffling roller past Rusie which the third baseman grabbed too late to get the runner either at first or second. Hanlon could see that Rusie was boiling.

The third man up laid one right in front of the plate, and it rolled so slowly that Rusie, running in to grab it, sprawled all over himself. He jumped up and shot the ball to third, hoping to force the runner from second. His throw was high. The ball went over the third baseman's head and was lost

in the grass. Three runs came in. Hanlon immediately gave orders for all to swing away. The damage had been done. Rusie was whipped—another victim of the psychology and savvy which Hanlon and his lieutenants, Captain Robinson and John McGraw, were employing to make baseball history.

That is what made the Orioles great. Some latter-day fans, recalling the club which won three straight pennants in the old National League, when the loop was composed of twelve teams, called it "teamwork." True, there was teamwork, but far beyond that was an aggressiveness, deception and baseball sense many feel was never brought together again on any ball field.

The 1896 Orioles came through with the best-won and -lost record of the Oriole nines which played in the National League from 1892 to 1899, winning ninety and losing thirty-nine. They also won the Temple Cup, progenitor of the World Series, in 1896, smacking down the Cleveland Spiders in four straight games. The team of fifty years ago was the only Oriole club which won both the pennant and Cup series.

Cincinnati that year fought, bare fang and knuckles, with Baltimore for supremacy. For weeks there was never more than eight or ten percentage points between them. Late in August, the Reds ventured to Baltimore, pleas of home fans ringing in their ears, to bring back the pennant. The town turned out and gave them a conqueror's send-off. They came to Baltimore cheery and confident, but they crept home defeated, humiliated, woebegone, their pennant dreams blasted. It was not until Pat Moran's outfit, twenty-three years later, that Cincinnati finally pushed through a winner.

The first game of the crucial 1896 series was on August 27 at Union Park, the high board fence of which marked the Huntingdon Avenue and Greenmount area. Cincinnati sent Johnny Foreman to the hill. John was a Baltimore boy. The Orioles gave him no sectional or home-town courtesy, but fell, instead, on his every pitch. Frank Foreman, his older brother, came in to relieve him. Frank also was drubbed. The Orioles took the next two games and the series, polishing off Big Brother Frank again in the process. The Reds dropped from first to third place.

The Philadelphia Club was the team most beloved of the Orioles. In 1896, Baltimore swept every game of the season with the Phillies. That success was borne over to the following year, and it wasn't until the pennant race was almost over that Philadelphia managed to remove the Indian sign.

Just before the series with the Reds, Baltimore went to Philadelphia in dire need of any help their Philadelphia cousins could give. On August 17, Al Orth held the Orioles to one run in seven innings. Hanlon's men managed to tie the score in the eighth, and in the ninth, with two out and the sacks untenanted, Hoffer and Kelley singled in succession. Then Keeler, a quiet fellow who stood out among the noisy, scrappy Orioles like a Sunday school boy at a pre-race meeting of touts, lifted a Texas leaguer over the head of the second baseman. It was too far out for the infielder to get, and too far in for Hulen, the right fielder, to nab. The ball fell at Hulen's feet. The Orioles won.

The misfortune infuriated the Phillies. They went into the second game and slammed the ball all over the lot. When the Orioles came to bat in the ninth, the score was 15 to 8 against them. Their case looked hopeless. However, they managed to eke over two runs before a man was put out. Then Kelley and Brodie both flied out. With the score 15 to 10 in their favor, it looked as if the Phillies had finally broken the jinx. But before they knew it, the Orioles had sent across four more runs and had men on second and third.

Keeler came up. He gripped the bag as he had in the last inning of the preceding game and poked the ball into short right field again. Hulen tore in, threw himself at the ball, grabbed it, juggled it and let it fall. Two runs scored and the Orioles won 16 to 15. "I try to hit 'em where they ain't," said Willie Keeler, greatest hitter on a team which the silver-thatched fans, who gather in neighbor-

hood bars in Baltimore, will tell you was the greatest of all.

Putting that club together was Hanlon's work, for he was without peer as a dealer in baseball muscle and brain. In 1892, Baltimore's first year in the National League, the club won forty-six and lost 101, having aboard one pitcher with the dubious honor of losing thirty-nine games. The following year, owner George Vonderhorst, who had delved into baseball as a spendid means of selling beer to patrons, replaced George Van Haltran with Hanlon.

The 1893 team came in eighth, winning sixty and losing seventy, but Hanlon, who had bought heavily into the Orioles, was looking ahead. A native of Montreville, Connecticut, he had starred for the Detroit Tigers in the eighties, had managed the Pittsburgh club in 1887 and had toured the world with Al Spaulding in 1888. When he went to the Orioles, Hanlon found only three players he liked—McGraw, still in his teens, Robinson and pitcher McMahon.

Hanlon sniffed for talent and found Jennings, one of the greatest of all shortstops, whose rallying cry "E-e-eyah!" was to echo for years over baseball diamonds. He swapped Louisville two players for Jennings. Then he picked up Bill Clarke, the pitcher, and Reitz, a classy second sacker. He plucked Walter (Steve) Brodie from St. Louis, and had a man who hit over .300 for five seasons. Next he rounded up Willie Keeler and Dan Brouthers from Brooklyn. Keeler was to top .300 for thirteen seasons (including a fantastic .432 in 1897). From 1894 to 1901, he collected more than 200 hits and 100 runs each season.

The 1894 Orioles were picked to finish in the second division. The team brought the sarcasm of the baseball world down on it for its Southern training trip that year, but it was in the Deep South that Hanlon introduced some of the plays which were to revolutionize the game. One of the first of these was the hit-and-run play.

Far and wide, the training trip was branded as a "goofy venture." Yet when they opened in New York that year, the Orioles swept four straight from the Giants and turned in thirteen hit-and-run plays during the series. John M. Ward, the Giant's manager, was so disgruntled that he denounced Hanlon and threatened to bring him before the league moguls. "It's a new game," Ward howled, "and it's not baseball."

Nobody stopped Hanlon, however, and he thought so little of his opponents' ability to break up the play that he would take his team out to the park early and demonstrate to the fans how his men worked their tricks. Brodie would cavort while shagging flies, catching them behind his back. And McGraw and the others would jockey the other club in practice, until they had their rivals mad enough to eat the bats. That stunt worked over and over again.

The Orioles caused many a rule to be changed, and McGraw was responsible for more than his share. He and other Orioles would stand at the plate and foul off delivery after delivery, until the opposing pitcher blew up. So foul balls became strikes on all but the third strike. Coaching at third, McGraw was a menace. With a man on first, he'd often take off from his coaching spot, running like mad for the plate. The pitcher, rattled by the sudden delusion that a man had been on third, would toss wildly to the plate. The man on first thus easily stole second. To curb such tricks, coaching boxes were introduced, and the coach had to stay put.

Another McGraw maneuver brought about the use of more than one umpire. McGraw would hook his mitts onto the belt of a runner on third, preventing him from scoring, while the umpire was watching the ball's flight. So the league brought in two umpires.

In a game with Patsy Tebeau's Cleveland team in '95, McGraw gave the rule makers more to think about. Joe Kelley hit a grounder to the shortstop. McGraw, on second, waited for the throw to first and then scooted across the diamond from second to home without the formality of even approaching third base. Both umpires had missed the play. The arbiter at home said he would call McGraw safe if his brother ump would attest McGraw had touched third.

McGraw, meanwhile, stood politely by the Oriole bench while the fans yelled "Muggsy" at him, a term he loathed. Finally, the umpires decided he was out. McGraw blew up. They tossed him out of the game, and Carey, the first baseman, was

sent over to replace him at third. Tebeau claimed Carey's glove was too large. The argument was settled through use of a tape measure. As soon as the game got going, it was stopped again. The umpire was waving to the stands. There was McGraw, surrounded by a protective fortress of Baltimore fans. Tebeau said McGraw was stealing their signals. Hanlon was the only one who could get McGraw to leave the park so that the game could be resumed.

Under Hanlon, the Orioles perfected the hit and run, the bunt, the sacrifice hit and the chop hit. The chop has been credited to Keeler and McGraw, but old-timers still insist Robinson fathered it. The batter smashed the ball down, forcing it to bounce many feet in the air. Men like the speedy Keeler would be almost to first base on such a high-bounding ball, while the infielder waited for it to come down. In addition, the ball was hard to catch, because it had a deadly spin. In Baltimore, there are those who still believe that the Orioles had hidden a block of marble close to the ground at Union Park, so that they would be assured of an honest shake when they attempted the chop.

Just as the Orioles were fighters afield, they were bitter-enders. Hanlon's maxim, "A game is never over until the last man's out," kept them hooting and trying until the final second. Any time it appeared they had a rise out of an opposing player, the Orioles tantalized and "tortured" him.

Baltimore, which in Civil War days was labeled "Mob Town" because the citizenry attacked the

Massachusetts State Militia while it was changing trains, had its old name revived in a baseball sense. Such oldsters as Walter Cox, who often sat with the Cleveland team when his uncle, Packard Childs, was playing second for them, relate that Oriole fans and players alike howled on every play.

The town went completely off its collective nut that September night in '94 when a telegram came through, announcing laconically: Baltimore 14, Cleveland 9. Reduced to utter essentials, the news said that Baltimore had taken its first league title, nosing out New York and Boston. The lowly Orioles had parlayed fire and cleverness into a pennant.

In the closing days of July, after setting a stiff pace, Hanlon's team had lost seven straight games and dropped to third place. There they were when August rolled around, facing them with a tough road trip west. Post-mortems were held. The team had cracked, everyone said. They didn't consider the amazing power of Hanlon's inspirational leadership. The Orioles piled up eighteen straight victories and won twenty-six of their last twenty-eight games.

To welcome her champions, Baltimore threw on her best dress. Bunting adorned the business houses. Pictures of the players went into the windows of all shops. On September 26, the day after the great news, employers let the baseball fans off for the day.

Trolley men clanged the bells of the horse cars. Horns and cowbells blasted and tolled. Clergy and medicos, office workers, store clerks, warehouse-men, longshoremen, brewery employees—everyone joined in the din.

All along the route home from Cleveland, the Orioles captivated the countryside. A great banner, "Baltimore Baseball Team, Champions of 1894," bedecked the train. There were stops at Martinsburg, West Virginia; at Piedmont, West Virginia; and in Cumberland, Maryland, where thousands turned out to greet them. On Wednesday, October 3, 200,000 persons lined the downtown streets to cheer Hanlon and his men, swarming about the carriages which carried the manager and Captain Robinson.

Old-timers say that there was nothing like it in baseball before and there has been nothing since.

After repeating as champions in '95 and '96, the Orioles fell to second place in '97, though they again won the Temple Cup. They were second again in '98, and after Hanlon had gone on to manage Brooklyn, they finished fourth in '99, their last year in the league. By that time, after having made $50,000 with his '94 team, $25,000 with his '95 team and a good deal less in '96, '97 and '98, Hanlon felt the Orioles weren't drawing the paid attendance they should. For purely financial reasons he shifted over to the Brooklyn Superbas. Baltimore was dropped from the National League after the '99 season, going out with Louisville, Washington and Cleveland.

McGraw, Robinson, Kelley, Jennings, Keeler and others went on to further glory, leaving their marks as managers and great players, and using again and again the "inside" baseball they learned under Ned Hanlon.

The Square Root of Crazy

by ARTHUR DALEY

CALIFORNIA, LOS ANGELES IN PARTICU-
lar, is inhabited by what was once described in
this magazine as "loonies in an orange bin." Consequently, the announcement that the Dodgers
were leaving Brooklyn for L.A. was received by
Californians with an air of righteous complacency.
Where else but in the City of the Angels could
such a discombobulated group of individualists be
at home?

There is, of course, only one answer to this
rhetorical question: Brooklyn, where the Dodgers
had lived for sixty-seven years. But now that the
union has been joined, the Dodgers and California
linked like Romeo and Juliet—or more appropri-
ately, like Burns and Allen—there is at last the
opportunity for seizing a historical perspective on
the wacky Dodgers, and how they got that way.

Brooklyn, not unlike California with the possible exceptions of space, accent, temper and cli-
mate, has always encouraged its rhubarb nine with
a sort of fatal desperation. "Wait 'til next year!"—
that most notable of all Dodger slogans—was born
there, as Brooklyn fans have trooped faithfully to
the ball park, year after year, in the full knowledge that they were fated to meet with frustration.
There was one season, even, when a large banner was defiantly unfurled during the first inning
of the opening game, reading "Wait 'til next year!"

In no other ball town has such dampened enthusiasm prevailed quite so fervently. Many years
ago, before the development of radio, a cab driver
sat awaiting the end of the game on the street outside Ebbets Field. Suddenly there was a roar from
the crowd.

"What happened?" the cabby hollered to an on-
looker.

"The Bums has got three men on base," yelled
the fan.

"Which base?" asked the cabby coldly.

His attitude was typical, and dates back to the
first mishap in the Dodgers' history, naturally oc-
curring at their first game at Ebbets Field, on
April 5, 1913. Faithful fans arrived early that day
and waited—and waited. Someone had forgotten to
bring the key to open the park. Finally, the customers gained admission and settled down for the
flag-raising ceremonies in center field. Playing magnificently, the band assembled at the base of the
pole, where another discovery was made. Someone had forgotten to bring the flag.

In many respects, the key figure to the Dodgers'
glorious disregard of conformity centers about the
Falstaffian Wilbert "Uncle Robbie" Robinson, the
former great catcher on the Baltimore Orioles of
sainted memory. At that time, he was among a
group of fire-eaters—John McGraw, Hughie Jennings, Wee Willie Keeler and all the rest. In fact,
Uncle Robbie still holds the record of seven hits
in one ball game.

While legend pictures him as being a clownish
manager, he was not. He was a good one, although
occasionally unorthodox, with an unerring eye for
appraising pitchers. He also had an uncanny knack
of getting the most out of retreads, the ballplayers others had discarded. His one big quirk
concerning pitchers was his insistence that they
be big.

"Little guys don't scare nobody," he used to say.
It was always incomprehensible to him that Dick
Rudolph, a tiny pitcher for the Braves, could be-
come a twenty-game winner.

"How can that high-school kid beat anybody?"
he used to ask. At the time Rudolph had graduated from Fordham University and was bald as an
eagle.

So strong were Robbie's convictions that the
fans were amazed one day when he started a rookie
pitcher and left him in the game long enough to

67

take an unholy shelling. But as soon as the boy was yanked, the Brooklyn manager strode purposefully over to the box where Ma Robinson, his beloved wife, was sitting.

"I hope you're satisfied now," he said bitterly. "I started that kid like you suggested. Maybe now you'll do less second-guessin'."

But everyone second-guessed Uncle Robbie. He'd argue strategy with cab drivers and fans. He'd argue with baseball writers. There was one period when the team was in a slump. So he let the writers pick his line-up and batting order.

Every once in a while the good-natured Uncle Robbie would try to crack down. "Listen, you guys," he announced to his addled heroes one day. "There's too many missed signals and bonehead plays on this ball club. So I'm startin' a Bonehead Club. Anyone who pulls a rock has to pay ten bucks into the kitty." His ultimatum delivered, Uncle Robbie stalked majestically from the dugout—and handed the umpire the wrong line-up.

Shortly thereafter the ineffable Babe Herman offered an idea.

"Uncle Robbie," he said, "everybody's missing signs. That's what's causing all the trouble. The hell with them. Let's play ball without signs." So the Dodgers played for a week without any signals at all.

Robbie was not too much help in the signal department, whether the Dodgers used them or not. One day he flashed the bunt sign to Zack Wheat, his best hitter, and Zack belted the next pitch over the fence for a home run. Uncle Robbie was coaching on third and he gave Wheat an affectionate whack on the pants as he jogged past.

"Attaboy, Zack," he shouted, forgetting that Wheat had disobeyed orders.

On another occasion, Zack Taylor opened the ninth inning of a scoreless tie with a rousing triple. Uncle Robbie was dancing an elephantine jig at third base in unrestrained glee. "Put 'er there, kid," he shouted happily, stretching out his hand for a handshake. Taylor stepped toward his beloved leader to accept congratulations—and was tagged out.

Life with the Dodgers seemed eternally like that. Distortions have so crept in, however, that not all the lies they tell about the Dodgers are

necessarily true. The lowest and most despicable canard of all is that Babe Herman once tripled into a triple play. This is a damnable falsehood. The Babe only doubled into a double play. However, if there had not been one out at the time, it would have been a triple play.

This was the day when Mickey O'Neil, an aging catcher, thought he should begin preparing for the future. So he offered to coach at one of the bases.

"Sure," said Uncle Robbie magnanimously. "Coach at third base. Nuthin' ever happens there anyway."

Here was the setup. With one away Hank DeBerry was on third. Dazzy Vance was on second and Chick Fewster was on first when our hero stepped to the plate.

The Babe uncoiled that long body and lashed out a tremendous shot to the outfield. DeBerry scored easily. But Vance passed third base and, fearing that the ball would be caught, began to backtrack. The fleet Fewster kept tearing and the Babe ran as only he could, head down and hell-bent-for-election.

Suddenly all three were unaccountably congregating around third base, a happenstance which caused Uncle Robbie to mutter, "That's the first time those guys ever got together on anything all season."

At any rate they all started traveling in several directions. At least three base runners were tagged in the ensuing confusion.

The big, gangling Herman resented stories about his squirrelish tendencies and once complained to Frank Graham, the author of the valued history *The Brooklyn Dodgers*, that he had a wife and family to support and that slurs on his reputation injured him. The promise was made that the Babe henceforth would be pictured as a model of circumspection, sanity and intellectual brilliance.

"Thanks," said the Babe, fumbling in his pocket before pulling out a charred cigar butt and sticking it into his mouth.

The writer whipped out some matches. But before he could strike a match, smoke began curling from the cigar butt.

"Never mind," said the Babe nonchalantly. "It's lit."

The Babe was a tremendous hitter—he holds the

all-time Dodger mark of .393—but he was no Joe DiMaggio as a fielder. There was one favorite line that the baseball journalists used. It was:

"Babe Herman made a sensational catch of an easy fly ball."

Although there always were persistent rumors that Herman often had been hit on the head by fly balls, it took a crack reporter like Tom Meany to run that fabrication into the ground. Tom boldly asked the question.

"That's a joke," said the disdainful Babe, "but it ain't funny. I'll promise you this: if I ever get hit on the head by a fly ball, I'll walk off the field and never come back."

"How about getting hit on the shoulder, Babe?" asked Tom.

The big blond thoughtfully studied his cigar and responded like the forthright gentleman he's always been.

"Oh, no," he said. "On the shoulder don't count."

During the wartime man-power shortage, the Babe was invited to rejoin the Dodgers even though he then was forty-two years old. In his first time at bat in eight years, he rifled a single to right.

The worshipers in the Ebbets Field stands pounded their palms and yowled in delight. The Babe waved condescendingly to the peasants on his way to first base, tripped over the bag—and fell flat on his face.

Until such slick fly-catchers as Pete Reiser, Duke Snider, Carl Furillo and the like moved into the Dodger picture within the past couple of decades, Brooklyn outfielders usually gave their fans palpitations whenever a ball was hit beyond the infield.

On one notable occasion Frenchy Bordagaray went tearing across the Ebbets Field turf in ardent pursuit of a fly ball. His hat blew off. Frenchy stopped, picked up his bonnet, clapped it back on his head and still made the catch.

Quite in keeping with the Brooklyn tradition—although an infinitely superior ballplayer to most of the zanies—was an outfielder who joined the club in 1912, a guy named Casey Stengel. He engineered one of the most famous of all baseball pranks.

From time immemorial Dodger fans have always booed those they love the most. Casey, on this day, was no exception. Stengel stepped up to bat midst a cascade of boos, doffed his cap to the fans, and a little sparrow spread its wings and flew away from the top of Casey's head.

Casey's outfielding abilities had worried Uncle Robbie in those early days; he always caught the ball but he didn't look good while doing it.

"Why the hell do you stagger like that?" demanded Uncle Robbie. "You give me heart failure every time."

"I catch it, don't I?" said Casey.

"Yes," said Robbie, "but with a rump like that and legs like that, you shouldn't be a ballplayer. You should be . . ."

His voice faded away as he groped for words.

"What should I be?" asked Casey.

"I'm tryin' to think," said Uncle Robbie. "But I give up."

But Uncle Robbie could be considerate when the basic needs of his men were concerned. The Brooks were in the middle of a rally when Chick Fewster began hammering with a bat on the dugout steps, whooping it up in traditional fashion.

"Cut that out," ordered Uncle Robbie.

"Why?" asked the astonished Fewster.

Uncle Robbie nodded toward the far end of the bench where Jesse Petty, the pitcher, was slumbering peacefully.

"I don't want to wake up old Jesse," he said.

Other measures of Robbie's compassion extended to kids. Before the game one day Babe Herman's son, Bobby, was not only in the dugout, but the little fellow was sitting in Uncle Robbie's lap. The manager had always been very fond of the little tyke. But suddenly Uncle Robbie dumped the boy on the ground.

"What's the matter, Uncle Robbie?" said the startled youngster.

Uncle Robbie transfixed him with a baleful glare. "Why ain't your old man hittin'?" he asked.

The Babe often brought little Bobby to the ball park with him. It not only made for a happy father-and-son relationship, but it gave the boy's mother some extra freedom. She had dinner ready one night when in strolled the Babe, all slicked up after his postgame shower.

"Where's Bobby?" he asked.

"Where's Bobby?" she echoed, a quaver in her voice. "You brought him to the ball park with you."

"Holy smokes," said the Babe. "I forgot all about him. I musta left him there."

A fast-talking salesman nailed the large Mr. Herman outside Ebbets Field one afternoon, and gave him a quick spiel.

"If you buy this encyclopedia," he said, "it will help this handsome little boy with his education."

"Nothing doing," said the Babe nonchalantly. "He don't need an encyclopedia. He can walk to school."

It's at least a parenthetical note to remark that Bobby did very well without the encyclopedia. He became so brilliant a student at the University of Southern California that he now is on the faculty there, teaching higher mathematics.

Uncle Robbie once tried to do some teaching himself. The Dodgers had foozled so many bunts that he ordered an extra practice. He'd teach them how to bunt. For all of his elephantine size, Robbie was nimble enough on his feet and he once had been an expert hitter.

"I'll show you guys," he said. There was a snicker from the players and Robbie bristled.

"Listen," he said. "When I played on the old Baltimore Orioles, I could bunt as good as John McGraw or Wee Willie Keeler or Hughie Jennings or any of them. Somebody get out there and pitch. I'll show you."

"Gimme the ball," said Duster Mails. The players gathered around the batting cage. Duster went to the mound. Uncle Robbie looked like the circus fat man in a baseball suit as he stood at the plate, bat in hands.

It's almost impossible to bunt a ball that's pitched high. So the mischievous Duster fired in a high one to Uncle Robbie. The manager deftly dumped down a perfect bunt.

"See," he said to the astonished players. "It's just like learnin' to ride a bicycle. Once you learn you never forget."

Up stepped Sherry Smith to try a bunt. The ball slipped as Mails threw it. It struck Smith between the eyes. So ended the lesson for the day. Only the

Dodgers could do things like that.

The parade of characters who wore Dodger uniforms is an endless one. Not the least of them was Clyde Day, a huge pitcher from a hog wallow in Arkansas which was called Pea Ridge. Naturally enough, he became known as Pea Ridge Day. It was his habit whenever he struck out a batter to give with a hog call.

The Flatbush Faithful took a vast fancy to this and soon everyone in the stands joined Pea Ridge in his hog call. Uncle Robbie put up with this as long as he could. Then he put a halt to it.

"A man has no right to be sillier than God intended him to be," said Uncle Robbie. The philosophy was sound except that the Dodgers have always been beyond the reach of philosophy.

It was in 1932 that an era ended. Uncle Robbie's contract was not renewed. But before we continue with the chronology, it might be well to interpose that the Dodgers eventually got around to giving their colorful manager the recognition he deserved for his vast contributions to Brooklyn baseball. So a plaque was suitably inscribed and unveiled one day in center field.

It was a noble plaque they unveiled for Wilbert Robinson—except that they spelled his name wrong. It came out "Wilmer Robinson." You'd almost think Uncle Robbie had engraved it himself in one of his more absent-minded moments.

But Uncle Robbie's departure didn't "cure" the Dodgers.

In 1946 the Brooks became involved, naturally enough, in the first postseason play-off the major leagues ever had. Just as naturally they lost it, the Cardinals winning.

A year later their manager, the fiery Leo Durocher, was suspended by Commissioner Happy Chandler, and was forced to sit out the campaign. Nothing like that had ever taken place before.

This was one time when Durocher failed to exercise the prescience he thought he had. It was Leo, you know, who once scorned a warning to beware of the unforeseen.

"There ain't gonna be no unforeseen," he boasted. The language was Brooklynese. So was the thinking.

Charlie Dressen, another Dodger manager, also

was oblivious of the unforeseen in 1951. That's when he had a thirteen-and-a-half-game lead in mid-August—and blew it. So the Brooks went into another play-off, this time against the Giants. They lost it in typical Dodger fashion: Bobby Thomson hit a three-run homer in the ninth to beat the foe from Flatbush 5 to 4. Only Brooklyn could have been victimized in such fashion.

Does it ever stop? Evidently not. A year later another pixilated high spot was reached in the World Series when a Brooklyn pitcher lost sight of a ground ball in the sun. Ballplayers have been known to lose fly balls when blinded by the sun. But it took Billy Loes, a throwback to the Daffiness Boys of Uncle Robbie's day, to do it the upside-down way.

Limitless is the Dodger predilection for the unusual. The first and only perfect game ever pitched in the annals of the World Series was tossed by Don Larsen of the Yankees against you-know-who. Could it have been otherwise?

Ever since baseball was invented all sorts of natural phenomena have halted major-league games. They have been canceled because of rain, snow, sleet and cold, but never, never, never—at least until that year—by anything as outlandish as fog.

On one memorable occasion that spring, however, a pea-soup mist settled over Ebbets Field. Although detractors, such as Giant fans, have eternally insisted that the Dodgers have always been in a fog, no game could be played.

"Game called pending results of the fog," intoned Tex Rickard, the priceless Brooklyn announcer, over the public-address system. Whereas the proper and snooty New York Yankees have an elocution instructor giving their announcements with pear-shaped tones and grammatical preciseness, in Brooklyn they use a malaprop.

"My people unastan' wot I say," declares Tex with dignity.

They understood him fully when he announced: "A child has been found lost."

His most unforgettable announcement beyond question came when he discovered that front-row patrons were draping their overcoats across the railing.

"Attention, please," came Tex's voice over the loud-speaker. "Will everyone in the front row kindly remove their clothing. . . ."

There never have been fans quite like Brooklyn's. Even the secondary nickname of "Bums" evolved from the peculiar way Dodger rooters addressed their heroes.

"Ya, bum, ya" was never meant in a derogatory sense. It was an expression of affection which eventually was made respectable by Willard Mullin's wondrous cartoon of the Brooklyn Bum. The term was used in the same jealous fashion of a father angrily berating his son. It was meant for family use only, not for outsiders.

Many years ago a Dodger fan become embroiled in a violent saloon argument with a drinking companion who dared to disparage the Brooks in Brooklyn. The Dodger fan whipped out a pistol and shot the calumniator. This, presumably, came under the general heading of justifiable homicide.

There's always been something of an Alice in Wonderland motif to the Dodgers and to Brooklyn. Everything always seemed to get "curiouser and curiouser." And now the Dodgers are in Los Angeles, where curious things also have been known to happen, including many of dubious sanity.

Playground for Heroes

by W. C. HEINZ

ON THE NORTHEAST FRINGE OF NEW York's Manhattan Island, where the Harlem River separates it from the Borough of the Bronx, there are seven and a half acres of flatland which are slowly receding into the river from which they were claimed. They are surmounted by an eight-story, green, concrete, wood and steel grandstand, built in the design of a horseshoe and seating 52,000 persons; and the whole is known as the Polo Grounds.

Polo never has been played here—the name comes from a now-vanished sward at 110th Street and Fifth Avenue, where James Gordon Bennett, the multimillionaire newspaper publisher, played the first American chukker—but almost everything else has. In 1923 the stadium was the scene of what boxing *aficionados* consider the greatest prize fight of all time. In 1951 it saw the most exciting single blow in the long history of baseball. And through the years it has housed about as much great football as any other stadium in the land .

Major-league baseball was played here longer than anywhere else—it came to Manhattan Field, now a parking area directly south of the stadium, in 1891. From 1891 through 1896 Yale played Princeton at football in Manhattan Field, and for three years in the nineties the Coaching Club made it the home of America's most distinguished horse show. In the summer of 1923 five world-title fights were held at the Polo Grounds, and there on September 23, 1937, four world champions defended their crowns on the same card. The field saw rodeos, circuses, auto racing, the Roller Derby, soccer, Gaelic football, hurling, exhibition tennis, track and golf and religious rallies.

The largest crowd ever to attend an event in the Polo Grounds poured in on the night of September 14, 1923, when 82,000 persons paid $1,188,603 while several thousand more paid nothing to see Jack Dempsey defend the heavyweight championship of the world against the 216½-pound Argen-

tinian, Luis Angel Firpo, the well-known Wild Bull of the Pampas. On the street outside they turned over wagons selling the cheaper seats and standing room, and inside they saw the fight against which all other great matches have since been measured.

"Dempsey thought he had a sucker," says Jersey Jones, veteran boxing writer of *The Ring* Magazine. "He walked into Firpo and Firpo hit him with a right uppercut and Dempsey's knees went. That started it." After the less than four minutes of fighting the boxing writers caucused to decide the number of knockdowns. They finally agreed that Firpo had been down ten times and Dempsey twice.

In the first round Dempsey, shaking off the opening punch, put Firpo down seven times. Then he caught a long right on the chin and sped backward through the ropes and off the ring apron onto the typewriter of Jack Lawrence, of the New York *Herald Tribune*. Lawrence, with the assistance of a Western Union telegraph operator and Hype Igoe of the New York *Morning World,* shoved him back into the ring, where Firpo put thirteen consecutive right hands on his head before the bell rang.

It has come down through the years that in the minute between rounds, Dempsey was the calmest man in his corner, possibly in all of the uproarious Polo Grounds. Jack Kearns, his manager, and Jerry (The Greek) Luvadis, his trainer, had trouble finding the smelling salts, which Kearns had pocketed when he saw his property propelled out of the ring, but when the bell sounded again Dempsey was once more the aggressor.

"What round was that?" Dempsey had asked Kearns in the corner.

"The first!" Kearns yelled at him. "Snap out of it."

When the fighters came together for the second round Dempsey dropped Firpo with a left to the jaw. Firpo got up and went down again from a combination of punches. His second time up he was floored by a left hook, writhed on the canvas, rolled over on his back and was counted out with only fifty-seven seconds of the round gone.

Lawrence's typewriter, wrecked as Dempsey landed on it, was exhibited in a store window for months afterward. For years there were hundreds of people who claimed the honor of having helped the champion back into the ring (for which Dempsey should have been disqualified)—just as today there are dozens of honest men who will tell you that they caught the ball that Bobby Thomson, the Giant third baseman-outfielder, hammered into Section 35 of the lower left-field stands on October 3, 1951.

It happened in the third and final play-off game between the Giants and the Dodgers for the National League pennant. The Giants had been thirteen and a half games behind the leading Dodgers on August 11, had tied with them on the final day of the regular season, had split the first two play-off games and were down, 4-2, with one out and two men on base in the ninth inning when Thomson swung at the high pitch he should have let go by for a ball. The game was over, the Giants had won, 5 to 4, in the most dramatic finish in the seventy-five years of major-league play, and the next day the baseballs started to roll in.

"I was going into the park for the start of the World Series," Thomson says, "when a guy ran up to me and showed me his ticket stub to prove he was sitting in the right place to get the ball. He showed me the ball and said, 'I'll be very glad to give it to you if you'll get me a ball autographed by the team.' I ran in and I hollered to Eddie Logan, 'Hey, Eddie, give me a ball. There's a guy out there's got the ball I hit.' Logan said, 'Go look in your locker. There's three or four others there right now.'

"So I don't have the ball," Thomson says, a little sadly, "because if I did have it I'd always wonder if this is the one."

Eddie Logan was the Polo Grounds clubhouse man. He began there in 1930 under his father, the late Fred Logan, who once tried to make a clubhouse boy out of a lad named William Bendix, who decided to become a movie actor instead. As overseer of the home team's quarters during the baseball and football seasons, Eddie Logan had a valet's objectivity toward his masters, the sports world's heroes.

"One day," he recalls, "Mel Ott booted one. When the game was over he was one of the first into the clubhouse, because he only had to come in from right field. He hid in a toilet booth and when McGraw came in he said to my old man: 'Get the key and lock the door.' He kept Mel in there and wouldn't let Pop open the door. I was just a kid at the time.

"We had a center fielder once who was a real nickel-nurser. He'd eat only on the road, where the club pays the bills. He wouldn't eat when we were at home, and one day he dropped, right in the clubhouse here, from malnutrition.

"Speaking of money," Logan said, "the day Ace Adams went to the Mexican League he came in here to say good-by to the fellas and he had sixteen thousand bucks on him. I'll never forget it. He had it stuffed in all his pockets and even in his hat."

In 1942 the Giants bought Van Lingle Mungo, the pitcher, from the Dodgers. There was some speculation as to what would happen when he joined the Giants because he and Dick Bartell, the Giant infielder were announced enemies. "I put Mungo's locker next to Bartell's," Logan says. "When Mungo walked in I walked right up to Bartell with him. I said, 'Dick, I want you to meet Van Mungo. Van, this is Dick Bartell.' They just stood there, looking at each other, and then they both looked at me and started to laugh. They became the best of friends."

The most riotous celebration ever seen in that clubhouse happened, of course, after Thomson's home run. Grown men became incoherent and fiddled around like delirious children.

"Everybody was going nuts and the fellas even kissed me," Logan says. "That usually doesn't happen."

Walter O'Malley, president of the Dodgers, came in to congratulate Horace Stoneham, owner of the Giants. Chuck Dressen, the Dodger manager, shook hands with Leo Durocher, the Giant manager, and John (Senator) Griffin, the Brooklyn clubhouse man, walked up to Logan.

"He shook my hand," Logan says, "and he said, 'If anybody had to beat us, Eddie, I'm glad it was you.' It was the nicest thing ever happened to me. I couldn't say anything. I choked up."

Practical joking from the athletes is most serious among professional football players. One day the football Giants threw a police sergeant who was watching practice over the Polo Grounds goal posts. On another occasion, Steve Owen, the coach of the Giants, released six of his biggest men from practice to wait for a large lineman who had an aversion to soap and water and would duck out without showering. When he came in, they stripped him, held him to the floor and worked over him with soap powder and brooms.

"Another time," Logan says, "Jim White and Steve Filipowicz were setting a trap for Red Smith, the assistant coach. Filipowicz took a pail of ice water up on the stairs to the shower room. White sat on the rubbing table and he was supposed to give the signal when Red came through. Steve Owen came through instead, and White raised his hand and Filipowicz let the water go.

"Steve was standing there with nothing on and he didn't even flinch. He just said: 'There's certain people around here who want to play. We'll put the pads on tomorrow and if they don't get all the play they want then we'll do it again the next day.' One day was enough."

The toughest single game, though, was collegiate —the 1919 Dartmouth-Pennsylvania game, won by Dartmouth, 20 to 19, in which both sides were peopled by hardened veterans of World War I.

"Dartmouth," says Lou Little, the Columbia University coach who played right tackle for Penn in that sample of trench warfare, "had Jim Robertson, whose leg was broken, Laddy Meyers, who went out with a broken collarbone, Swede Youngstrom, Jack Cannell, Cuddy Murphy, Bill Cunningham, the Boston sports columnist, and opposite me was Gus Sonnenberg, who became a pro wrestler. Our captain was Bert Bell, who became the head of the National Football League.

"Our tackle playing opposite Murphy was John Titzel and he spoke to me about Murphy and between plays I went across to the other side of the line. I said to Murphy, 'Look, why don't you just play football? Why don't you leave this man alone?' Murphy didn't say anything. He just let a spray of tobacco juice fly right by my nose. I turned to Titzel and said: 'Look, John, I've got all I can take care of over on my side with that Sonnenberg. You handle it over here.'

"I started out without thigh- or headguard," Little says. "After the first play I got my headguard on in a hurry and between halves I could hardly get my thighguards on, I was so swollen. 'Tiny' Maxwell was one of the officials and he and Doc Spears, the Dartmouth coach, got into a fight. They lost six men, we lost one with an injury and one put out by the referee."

Owen, who has been with the football Giants since 1925 as player and coach, thinks that the roughest pro game in his time was the 1927 National League title affair in which the Giants beat the Chicago Bears, 13-7. The Giants had to stop Bronko Nagurski and Red Grange, and Owen played sixty minutes at tackle against Jim McMillen, later claimant of the world's heavyweight wrestling title. When the final gun ended the laying-on, Owen and McMillen, exhausted, slumped to the ground, smiled and reached over and shook hands.

"The Bears had a first down on our one-yard line," Owen says. "They sent two fullbacks into the line and both were carried off, and on fourth down they were back on the ten."

Only once did Army and Notre Dame meet at the Polo Grounds, and that was in 1924, when Notre Dame won, 13 to 7. Up in the press box as the game ended Grantland Rice, who had exchanged seats with Jack Lawrence at the Dempsey-Firpo fight the year before, thereby renouncing one claim to fame, was staking out another. He was writing what was possibly the most colorful lead ever composed about a football game and coining one of the great trade names of sports.

"Outlined against a blue-gray October sky," he wrote, "the Four Horsemen rode again. In dramatic lore they are known as Famine, Pestilence, Destruction and Death. These are only aliases. Their real names are Stuhldreher, Miller, Crowley and Layden."

At South Bend, Indiana, a few days later a photographer named Harry Elmore hired four horses. On them he posed the four backs: Harry Stuhldreher, Don Miller, Jim Crowley and Elmer Layden. The nation's newspapers carried the picture and the caption: "The Four Horsemen of Notre Dame."

The natural meander line of the Harlem River is home plate at the Polo Grounds. Several years ago the land under the stadium had to be raised in some places as much as twenty inches to repair the river's subterranean depredations. The land is owned by the family of Mrs. Harriet G. Coogan.

The present grandstand—ideal for football and boxing but something less than perfect for baseball because it demands the shortest foul lines in the major leagues—was designed by the late William Foster, a Philadelphia architect, and built in the summer of 1911. The old wooden stands had burned on the night of April 14, 1911, after the opening game of the Giants' home season.

From home plate, painted before each game with quick-drying white enamel, it is 475 feet—the longest reach in the major leagues—to the monument erected in deepest center field to the memory of Eddie Grant, the pipe-smoking Harvard man who became a Giant infielder and four years later gave his life in the Argonne Forest. It is only 280 feet to the left-field stands and only 258 to those in right field, however, and because of these peculiar dimensions there is a peculiar Polo Grounds style of play.

"With the short foul lines," said Bobby Thomson, "outfielders tend to bunch in the middle. I play hitters more straightaway here, and you don't care if somebody gets a good piece of the ball because you can go back so deep in center."

With the near-by stands beckoning in short left and right fields, batters become home-run conscious. At the end of almost every home stand the Giants' hitting tapers off because the batters have been trying for the seats.

"You have to be careful here," said Sal Maglie, the Giants' ace right-hander. "You have to have good control, and you can't pitch inside to a hitter unless you have something on it. If I have my control and keep the ball away there's very few can pull it. Everybody who comes in here tries to

pull the ball, and that can be an advantage if you know how to use it. Of course, you lose more heartbreakers here, too, with those handle hits for short home runs."

Only one man has ever hit a ball into the present bleachers during a major-league game. In 1933 before a preseason exhibition game between the Detroit Tigers and the Giants, Schoolboy Rowe, then making his entry as a major-league pitcher, hit a ball into the left-field bleachers. In 1949, just before he joined the Cleveland Indians, Luke Easter bounced a ball out of right-field bleachers in a Negro National League game.

According to Polo Grounds habitués, the hardest ball ever hit in the park was propelled by Johnny Lindell, the Yankee outfielder, off the delivery of Montia Kennedy of the Giants in an exhibition game in 1949. It landed deep in upper section 39, more than forty feet above and about twenty feet beyond a spot on the ground in left field, 450 feet from home plate.

It was in the Polo Grounds in the All-Star game of 1934 that Carl Hubbell, the Giant left-hander, struck out Babe Ruth, Lou Gehrig, Jimmy Foxx, Al Simmons and Joe Cronin in succession. Bill Dickey, the Yankee catcher, then singled, and Lefty Gomez, the Yankee pitcher, came up. Before taking his stance to strike out, he had a word with Gabby Hartnett, of the Chicago Cubs, who was catching for the National League. "You are looking at a man whose batting average is one-oh-four," Gomez said. "What the hell am I doing here?"

From 1913 through 1922 the New York Yankees shared the park with the Giants, and on August 16, 1920, in a game against the Cleveland Indians, Carl Mays, the Yankees' submarine-ball pitcher, hit Ray Chapman, the Cleveland shortstop, on the head with a pitched ball. Early the following morning Chapman died.

On that day Ty Cobb was quoted in an Associated Press dispatch as saying that Mays should be run out of baseball. Later he denied the story, but that cut no ice with the Yankee fans who came out to the Polo Grounds several days later to see the Tigers play the Yankees.

"The place was packed," recalls John Drebinger

of the New York *Times.* "During batting and fielding practice there was no Cobb. As they were marking out the batter's box he came out onto the field and when he did the place filled with boos. With everybody in the stands booing, he walked up to the press box, which was behind home plate then, on a level with the field, and took off his cap to the writers. Then he walked to the dugout, put his thumb to his nose and saluted the crowd. That day he got four hits. They never did get him out."

The man with the longest period of service with the Giants was Edward T. Brannick, sometimes identified as "the first white child born in the Polo Grounds." Actually Brannick was born at 441 West Thirty-first Street, in the early 1890's and rose from office boy under John T. Brush in 1905 to club secretary in 1936.

There is no standard measurement by which fielding plays may be assessed, but Brannick said the finest play in his years in baseball was the double play that ended the 1921 World Series between the Giants and the Yankees. "We had the Yankees one to nothing," Brannick said, "and one out in the ninth. They had a man (Aaron Ward) on first and the batter (Home Run Baker) hits a ball that knocks Johnny Rawlings down off second base. While Rawlings is on the ground he grabs the ball and throws to George Kelly at first and Kelly throws a strike to Frank Frisch who is not on third but rides in with the runner for the double play."

It was Brannick's opinion that the greatest player ever to perform at the Polo Grounds was Honus Wagner, the bowlegged long-armed, ham-handed shortstop of the Pittsburgh Pirates. He had a favorite play here, too. "It was around 1907," he said. "I was a ball boy. The score was one to one with nobody out. Wagner gets a base hit. Then he steals second. McGraw is going crazy, hollering: 'Get him back. Chase him back!' Wagner had a way of moving his feet on the base lines like a guy playing piano moves his hands up and down a keyboard. Either George Wiltse or Iron Man McGinnity was pitching for us. He throws back to second two or three times. On the next throw back, Wagner goes. Bill Dahlen takes the throw and fires to Arthur Devlin, who has Wagner off third, but Wagner hops over Devlin's hands and gets the

bag on the other side. He scores on an outfield fly, and they win the ball game, two to one.

"People ask me," Brannick said, "why I think Wagner was the greatest ballplayer. That's why. He could do everything. That was the greatest piece of base running I ever saw."

John Drebinger, who watched baseball at the Polo Grounds for fifty years, says the greatest catch he ever saw there was made by Jigger Statz, then an outfielder with the Dodgers. The year was either 1927 or 1928. "I was traveling with the Brooklyn club then," Drebinger recalls, "and coming north from training Statz had made a great catch in Birmingham. The Dodgers were playing the Giants in the Polo Grounds and I was in the press box telling Boze Bulger about it. I was explaining to him how Statz had been running at full speed with his back to the ball when he just crooked his elbow back and caught the ball without looking. Bulger said: 'Go on. Nobody can catch a ball like that.' I said, 'No? Look!' It was the eighth inning and Bill Terry had just driven one out near the clubhouse steps. There was Statz, running like crazy with his back to the ball, and then he crooked his elbow and damned if he didn't do it again."

Athletes have risen to great heights at the Polo Grounds, but a few have fallen to substantial depths. In September of 1924, Cozy Dolan, a Giant coach and John McGraw's bodyguard, and Jimmy O'Connell, an outfielder in his second year with the club, were banned from baseball for life by Judge Kenesaw Mountain Landis, commissioner. O'Connell was charged with offering Heinie Sands, the shortstop of the Phils, $500 if "he would not bear down" in a Series with the Giants. O'Connell admitted it, and said Dolan had put him up to it. "I don't remember," was all Dolan would say.

In 1908 Bill Klem, most famous of all baseball umpires, was offered a bribe at the Polo Grounds before a play-off game between the Giants and Cubs for the National League pennant. Klem testified at a meeting of league executives, and his testimony was corroborated by Jim Johnstone, the other umpire, that the offer was made by Dr. William Creamer, the Giants' physician. The doctor entered a denial, but was barred from all major- and minor-league ball parks for life.

The play-off game was necessitated by what

was probably the most colossal "boner" in baseball history, but it was really only a pretty technical mistake. It happened on September 23, 1908, with the Giants and the Cubs in a tight struggle for the league lead. The score was tied, 1-1, when the Giants went to bat in the ninth inning. With two out, Moose McCormick, an outfielder, was on third base, and Fred Merkle, the first baseman, was on first. The batter, Al Bridwell, the shortstop, lined the ball into center field for a hit.

McCormick ran home with the "winning" run, and the crowd started to swarm onto the field. Merkle had started for second base, but now he saw McCormick cross the plate. He stopped short of second and headed for the clubhouse. Johnny Evers, the Chicago second baseman, went looking for the ball.

According to Evers, the throw from the outfield had rolled over to the third-base coaching box, where McGinnity, the Giant pitcher who was coaching on third, picked it up. He was about to throw it into the stands when Evers and Joe Tinker, the Chicago shortstop, jumped him.

McGinnity broke loose and heaved the ball into the crowd. Evers later said it was caught by a tall, thin, middle-aged man wearing a brown bowler hat. He may have been middle-aged when he caught it, but he was an old man when he left the park. Harry Steinfeldt, the Cubs' third baseman, and Floyd Kroh, a Cubs pitcher, ran over to him, begging for the ball. When the customer refused to part with his souvenir, Kroh hit him on the head, driving the bowler down over the gentleman's eyes, while Steinfeldt grabbed the ball and threw it to Evers. Evers, the crowd milling around him, stepped on second base for the force-out, while Hank O'Day, the umpire, watched.

In the press box the sports writers had already flashed the news that the Giants had won, 2 to 1. They hadn't. The game was declared a tie. The two teams finished the season with the same record, and the Cubs won the play-off and the pennant, 4 to 2.

In 1917 the Giants lost the World Series to the Chicago White Sox after Heinie Zimmerman, the Giants' third baseman, with ball in hand, chased Eddie Collins, the White Sox second baseman, momentarily trapped off third, across the Polo Grounds home plate. Walter Holke, the Giants' first baseman, had failed to cover home; the only man behind the plate was Bill Klem.

"Who the hell was I going to throw the ball to?" the frustrated Zimmerman said later. "Klem?"

Though he stood only five feet six inches, the most imposing man ever seen in the Polo Grounds was John Joseph McGraw, who was born in Truxton, New York, on April 7, 1873, and died in a hospital in New Rochelle, New York, on February 25, 1934. He came to the Giants from the Baltimore Orioles in 1902, as manager and shortstop, and he managed the team thirty years. McGraw's Giants won ten National League pennants, appeared in nine World Series and won three of them.

McGraw was almost as quick with his fists as he was with his tongue; outside New York he was probably the most hated man in the history of baseball. But everybody who hated him respected him, not only for his ability but for the hard core of integrity behind his highly combustible exterior.

Some of McGraw's fire rubbed onto his Giants, and some of the best fights in the history of baseball occurred at the Polo Grounds. In 1922 in a game between New York and Philadelphia, Ralph Shinners, a Giant outfielder, who in an earlier game had been hit on the head by a ball pitched by George Smith, a former Giant then with the Phils, slugged Smith to the ground as Smith, knocked out of the box, was walking out to the clubhouse. McGraw was in on that one—he had sensed what was about to happen and had taken a short cut through the stands.

That same year Earl Smith, the Giant catcher, slugged Cozy Dolan, the Giant coach, in the Polo Grounds clubhouse. Smith, among others, suspected Dolan of being a stool pigeon for McGraw, and gave Dolan a classic beating while the rest of the team looked on, counting for the knockdowns.

McGraw has been gone from the Polo Grounds bench for years, but for a long time some of him remained. It was still impossible to look from the Giants' dugout into the visiting dugout—McGraw, violently opposed to any fraternization between players of opposing teams, insisted that the architect design the dugouts that way—and there was still on the bench at the end nearest the water cooler a green wooden box about eight inches high. It was put there so that the squat McGraw could see his outfielders over the hump of the diamond.

The Giants, moreover, until they gave up residence, hoisted a blue pennant signifying victory or a red and white one mourning defeat from a pole on the clubhouse roof after each game. Gone, however, from the green outfield walls was the advertising of McGraw's day, including a sign which

changed slightly with the outfield personnel of the Giants but always made reference to a Giant hero. Around the time of World War I, for example, it read:

"Last year George Burns, Giant left fielder, caught 512 flies.

"Last year TANGLEFOOT caught 15,000,000,000 flies."

Babe Ruth's Greatest Moment

by JACK MILEY

THERE'S NOTHING THE MATTER WITH baseball today that another Babe Ruth couldn't cure.

For when this fabulous fellow trudged into the shadows of retirement, dragging his booming bat through the dust at his heels, our theater of American sports lost an actor who may never be replaced.

It is already more than three decades since the greatest Yankee of 'em all—not to mention the most colorful character a century of our national pastime has produced—was at his bombastic, belting, slambang best. And that, my friends, was tops in any league.

For the Babe was not only an amazing athlete— a thick-thewed, contemptuous, cocksure colossus of clout who made more records than a phonograph factory—but he was also an accomplished actor, a Barrymore of the bat, a thumping Thespian of the greensward.

While your ballplayers of today stand out there on the field, apparently engrossed in ponderous thought, they are probably figuring their income taxes.

But in the Babe's time it was different—and so was he. Ruth was not the type to fret over money. So he frolicked around in the outfield, with his blubbery torso bobbling above his spindly legs, razzing the fans, encouraging his teammates and shouting delightful unprintables at his opponents. In short, the big fellow enjoyed himself; he had fun and the customers loved it—and him.

Although his whole career, on and off the field, was one continuous and highly theatrical performance, the Babe really reached his histrionic height one autumn afternoon in Chicago, when he audaciously announced to 50,000 people that he would knock one of his famous home runs all the way to hellangone out of Wrigley Field.

The date was October 1, 1932. It was the third game of the Yankee-Cubs World Series. The Yanks had won the two opening games in New York and had invaded Chicago to conclude their clean-sweep blitz. Feeling between the two teams was bitter because Ruth, always a fast fellow with a dollar, had publicly announced the Cubs as "a lotta cheapskates" for confining their World Series money to twenty-four shares and dealing out the popular Rogers Hornsby, their ex-manager, and a few others in their divvy of surplus sugar.

The big dramatic moment was the Yankee half of the fifth inning, with the reliable Charlie Root on the mound for Chicago. Cub players and fans alike had been riding Ruth, who had homered into the right-field stands with two aboard in the first. The Chicago rooters had been pegging lemons and other missiles at the Babe as he patrolled his outfield post. He in turn had tossed a few choice observations about Chicagoans in general and Cub followers in particular over his big, fat shoulder and guffawed heartily at his tormentors during this exchange of repartee.

But the Cub players didn't stop there. They lined the dugout steps and speculated loudly and unfavorably as to the Babe's paternity, if any. He contented himself with thumbing his flat button nose at the Cub bench and emitting through his thick, pursed lips raucous sounds known as the Bronx cheer. Ruth also flipped up a few pennies toward the Cub dugout and shouted: "Split those up among yuh, pikers!" All in all, it was good, clean fun.

There was one down in that fateful fifth and the score was tied, 4-4, when the Great Man, with his peculiar little mincing stride, stepped into the batter's box after tapping the dirt from his spikes, cocked his yellow bat menacingly and grinned at the Cub hurler.

The smile faded from his punkin face as Root whipped a strike past him. The stands went wild. The Cub bench unleashed a new barrage of insults at the Babe. But the ham came out in him. Ruth the batter became Ruth the actor. He held up one thick, browned forefinger, about the size and hue of a hot dog. That, indubitably, he pantomimed to the populace, was strike one.

A ball intervened. The Great Man didn't even deign to waggle his wagon tongue bat at it. Umpire George Magerkurth jerked his right arm upward and shouted "Strike Two!" The fans jeered and howled and the Cub bench jockeys really razzed Ruth. This time the Babe majestically held up two fingers and shook them toward his dugout taunters.

And then he made the most dramatic and daring gesture ever seen in a World Series. Leering at his hecklers, he pointed to the flagpole to the right of the scoreboard out in center field and promised in unmistakable pantomime that he would hit the very next pitch there or thereabouts.

Ruth wrapped his big, hamlike hands around the end of the bat handle and dug in with his spikes as Charlie Root wound up. The pitcher had him in the hole and could afford to waste a couple of balls on him. But the way the Babe exuded confidence you'd think it was he who had Root out on the limb. But bad ball or good one, right in the groove or low and outside, the Babe had promised his ill-wishers he was going to hit that next pitch or break his back swinging on it. So the minute Root let fly with that spheroid, the greatest batsman baseball has ever seen "swang on it" right from his heels, with his whole heart and soul.

Wham! That ball took off like a rocket! It soared high, wide and handsome straight out where Ruth had indicated he would send it; it finally lost altitude and hit an office building outside the Park. While the press coop statisticians didn't get out their tapes and measure it, this Herculean homer is still cited as the longest hit ever made at the Cubs' Park.

The minute Ruth fulfilled his prodigious promise, he stepped from his role as hero—or villain, if you had happened to be a Cub fan—and became boisterous Babe, the comedian. He flung down his bat and galloped around the base paths, gesticulating and making derisive motions at Cub players and rooters alike. His big, bobbling belly shook in uncontrollable merriment as he jogged over the sacks, pausing briefly at each to address a few indecorous outbursts to their custodian. Tears of happiness streamed down his fat, brown cheeks and his Falstaffian roars echoed in the Yank dugout for minutes after he sank in hysterical exhaustion on the bench as his New York teammates ganged him and whacked him black and blue.

This, then, was Ruth's greatest hour. With Lou Gehrig hitting a homer—his second, too, for that afternoon—before the crowd had recovered from the Babe's feat and the Yanks sweeping the Series next day, that afternoon of October 1, 1932, was easily the outstanding achievement of his star-studded career. Like Houdini, the magician, who attained his zenith when he made an elephant disap-

pear on a Broadway stage, what could the Babe have done for an encore after that terrific feat against the Cubs?

Luck Goes to Bat

by FORD FRICK

THE NEW YORK YANKEES WERE PLAYing the St. Louis Cardinals at Avon Park in Florida. The score was 3 to 2 in favor of the Cardinals. It was the eighth inning and the Yankees were batting. Two men were out and the bases were full.

Babe Ruth sauntered forth from the dugout and a hush of tense expectancy settled over the fans. Even though this was only a preseason practice game, the crisis was so acute and so full of interest it might just as well have been the deciding contest in a World Series—so far as the fans were concerned, or so far as Ruth himself was concerned.

Any kind of a base hit meant the ball game for the Yankees, and the Babe and the fans both knew it. Day in and day out, the fans plunk down their money in hope of getting a thrill from a situation such as this, and the players dream of such an opportunity to demonstrate their prowess.

The Babe paused before the bat rack. He took his time, as a great man about to cope with a grave emergency is entitled to do. After solemn deliberation, he picked out his bat, hefted it and strolled toward the plate. Just as he was about to take his stance, he caught sight of a Negro boy standing near the Yankee dugout.

The Babe put down his bat and beckoned to the colored youngster, who promptly trotted forward, eager and grinning. While the fans stared down, for the most part utterly mystified, the King of Swat performed a peculiar ceremony. He placed

his hands on the Negro's head, as if conferring a title or bestowing a benediction, and earnestly rubbed his fingers through the woolly black hair.

The fans were fascinated, but few of them knew what it was all about. Perhaps the Babe was merely wiping perspiration from his hands in this grotesque manner, exercising thereby the prerogative of his greatness and indulging his sense of humor— as the lords of the manor used to do in medieval days when they cleaned their greasy fingers on the flowing locks of their vassals in lieu of table napkins.

Then the Babe went to bat—struck out on three pitched balls! After the third strike went zipping past, the Babe whirled around and took out after the colored lad, chasing him under the grandstand and out of the park.

The fans howled with glee. From those in the know the word went around that the Babe's wrath wasn't caused by striking out so much as it was the failure of one of his pet superstitions. Many ballplayers believe if they rub the head of a colored boy that luck will go to bat with them—and for them.

As a class, ballplayers are exceptionally prone to be superstitious, and the Babe was one of the most susceptible. For instance, he always insisted upon warming up with a certain selected player before each game. Benny Bengough was once his favorite. Then he went into a hitting slump and Benny was blacklisted. For a time Eddie Bennett, the mascot,

LUCK GOES TO BAT 81

was his choice. Later he switched to Earl Combs, and afterward to Bill Dickey. But the job never lasted long. Every time the Babe went into a slump, he demanded a change.

Another one of Ruth's superstitions dealt with opening mail. He simply refused to open it himself, insisting that brought him bad luck. Naturally he received a vast amount of mail, which accumulated unopened in his locker until someone—Doc Woods, the trainer, for instance—found time to sort it for him.

On one occasion Steve O'Neill, who was catching for Cleveland at the time, sent Ruth a telegram asking him to speak before a boys' club. Knowing that Ruth was always ready to co-operate in any welfare work for boys, Steve was very much surprised and disappointed when the Babe failed to show up. Several weeks later when Steve was in New York he demanded an explanation.

"What's the big idea of standing me up that way? Didn't you get my telegram?"

"No," Ruth replied, fumbling through a huge stack of mail in his locker. "It must have got lost. Oh, I guess this must be it."

"Well," O'Neill insisted, "that's all right about that one, but what about the second one. Didn't you get that either?"

"Oh, sure!" the Babe blustered. "I got that one all right. I answered that one."

"Oh, yeah?" O'Neill retorted. "Well, you're a big liar. I didn't send another one."

Many baseball superstitions center around bats. Frank (Wildfire) Schulte of the old Cubs had a special pet bat which he called Black Betsy. No other player was permitted to touch it, much less use it. Schulte himself only used it on coming to bat when there were two out and the tying or winning run was on base. Then it was his big medicine, his heavy artillery that seldom failed him.

"Mixing up the bats" is a common practice among big league players when a team is in a hitting slump. But if the team happens to be hitting, woe betide the unfortunate bat boy who permits the bats to get out of alignment as they lie in a perfect row in front of the dugout! For the players will tell you, the same mixing of bats that has the power to bring a team out of a slump is just

as effective in stopping a rally, should that mixing occur—accidentally or otherwise—while the team is hitting.

Lefty Gomez was another player who had his own private little superstition. He was about to take the mound against the Washington Senators in a certain game at the Yankee Stadium. He got his final instructions from Manager Joe McCarthy, took a final drink of water, and started up the steps of the dugout. Suddenly he stopped, horrified.

"Where's that flat fungo bat of Burke's?" he demanded. "Who moved it?"

For a moment no one spoke. Then the bat boy, flushed and nervous, produced the bat—a practice bat, which is short and light, so the batter can hold it in one hand while tossing up the ball with the other, and which has a flat surface, so the batter can place the ball out into the field to whatever man he wants to.

"I put it over here," the bat boy explained. "I forgot!"

"I ought to box your ears!" Gomez declared.

Then he solemnly placed the bat at the very end of the bat rack, flat face up, and went back for another drink of water. When he emerged from the dugout again, he took care to step lightly on the bat's flat surface as he went out to the mound.

Lefty didn't go very well that day. He was wild and in the third inning a line drive from Goslin's bat drove in three runs and took Lefty out of the ball game. He walked across the field disconsolately, threw his glove into the corner of the dugout and sat down on the bench, muttering to himself.

"That bat jinxed me," he told Joe McCarthy. "I knew I was licked when I saw the kid had moved it. I was a cinch to lose." And Gomez meant every word he said. He believed implicitly that the only way he could ward off the jinx was to step on the flat surface of that fungo bat, with elaborate unconcern, as if merely by accident.

If a player finds a pin, that means a base hit. A load of hay also signifies good luck. So does a load of empty barrels, and when the players see a load of empty barrels they immediately remove their hats. John McGraw, the wise and cagey manager of the Giants, once used that superstition to help him win an important series.

The Giants were playing the Cubs in one of those old-time, uproarious pennant-making affairs. The afternoon of the first game as the players were assembling in the clubhouse a truck load of empty barrels went creaking and rumbling down the street.

"Oh, baby! There's luck," one of the men commented. "There's a flock of base hits for this afternoon."

Fired by the omen, the Giants won the game. The next day another load of empty barrels went past. Again the players were elated and again they won. For the rest of the Series, it was the same each day. Some one saw a load of empty barrels—but no one noticed that they were the same barrels each time!

After the series was over a swarthy Italian laborer appeared at the door of the clubhouse and asked for McGraw.

"Not in yet," Roger Bresnahan responded. "What do you want with him?"

With copious gestures and broken English, the Italian explained that he wanted his money. McGraw had hired him to bolster up the confidence of the team with those barrels, and he wanted his money. I guess he got it all right. He deserved it.

In the days when Eddie Collins was second baseman for the Philadelphia Athletics, he had two cherished superstitions. When batting, he would park his chewing gum on the button of his cap, returning it to his mouth only after two strikes had been called. Also, he had a lucky undershirt which he wore in all World Series and championship games for ten years or more. That old shirt, tattered and torn, patched and repatched, was Eddie's ace in the hole all through his big-league career.

Ted Lyons, the White Sox pitcher, and George Pipgras of the Yankees had a superstition they picked up from old-timers. When they left the pitching box at the end of an inning they put their gloves down most carefully, palm up with thumb crossed over and fingers pointing meticulously toward the dugout. That's because in the days when the spitball was permitted, pitchers parked their slippery elm in their gloves between innings, laying out their gloves in that manner. Pipgras got the habit from Urban Shocker, perhaps the most superstitious player who ever wore big-league

spikes, and Ted learned it from the veteran Urban Faber.

Tony Lazzeri of the Yankees and Hughey Critz of the Giants had similar superstitions. When they took the field they always walked over and moved the opposing second baseman's glove a few inches from where it was tossed. Critz, in addition, always picked up a pebble from the infield at the start of every inning.

Gabby Hartnett, catcher for the Chicago Cubs, traveled far out of his way to avoid stepping between the catcher and the umpire when he went to the plate. If Gene Robertson, once with the Yankees, succeeded in getting a hit on his first time at the plate he would thereafter studiously retrace his identical steps on each trip from the dugout. Eppa Rixey, the elongated left-hander of the Cincinnati Reds, after losing a tough game always broke up a chair in the clubhouse—a rather expensive gesture, incidentally, for a tail-end club such as Cincinnati. Fred Toney, the old Giant pitcher, who worked in the days before sanitary drinking fountains, used to crash the water bucket to pieces after a bad inning.

It's been a long time since the inspired Boston Braves of 1914 walked away with the National League pennant and a world championship, but veteran players still insist that there was the luckiest ball club in history.

"I never saw such a gang of baseball misfits," John McGraw once remarked. "They were the dumbest-looking ball club I ever saw. Yet they ran off with the pennant—the lucky stiffs!"

Those Braves were a superstitious lot—and the most superstitious man in the outfit was Manager George Stallings. Bits of paper or peanut shells, scattered about the ball park, were Stallings' chief hoodoo. Nothing, he believed, was a more potent omen of bad luck. During those hectic pennant days it was no uncommon sight to see Stallings, hatless and coatless, down on his knees in front of the bench, picking up stray bits of paper and peanut shells that had landed there from the stands.

Opposing players knew Stallings' superstition, and nothing delighted them more than to tear up a score card and surreptitiously strew the fragments in front of the Braves' bench when Stallings wasn't looking. For a time George hired Oscar

Dugey, ostensibly as a coach. But Oscar's real job was to keep the bench clean of all trash. Dugey still maintains that in his two years with Stallings he completely ruined his arm shying stones at pigeons that flocked around the bench to get the peanuts thrown by opposing players.

Stallings also had another superstition that was ludicrous, but painful. If a batting rally started he wouldn't change the position he was accidentally caught in, until the rally was over—no matter how cramped and uncomfortable his position. Sometimes he would be caught looking at the stands. He'd hold that pose like a statue. Sometimes he would be stooped over and have his back to the play. That didn't make any difference. He'd hold it. Sometimes he would be caught gazing at the sky.

When he was caught like that, and couldn't see what was going on out on the field he would be miserable. He was always wrapped up in the game. So he would call a substitute, and have the substitute tell him every pitch, every move, every single detail.

Once he was caught crouched down in a corner of the dugout picking up a match. On that occasion the Braves batted all the way around. Stallings wouldn't move, and for fifteen minutes he suffered agony. At the finish his leg was so cramped that he had to be carried to the clubhouse and given a massage.

Thus, luck goes to bat.

OUT AT HOME by Fletcher Martin

4
HORSE RACING: THE SPORT OF KINGS

No animal (excepting woman) has so inspired man to extravagance as has the horse. It has been a favorite with artists and sculptors since the age of Pericles because of its grace and strength. Pride inevitably first provoked challenges between owners, and it's been a matter of opinion ever since. The horse has pulled chariots, surreys, milk wagons, stagecoaches, and carried monkeys, pony-express riders, Lady Godiva and the hopes of millions of fanciers as it galloped through the centuries. Here are three great horses and their greatest moments: Man o' War in the Dwyer Stakes as backed by Grantland Rice; Dark Secret, touted by one of the greatest of all horse trainers, "Sunny Jim" Fitzsimmons; and the incredible Dan Patch, the pacer that trotted faster than runners. Up are two great men: Eddie Arcaro, who has won more stake races than any jockey who ever lived, and Tod Sloan, who revolutionized saddle racing, won two million dollars, dined with kings and was the inspiration of George M. Cohan's "Yankee Doodle Dandy," a great man who—like Humpty Dumpty —had a great fall. Last, for all those who long to cry, "Foul!" and have their horse put up first, a journalistic classic: Arthur Daley's yarn of the reporter who, alone out of 40,000 fans, saw the incident in the 1933 Kentucky Derby which almost caused the only disqualification in its history, and lost his job because of it. Read 'em and pick 'em.

Big Red: "The Mostest Horse"

by GRANTLAND RICE

JULY 10 BACK IN 1920 WAS TO BE BIG Red's major test. Big Red was better known as Man o' War. On this day, in the Dwyer Stakes at Aqueduct, Big Red was to run against Harry Payne Whitney's John P. Grier over the mile-and-one-eighth route. It was superhorse against superhorse, and Man o' War was conceding John P. Grier eighteen pounds, 126 against 108.

There was a feeling long in advance that this was to be one of the great horse races of all time. It was.

raw breaks and ragged luck happened to him.

But the Whitney starter, John P. Grier, trained by James Rowe, had been working in record time, and I can name you more than a few big gamblers who went broke backing him at five to two. They were still not quite sure that Man o' War could be as good, or as great, as he proved to be. At any rate, there was a sweep of feeling in the big crowd that track history was in the making—track history that has never been equaled or approached.

MAN O'WAR BEATING JOHN P. GRIER
by Frank Voss (In the Dwyer Stakes at
Aqueduct, July 10, 1920)

Man o' War, son of Fair Play and Maluba, owned by Samuel Riddle, trained by Louis Feustel, could look back on over two centuries of flawless pedigree. His only defeat as a two-year-old—the only race he ever was to lose—had come from Upset at Saratoga the year before, when everything in the way of

They were off. Clarence Kummer, riding Man o' War, broke with Big Red's usual thunderbolt rush. But Ed Ambrose on John P. Grier matched this first wild charge to blend the two horses into one picture.

Now they were under way—and still they were

head and head. While the odds were against John P. Grier this afternoon, he was matching pace for pace the best that Man o' War had to offer. They came to the first quarter in 23 and 2/5 seconds, dizzy time by any standards. And still they were eye to eye.

Now they rushed to the five-furlong pole in the sensational time of 57 and 2.5. A handkerchief could have covered both noses. Without a split second's faltering on either side, they came to the six-furlong spot, still head and head, still stride for stride, in the world's record time of 1.09 and 2/5.

Here was the horse race of all horse races. You can imagine here the heart-cracking excitement of those who had backed one horse or the other. Six furlongs—a world's record—and neither had slipped a stride. Then they came on to the mile in 1.35 and 3/5, equaling the world's record, still racing as a team, still head and head, eye to eye, stride for stride.

Who would break first? The stretch alone could tell the story of this historic race. Here were two horses that had been breaking records from the first jump through the killing mile. Neither had been able to pick up as much as half a length. They might have been a team painted on canvas.

But now they are in the stretch—the crucial point of every contest, no matter what the game. Before the race, owner Samuel Riddle had given Clarence Kummer just one order: "Lay alongside of Johnny Grier—use the whip only when you need it. Just once is enough—if you have to."

As they came to the sixteenth pole, John P. Grier put his nose in front. At this moment a wild shout came up from the big crowd—"Grier wins—Grier wins—Man o' War is beaten!" And just at that moment Kummer, Man o' War's jockey, responded to orders.

He called upon the whip. As Kummer struck Big Red, the giant horse took just one great forward leap. He became a thunderbolt. Kummer later admitted Man o' War almost shook him from the saddle. With a stride of twenty-four feet against the normal thoroughbred's stride of eighteen or twenty feet, Big Red went to the air. From his position back of John P. Grier, himself a great horse,

Man o' War with that one whiplash took a full half-length lead. He was something shot from a gun. In just one jump he was out in front, charging on to beat John P. Grier by almost two lengths as he gave racing a new world record.

Man o' War had run the mile and sixteenth in 1.49 and 1/5. Carrying 126 pounds, he had smashed the record for the distance set by Borrow in the Brooklyn Handicap three years before, when Borrow carried only 117 pounds.

This was Man o' War's greatest race. In his racing career of two years he met no older, no handicap horses. He faced no such competition as Exterminator through five or six years. But he was the greatest of all time as a two- and a three-year-old. He was the king of all sires, with a record crop such as this: Crusader, Mars, American Flag, Scapa Flow, Edith Cavell and War Admiral, to mention only a few.

But Big Red's greatest performance was against Johnny Grier, Harry Payne Whitney's favorite horse, when both continued to break world's records until Kummer called on the whip down the stretch—and Big Red went on to a new world's record.

The criterion is that through the years they are still comparing thoroughbreds with Man o' War. Man o' War and no one else. For here was the Thoroughbred Thunderbolt, in all racing history —"The Mostest Horse."

Deep Through the Heart

by JAMES E. "SUNNY JIM" FITZSIMMONS

IT'S A COLD RAINY SATURDAY AT BEL-
*mont Park. The track is mud, pocked with puddles
for the 1934 running of the two-mile Jockey Club
Gold Cup race. . . . This large crowd is tense as
the three starters come up to the post. There's
Dark Secret from Wheatley Stables, Faireno from
Belair Stud and Inlander from Brookmeade Stables.
. . . Both Dark Secret and Faireno, although
owned by separate interests, are trained by "Sunny
Jim" Fitzsimmons. . . . They're at the barrier now—
and they're off! . . . Dark Secret leads with Faireno not quite a length behind. Inlander is fading
fast. . . . Faireno is sticking to Dark Secret like a
leech as they head into the stretch for the first
time. Inlander is out of it. . . . They're in the
back stretch again with Dark Secret still out in
front by a length. . . . Now they're thundering
for home. Dark Secret and Faireno! They're at the
sixteenth pole. Dark Secret on the inside lurched
badly, but Jockey Kurtsinger is pulling him together. . . . At the finish line—it's Dark Secret by
a neck! Dark Secret, the winner, is floundering
now . . . he's going down on his right foreleg. . . .*

I suppose there are many ways to measure greatness. In humans, the yardstick may be individual
courage, the ability to carry on despite extreme
handicap. Horsemen measure thoroughbreds by
the same quality.

Above all else, the thoroughbred is bred to do
one thing—RUN. In a good one, the life message—
to reach the finish ahead of the field—is the all-driv-
ing force, transmitted from his blood, heart and
lungs to his animal brain. There are instances when
this drive takes over to complete the job when the
legs are no longer there to carry the weight. . . .

The first time I saw Dark Secret was in May,
1931. A two-year-old by the Kentucky Derby winner, Flying Ebony, the youngster was being un-
loaded from a van at Wheatley Stables at Aqueduct. Owned by Mrs. J. S. Phipps and her brother,
the late Ogden Mills, he looked a touch on the
small side; but he had plenty of bone. Bone in a
horse is akin to stout legs in a man. A bay, ticked
with gray, he was bred by the late Gifford Coch-
ran's Shandon stud.

DARK SECRET'S LAST RACE by Harold Von Schmidt

Our first "work" on him was late that month
when we caught him at two furlongs. There was
little to indicate he was anything special. But as he
began moving, Dark Secret gave every indication
that he was geared for distance. Some thoroughbreds like the short, fast haul; some are gaited for
longer tests. I especially like that disposition for
distance. One thing is certain: you can't rate a
horse strictly off his bloodlines; you can't read his
heart by just looking at him.

That year, Dark Secret won two out of eight.

The next he won the Kenner Stakes, among others. At four, he won the Brooklyn, Empire City and Manhattan Handicaps, the Jockey Club Gold Cup at Belmont.

His fifth year, 1934, was the climax. Three days before defending the Jockey Club Gold Cup, he again won the Manhattan Handicap, a mile and a half, in 2:29 1/5 with 122 pounds; and just before that he won the Saratoga Cup.

All told, the book shows that he won twenty-three of fifty-seven starts with thirteen seconds and six thirds.

I watched the Jockey Club Gold Cup from the infield. Just beyond the finish line, the late Charlie Kurtsinger, the jockey, was easing up rather abruptly when suddenly Dark Secret bobbled and went down on his right foreleg. The jockey jumped off, spotted me and cried, "Mr. Fitz, I was afraid he was going to fall on his head. I think he hit a hard spot about a hundred yards from home. Something gave way, maybe a tendon, but he was still rolling and I tried to pull him together. We reached the finish and he went for good."

Thunderstruck, I noticed Dark Secret's right foreleg dangling. It must have snapped completely in those last few strides. The colt was suffering from a multiple fracture of the cannon bone directly above the ankle, and Doc Masterson advised that the only humane thing to do was destroy Dark Secret at once.

Several days later, from the Doc, I learned what had happened. Inside the sixteenth pole, Dark Secret's left leg had bowed (tendon rupture). The lurch the jockey felt in those final strides was the horse shifting his weight to the sound right leg—the one that literally exploded a few strides later! But it didn't prevent him from struggling on—to get his nose somehow under that finish line ahead of Faireno.

That's the quality I was talking about—it's the courage in a thoroughbred heart.

Million-Dollar Horse

by ROSCOE MACY

IN THE OPENING DECADE OF THIS CENTURY a crooked-legged mahogany bay pacer—a harness horse—grossed an estimated million dollars for his owner in seven years of exhibition races and in indirect returns.

Just get a few veterans of harness racing talking about Dan Patch, and watch the superlatives fly. "He was the speediest creature that ever wore harness." "In or out of harness, he was the most intelligent horse I ever saw." "A kinder, wiser, finer-dispositioned horse never lived." Dan Patch had the largest and most faithful popular following of any animal in racing history.

At the height of The Patch's career, there was a Dan Patch cigar, and toy stores everywhere featured Dan Patch sleds, coaster wagons and hobbyhorses. One manufacturer advertised the Dan Patch washing machine, warranted to turn out a clean tubful in two minutes. As state-fair attractions, Teddy Roosevelt, William Jennings Bryan and the fireworks display "Burning of Moscow" ran poor seconds to this lovable horse.

Even after The Patch was retired to stud, throngs of the faithful made pilgrimages on the Dan Patch Railroad out of Minneapolis just to gaze at him in his stall as he munched his oats, had his coat curried or took his regular after-luncheon nap. "Men, women and children," declared an article in *The*

Harness Horse, "seemed content just to see him—as if he were George Washington or Abraham Lincoln."

The saga of Dan Patch had its beginning in an ill-judged wink. Big, smiling Dan Messner, village storekeeper at Oxford, Indiana, pushing into the horse ring at a dispersal sale, flickered his eyelid as a greeting to his friend, the auctioneer. He was astounded a moment later to hear the latter shout, "Sold to Dan Messner for $255!"

Dan was what they called, in 1894, a "dead game sport." He paid over the money, then ruefully inspected his purchase—a lame, decrepit, old mare named Zelica. She had good racing blood in her, yet in all her life had been entered in but one match, which she lost. She was a standard-bred, though, and the first Dan had ever owned. A few miles away across the Illinois state line the famed and temperamental Joe Patchen, briefly holder of the world's harness record, was in stud. Dan decided to invest $150 in breeding his mare to the former champion.

The week Zelica foaled—in March, 1896—Dan was absent on a business trip. But one look at the depot idlers' faces as he stepped off the train was enough to tell him that his money had gone up the flue. At the livery stable he studied the gaunt, scraggly colt and sighed. The things that were wrong, he saw, were not the sort an animal outgrows. For racing the colt's knees were too knobby and his face too amiable. Kind of a friendly little cuss, Dan thought; might make a pretty fair delivery horse someday.

Messner christened his colt Dan Patch, after himself and Joe Patchen, then left the colt's handling to Johnny Wattles at the livery barn. Johnny soon came to set great store by his charge, often neglecting the livery business to see that young Dan had his daily workout with a racing sulky.

That Dan Messner had no hope of salvaging his investment through track earnings is indicated by the fact that The Patch was a four-year-old before he competed in his first race. Worn down by Johnny's persistent urgings, Messner finally matched the horse with two speedsters of modest reputation thereabouts.

The race was held in the summer of 1900. Only a few neighbors were present to see the bay stallion win in straight heats under wraps. Dan Messner scratched his head, shook his stop watch and looked again. "Hmm! Reckon mebbe we got something here after all, eh, Johnny?"

That same year, after a brief training stretch under the veteran driver Myron McHenry, the Messner stallion was entered in his first big-time match at Lafayette, Indiana. Here was real competition, a dozen seasoned pacers, some of them with wide experience around the Grand Circuit, the big-money tracks of the nation. Rated as top-heavy favorite by the bookies was the rugged speedster, Milo S. No one even looked at Dan Patch.

The track would not accommodate a single-tiered start with so many entrants, and McHenry drew a position in the rear rank. The big bay, confused at finding himself hemmed in by so many other horses, was lost in the ruck during the early stages of the race. Then, near the halfway mark, he broke to the outside of the thinned-out line and sped past the others. But the recovery was too late, the homestretch too short. Milo S. nosed out a victory.

And that, it turned out, was an epic loss. Dan Patch won the next heat in the remarkable "maiden" time of 2:16, then went on to win the third and fourth heats, and thus the race. In those days the first horse to capture three heats was the winner. Never again, to the close of his career, did the pacer lose even one heat in a fair field. One other lost heat was recorded the following year, but under circumstances so suspicious that Dan Patch's driver was severely grilled by the judges.

After half a dozen of those effortless wins, Dan Messner began to suspect that he was a trifle beyond his depth. The sudden death of a well-known colt by poisoning convinced him ownership of a miracle horse was not for a country storekeeper. He listened to an offer of $20,000, and Dan Patch became the property of M. E. Sturgis. Johnny Wattles wept.

In 1901 and 1902, The Patch racked up an unbroken winning streak of eighteen races around the Circuit, and at Providence, Rhode Island, on August 29, 1902, he became the second horse to break two minutes for a mile. His mark was 1:59½, a scant quarter second short of the world mark set by Star Pointer in 1897.

With the aging Star Pointer in retirement, no horse anywhere could give Dan Patch a run for the money. Sturgis began to notice that track managers shifted uneasily when he filed his entry for coming events. Fans loved The Patch, but they clamored for real races, with suspense and close finishes. Those who liked to bet could find little fun in wagering on the second-place winner. Amazingly, though, Dan Patch's days of greatest fame were ahead.

Throughout the latter part of the 1902 season a quiet, soft-spoken individual in frock coat and black derby was noticed trailing the horse around the circuit. He held a stop watch on the races, but turned a deaf ear to gamblers' tips. He neither smoked, drank nor showed up at the track on Sundays. In December, he was identified in a startling news item. Marion Willis Savage, a Minneapolis stock-food manufacturer, had paid Sturgis the stupendous sum of $60,000 for Dan Patch!

Sturgis had a hunch that he had given the purchaser a mild shellacking, not suspecting for a minute that he was to be overheard less than three years later pleading with Savage in The Patch's stall: "Look, M. W., you gave me three times what I paid for the horse. Say the word, and I'll write you a check today for three times what you paid me." The offer was turned down.

Farm-bred Marion Savage, founder and owner of the International Stock Food Company, was a born promoter. He had built his firm into a million-dollar concern, but saw a vast untouched market for his product. In the spring of 1903 he introduced a new advertising technique: he advertised his wares with a race horse—a horse that turned out to have a miraculous sense of drama.

Preceded by posters picturing the bay pacer and featuring International Stock Food, Dan Patch was entered in a trial against time at Brighton Beach, Massachusetts, on opening day of the 1903 Grand Circuit. The spectators grumbled, and settled back in their seats, for such events were notoriously dull. This time a surprise was in store.

The pace-setter, a running horse hitched to a modified type of sulky called a speed cart, galloped along in the lead, with the star of the show immediately behind. A second bangtail ran neck and neck with him on the outside. The runners strained and their drivers urged them on, but the big bay matched them pace for gallop. The crowd sat up. As the three horses swept around the final turn and approached the straightaway, the second runner began to drop back. Dan Patch swung out and edged up, foot by foot, to overtake and pass the pace-setter. Suddenly a fresh runner charged onto the track. He fought to take the lead—but the steady clop-clop-clop of the pacer never faltered. The crowd was in a frenzy. It roared its enthusiasm as The Patch crept into the lead and finished first.

That summer the eastern racing crowd went wild over Dan Patch. His eye on a wider audience, Savage then entered the horse at a number of state fairs in the Midwest and Southwest, cheerfully accepting opening day or Saturday—both traditionally poor drawing days—as Dan Patch Day. He would sign for a percentage or accept all of the gate receipts above the highest sum taken in on the corresponding day of any previous year.

To each area, on the signing of a contract, Savage dispatched an army of advance men, to plaster the countryside with bills describing "Dan Patch, the Wonder Horse." Advertisements in local farm journals invited readers to send postage for the pamphlet "The Racing Life of Dan Patch" (stock-food literature to be included free), and thousands rushed to the post office. Evenings, the local folk congregated in barbershops, drugstores and pool halls to praise the pacer that had shown his heels to the best horses any of the Eastern slickers could round up, that was "gentle as a woman and wiser than most men."

And wise The Patch was. There were no starting judges in exhibition races, the take-off being left to the judgment of the driver—in theory. But driver Harry Hersey, who held the reins in some of Dan Patch's fastest races, said that *he* never controlled the start: "When Dan was ready, he just gave a certain jerk on the reins, and that was my cue."

Before the campaign ended, every villager, every farm family had determined to see the Miracle Horse, come Dan Patch Day at their state fair. Trains were jammed and dust clouds swirled for miles over the roads leading to the fair grounds. At one fair the entire countryside was drained of its inhabitants on Dan Patch Day. That evening the managers discovered that they owed Marion Savage $21,000 as his share of the gate!

And if some spectators came to scoff, they left the grounds hopelessly smitten with the intelligent, lovable horse. His trick of bowing right and left —"If you've been there before, he'll recognize you and bow," the advance agents promised villagers—made them come back and back.

In 1904, The Patch traveled 10,000 miles in his private railroad car, played to 600,000. On his return home that winter, he was met at the Minneapolis station by a brass band and escorted down Nicollet Avenue by 200 paraders.

The Patch reveled in his gaudy role. He was

known as an out-and-out camera hound, but with such frankness and naïveté that nobody ever held it against him. Murray Anderson, his trainer for years, called attention to the fact that among the thousands of still shots of Dan Patch, it is almost impossible to find one in which he is not facing the camera.

As he stepped onto the track, the band playing, Dan Patch liked to turn his head and scan the crowd. "You know what he was doing when he turned that way?" asked Ed Hanson, long a handler in the Savage Stables. "Counting the gate, that's all. Just go through the books and see how he always made his best marks before the big crowds. There were 80,000 at the Allentown track the day he set two world records for a half-mile course. At Lexington, Kentucky, in 1905, some 45,000 saw him do 1:55¼, for thirty-three years the fastest accepted mile in harness. Then there was that day in 1906 at Hamline track in St. Paul . . ." That was the day—some said there were 93,000 in the crowd—when Dan Patch stepped off a mile in the phenomenal time of 1:55, a mark which, barring an unrecognized 1:54½ claimed in 1913 for the trotter Uhlan, has never been broken and wasn't equaled until 1938.

Meanwhile, the turf governing bodies had legislated against exhibition trial records, especially behind a windshield. The authorities called the sailcloth stretched between the wheels of the pace-setting sulky a windshield; owners of exhibition horses, nearly all of whom had adopted the sailcloth, called it a dirt shield, a protection from flying clods thrown up by the pace-setter. Thus the 1:55 mile at Hamline, done behind a dirt shield, was never officially recognized. Savage, highly indignant, renamed his farm the International 1:55 Stock Farm.

Down the years, record after record fell beneath the hoofs of the genial bay. As the hero walked off the track after a triumph, people tried to reach him to pluck hairs from his tail as souvenirs. Old Man Nash, the "official" farrier of the Savage stables, sold thousands of "genuine Dan Patch horseshoes" at one dollar each. "Dan Patch," exclaimed *The Horse Review*, "is so phenomenal as to defy comparison."

But Dan Patch's fastest race, up to a point, did

not result in a record. At Lexington, Kentucky, in the fall of 1908, The Patch passed the half-mile mark in 56½ seconds! The crowd gasped, for the bay customarily paced both halves in approximately equal time, and this, at that rate, would be a 1:53 mile, something the experts had always thought impossible. The third quarter was rattled off in 28½ seconds, bringing the time at three quarters to 1:25. At Hamline track, the day of the phenomenal 1:55 mile, the stop watches had said 1:27 for three-quarters. And Dan's last quarter was usually his best.

But suddenly reliable old Cobweb, the pace-setter, broke in midstride. Plainly distressed, he swerved to the right, so that The Patch had to swing far out to round the leading sulky. The mile was finished in 1:56¼. After the race Cobweb's handlers discovered he had broken a small blood vessel over his eye. A minor accident, one that would not happen once in a million times, had prevented what might have stood for all time as the fastest mile in harness.

Finishing an exhibition mile at Los Angeles in 1909, Dan Patch went lame. Next day, in a newspaper piece headed "The Curtain Call of a Champion," a reporter wrote a tender story of the hush that settled over the multitude when the great pacer limped up to receive the floral wreath, of the tears that swam in many an eye as he hobbled off toward the stables.

In 1910 Dan Patch was retired to stud on the International 1:55 Stock Farm. There he held court in a palatial stable. And there, by a curious coincidence, Marion Savage and Dan Patch were both striken ill, each with a mysterious heart ailment, in July of 1916. Just as mysteriously, a week later, they passed into the other world together.

Heady Eddie

by AL STUMP

AFTER THREE MONTHS OF STEADY CAMpaigning on New York tracks a while ago, with the screech of 50,000 horse players beating on his ears, Eddie Arcaro felt the need for a change. Slipping away to a near-by airfield, Arcaro zoomed up and away from this worrisome planet. For an hour the king of the jockeys enjoyed a solo spin in his private plane. He was relaxed, whistling a gay tune and for once without troubles as he glided in to land at Roosevelt Field.

He was still fifty feet in the air when a treacherous cross wind gripped his light monoplane, which promptly nosedived at the runway. Arcaro's feet frantically jabbed at the elevator controls, but something went wrong. An instant later there was a splintering crash.

It was a spectacular crack-up, befitting a leading daredevil. The trim Cessna smacked into the landing strip, bounced high, did three cartwheels and wound up a pile of junk. Rescue crews rushing to the spot expected to find Arcaro crushed. But he climbed unhurt from the wreckage, dusted his expensive flannels and strolled away with all the aplomb he has often demonstrated after falling horses have thrown him beneath steel-shod hoofs.

Explaining the accident, Arcaro needed only nine words: "I found out that my legs are too short."

It was a considerable admission. Unlike other jockeys, Arcaro, who weighs 114 pounds and stands five feet three inches high, has never considered himself a small man. In his own mind,

Arcaro bulks as huge as Joe Louis, Johnny Mize or Man Mountain Dean. It took the near-fatal New York plane mishap to make him admit anything else.

"Before that, all the time I'd been flying, I actually didn't realize they built planes for taller guys," he said. "But in the pinch, when that wind hit me, I didn't have enough floor-board reach. So I gave up the sky stuff for good."

Arcaro showed his confidence in many ways as he rounded out his twentieth year on the turf. Most race riders compensate for their lack of size by marrying Amazon types who tower above them, by padding their suits, elevating their shoes and wearing gaudy clothes that shout: "Look—I'm important!" Arcaro's wife Ruth, a beautiful blonde ex-model who eloped with him to Elkton, Maryland, in 1937, is about his height. His $200-and-up tailored suits are models of restrained good taste, and he walks on his natural keel. He rarely raises his voice and he forgot how to swagger in 1938, when he won his first Kentucky Derby. Beyond any need of flamboyance, he is Heady Eddie, a triumph of brains and applied energy over a cutthroat business which produces some of the most extroverted and frustrated athletes in the world.

Arcaro is beyond any question the greatest American jockey of modern times. The olive-skinned, black-haired booter with the big beak has won everything there is to win on the track.

Aboard Lawrin, Whirlaway, Hoop Jr., and Citation, he has galloped home first in four Kentucky Derbies—another Arcaro exclusive.

Arcaro is one of the highest-paid sports stars of the day. His 10 per cent of stakes winnings, his other riding fees and the considerable sum bet for him by owners—the "extra little incentive," stablemen call it—were estimated at around $150,000 annually in 1951. Arcaro lives like a prince of the realm in a costly home at Rockville Center, Long Island. Even the movie queens in the Santa Anita boxes blink at the mink Ruth Arcaro trots out on a chilly day. The Arcaro retinue includes a business manager, an agent and a valet. It's nothing for Eddie to slip a needy race tracker $500 and—"pay me before you die, pal."

Not so long ago, however, Eddie Arcaro was a broke, hungry and all but friendless kid hanging over a race-track rail in Mexico. His rise from that bleak beginning is easily forgotten by those who see him only as a Rockefeller in nylon breeches and boots.

George Edward Arcaro was born February 19, 1916, in Cincinnati, Ohio. Edward didn't like school, but he was nuts about horses, so when he was thirteen his father got him a job as exercise boy and stable hand at Latonia Race Track for Tom McCaffrey, a shrewd horseman and wealthy shoe merchant. Trainer Odie Clelland taught the boy something about racing, and in the winter of 1930, Eddie went to Hialeah with the horses, but Clelland never gave him a mount in a race, and in the spring of 1931 McCaffrey turned him loose.

For several months, Eddie was a free-lance exercise boy, working horses at fifty cents a throw—often on credit—for the gypsy stables at Latonia. Toward the end of the season, his father persuaded a local horseman to give Eddie a chance, and trainer Alvin

Booker sent his new jock to Thistledown, Ohio, where Eddie rode his first race. According to Bill Brennan, who handled Booker's horses on the Ohio circuit, Eddie beat the whey out of his mount and finished second—despite orders that the beast was running for education only and was not to be punished. Too much effort too early in the season wrecked the horse for the meeting, and Eddie learned to obey orders.

Booker shipped his horses and his fifteen-year-old jockey to Agua Caliente in Mexico in the fall of 1931. Cheap mounts were plentiful there, and Arcaro rode more than a hundred before he managed his first winner, a selling plater named Eagle Bird, the best of Booker's horses. When the meet closed, nobody wanted the kid from Kentucky except a gypsy horseman, Clarence Davison. "About then I was flat broke, but too full of pride to write home for money," Arcaro recalls. "Ma would sneak me a ten-spot in the mail now and then to keep me eating. But without Davison, I'd have been all washed up."

In memory, Arcaro plants roses on Davison's grave. The big, rough-talking horseman liked Eddie's willingness to perform every dirty chore around the barn and bounce back for more. He and his wife took the boy into their home, put him under curfew, watched his physical condition and his race-track associates. During his three years with the Davisons, Arcaro had no dates, no cigarettes and no liquor.

When the stable moved to Tanforan Race Track at San Bruno, California, Davison gave Eddie a professional education. He taught the boy pace by putting him head-and-head with the first-string jockey and working them various distance at specified speeds. He crammed it into Arcaro that a thoroughbred will run not more than three-eighths of a mile at top speed, and taught him about rating—the art of holding back a horse early in a race without punishing him. He showed the green youngster how to sit quietly in the gate, then help a horse get out on top, and how to pick the best footing around the track. In the matter of the whip, Davison, a rough-and-tumble character of the precamera days, advised, "Let them other jocks see it under their noses—that'll keep 'em from shutting you off or pulling a leg lock."

Under Davison's iron rule, Arcaro grew into a snarling, scrapping demon. Racing officials marked him down as a rough and dangerous rider. Recalling those days, a Washington Park official described Arcaro as "a kid who either had to be awfully lucky or get killed."

Eddie sometimes went out of his way to make trouble for himself. At Arlington Park, he once found himself on the rail, hidden from the judges, in a head-to-head stretch battle with jockey Jack Westrope. Carefully, he slid his foot out and clamped Westrope in an expert leg lock, holding Westrope's mount a whisker behind his own to the finish. Westrope lodged a protest, and the stewards called Eddie to their aerie.

"Did you interfere with Westrope?" they asked.

"Not so's you'd notice it," Arcaro answered, accurately but unwisely. He was set down for the remainder of the meeting.

Arcaro's boyhood was literally a blend of blood,

sweat and tears. At Washington Park's "glorified bull ring," on June 6, 1933, he had his first scrape with sudden death. He was laying up front when his mount, Gun Fire, buckled his legs and went down. Eddie was thrown forward. Seconds after he hit earth, the horse behind galloped over his backbone. Result: a concussion, a punctured lung and two fractured ribs. Other accidents followed and Eddie remembers all of them. "Show me a jock who isn't scared to death after a bad fall or a close shave and I'll show you a freak," he once said. "I still have plenty of shaky moments."

In 1933, Arcaro rode 132 winners, and he started 1934 with a string of conquests at New Orleans. When he returned to Chicago, his riding caught the attention of the late Warren Wright, who was then building his mighty Calumet Farm. Wright bought Arcaro's contract from Davison for $6000, and boosted Eddie's salary from $50 to $350 a month, plus 10 per cent of his stakes winnings. Arcaro moved from the cheap and infirm to the finest horses bred.

By the summer of 1936 Calumet was paying Arcaro $750-a-month basic salary, but that fall Eddie received a better offer: $1000 a month from Mrs. Payne Whitney's Greentree Stable, one of the great names of American turf.

When Arcaro reported to Greentree, to start an association that lasted ten years, he was the highest-paid exercise boy in the world. For the time being, he wasn't a jockey: the stewards at Pimlico had suspended him for six months for pushing one horse and colliding with another in the Pimlico Futurity—a suspension later lowered to four months when Arcaro came up with a racing newsreel that proved him innocent. This was the first of three deserts Arcaro had to cross while he was Greentree's contract rider. The second came in August, 1941, when he was suspended for the rest of the calendar year. The charge was that Arcaro, riding one part of a three-horse entry in Saratoga's Grand Union Hotel Stakes, had run interference for his friends, blocking out horses that had a chance for the marbles.

Eddie's longest and driest desert opened up beneath his feet after the Cowdin Stakes at Aqueduct on September 19, 1942. He had the leg up on the favorite, Occupation, and a post position next to Vincenzo Nordase, on Breezing Home. At the start, Breezing Home lunged over and tossed Occupation off stride. Arcaro, sure the interference was deliberate, rose to a boil and set out after Nordase. When he caught his man he bore into the rail and tried to knock Nordase off his horse; and when the race was over he held a blasphemous but bloodless fight with Matt Brady, Breezing Home's trainer. The stewards called Eddie to attention, and he went to the judges' stand, still blazing mad. He told the authorities he was sorry only that he hadn't thrown Nordase into the infield, and they promptly slapped him with an indefinite suspension. Ten days later the Jockey Club revoked his license, and it was not until September 19, 1943, a year from the effective date of the initial suspension, that the Jockey Club granted his application for reinstatement. Since then, Eddie has been a reasonably good boy.

Arcaro got his first big break in 1938, when Wayne Wright, Lawrin's jockey, decided that his horse wasn't going to win the Kentucky Derby and that he could pick up a piece of change riding in New York on Derby Day. "Plain Ben" Jones, Lawrin's trainer, offered the mount to Arcaro; since Greentree had nothing going in the Derby, Eddie was free to accept it. Privately, he agreed with Wright, and was reluctant to go; but Jones' power of persuasion, plus the fact that Lawrin finished second in the Derby Trial on the Tuesday before the classic, sent him to Louisville. He never regretted the trip.

Before the race, Jones told Arcaro that Lawrin would give him an eighth of a mile in eleven seconds whenever he decided to make his move; the timing was up to Eddie. Arcaro stayed in fifth place, saving gobs of ground along the rail, for three-quarters of a mile. At the mile, he was second, and when he gave Lawrin the juice, the colt scooted to the top. He was leading by three lengths at the head of the stretch, and he still had a length on the fast-closing Dauber at the end. To the customers, Lawrin's victory was worth $19.20 for $2; to Eddie the net was $4705 and a fortune in happiness: he had reached the top.

Arcaro picked up his second Derby in 1941, on Whirlaway, one of the most colorful—and one of the dumbest—horses in racing history. Here again Jones, who was now working for Calumet Farm, had a job convincing his jockey, because Eddie considered Whirly, who had a nasty habit of bolting to the outside of the track, a potential man-killer.

At Louisville, he learned that Jones had solved Whirly's problem. Working on the theory that Whirly got befuddled when he found himself out in the middle of the track with nothing but turf all around, Jones designed a one-eyed blinker that allowed the colt to see the inside rail but not the outside dirt. "You just keep him back, away from the other horses, and don't get nervous if it looks like we're licked," Jones ordered. "Some place in the race he'll be in front—and I'll bet it's the last eighth."

To Arcaro's surprise, Whirlaway "ran as if he'd talked to Jones." He was sixth, eighth, then sixth again nearing the mile; but he exploded in the last quarter. He blazed past the leaders, won by eight lengths and set a new track record of 2:01⅖. Whirly went on to cop the Preakness and the Belmont, giving Arcaro his first Triple Crown.

Throughout the forties, Arcaro rose in reputation and riches. He won his third Kentucky Derby in 1945 with a front-running race through the mud on Hoop Jr., and in 1946 he decided he was secure enough to break his ten-year connection with Greentree. He was a free-lance rider when Jimmy Jones, Ben's son, called him to Maryland in 1948 to ride the greatest horse since Man o' War: Calumet's Citation.

Eddie's first race on the big brown colt was an unimportant six-furlong prep for the Chesapeake Stakes—and he lost it. He got revenge in the Chesapeake itself, winning by four and a half easy lengths, then piloted Citation to an easy win in the Derby Trial and came to the Derby an overwhelming favorite. In the Kentucky classic Eddie let Coaltown, Citation's stablemate, chase off to an eight-length lead, then roared up and ahead to win handily by nearly four lengths.

That year Arcaro and Citation swept five $100,000-added events, including Eddie's second Triple Crown, and the Italian Imp rounded out the season by bringing Talon home by a nose in the $100,000 Santa Anita Handicap.

In his twentieth racing year, Eddie rises late, has toast, juice, ham and eggs. Other jocks must endure a near-starvation diet; Eddie's weight remains at 114 pounds on a normal intake of food. After breakfast, he digests the *Racing Form* to get a line on the horses he must beat that day. He spends some time with his children, Carolyn and Edward Robert. Then he may practice a few chip shots to his private putting green. At noon, clad in expensive gabardine and cashmere, he drives in his Cadillac to the track. Everybody knows him and shouts a greeting. Surprisingly, Eddie is popular with the other jocks.

With almost 15,000 rides and more than $11,000,000 in purses behind him, Eddie says that one of these bright days he's going to hang up his tack and spend the rest of his days bonefishing and golfing in Florida. Nobody believes him for a moment.

Once at Santa Anita, Heady Eddie rode a horse named War Coin which crossed the wire, continued a few strides, and dropped dead. "When Arcaro does that, I'll believe he's finished," said a man in the press box. "But no sooner."

May 2, 1953: Dark Star Upsets Native Dancer in the Derby

The hustlers, holding juleps, as they elbowed
past pickpockets and country boys,
were chattering, "Sure thing.
The Dancer's sure."

Blocked at the start,
whipped at the finish,
the sure thing closed like fury come too late.

"Twenty-five to one," the hustlers said,
holding their juleps,
"And, say, what was the name of
the pig that beat him?"

The Man Who Talked to Horses

by ALBERT ABARBANEL

EARLY IN NOVEMBER, 1933, A FIFTY-nine-year-old pauper was admitted to a charity ward of the Los Angeles County Hospital. Death was inevitable; an examination showed that the man was in an advanced stage of cirrhosis of the liver aggravated by chronic alcoholism.

The doctors looked at his name on the chart—James T. Sloan—and shrugged. It meant nothing whatever to them. If there was anything at all unusual about this doomed derelict, it was his small size; he was less than five feet tall and weighed under a hundred pounds.

But others remembered him and traced him. Five weeks later, anonymous friends arranged for the transfer of the little man to Sylvan Lodge Hospital, where he was made as comfortable as possible and provided with whatever little luxuries he could use. Two weeks later, on December 21, he died.

This was the tragic end of Tod Sloan, who in his heyday was unquestionably the greatest jockey of all time. Inventor of the "monkey seat"—that huddled crouch far up and forward on the horse all jockeys employ today—he was, for a few brief years, close to unbeatable. Even when he rode an inferior mount, the betting switched in his favor. In one meteoric decade Tod Sloan earned, gambled and drank away several million dollars in the United States and Europe. At his peak, he was the pet of royalty, the nobility and café society; the Prince of Wales (later King Edward VII) offered 6000 guineas for "first call" on his services for a single season.

There were "Tod Sloan" cravats and cigarettes. Women pursued the little man madly; on numerous occasions they mobbed him and literally tore his cloak to shreds, which they kept as souvenirs. He was married to two of the most beautiful women on earth, the diminutive, scintillating mu-sical comedy star Julia Sanderson, and the legitimate actress Elizabeth Saxon Malone; both marriages ended disastrously.

There was something uncanny about him. Many people believed that he could talk "horse language," while others thought him more horse than man. With some reason, he was variously compared with a horse, monkey and plain fool. It is certain he was a complex, twisted personality—a strange sensitive creature whose next move was never predictable.

Before he was twenty-three, Tod Sloan was undisputed king of the turf. Then, at the height of his fame, he made the mistake of assaulting a waiter with a champagne bottle on the lawn terrace of England's fashionable Ascot Heath. The incident provoked such notoriety that at least 10,000 persons claimed afterward to have been present—and recounted their own versions. Tod always insisted that the waiter had been bribed to annoy him. But implacable Fate had turned against him; after that, everything he did seemed doomed to failure. He was barred from many tracks, and the last decades of his life were spent miserably as a racetrack tout, gambler and drunkard.

The inventor of the monkey crouch was born in Kokomo, Indiana, on August 10, 1874. He received the nickname "Tod" from his father, a barber who had attained officer rank in the Union Army during the Civil War; Tod said it was a corruption of "toad." At thirteen, Tod weighed only fifty-six pounds.

Tod did not always have his magic with horses. As a child, he not only disliked them; he hated them. Just the idea of them scared him. Tod never threw leg across a horse until he was twelve—and then only because he was forced to ride to a funeral on a borrowed mare.

They made it to the cemetery all right, but on

the return trip the mare bolted and gave young Sloan a thorough shaking up. "I swore to myself then and there that if I ever got off alive I would only look for a horse after that in zoological gardens," Tod always declared afterward. He believed firmly that the shrewd mare had sensed his fear and had "taken him for a ride" out of sheer cussedness.

"I hadn't learned 'horse language' then," he added.

Tod's mother died when he was five, and a few weeks afterward his father was sent to the soldiers'

ally. As he became accustomed to the animals, his earlier fear vanished, and he discovered his odd ability to "talk" their language. He was able to make friends with supposedly vicious, outlaw horses. One such animal that nobody else could even approach followed him around and ate anything Tod offered him. Even if the food was something the horse disliked, he'd eat it after Tod pretended to take a bite.

Cassius was determined to become a jockey, and presently Tod got the same idea. When he was fourteen, the prominent trainer Johnny Campbell

frank Boyd

home. The four Sloan children—Cassius, Fremont, Tod and Molly—moved into an abandoned cabin, begged for their food and wore clothing they salvaged from the city dumps. Inevitably they drifted apart; Cassius and Fremont found work as livery-stable exercise boys and Molly got a job as a bareback rider in a circus. Tod was adopted, and sent to school, but was a frequent runaway. For a time he worked as a farm hand, swept out saloons, begged handouts from door to door and lived a hobo's life in the "jungles." Briefly he was a helper for an itinerant balloonist known as Professor A. L. Talbot. That job ended abruptly when the "Professor" wanted the thirteen-year-old lad to jump out of the balloon in a parachute.

Finally Tod trailed brother "Cash" to Kansas City, where he too found work leading horses around after a workout to cool them down gradu-

—who considered him half horse anyway—allowed him to practice on Viking, a promising colt.

The instant Tod was astride, Viking set off at a dead run. The animal didn't stop for three and one-half miles, and then he was streaming lather from every pore. Campbell was furious; he was certain that the colt was ruined. "Keep out of my way," he warned Tod. But after he calmed down he gave the boy a second chance.

Six years later, Tod discovered the "monkey seat." The horse he was riding bolted, and in trying to pull him up, he got out of the saddle and up onto the neck of the horse. He hung on with everything he could—the reins, his toes, his knees. Everybody who witnessed the wild ride roared with laughter. "Look at the little monkey," they shouted.

But Tod had noticed that the horse had run

with great freedom, a long stride, a minimum of effort, actually seemed to enjoy the odd placement of weight. And it was easier for Tod to control him, too.

Tod told the trainer that he believed he had discovered a more efficient riding position, and he was allowed to experiment with shorter reins and stirrups. Tod practiced the new "monkey crouch" while exercising the horses, and finally used it in a race. Jockeys and crowd alike were convulsed with merriment by Tod's queer jack-knife perch with his head almost on a line with the horse's ear. This was in 1894, when he was twenty.

Tod's rise to fame was meteoric. In 1895—the first year his monkey crouch was consistently seen on American tracks—he started in 442 races, of which he won 30 per cent. This was an incredible record, considering the poor quality of many of his mounts. The ridicule stopped. But, oddly enough, few attributed Tod's success as a jockey to his new posture, the most important factor.

Tod himself never tried to conceal where his advantage lay: "When the signal is given for the start I bend far over the forepart of the horse. Both my hands with short-held reins rest on the horse's neck. I never press myself among the leading horses. I permit another horse to make the pace and break the wind for me until shortly before the finish. I remain on the alert. When the distance is reached I bend still further over the forepart and use all my arts of persuasion. I use the whip only rarely. It pains me to chastise a horse."

Except for the slightly stilted phraseology, this was an accurate description of the skills and tactics of most jockeys of today. And it is generally conceded now that only one other jockey—Fred Archer —even came close to challenging Tod's supremacy. But Archer was the world's greatest exponent of the old; Tod was the discoverer of the new. For this reason, Tod is generally awarded the distinction of the greatest jockey of all time.

Tod swiftly became the favorite of wealthy sportsmen and high-plungers. His friends included William C. Whitney, then the most influential man in American racing; the multimillionaire Pittsburgh Phil Smith; Charles Fleischmann; John W. Bet-a-Million Gates (who made half a million dollars on him in a single race); John L. Sullivan; Buffalo Bill Cody; Charlie Hanlon.

Tod made fabulous sums. In one year, his track earnings exceeded $75,000. He also cleaned up on tips on the stock market; one such hint from Whitney to "buy American Tobacco Company shares and wait for the rise" netted him $110,000 in a few weeks.

When only twenty-three, Tod dressed in the height of fashion, lived in a $200-a-day hotel suite, maintained a staff of servants, smoked cigars especially made for him. There is little doubt that success went to his head.

Then, 1897, he made his first trip to England. Either through ignorance, defiance or both, he paid no attention to the convention which placed a jockey—no matter how famous—in the same social stratum as a servant. Arriving in London with two valets, a secretary and two employees whose sole job was to look after his financial affairs, he engaged the most expensive suite in the most costly and exclusive hotel. He had calling cards engraved with the name "James Todhunter Sloan"—and hinted that the high-sounding middle name had descended to him from illustrious British ancestors. He bought four matched horses and a rich phaeton.

He showed up for an important English race, the Cambridgeshire, wearing an opulent silken cloak over his jockey's uniform, a flower in his lapel and a pearl-gray derby perched jauntily on the side of his head. When the moment arrived for him to mount Mr. James R. Keene's St. Cloud II, he carefully tossed derby and cloak to a waiting valet and threw his half-smoked cigar to the ground, where it was scrambled for by admirers.

Ironically enough, St. Cloud II was beaten by a head. Tod always swore that had the race been photographed, the pictures would have shown his mount victor by a nose.

But the famous monkey seat soon proved its superiority. Tod proceeded to win the Rothschild Plate at Liverpool and the Tare Well Handicap at Newmarket. At Manchester he won four races in one day, and in his first month in Britain he came in first in twenty-one out of forty-eight starts.

The English newspapers began calling him The American Wonder Boy. He quickly attracted a following of "the best-known of the fair-weather crowd."

After the close of the 1897 English racing season, Tod went to Monte Carlo. He played roulette for six days and never lost.

Back home, he rode five winners at Ingleside track in San Francisco on March 21, 1898, and duplicated the quintuple triumph on May 28, at Gravesend. By August 1, he had come in first in 190 races. He bought a luxurious home and a yacht.

The American press viewed him with mixed feelings. Many reporters accused him of wanting to crash society, and were unfeignedly delighted when he went back to England in the fall.

There, however, he continued to win races. On September 30, at Newmarket, he rode in six races, won all but one.

The oddest fact about Tod's career is that some of the most reputable British gentlemen sincerely liked him and overlooked his frequent crassness. They introduced him to London's finest clubs, where he gambled for high stakes and frequently won.

Though he tried his hardest to prove himself the social equal of "quality," Tod was no bootlicker. When Lord William Beresford—who had first introduced him to English tracks by arrangement with William C. Whitney—presented him to the then Duke of York (later King George V) the ninety-nine-pound horseman pointedly failed to uncover. Later Lord William asked Tod: "Why didn't you remove your hat while the Duke was addressing you?"

"Because I am an American," Tod replied. "I don't understand such things."

The nautical and extrovert Edward, then Prince of Wales and later King Edward VII, took quite a liking to Tod. He let the American jockey ride his four-year-old Nonsuch in the Oaks, but the horse remained standing at the post. The identical thing happened with the same animal in the Cambridgeshire; Fate seemed determined to thwart the little man when it came to the triumphs he wanted most to achieve. However, Tod rode Non-

such to victory in the Old Cambridgeshire, and went on to ride a good many winners for the Prince of Wales.

Tod was pitifully proud of the Prince's casual friendship. He scrapped his entire wardrobe and had an outfit made by the Prince's tailor. This provoked fresh resentment among those who considered him a pretentious buffoon who sought to force himself into circles where he did not belong.

So far, he had acted merely in bad taste, but now he committed two really grave breaches of etiquette. By this time he owned as well as raced horses, and he made the mistake of "pushing himself through a gathering of nobility" to outbid royalty itself for a promising yearling.

Then, in 1899, came the disastrous "Ascot incident."

Most versions of this affair are in agreement—up to a certain point. Tod had finished riding for the day, and had changed into a white yachting suit. He sat on the terrace at Ascot Heath and ordered a small bottle of champagne. Presently a burly waiter—accounts generally agree that he weighed 250 pounds—bumped against his table, knocking it over. Tod jumped up, champagne bottle in hand. A glass of brandy the waiter was carrying was spilled on his resplendent uniform.

A furious altercation followed. The waiter, the newspaper accounts admitted, was insulting.

Tod claimed the waiter had been about to assault him. And it must be remembered that he was a very tiny man. His version was that, having his champagne bottle in his hand, he made a "light jab" at the waiter "with the neck of it, meaning just to give him a reminder. His lip was cut, not badly but enough to draw a little blood. The whole thing at that time seemed a simple annoyance."

Tod also insisted that a man sitting near by had promised the waiter "five shillings if he would upset the table and the champagne over me and my suit."

But the British press charged that Tod had been drunk, had "heaved" the bottle at the waiter—and emphasized that the man had been injured enough to necessitate a trip to the hospital.

Long-repressed resentments boiled into print.

An *Evening News* writer declared, "There is in the whole of the English empire only one licensed jockey who could commit such an outrage against good manners when a guest of a reputable club. It is superfluous to give his name."

Tod's English supporters came magnificently to his defense. Lord Beresford stated publicly, "Before you judge him too harshly, think of what he has gone through. He was first made a popular hero and latterly a tide of opposition has set in against him, presumably because people have lost money."

And the Prince of Wales requested Tod to return to England as his personal jockey, and guaranteed 6000 guineas for first claim on Tod's services!

But the resentments had grown too great. Rumors were rife that Tod would throw a race for a price; finally he was charged with having attempted to fix a race in cahoots with an Australian jockey. The Jockey Club "intimated" that it was "advisable" for him not to apply for a renewal of his license. Tod was now drinking heavily; he refused to ride for Lord Derby because he had been "dissipating and drinking too much to give a good ride."

In 1901, Tod was barred from English tracks. He raced sporadically after that; in the United States, for example, he won the Futurity that same year. But in May, 1903, he got in trouble with the French Jockey Club. Rose de Mai, which he had ridden a few days before the race, won the Prix de Diane after it had slid back in the betting from 4 to 1 to 12 to 1 because of a rumor that the filly had a cough. Four days after the race, Tod was warned off the turf on the charge that he had exercised the filly illegally. He sued the Jockey Club, won vindication and a $40,000 verdict.

But his interest in riding was gone, and he turned to grandiose attempts to get rich in other ways. Actually he was well off; despite his extravagances and drinking he had a fortune estimated at more than $1,000,000. With French auto-racing driver Henri Fournier, he started an automobile business in the United States. It went out of operation in less than a month, during which Tod lost $150,000.

He put $40,000 in a legitimate theater and lost that. For a short time he ran a bar in Paris. He gambled recklessly in every casino in Europe; in one afternoon he lost $31,000 betting on horse races, and in the same evening he dropped $30,000 more at cards.

He was broke many times. Once, when he was down and out, he attempted to make a comeback as a jockey, riding for Edward Corrigan in New Orleans. But other jockeys were using the monkey seat now. He was also overweight. He was beaten badly.

He went into partnership with John L. McGraw in a Herald Square billiard parlor, from which he drew fifty dollars a week. In his spare time he haunted the race tracks, working as a tout or tipster. In 1906 he was sued for $4000, lost the judgment and had to admit he couldn't pay.

For more than three years he had courted the diminutive and exquisite Julia Sanderson and finally, on September 21, 1907, she married him. Before midnight on the wedding night she walked out of his apartment and returned to her mother's home. She was granted a divorce in 1913.

Tod never could resist the lure of England, going back several times. By 1915, however, the British had had enough of him; they deported him as an undesirable alien. The specific charge was "maintaining a gambling house." He went to Paris and attempted to join the French Army in World War I, but was turned down, perhaps because of his size.

Drifting to San Diego, Tod ran a real-estate business for a while. In 1920 he married the stage star Elizabeth Saxon Malone, and she bore him one child, a daughter. But, in 1927, she divorced him on grounds of "mental cruelty and habitual intemperance."

He frequented the race tracks incessantly. Sometimes, to old acquaintances, he'd drop hints of his broken dreams. "I always wanted to settle down and enjoy a gentleman's life," he said once. "Buy a stable of horses and train them. That's by far and away the best thing you can do."

In maudlin moments, Tod liked to reminisce about Edward, who had long since attained the British throne, ruled briefly and died. Tod always denied that the Prince had been to blame for his "swelled head." On the contrary, he insisted that "the Prince put me at my best and made me hope to live up to what I ought to have been, but what I was not."

Tod gravitated to Hollywood. People who remembered his former glory helped him to get bit parts in various pictures.

On August 24, 1932, Tod was arrested in Los Angeles as a result of what was perhaps his most bizarre venture. This was a "turtle race" which he promoted in company with fourteen others. Two hundred bettor-spectators paid two dollars a ticket each for the privilege of watching 100 turtles "race" 100 feet and the chance of winning the "pool." Tod and his fellow promoters were charged with "operating a gambling device by the option system." Apparently, however, they got off without punishment.

It took death to bring Tod into the news again.

Tod Sloan was a strange man, an enigma. One thing is certain, he suffered more than most. Maybe it's best, now, to remember that, whatever his faults, he always went out of his way to be friendly with horses. Maybe it's best—the next time you watch the running horses—to note the monkey seat of the jockeys and think for a moment kindly of poor, tortured Tod Sloan, who talked to horses

in their own language, revolutionized saddle racing and, through some inner compulsion, drank himself to death.

SEABISCUIT: A Lithograph by C. W. Anderson

My Old Myopic Kentucky Home

by ARTHUR DALEY

IT IS DEEMED HIGHLY IMPROPER FOR one jockey to whip out his bowie-knife in the Kentucky Derby homestretch and thoughtfully carve his initials on another jock's epidermis. If that ever were to happen, the stewards would frown disapprovingly and exclaim in shocked tones, "Naughty, naughty!"

As far as neutral observers have been able to figure out, there is only one sure offense meriting disqualification in the classic Run for the Roses: to assassinate the Governor of Kentucky at the sixteenth pole.

Frequently the Derby is the roughest riding race of the year. But never was it rougher or the fouling more flagrant than in 1933 when it became a wrestling match on horseback. However, the only person in the entire cast of characters to be disqualified was an innocent bystander, Bryan Field, then a sports writer who doubled in brass as a radio broadcaster. He became *persona non grata* and was invited *not* to broadcast the classic the following year.

In a way this is as much the story of the sharp-eyed and observant Field as it is of the two villains in the piece, jockey Don Meade and jockey Herb Fisher. There were 40,000 witnesses in the sprawling Churchill Downs stand that day and Field was the only one to notice the fouling tactics, the only one to call it. The stewards missed it. The other newspapermen missed it. The other broadcasters missed it.

Yet even he might have been hooted down and the true facts never brought to light had it not been for the enterprising (and lucky) photographer who "bootlegged" a picture of the finish. That one was the convincer.

But suppose we start, more or less, at the beginning. And we have to start with Field, later vice president and general manager of Delaware Park. However, he was just a thirty-year-old stripling back in 1933, the youngest and least experienced of the racing experts, as well as the newest of the radio broadcasters. Those are serious imposts for a sport which requires as much technical knowledge as the hoss game demands.

His one compensating factor, though, was that he was an excellent reporter and shrewd observer. Hence even the august New York *Times*, which hates error as the devil hates holy water, did not hesitate to give him its turf assignment. Nor did the fledgling Columbia Broadcasting System hesitate to offer him as a counterattraction to the mighty Graham McNamee of the National Broadcasting Company on the theory that Field's crisp, reportorial style of air-wave presentation might be preferred to the McNamee hoop-la.

There were thirteen starters in the Kentucky Derby that cloudy May afternoon of 1933, and Ladysman was the favorite. The betting gentry also held Mrs. Silas B. Mason's Head Play in considerable regard, while the wagering on Colonel E. R. Bradley's Broker's Tip was partly sentimen-

tal and partly due to the fact that Bradley had had remarkable success in the Run for the Roses. There could be no other reason for going overboard on Broker's Tip because he never had won a race in his life.

Like all Kentucky Derbies, however, this one generated just as much traditional excitement. The same carnival spirit was in the air, the same eager and bustling crowds, the same feeling of feverish anticipation and the same sensation of brittle tension as the horses began their solemn parade to the post. There even was that same peculiar tingling along the spinal column as the band played "My Old Kentucky Home!"

Once again the thunderous cry of "They're off" echoed and re-echoed as it cascaded down from the white stands with their steepled towers and rumbled across the crowded infield to the barns scattered along the backstretch. From the gates at the head of the grandstand straightaway the thirteen starters leaped in a mad scramble which saw them all edging gradually over toward the rail in a frantic rush to be first to the turn.

Head Play, breaking from the middle of the pack, flashed around that turn on top, while Broker's Tip had to struggle to keep from the parade's rear guard. There's no point in mentioning the contenders in between. These are the only two who are important.

Into the backstretch the field whirled, the rata-plan of hoofs on the hard and cuppy Churchill Downs track swallowed up by the excited hum of the crowd. Fisher kept Head Play in front into the final turn, but Meade kept saving ground on Broker's Tip by clinging to the rail. The distance between them, once almost ten lengths, had dwindled to two and a half around the far turn. They hit the homestretch a head apart.

The din of the shouting, straining crowd was terrific. Men and women stood on tiptoes, on chairs, on boxes, fighting to get glimpses of the action far down the track. But high on the grandstand roof in a radio booth was Bryan Field, cool and detached. His high-powered binoculars brought the two horses right into his lap and he called 'em as he saw 'em. And he saw plenty.

Just beyond the three-sixteenth pole Meade veered out from near the rail to force Head Play to go wide. Simultaneously Fisher swung his mount in to squeeze Broker's Tip against the pole. And it was Meade, who later was to become one of the turf's stormy petrels, who was the aggressor.

The two steeds bumped and everything that happened thereafter happened within the fleeting space of some fourteen or fifteen seconds. Fisher's left arm shot out from his shoulder as he pushed Meade off. Meade grabbed Head Play's saddlecloth with his right hand and Head Play seemed to falter. Fisher's whip angrily flashed down on Meade's head. Meade retaliated in kind. The two jockeys flailed each other with their bats and they swept over the finish line with Fisher clutching the saddlecloth of Broker's Tip and Meade grasping Fisher's shirt at the shoulder.

Into Bryan Field's microphone poured a vivid description of every gesture and every act of the two roughriders. He announced the winner as being Broker's Tip by a nose, but added: "However, the fouling was so flagrant that I'm sure there will be a disqualification."

Intently he watched the horses return to the saddling enclosure, paying particular attention to Fisher because the number of Meade's mount was going up on the board as the winner. He saw Fisher look bewilderedly around him, tears of anger streaming down his face. Crowds were pouring across the track to the infield where the presentation ceremonies always take place, the traditional draping of roses around the neck of the winning horse.

The stewards now do their observing from the grandstand roof, but that year they operated out of a tower in the infield. And Fisher was trying to find the stewards to lodge his protest. The little jockey pushed and fought his way through the milling multitudes. But as he approached the stewards he met only with rebuff. The observant Field noted one of them gave Fisher a backward wave of his hand in dismissal. There was to be no disqualification that day. Fisher tried to take it out of Meade's hide in the jockey room afterward. Their fight was ferocious but brief as willing hands pulled them apart.

However, the instant the race became official, broadcaster Field changed roles. He became reporter Field, the gentleman from the *Times*.

Downstairs he rushed to his typewriter, pausing only to pick up a copy of the official chart. Unbelievingly he stared at the footnotes. There was no mention of even the slightest foul.

"That was the most flagrant fouling I ever saw," he muttered.

"You're crazy, Bryan," scoffed a writer. "I didn't see any foul."

Cautiously and still unbelievingly, he asked a few questions in the press box. Nope. No one had noticed any foul tactics. The rival broadcasters came downstairs. Nope. They'd neither seen any nor mentioned any on the air. The unanimity of opinion was enough to shake the confidence of even the most stubborn.

But Bryan Field is nothing if not tenacious. After all he'd seen it all with his own eyes, hadn't he? So he doggedly began his story with the phrase, "In a bristling, fighting finish on horseback . . ." and in the first paragraph dropped the phrase "flagrant foul."

The sports editor of the New York *Times* then was the late Colonel Bernard S. Thomson, a man who knew the turf better than any sports editor in the country. He also knew the dangers of indiscriminate, unsupported charges of foul, and the telegrapher sending Field's story suddenly stopped as his wire went dead. A message was about to come from the New York end.

"Are you sure of your finish?" clicked the keys. "What's this foul riding and whips? The Associated Press story makes no mention of fouls. Are you sure?" It was signed simply, "Thomson."

"Tell him I'm sure," snapped Field to the telegrapher, but he was aware his confidence had been severely shaken. Could he have been that egregiously mistaken?

It didn't help any when a message from his boss arrived a few minutes later, bearing his pointed warning, "I fear your zeal has been excessive."

Hours afterward Field had finished writing. He'd poured forth some 6000 words and with each sentence his bubble of confidence was getting a new pricking. Churchill Downs was deserted, looking like a picnic grounds after the picnickers had departed. A scared and worried Bryan Field gathered his notes. Suddenly that long-silent telegraph key began to click a new message.

"Neither the first edition of the *Herald Tribune*," it began, "nor the *Racing Form* mentions a foul on the stretch. I'm afraid you are in error. Please phone me long distance tonight." Field waited for the tip-off word. Colonel Thomson always prefaced his signature with the word "Regards," unless he was in anger or displeased. It did not come.

"That's it," said the now very frightened reporter. "I'm going to be fired for this."

He walked to the dining room, where steak dinners were awaiting gentlemen of the press. Again he asked his fellow reporters about the foul. Again no one had seen such a thing. A waiter whisked a succulent steak in front of him. Field pushed his chair away from the table. He hadn't eaten since breakfast, but he had no appetite.

Silently and alone he made his way from Churchill Downs. There were no trolleys at the main gate, no taxicabs. Nothing.

Field began to walk the long, long way back to Louisville, accompanied by agonizing thoughts. He saw his career nipped, jobless, with a wife and two sons, too disgraced ever to get another job anywhere. No newspaper or radio station will put up with an inaccurate reporter.

A taxicab driver finally hailed him and brought him to his hotel. He went to his room and reached for the phone. Vast was his relief when he was told all the long-distance lines were busy.

For ten minutes he paced madly up and down his room. Then he asked the bell captain to send up all the newspapers he could get. The bellhop handed over the papers perfunctorily and instantly was startled out of a year's growth.

"Yowie!" screamed Field in an involuntary gasp of elation.

That newspaper was the Louisville *Courier-Journal*. Field tenderly and gratefully kissed its rotogravure section before spreading it out on the bed for his eyes to devour. Most of one page was occupied by a picture. And what a picture it was!

Newspaper photographers had long wanted to snap a Derby picture from the infield, right near the finish line. However, there was a long-standing rule at Churchill Downs that pictures were not to be taken from this point. Wallace Lowry of the *Courier-Journal* decided to take a gamble and bootleg his picture.

His plan was to wait until all attention was centered on the horses at the post for the Run for the Roses, then walk across the track and plant himself for the shot. It was his intention to lie flat on his stomach, focus his camera at the horses coming down the stretch on their first time around, then roll under the fence as the horses went by. When the horses neared the finish line, he planned to roll out again, check his focus and shoot the picture as they crossed the finish line. He had tried this experiment in 1932 and it had failed.

In 1933 the racing gods were kind to Lowry—and, in a left-handed sort of way, to Bryan Field, who reached for the phone, anxious to get through his long-distance call to Colonel Thomson in New York. The old fire and confidence gushed through his veins. Now he had the proof he'd lacked.

Spread boldly across the *Courier-Journal* was the picture, so clear that there could be no mistaking it. Fisher's left hand was clutching the saddlecloth of Broker's Tip. Meade's arm was grasping Fisher's shoulder.

That first edition of the *Courier-Journal* turned the newspaper world topsy-turvy. The racing experts had to rush back to their typewriters, kill their stories and write new ones. The stewards, confronted by evidence they could not ignore—they could ignore Field's broadcast and original story because he could not prove them—unprecedentedly met on a Sunday. They suspended Fisher for thirty-five days and Meade for thirty days.

But they disqualified no one. Bryan Field was the only one to get disqualified, being set down for two years as a broadcaster before he was permitted to resume for the 1935 Derby.

5

AUTO RACING: HELL ON WHEELS

THERE ARE THOSE WHO WOULD DISPUTE THAT RAC-*ing automobiles is a sport at all, would contend it is a form of insanity. But if sport can be defined at all, we would venture our definition in which it most certainly must be included. Sport is a contest, a microcosm of life in which is condensed all of the risks, challenges, skills, thrills, disappointments and exultations of man's course along the road which ends inevitably in death. Behind the wheel of a racing car, life is so compressed that it may well end around the next hairpin turn. One does not participate in sport for the money, though it may be there as a reward at the finish. Most of us are not physically capable of enduring professional competition, but even granted such gifts something more is needed: the itch, the urge to "give all to-day, and damn tomorrow." Impatience with the*
long journey of life makes great men of sports capable of reducing the experience into hundreds of dehydrated capsules, of specific length: sixty minutes of a football game, nine innings, fifteen rounds, eighteen holes, or the Indianapolis 500 miles. Speed, then, is the essence of sport, and the fastest sport on earth is on four wheels. Here are four hell-bent pioneers: Barney Oldfield, Bill Hilliard, George Robertson, and Ralph de Palma (the account of the latter, incidentally, by a great driver himself, Captain Eddie Rickenbacker); a profile of the greatest driver of modern times, Juan Manuel Fangio; and a personal reflection on the great moments of a race by Stirling Moss. In addition we give you a great car, a blueprint of Ferrari, machine, myth and the man behind it. Come along for the ride?

Barney and the Green Dragon

Through the year 1904 a daring young man in a green leather helmet and suit was barnstorming the country in a roaring green monster. At county fairs and carnivals—on half-mile weed-grown dirt tracks, mile dirt ovals, straightaway roads, sand courses at low tide—from Brighton Beach to Fresno—Barney Oldfield in his low-slung Peerless Dragon was breaking local records, world records, his own records.

Sometimes there would be a race. Other professional "chauffeurs" were beginning to show up around the country and unload their racers from flatcars. Such names as Earl Kiser, Webb Jay, Herb Lytle, Charlie Burman, Louis Chevrolet and, later, Wild Bob Burman, Ralph de Palma and Eddie Rickenbacker.

Sometimes there would be just an exhibition. But the great favorite was Barney Oldfield, the cocky daredevil who crouched rigidly under the wheel behind the long hood, a cigar clenched in his teeth and death at his elbow, as he went streaking around the ovals in a storm of dust.

It was at the Empire City track, near Yonkers, New York, on October 29, 1904, that Barney Oldfield ushered in a new period of automobile racing. Three weeks earlier he had finished third in the Vanderbilt Cup Race at Brighton Beach. Winner had been the Frenchman, Bernin, in a Renault owned by W. Gould Brokaw. Paul Sartori, an Italian, had come in second in a Fiat owned by Alfred Vanderbilt.

At Empire the first heat was won by Sartori. Oldfield and his Green Dragon took the second heat from Bernin. So it was Oldfield and Sartori in the final.

But Oldfield left Sartori and the big, black Fiat in the dust, doing the ten miles in nine minutes and twelve seconds. A world's record from a standing start.

The Green Dragon of 1904 wasn't Oldfield's first car, nor for that matter, his first Green Dragon. In

GANGWAY FOR BARNEY OLDFIELD by Peter Helck

1902 Henry Ford, in disgust, had sold his half interest in two racing cars which he had built with Tom Cooper. Oldfield, after a career in bicycle racing, was working as a mechanic for the pair. He went along with Cooper, and it was at the tiller of one of these cars, the old 999, that Oldfield took the five-mile Manufacturers' Challenge Cup Race at Grosse Point from the millionaire amateur Alexander Winton.

Automobile racing in this country during the late nineties was principally a newfangled sport for the rich men of New York. Men such as W. K. Vanderbilt, W. Gould Brokaw, Frank LaRoche, H. L. Bowden imported fast cars from abroad, usually drove them themselves. Later Winton got interested in building cars and won many races in his own models. In 1903 Oldfield signed a contract with Winton under which Winton was to furnish a car, a mechanic and transportation. Oldfield was to pay his personal expenses and keep all the money he won in meets.

Unlike the millionaire amateur, Oldfield had to make it pay to stay in the game. Canny in publicity and always giving the crowd a spine-chilling ride for its money, Oldfield soon built himself into a name that spelled dangerous glamour to the public. He was frequently in trouble with the A.A.A., for participating in unsanctioned meets and for signing up for two meets on the same day—then taking the one which offered the best money.

Oldfield became associated with the Peerless Company after he had been reinstated from his first suspension in 1904. While a new car was being built for him, he drove a remodeled racer—Green Dragon No. One. This car ended up a heap of junk in one of the worst crashes of his career, when he went through a fence in St. Louis, killing two spectators and banging himself up, breaking three ribs. When he was able to race again, he started out in his new car—the Green Dragon No. Two—on his record-smashing tour of 1904.

Ahead of him lay more years of speed and close calls, more cups, more medals, more records—faster and faster cars. But it wasn't just the money and it wasn't just the glory that kept him on the tracks. As he said afterward: "I didn't need to throw dice with death on the track to make a living. . . . Racing gets in the blood."

Climb to the Clouds

by JOHN LEATHERS

It is 7:56 A.M. on July 18, 1905. A palpitating, two-year-old British race car stands poised on the drive of the Glen House in Pinkham Notch, her nose pointed toward the Mt. Washington carriage road. Her thundering exhaust stops all conversation about her as tense Bill Hilliard, her twenty-six-year-old driver, awaits the megaphoned word of starter Butler. "You have two minutes." The low-speed gears grate into mesh. "One minute." The exhaust note rises under Hilliard's eager foot. *"Go!"* An earsplitting bellow bursts from the Napier's engine, rearward spectators are showered with gravel, and the big machine rushes across the Glen House green and, grazing the tollbridge rail, is swallowed by the foliage screening the sharp rise beyond.

As Hilliard's exhaust fades out, a buzz of comment arises on the sunny lawn. Will this green kid of twenty-six from Boston, Massachusetts, beat the marks of F. E. Stanley and the seasoned amateur Harry Harkness? "Hell, yes!" Colonel Wood, owner of the Napier, is speaking. "Hasn't he already taken the Bay State A. C. championship, and beaten them all in the Worcester climb? Why, at Readville, this boy . . ."

Conversation is interrupted by a message telephoned from the two-mile post: "Napier just passed, going great guns. Time—four minutes, seven seconds flat." Colonel Wood smiles broadly.

While the thundering machine races upward, bouncing over water bars which throw driver and mechanic momentarily from their seats, and skirting for breathless moments the edge of thousand-foot declivities, let's look at the scene on the mountaintop.

Here, under the lee of the old chain-moored barn, the leaders of motordom bask in the sunlight. Long Island millionaires James L. Breeze and Harry Harkness, mountain record holders of 1904, know the hazards which the intrepid Hilliard is at this moment braving. Charles Soules, Pope-Toledo crack, and F. E. Stanley, adherent of steam, sit complacently in their cars. Their records of approximately thirty minutes will take a bit of beating. The din of the Napier's exhaust rumbles up from the seven-mile post. President Lewis Speare and secretary John Kerrison of the Bay State Auto Club man the timing gear, and spectators jump to their feet, watching the turn where Hilliard will appear. Into full view shoots the green Napier, her driver fighting the loose rocks, and mechanic Townsend holding on for his life. Who can doubt that this is winning speed?

A crack from Mr. Reeves' pistol and the cutting of the Napier's motor signal the end. A brief message quivers down the eight-mile copper thread to the watchers at the start: "Hilliard finishes, time 20:58 2/5, a new record for the mountain."

Previous chapters of the history of this record are not less adventurous. The eight-mile carriage road, ascending nearly 5000 feet, represented a challenge to Jacob Vanderbilt as early as 1883, and his record, with six horses and a light carriage, was one hour, seventeen minutes.

In due course came the automobile, and in 1899 Freelon O. Stanley, of Stanley Steamer fame, made a matter-of-fact approach to the problem by touring from his Newton home in a tiny six-horse-power steamer, with a side trip to Washington's summit in two hours and ten minutes. He may be excused for not beating the horse, for he had to stop to jack up his rear wheels every two miles. Water consumption was unprecedented, and his water pump was hooked to the engine crosshead, hence the necessity for idling. For 1903 the record was one hour, forty-six minutes, made by L. J. Phelps in a model bearing his name. In June of 1904 Otto Nestman drove a diminutive two-cylinder, seven h.p., crank-steering Stevens-Duryea for a forty-eight minute, thirty seconds record.

Nestman's record was one month old when F. E. Stanley, brother of Freelon, opened the throttle of his six-horsepower, 800-pound vehicle on the Glen House drive and arrived at the summit, through a cloudbank, in 28:19 2/5 minutes. He was demonstrating the greatest four-wheel hill-climbing machine of its weight and horsepower for twenty years to come, the direct-geared Stanley Steamer. This mark stood for just five hours, forty-six minutes. Harry Harkness, Long Island amateur, made a spectacular flight up the mountain on the same day in 24:37 3/5. His car's weight was three

times, its horsepower nine times, and its price twenty-seven times that of the Stanley.

Mt. Washington was repeatedly climbed without a fatality, but there were near misses aplenty. On the second day of the 1904 climb, A. E. Morrison shot past the six-mile post in a high-powered Peerless touring car. A bitter rival of F. E. Stanley, Morrison was bent on gaining the four seconds by which he had lost the day before. Entering a turn near the Gulf of Slides, the Peerless leaped from a water bar, and was air-borne for her full length, the resulting skid loosing a small avalanche of rock into the ravine below. Straining his eyes into the haze ahead, Morrison was confronted with disaster. Number 14 Oldsmobile, stalled in the narrow path, was crowded against the bank; opposite her was a fog-blanketed drop of unknown depth. Morrison decided to go through. With foot hard down, and eyes glued to the wheels of the Olds, he left a bare coat of paint between them and his flying car, and let Fate take care of the offside wheels of the Peerless.

A long rasping slide on front axle and rear housing brought the Peerless to a stop, her wheels overhanging the ravine. Her twisted frame had broken a radiator bolt, and fan and radiator were thrust against the motor.

Such trifles, however, did not stop Morrison. It is on the record that he pulled his radiator into place, got the car on the road again by means unknown and rushed across the finish line in 29:6 4/5—and for years his favorite gripe was the loss of those four seconds.

The succeeding year saw the brilliant performance of Hilliard, which ended the official trials over the old and rugged track, as it ended also the records of Breeze, Harkness and Stanley. The road was subsequently widened, and with the 350 water bars eliminated, Cannon Ball Baker, in 1928, reached the top in thirteen minutes, twenty-six seconds flat.

Ten years later, in 1938, a new chapter was written by Lemuel Ladd, an amateur from Brookline, Massachusetts. Under the auspices of the Automobile Racing Club of America, he shot his Ladd-designed V-8 special up the carriage road in 12:17 3/5, for an international free-for-all mark.

SULGRAVE MANOR: Henry Austin Clark's 1916 Pierce-Arrow

PRESCOTT HILL CLIMB: 1914 Vauxhall

8-Litre 1930 Bentley: Cambridge

Robertson Comes Through!

by PAUL GALLICO

"CAR COMING! CAR COMING!"

With a rumble and exploding clatter, the big buzz boxes from hell on wheels, driven by masked demons from the pit, came thundering down the old Jericho Turnpike on Long Island, jouncing and bounding on the chewed-up, rutted, narrow dirt road, screamed into the curve, rounded the bend on two wheels, the slender pneumatic tires screeching, gears grinding and clanking, and with a flash of flame, a spurt of mud and a stink of gasoline vanished down the road.

"Did you see 'em? They were goin' more'n a mile a minute! Ain't no one goin' to ketch that George Robertson. Hurrah for our own Robbie! That there Eyetalian car better get off'n the road when Robbie wants by. . . ."

Granddad will remember the day. It was Saturday, October 24, 1908, the great milestone in American sport, when George Hepburn Robertson, twenty-three-year-old American race driver, piloting a 120 h.p. Locomobile, won the Vanderbilt Cup Race over the 258.06 mile course at Hempstead Plains, Long Island. It was the first time in history that an American, driving an American-designed and -built car, had won America's own racing classic.

October 24, 1908. The North Pole was still to be discovered and the Panama Canal was being built. The Wright brothers had invented a flying machine in which no one had much faith. Women autoists wore long linen dusters down to their ankles and veils to hold their Gibson hats in place while scorching along at twenty miles an hour. And George Robertson and his Locomobile once and for all ended the invincible supremacy of the foreign cars over the thunder-wagons of American make.

Among the European cars that Robertson whipped on that day of days were an Isotta, three Mercedes and a Renault. The entry that finished second, one minute and forty-eight seconds behind Robertson and his Loco, was the Italian Isotta. It was that close.

What days, what times, what memories! The old smoke- and fire-belching Locomobile, with the number 16 painted on the broadside of its hood, went from racing to the barn of Peter Helck, the artist whose brush brought to life the stirring moment when George Robertson, Helck's lifelong friend, rounded the Westbury Turn and pulled away from the speedy Isotta.

Two hundred and fifty thousand spectators got themselves out onto Long Island the day of the race, starting long before dawn, by automobile, by the steam-drawn Long Island Railroad, by horse and wagon and on foot, distributing themselves over Hempstead, Jericho, Garden City, Mineola, Westbury and Plainfield. Plutocrats paid fifty dollars to park their autos in vantage places by the grandstand, only to find when they arrived there that they had been sold out and their view utterly blocked by thousands of spectators on foot.

The New York *Times* chortled with delight over the fact that at that particular race one could get a plate of clam chowder for twenty-five cents and a cup of coffee for ten cents at a tent near the grandstand, with Greeks peddling bananas at two for a nickel, and at the same time waxed bitter over the Long Island Railroad, complaining that: "The Long Island Railroad is probably past reform, but it does seem as if any railroad with such an opportunity before it would have felt some pride in trying to make a record. Three hours is too long a time to take in getting from the grandstand to Long Island City."

The announcer was a leather-lunged hero named Pete Prunty who bawled the news of approaching cars through a megaphone. Nineteen cars were

117

entered in the race. Not more than half of them finished. Several caught fire. Nobody was hurt, though spectators swarmed over the track after each car passed with no regard for the danger of those approaching.

George Robertson, a truculent, hard-driving daredevil, threatened to drive right over any car that wouldn't give him road when he wanted to pass, and the other drivers knew he meant it. He got road.

On the last lap he was a few seconds under four minutes ahead of the big Isotta driven by Herb Lytle and had the race won. With a groan of despair the crowd heard Pete Prunty bawl through his trumpet that Robertson was off the road at Fairfield with a blown tire.

But less than two minutes later, the huzzahs and hurrahs arose when old Stentor shouted that Robbie had swapped tires in one minute and forty-eight seconds, thanks to those new demountable rims.

Would he be able to hold his slim lead? Swaying and straining to catch the first glimpse, the crowd waited in anguish. Robbie was nowhere in sight.

At last the flame-throwing, smoke-spitting, wheezing Loco showed over the top of the rise and a scream of delight and welcome broke from the throng. Robertson flashed across the finish line, the winner by one minute and forty-eight seconds.

What men! What times! What a race!

Ralph de Palma's Glorious Failure

by CAPTAIN EDDIE RICKENBACKER

THE SAME DAY I SAW A PICTURE OF Ralph de Palma pushing the gray Mercedes up to the finish line at the Indianapolis speedway in 1912, I read in the newspapers that a young R.A.F. ferry pilot had flown across the Atlantic in less than six hours.

I thought to myself: it's all a question of where you're going and what the competition is. The airman left Newfoundland and presently turned up in Scotland, saying the trip was uneventful and all the winds were tail winds. De Palma, on the other hand, chased around a two-and-a-half-mile track for more than six hours and after nearly 500 miles ended up exactly where he had started. Clear to the end he was the fastest thing on earth that day; then a piece of metal failed and in the time it takes a piston to travel seven inches he was re-

duced from a sure champion with $20,000 in prize money in his grasp to an empty-handed tail-end Charlie.

That would have crushed most men. But de Palma answered with a show of character that will be remembered as long as the concrete foundations of the Indianapolis Speedway stand. I was there and saw it all. And I can't help thinking that if the other Italians had been like him, we'd probably still be fighting in Halfayah Pass.

We go back many years. Mr. William Howard Taft was in the White House; Franklin D. Roosevelt was an unknown New York assemblyman; Christy Mathewson was the sporting hero of the day when de Palma appeared at the 500-mile Memorial Day race with a Mercedes that had the gleam of something taken from a Tiffany showcase.

De Palma had raced the car in Europe. The German builders had given it a watchmaker's care. It hugged the ground and could do 120 miles an hour on the straightway. But Ralph, besides being a sweet character, and real gentleman, was known to have a heavy foot. He always gave the customers what they wanted, but machinery will take only so much and the breakdowns and spills that came with monotonous regularity gave him the reputation of a hard-luck guy.

Twenty-four cars came up to the line that morning, driven by some very fine sportsmen. Looking over an old entry list, I was surprised to find how many are gone. Hughie Hughes, Howdy Wilcox, Matson, David Bruce-Brown, Harry Knight, Bob Burman, Spence Wishart—all were killed, sooner or later, on the track. Wishart was killed a hundred feet in front of me at Elgin, Illinois, two years later. He blew a tire, rolled over and over and died under the car. Both he and Bruce-Brown were "gentlemen drivers," part of Willy Vanderbilt's Long Island crowd of millionaires—wonderful drivers and great sports.

Bob Burman was the popular favorite. A rangy, broad-shouldered, handsome guy, he drove a car out to his measure—a Cutting with a whopping piston displacement. He'd spent a fortune on it. But the grease monkeys in the pit thought it would be a tossup between him and Bruce-Brown of the National team. Working with Bruce-Brown were Wilcox and Dawson, the latter a test driver for the old Marmon company. Bruce-Brown was all hell-for-leather. The strategy called for him to run the rest of the field to the ground; then one or the other of his teammates would come up from nowhere and win. However, that was not the way things worked out.

There were several other men who packed plenty of horsepower. Hughes showed up with a brand-new yellow Mercer equipped with wire wheels and a counterbalanced shaft—revolutionary stuff. The man I personally picked to beat was Tetzlaff, a crafty and experienced driver, a real money player. Tetzlaff had an old Fiat with beer-keg cylinders and a double chain drive geared two and a half to one. Alongside the new cars, it looked awkward and top-heavy. But every cylinder explosion made that Fiat jump twenty feet.

I remember the bands were playing "Everybody's Doin' It Now" as we lined up. So as to get the pack off to a flying start Carl Fisher took us around once in a gray Stoddard-Dayton roadster; then he scooted out of the way as the speedometers touched sixty. The morning air was fresh and cool. But in a few minutes the cockpit was as hot and noisy as a foxhole.

De Palma worked out in front in the third lap. The two millionaires' sons, Wishart and Bruce-Brown, were close on his tail and Tetzlaff bounded along in fourth place like a jack rabbit in his Fiat. I was in trouble from the start. My engine wouldn't put out the r.p.m.'s and I was lapped on the fifth lap.

De Palma pushed eighty-three miles an hour—a lap in one minute and forty-nine seconds. He was playing for keeps. The pace was too fast for Knight. On the sixth lap, his Lexington blew a cylinder and he was through. A couple of minutes later Ormsby's Opel was forced off the track with a busted connecting rod. On the twenty-fifth lap, Bruce-Brown had to go it with broken piston rings. My turn came on the forty-third lap—a broken valve.

So with nearly 400 miles still to be run, I joined the spectators. I could have used some of the prize money, but if I had to look on, this was certainly the race to see. De Palma was driving with plenty of style, hurling across the turns with little loss in speed. His pit work, too, was the best on the track. The rest of us were lucky to change a tire and clear the pit in sixty seconds. Ralph was in and out in thirty. He looked fine and you felt nothing could stop him. The clockwatchers spread the word that the records were going by the boards. Two days of rain had cooled the brisk track and tires were lasting longer, the cars were going faster. The crowd, which always goes for the winner, gave Ralph a cheer every time he went by the grandstand.

But the wise guys in the pits remembered the heavy foot and said "Wait." De Palma, with Mulford, was putting on an iron-man performance. The National and Stutz teams kept relieving their drivers. But de Palma and Mulford slugged it out alone.

Eddie Hearne quit with a burned-out crankshaft bearing on the fifty-fifth. On the sixty-third the McFarland Six blew a tire, slapped into a wall and shed two wheels. Four laps farther on, Disbrow's Case folded up. Then, in quick succession, a Stutz somersaulted off the track, a connecting rod went through the crankcase of a big red Simplex and the carburetor of a Marquette-Buick caught fire. At 200 miles only fifteen cars remained in the race. De Palma out in front, Tetzlaff second. Joe Dawson in a stock car was in third place as if he were glued there.

Between 200 and 300 miles—what we called the third century—Dawson worked into second place, just ahead of the Fiat whose leaps were getting shorter. A tire change and a touch of engine trouble brought de Palma's average speed down from nearly eighty-four to under eighty miles an hour. Meanwhile, three more cars dropped out, Wishart with a split water connection, Matson with a broken crankshaft and Anderson with a burned-out connecting rod.

The sun climbed high. You could smell rubber burn as it shrieked over the hot bricks. The pit crews started to flag in the crews at the first sign of wear on the threads. God, it was hot. I used to envy the Detroit and New York sports in the seven-dollar seats. The grandstand roof shaded them from the sun; they guzzled champagne which they brought in wicker hampers. Only once in my life did water ever again taste as good as the ice water in the galvanized iron buckets at Indianapolis.

De Palma kept his foot down on the floor. In the fourth hundred he raised the average speed to eighty-one miles and increased his lead to seven laps. By then Bob Burman was done for. He jockeyed Tetzlaff out of third place; then two tires let out and the big Cutting rolled over, but not fast enough to catch him. That left eleven cars. And with the Mercedes charging around the track making a noise like a battery of five-inch guns, and with that fine lead, it certainly looked as if de Palma had licked the jinx.

On the 197th lap, with only three to go, de Palma flicked up the speed. He was eleven minutes ahead of Dawson, only seven and a half miles and five and a half minutes to the $20,000.

The others were slamming around the track as methodically as Lionel trains; the racket kept up; the grandstand was emptying; everything was as it should be and then a hush fell and you could feel the question forming in 80,000 minds: "Where's de Palma?" Then the news came from the spotters in the backstretch. De Palma was in trouble; the Mercedes was hitting on two or three cylinders—a broken piston. Dawson caught the frantic signal from his pit men and poured on coal. The speed went up to ninety miles an hour. But Ralph, when he finally hove in sight, was crawling at dump-wagon speed and from the engine noises you would have thought it was being pounded with sledge hammers.

Ralph started to turn into the pit, but his men waved him out; if he shut off the engine, he was out for good. He went back on the track and crawled, like a hurt animal, up the street a way. The crowd groaned. He didn't reappear for a long time and Joe Dawson and the others kept going round and round. The next time he passed the pits, to start the 199th lap, he was making less than twenty miles per hour.

The books show that the flag went down in front of Dawson at 381.06 minutes—a new record incidentally. Ten minutes later Tetzlaff finished and won $10,000. And right behind him was Merz in Stutz, to take third place and $5,000. Then several others rolled home. About that time the Mercedes showed up in the backstretch. It was barely moving. Ralph was steering and pushing from the side, and his mechanic was shoving from behind. I'd say they pushed a mile and a half, clear to the finish line; while the field went by.

The rules say that the car must complete a race under its own power and so de Palma is down on the record book as not finishing. The popular legend is that he pushed the Mercedes to the finish line. Not quite. Technically, he was still one lap short. But 80,000 people were there; they saw the sweat on his face; they knew what was going through his mind; and I doubt that they cared about the missing lap. They roared out a cheer that has never been heard again in Indianapolis. You have to fail in a peculiar and wonderful way to earn such a cheer.

The Whirling World of Juan Manuel Fangio

by JOSH GREENFELD

IN THE RISKY SPORT OF GRAND PRIX racing, in the days before Juan Manuel Fangio gave it up, there was only one certainty, and that was that "the old man," as his fellow racers call Fangio, was the best driver who ever lived. For four consecutive years he was the World Champion Driver. From the time he captured his first title in 1951 he completely dominated the Grand Epreuve scene. His record of completing more than half of the 180 races he competed in speaks for itself.

Yet probably more out-and-out nonsense has been written about him than any other public figure. European auto journalists, in flights of epic fancy that almost scan, liken his achievements to those of an Olympian hero. And the popular image of Fangio on the Continent has grown to assume the classic pallor of a statue in a museum, awe-inspiring perhaps, but lifeless nevertheless.

American journalists on the Fangio story inject the human touch. They describe him as a "careful old daredevil"—whatever that may mean—who drives his car at speeds of more than 150 miles per hour with fussy meticulousness.

He wins, one gathers from these accounts, by employing a catalogue of clever tricks: he studies each circuit carefully before a race; during a race he never enters in a "dice"—a hubcap-to-hubcap duel; and he always plays cautiously in a race—laying back until all the dashing young hares fall to the wayside.

Then a "clinker" enters into the Fangio human-interest story. For somehow no writer can resist mentioning "Fangio's imperturbability," his "stone-faced and solemn detachment," until finally and ironically, drained of all his humanity and manliness, Fangio is returned to the same museum of natural mythology to which the European journalists had consigned him.

The simple fact is that Fangio employs the same tools as do his fellow drivers; the marvelous fact is that he applies them better. For example, the course of the Grand Prix of Monaco runs along the narrow, twisting streets of that picture-book Mediterranean harbor. On Boulevard Louis III there is a sharp right-hand curve away from the sea and then a plunge into a pitch-black tunnel. Suddenly confronted by the cold darkness, most racing drivers instinctively lift their feet ever so slightly from the gas. "But the old man doesn't," says Stirling Moss, admiringly. "He has such amazing confidence."

At Le Mans, years ago, eighty-one spectators and one driver were killed in Grand Prix racing's worst accident. Mike Hawthorn slowed down his Jaguar, coming in for a pit stop. Lance Macklin, on his tail in an Austin-Healey, swerved to pass him. Pierre Levegh, approaching from the outside, clipped the rear of the Austin-Healey with the front wheels of his Mercedes, brushed against the pit wall, skidded up the embankment and into the screaming crowd. Through it all Fangio streaked on in his Mercedes. A lap later, by managing to steer precisely and correctly through the confusion, he not only saved his life but, according to his fellow drivers, approached the quintessence of beauty.

The aesthetics of Grand Prix racing are grim, to be sure. During a race the only place a driver can really gain on his rivals is at a corner. However, in rounding corners at high speeds, drivers discovered long ago they simply couldn't let the car roll. But if they accelerated, the tail broke away and it became necessary to lock the front. They then hit upon the "four-wheel drift."

In the execution of the drift, racing's moment of truth so to speak, a driver approaches a curve from

HEINEMANN

the outside. He then steers as if to cut across the heart of it. At the right speed, on the right line, the pull of centrifugal force slides the car outward. Friction and gravity rush to the aid of the driver. The rear wheels, opposing the outward pull, push the car around the curve, the four wheels in perfect alignment, although they are slipping all the way.

Once the drift is initiated the driver is committed. He has guided those forces which he can control, the speed and power of his vehicle, into the realm of those natural forces he cannot control, inertia and centrifugal force. For a split second the efficacy of his judgment is severely tested. Herein lies the real beauty of racing.

And what marks the superb driver such as Fangio is his uncanny sense of precisely perfect line.

There are some purists who argue that Grand Prix road racing is the only valid twentieth-century art form. For the driver must deal with the twentieth-century preoccupations of speed, power, competition and destruction in terms of that most singular twentieth-century instrument, the automobile. And what is art, they insist, if not the precise expression of a society's fascinations?

Fangio himself, the Picasso, El Greco and da Vinci of "art" all rolled in one, shies away from these theoretical discussions. If you ask him why he drives he will simply say, "It is my passion."

However, the passion of Grand Prix driving is usually one associated with the world of daring

young men. Its lure for them is unmistakable. There is an intense exhilaration in driving a high-powered Ferrari or Maserati over a challenging circuit at breakneck speeds. And the driver, having chosen his fate, feels free and independent and very much a man.

The average driver rarely thinks about the possibilities of his own death. He develops a deep personal *mystique* which enables him to indulge his passion. If he is fortunate he will live to be thirty.

Most drivers are therefore young, adventurous, flamboyant, vain and seekers after notoriety. They are usually tall, graceful, and walk in an affected swagger, and will confide privately that they consider themselves half crazy.

Juan Manuel Fangio, however, is an anomaly, the exception that proves the rule. He is in his fifties, quiet, subdued, modest, and no lover of the limelight. He is stocky, his hair is thinning, and he walks with a lazy, rolling gait. He also considers himself quite sane. He is a mature man in a world of boys.

To fully appreciate Fangio one must understand the bizarre Grand Prix road show that rolls across Europe each summer, stopping in Italy one week, France, the next, then over to England and on up into Germany. During the winter it sojourns in Morocco, Florida, Cuba, Venezuela and Argentina. The caravan works a five-day week, from Wednesday to Sunday, and that is its sole association with the world of normality. Its dizzy entourage, aside from the drivers, consists of petty agents, skilled mechanics, hot-shot publicity men, cynical journalists, ambitious auto salesmen, garrulous gasoline-company representatives, untiring tire salesmen, international play girls and out-of-work polo players.

On Wednesday afternoon, the members of the circus panoply descend upon the best hotel in town, check into their reserved rooms, change from one sports ensemble into another and head out to the circuit for the practice trials. In some cities the circuits are roads that are usually open to normal traffic. In others they are especially constructed closed courses. But in all cities they vary greatly.

At the first trials, Fangio, a fierce competitor, rarely leaves the course until he turns in the fastest time for the day. From the very start it is as if he serves notice to the boys that he is the man. In the evening he sits like a patriarch in the hotel lobby, his wife Beba, a comely middle-aged brunette, beside him. The other drivers stop by; they defer to him as they try to speak in Spanish. Fangio is warm and good-humored as he doles out racing advice generously. And then at ten o'clock he rises and goes off to bed.

On Thursday and Friday, as the practice trials continue, the drivers familiarize themselves with their cars and with the special intricacies of the course. The international parasites familiarize themselves with the bars and with the special effects of the local beverages. (At Rheims it's champagne; at Nürburgring beer.) And each evening Fangio holds his quiet court.

Then on Saturday everyone rests. The drivers do not go out to the course. The parasites disappear from their favorite haunts. An awesome quiet, an expectant hush descends upon the town.

Sunday, Grand Prix day, bursts forth like an American Fourth of July. There is a holiday atmosphere everywhere. Early in the morning, from miles away, traffic begins to pour into the racing town. The grandstands of the course are bedecked with gala banners, country-fair style. Sprightly music issues out of loudspeakers. Concessionaires hawk food and drinks. In the infield, oil and tire firms have set up special pavilions. Electric-razor salesmen dispense free shaves. Beauticians give sample manicures. By three o'clock in the afternoon as many as 100,000 people are gathered. Some have come out of genuine *aficionado* interest, others simply out of morbid curiosity. For even on the most golden of sunlit Sunday afternoons, the specter of death is present.

The cars line up in grid formation, those with the fastest practice times up front. Fangio is usually in the middle of the first row. Freshened by more than twelve hours of sleep, he sits in a seat specially tailored to his measurements, wearing the required crash helmet, goggles and fireproof trousers pegged in at the ankles.

When the gun goes off there is an earsplitting burst of sound as the cars roar away in a mad scramble toward the first turn. Fangio shies away from the preliminary jockeying for position that

takes place, but after a few laps he begins to drive "my race."

Unfortunately for those who would like to emulate him, there is no set pattern to "my race." An expert mechanic, he has assessed the capabilities of his car during the practice trials. He has also made careful judgments about the personalities of each of his opposing drivers, their technical proficiencies and the performance levels of their cars in regard to the particular circuit. Therefore his tactics vary. One week he may front-run, the next week he lays back and a third week he may hang on, hubcap to hubcap, until he "dices" the opponent he fears most into submission. But each week as the season progresses, he taxes himself and his car to the breaking point for three long hours, during which he requires less road space, takes closer corners and exhibits better throttle control than any other driver. Nor does it seem to matter which make of car he is driving—he has won his championships aboard an Alfa Romeo, a Ferrari, a Mercedes and a Maserati; more often than not, he is the winner.

In triumph Fangio was graceful. Perhaps the reason Fangio can accept the accolades of triumph with so natural an ease is that his fame came to him casually and unexpectedly. For he did not achieve any measure of international renown until he was thirty-eight years old.

Fangio was born in the vicinity of Balcarce, a valley town in Argentina's table mountains, on June 24 (San Juan's Day), 1911, the fourth of six children in the family of an immigrant potato farmer and part-time plasterer.

His interest in mechanics came young. By the time he reached his early teens he was an eminently qualified grease monkey by reason of his apprenticeship at a local garage.

The turning point of his young life came when he was eighteen and had his first brush with death —but not the spectacularly sudden kind he would later encounter in road racing. Juan came down with a severe case of pneumonia and the doctors almost conceded his life. But his mother patiently nursed him back to health.

Until his illness Juan had been a gentle, withdrawing youth; following his illness he became an energetic, participating youngster. He joined the town soccer team and soon earned for himself a local reputation as a stubborn competitor. Then he served a year in the army at the cadet school, Campo de Mayo, outside of Buenos Aires, where he was chauffeur for the commanding officer.

By the time Juan returned to Balcarce he knew he wanted to be a racing driver. But Balcarce is a poor town and Juan was a poor young man who could not even afford a car of his own. Fortunately, because he had a mechanical background, he often was taken on as a *corredor* or co-driver in a race because he could also double as a repairman. But it was not until he was twenty-five years old that he had a racing car of his own.

He obtained a Ford, and he and his brother souped it up in a farmyard workshop until the only recognizable part of it that remained a Ford was the engine block. Every other part was catch-as-catch-can with a purpose: speed. "She may not have looked very pretty," Juan recalls, "but she hung together well enough to last the three hours of a race."

So intense was the concentration of Fangio when driving his Ford Special that he was completely oblivious to other events during a race. In 1938, competing in the crowded Tres Arroyos, Fangio was called in after the fifth lap. "What's the matter?" Juan demanded angrily of the officials. "Don't you know," they asked incredulously, "that five drivers have been killed here in a terrible accident?"

By 1940 Fangio had acquired a wealth of racing experience under the most primitive of conditions, but little else. That year, driving a Chevrolet coupe, bought through the contributions of his friends, he won his first race, the Gran Premio Internacional del Norte, a round-trip endurance test of 6000 miles from Buenos Aires to Lima, Peru. With his victory he earned a reputation in Argentine motor circles. But Argentina then was indeed a very thin line on the world auto-racing map.

Fangio won almost every long-distance race in Argentina until World War II put an end to racing there. Until 1948 he bided his time in the sleepy Pampas, driving a taxi in Balcarce to earn his living. In that year, when he was thirty-seven years old, he received his big break. It came, in a roundabout way, through Perón, who had be-

come interested in racing the year before. Perón, like all dictators, saw in the circus of Grand Prix racing an easy chance to gain international laurels.

At Perón's "suggestion" the millionaire members of the Argentinian Auto Club outfitted Fangio with a new Maserati. After an abortive start in 1948 (in a Simca-Gordini), Fangio launched his continental career with a vengeance the following year by winning six Grands Prix. He was on his way. A grateful government presented him with an outright gift of $30,000, he was acclaimed a national hero in Argentina, and a place was secured for him on the Alfa Romeo "Works" team for the 1950 season. And in 1951, as captain of the Alfa team, he drove to the first of his five World Championships.

Fangio since has become a very wealthy man. His annual income from road racing exceeded $100,000. The holdings that he has amassed in the last fourteen years include two service stations (one in Buenos Aires, the other in his native Balcarce), a 2000-seat movie theater in Mar del Plata, Argentina's plush resort, and two very lucrative automobile dealerships (General Motors and Mercedes).

A great deal of fiction has been written about the fact that there are two types of drivers, "safe" and "daredevil"; that whereas the daredevil gets killed, the safe, like Fangio, can go on indefinitely. Fangio himself, however, knew that the list of road racing's honored dead knows no such fine distinction. He understood the hazards of his profession full well. In 1952, at Monza, in the only serious crash of his career, he sustained broken neck vertebrae and head injuries. He has seen his self-appointed protégés, de Portago and Castellotti, "buy it." And he has been careful to keep his teenage son far from the madding circuits.

Fangio is that rare phenomenon of a human being: a man who has maintained his physical reflexes while garnering his mental experience. But the ultimate reason for his success must be assayed from deep within his character and attitude. ("With most of us," says Phil Hill, America's top road racer, "you can figure out a ratio of importance between man and car, say 25 per cent driver, 75 per cent car. With the old man the ratio is 40 per cent driver, 60 per cent car. He's got us beat by 15 per cent before we even start. It's something he's got inside.")

To most drivers, racing, as it was to De Portago, is a vice, the outer manifestation of some secret and inner guilt. To Fangio, the normal man, it was simply his avenue for controlled expression and self-assertion in an otherwise wild and whirling world.

I remember sitting with him in the paddocks behind the Maserati pit at Rheims one summer.

It was moments before the start of the Grand Prix. The other drivers were strutting about nervously. Fangio was nervous too, there were beads of sweat rolling down his forehead, but he sat quietly, chewing gum. Finally, it was time for him to walk out to his Maserati. He rose and, turning to me, shrugged and said, *"Laborar"* (To work).

Off he went in rolling gait, a skilled laborer on his way to work, even though his work might mean death.

The Day of the Race   by STIRLING MOSS

THIS IS THE RACE ITSELF, WHERE ALL the excitement that went before—everything that's gone before, the years that have gone before, the experience and the work—all come into being.

During the night that has gone before, you have tried—subconsciously more than consciously—not to think of the race, tried to relax so that you can sleep properly and not worry about gear ratios and so on, because all this should have been tended to before. There's really no point in worrying about the motorcar. You leave as much of this worry and responsibility to your mechanic, who tends the car with very great care always. And at this time there's really not much point in worrying about the race. You have discussed it the day before, after the practice, with the mechanics, team manager and possibly the other drivers. I'm usually a bit pessimistic with regard to the chances of the car because I think it is the easiest way.

Now comes the morning of the race, spent, in this case at a friend's pub down in Chichester, which is near Goodwood. I'll eat a pretty hearty breakfast because I won't be having any lunch: corn flakes or other cereal, bacon or sausage, eggs, maybe some kidneys, coffee and toast and marma-

lade. And then I would reckon to go right through the day until evening before eating anything else. I don't like to race on a heavy stomach. My wife doesn't eat a very big breakfast; she just sits and chats with me and generally takes my mind off the race—not that it normally worries me too much, anyway.

After breakfast, I start to dress and I hope again that the mechanics have properly prepared the cars; I make sure I've got my goggles with me, ear-plugs, crash helmet, equipment in case it rains, perhaps a jacket to put on after I get out of the car in case it's cold.

At the circuit, there are always lots of kids around waiting for my autograph—or I *hope* there will always be lots of kids around, because although an autograph may be a bit tiresome to give at times, when you're a bit pent up and waiting to get in the car and have a go, if the kids weren't there we'd miss them. It would mean perhaps that you weren't being as successful as you hoped to be. This is related to a fact that the Americans might find difficult to understand. In England, if you're asked what you do and you say you're a professional racing driver, you are accepted socially, and everyone thinks yours is a very creditable profession to be in; whereas I have the feeling that in America, if you say you're a racing driver, everybody sort of grabs at his daughter and rather frowns down upon you. But in England the racing driver does enjoy a very high position in sport. Our races are normally written up on either the first or third pages in our newspapers, not on the sports page. Racing drivers do get invitations to world *premières* and first nights and so on, and they're treated more as a polo player would be in the States. This is true even though over here, of course, ours is a professional sport, because there is money involved. Nevertheless, I would say that without exception all the drivers race primarily because they like it. There is no professionalism, if one accepts that in the way that some people refer to "dirty" driving.

Now I prepare to get in the car. I've got my jacket on, quite possibly because there's a bit of a wind; though the cars are warm inside, it pays to wear a jacket when you're standing around waiting. The car I'm about to drive is a 3.7 Aston Martin. I'm equipped with goggles—that's because I expect there will be no rain during the race. Otherwise, I would have on a visor, which is a sort of plastic screen that comes down from the peak of your helmet; most drivers find this to be the best form of protection against the rain. Goggles are very difficult to keep from steaming up and, in fact, to see through when there's driving rain.

Now we are at the last-minute, on-the-start line; the cars are running, and the mechanics are just doing up the bonnet, having checked to see that there are no oil or water leaks. A friend is leaning over and giving me last-minute best wishes, or perhaps telling me about something else that he knows: that there's a bit of oil on the first corner, and so on.

It's the last minute when one is trying not to be too tense. I will look down, check my goggles, see to it that they're sealed properly so that the wind won't cause sore eyes. I will read all gauges to make sure that there's nothing wrong with the car that I can see at the moment.

There's one minute to go now, and it's with this signal that mechanics have got to clear away from the track. If a car doesn't start properly, the driver will be morally obligated to wait until the race is completely under way and then the mechanics will be allowed to run out and push-start the motorcar. It's usually quite a flap at the one-minute-to-go; you'll find there are mechanics who are there when they shouldn't be, and there are photographers and officials standing in the way. The starter walks across the circuit, lifts his flag, then usually counts five or ten seconds, drops the flag, and the field is away, unless, of course, Harry Schell is driving, in which case he's usually away with about one or two seconds to go.

In this last minute of a racing driver on the line, your thoughts take many forms. One is to rather wish or pray that you may do well, that there may be no accidents, and another one is to watch your motorcar. You try to keep your mind off what might happen, you try to see that everything's all right in the cockpit and not get too het up. You check to see that your rear-view mirrors are O.K., and you just try to concentrate on what has got to happen in the ensuing minutes. The first few seconds from the start are terribly important, because it's very easy for one to be too pent up when the flag drops. If you're too excited, it's quite easy to make a mistake, stall the car, get too much wheelspin generally, make a mess at the start.

For maximum acceleration at the take-off point, you have to think of getting the revs correct. If you have a multiplate aluminum clutch, the take-off is absolutely instantaneous. It's impossible to slip the clutch and therefore more revs are usually required. The clutch is either in or out, you rev up, let up the clutch and the car has to go forward at that second. However, with the Ferodo clutch, it is possible to slip the clutch a bit and make an easier getaway, using fewer revs. To get the maximum acceleration, it's essential not to have too much wheelspin. And usually, with a racing car, we don't want to stay in first gear longer than necessary because it is sometimes a little difficult, if you go to maximum revs in first, to pull the gear across and get it into second.

Once away and after the first lap or two—which I normally like to take a little easier than the others in case there's oil on the course left by cars from previous races—I then try to get my car up to its maximum and myself up to my maximum as soon as possible. In other words, I like to go to the absolute limit of braking, the limit of road holding and cornering and of acceleration, and then, when I've got down to what I consider is just about my own limit and my car's limit, I see what revs I'm doing out of and around each corner. I then have a set factor as to what I consider is the best I can do. In other words, if I come out of a corner, shall we say, at 6800 r.p.m. and I think that I did it just right, then, later on in the race, if I find that I'm coming out only at 6700, I know that either the car is more difficult to drive or I'm getting tired and not properly concentrating on my job. A motor race is very, very tiring physically, and it is very tiring mentally, and to start losing a fifth of a second here and a fifth of a second there, which soon tots up to the odd second for a whole lap, is a very easy thing to do. You can do it even though you think you're still at your absolute ultimate limit. It's surprising how these fractions of a second slip away without one realizing. Therefore, in a motor race, it's essential to be driving as fast as you possibly can or as you possibly need to, shall we say, from the first lap or the second lap right to the finish. And if a driver can spin his energy out over the whole race and get the ultimate from himself, then the more he can give of himself, the more he can save in the motorcar. In other words, if he can go around the corner a little bit faster, he can save a little bit of the motorcar on the ultimate of acceleration by leveling the two out. It's a little difficult to explain. Let me have another go: if it's necessary to lap a circuit, shall we say, at ninety-five miles an hour, then it's best to do so by straining the driver and not the car. This is, of course, providing the driver can withstand the pace, but that's the driver's problem, and I do feel that one should be able to withstand a two- or three-hour Grand Prix even straining one's self to the limit all the time.

There's one interesting point which comes in here; quite often you'll find in practice that you may have ten cars within one second of each other in practice times for one lap; however, after ten or fifteen laps—even barring mechanical troubles —you'll find those same ten cars are very considerably spread out, certainly not within a couple

of seconds of each other. This is due primarily to the fact that there are people who can drive one extremely fast lap on a semifree course without other cars, and they perhaps can do this once or twice, but they find it considerably more difficult to keep the same pace minute after minute, lap after lap and in fact hour after hour. It goes practically without exception that very few races are won at an average speed anywhere near the average speed of the lap record. This, of course, is due to other things, too, such as oil on the course, having to lap other competitors, and the load of a full fuel tank which makes the car more difficult to drive. However, the fact remains that very few drivers are able to keep up their maximum, their personal and physical maximum, right through even a comparatively short Grand Prix of two hours or just over.

As we lap the track, all of us are going quite fast nevertheless. Now speed is only relative and quite frankly a driver shouldn't be frightened of speed. The things that frighten me are mainly things I don't understand. If one gets into a situation he's not sure he can handle, then one realizes he is out of his depth and is frightened. I worry for instance, if there's oil on the track, or if I make an error of judgment or if somebody else makes a mistake—if someone should spin around in front of me when I don't expect it, or something happens to the car such as a wheel coming off. These things take you by surprise, and until you get them under control they are definitely frightening. It gives you a tingling sensation in your hands and rather a cold sweat and a lump in the throat, difficult to describe, but anybody who has ever had real fear will know what I mean. To me, though, speed is exhilarating. When I go around a corner and I execute it in what I think is a reasonable fashion, I'm happy at what I've done. I get a tremendous feeling of satisfaction, the type of exhilaration that I imagine a golfer gets when he swings his club, hears that nice click when it contacts the ball just right and then watches the ball land right on the green, close to the pin. Although I'm not a golfer, I feel that must give him a tremendous sense of exhilaration. The same thing goes when you're playing table tennis and you get a shot which manages to pick the ball practically off the floor right when you didn't expect to make it.

Well, I get the same sense of exhilaration as the golfer or the table-tennis player in motor racing when I go around a corner. I get a tremendous feeling of satisfaction.

It isn't just the speed, it's also a matter of keeping your car glued to the road. Speed comes in because speed makes the gamble higher. It's rather like playing cards for matchsticks or playing for money. Obviously you get more out of the game when you're playing with higher stakes, and in motor racing you're playing with the highest stakes

of all. That's what makes it so vitally important to the driver concerned. Apart from this there is the tremendous spirit of competition—of beating the other man, perhaps of beating the lap record or beating the race average speed. Or perhaps the challenge simply lies in getting your car home, because quite often your car may be ailing, and to get it home is a tremendous personal achievement in itself. It's like taking a sick animal and coaxing it through its illness. You get the same thing with a car, because a car is almost human to a driver. And because of all these things motor racing is to me the greatest sport in the world.

The race is over now, and this one I've won, so the story has a happy ending. The first thing I'll do is tell my manager, Mr. Reg Parnell, what the car felt like and perhaps offer suggestions for improvements. Perhaps the car would run better with a higher or a lower third gear, and in my elation at having won, I'm explaining to him that the car is good but we mustn't stop here; let's go on and make it better.

(Eventually I put all this into the book that I always keep, which shows the axle ratio that I'm using, the tire pressures, the grade of plugs, what worth I'm getting out of what corner, so that in years to come, or maybe only in months to come, I can look back and say: *Right, I was going through that corner faster then, or slower then, and so on; I must have made improvements or perhaps I'm not going quite as fast as I should.*)

Then I'll explain much the same thing to my wife, but perhaps things are a little bit more personal, or a little bit closer to us rather than the motorcar.

We will pack up immediately and rush away to get out of the tremendous crush that comes after a race, the stiff unending questions that are fired at one. We will stop on the roadside for a cup of tea. It's nice now to be able to relax, just the two of us, and to discuss the race at length. If I've done well, I normally talk about the race up until two or three hours afterward. If I haven't done too well, then I still talk about it, I guess; but it's easier when you've won or when you've done what you consider is a good performance, because in motor racing it isn't always necessary for a driver to win in order to feel happy.

Then I may write a report of the race, because

occasionally I do reports for newspapers. Once in a while I may answer some mail that has followed me around from race to race and which is important that I answer.

Now it is evening and the race is forgotten, but subconsciously I'm bubbling over and perhaps rather excited inside, and I'm playing a game with my wife of tag, or whatever you call it in the States, and this is the nice side because, although I'm not thinking of the race, it's given me a boost which makes the day seem worthwhile and the evening as well. It's rather the way you feel, I suppose, when you've come out of the cinema and seen what you think is not only a good film but a happy film, and one that you enjoyed.

Finally, in a long race, a tough race, particularly if it's very hot, I lose about an inch around the waist and quite a few pounds of weight. Of course all this weight comes back that evening, because I drink many, many pints of water, and so my slimming efforts really are worth little.

And now, lastly, the most difficult part. If you have any measure of success—and this goes more for Juan Fangio than anybody else in the world— it is a fact that if ever you get in anybody else's motorcar, any circuit, anywhere in the world, whether it's a good car or a bad car, you are expected to go faster than that car's ever been before. Not only in that particular car, but in any other car of that mark—whether you know the circuit or whether you don't, whether you have the

stomach-ache or whether you haven't. These are the difficult things, and for a man like Fangio it must be even much more difficult. Everybody expects so much all the time.

The obligation to race is sometimes a burden. You've got to lead your team. You have the responsibility of the team and sometimes you don't even have the backing of the people there, because after all there are many drivers who are perhaps your junior and who would like to take your job.

Now my final ambitions. Naturally, the thing I'd like more than anything else in the world is to be world champion driving a British motorcar. And then later on—well, I'd like to be able to continue racing, be able to pick the races and the days that I want to race and the places I want to go to race, and not feel that I have the obligation of racing at my absolute ultimate every time that I get in a motorcar. It's a funny thing, but you know today when I pull the goggles down, I really feel that something inside of me says: *Come on, you've got to go.* I suppose that's much the same way as a horse feels when it gets the bit between its teeth, and I have this principle: that if I've got to go out and I've got to go around slowly for any reason, then I don't put my goggles down. Well, I hope that in the not too distant future I'll be able to pull my goggles down and not go fast unless I want to.

The Ferrari "Jinx"   by ROBERT DALEY

EXCITEMENT AND GLORY, SPEED, DEATH. These are the elements of motor racing, and in the years since the war no other marque has drunk of them so abundantly as the blood-red cars of Enzo Ferrari.

There are no roads where cars are raced which

have not known the banshee wail and frightening agility of Ferraris. They have sped to victory in Florida, Venezuela and Australia, through the soundless forests of West Germany, the chic and haughty streets of Monte Carlo, the mountains of Mexico, the deserts of North Africa. They have won races lasting two hours and they have won races lasting seven days. Four drivers' world championships and eight sports-car world championships have fallen to them in the last ten years.

No other marque can match the record in victories of the blood-red cars. Nor their record in death.

In Argentina in 1953, a Ferrari slewed into the mob, slaughtered five and maimed many.

In Italy during the 1957 Mille Miglia a Ferrari rocketed off the road and struck down fifteen more, four of them children.

In Cuba, during the 1958 Gran Premio, a Ferrari killed seven.

Five drivers under contract to the Ferrari factory, skilled professionals, have crashed to their deaths since 1955 alone. The 1959 record was unfortunately typical. In ten Grand Prix races two drivers were killed, two were injured severely, four cars were destroyed.

Another Ferrari, a privately owned, factory-tuned sports car, crashed into a Jaguar at night in the rain at Le Mans. Both caught fire. The Ferrari driver lived to race again. The Jaguar driver died.

The man whose cars bear the name that brings glory and death to so many is a mysterious figure—a recluse who never goes to races, who is rarely seen in public, who appears to suffer intensely each time a driver is killed, who protests that he loves his drivers like sons but then sends his cars out the next week anyway.

Enzo Ferrari in his sixties is a stern, unapproachable man. All who come in contact with him defer to him. No one sits down until he does. He has no intimates. He is addressed only as Commendatore, the rank to which he was raised by the Italian king in 1939 in recognition of the glorious victories he had won for Italy.

Commendatore Ferrari was born in Carpi, a northern Italian village nine miles north of Modena, the present capital of the Ferrari kingdom, and was a mule-shoer in the Italian army during World War I. After the war he had a short, undistinguished career as a race driver, taking over in 1925 as team manager for the Alfa Romeo factory. When Alfa quit racing, Ferrari bought a team of their cars and raced under his own name. Most of the great drivers of that epoch worked for

him—Nuvolari, Varzi, Compari—and several died.

In 1939, Ferrari came to Modena to build his own cars. War began. Worried about possible bombings, he quickly moved to Maranello, ten miles west, and spent the war making machine tools.

The first Ferrari cars appeared after the war. It is said that the transition from toolmaking to cars was made thanks to the devotion of workers who labored on the cars after hours. This is part of the legend which surrounds Ferrari, and may or may not be true. The legend also has it that he is autocratic, demanding that the job must be done his way or not at all. He has run through half a dozen chief engineers and three team managers in the last few seasons. Harry Schell, an ex-Ferrari driver, called him "an impossible man to work for." But it is also true that some around him regard him with extraordinary devotion. His team manager and former secretary, Romulo Tavoni, has worked for him ten years and always speaks of him in a voice charged with respectful awe.

Today Ferrari's factory domain covers an area equivalent to two city blocks, and no one enters it without a pass.

There are about 300 workers, and production in 1960 reached one car a day, with commercial models selling for somewhat under $15,000. For a long time output was only 200 cars a year, and those who bought them at such a high price were clients, not customers. Clients alone intruded upon the privacy of the Commendatore. Many were famous: Ingrid Bergman, Roberto Rossellini, Prince Bernhard of The Netherlands, James Stewart, William Holden, Zsa Zsa Gabor. These people mean nothing to Ferrari, but he has autographed pictures of them in his waiting room to impress other prospective clients, and the celebrities share wall space with shots of Farina, Fangio, Ascari and Hawthorn, all of them world champions (the latter two are dead), sliding around corners at Monza or the Nürburgring.

Ferrari has made himself inaccessible to reporters, with the result that his press in Italy has been consistently terrible.

Journalists who arrive at his door are told to write out a list of questions and that Commendatore Ferrari will answer them by mail.

However, exceptions are made for representatives of magazines Ferrari feels are read by potential buyers of his cars, or for some few automotive journalists he especially respects.

When under fire in the press he remains aloof, indifferent. But he will not permit his beloved cars to be smeared. When Luigi Musso, last of the Italian drivers, was killed in 1959, the entire nation was plunged into mourning, and Ferrari was accused of having sent Musso out in a car that was mechanically unsound. At this, Ferrari lashed back angrily, charged that Musso had been going too fast and vowed that he, Ferrari, would never race again in an Italy which did not appreciate all he had tried to do for it.

Ferrari has often threatened to abandon racing. In 1953, feeling the financial pinch of competing against major factories like Jaguar, Lancia, etc., and knowing Mercedes was due back the next season, he announced suddenly that he could not go on. As Ferrari quite possibly expected, the giant Fiat Company promptly offered him a yearly subsidy of 50,000,000 lire ($81,000) if he would continue to uphold the honor and prestige of the Italian automotive industry.

The Commendatore also abandons racing almost every time a driver is killed, sometimes calling in all his cars but always reconsidering in time for the next race.

Some days after Peter Collins was killed a few years ago, his widow came down to Modena to call on Ferrari. Ferrari never goes to his drivers' funerals and he had been represented at Peter's only by a wreath. But now he began to tell Louise Collins how much he had loved Peter. Peter had been his favorite. Louise started to weep. Ferrari began weeping himself. The Grand Prix of Italy would be his last race, he told Louise. He would run it in honor of Peter Collins. He would end his long absence from races and Louise should sit beside him in a box at Monza and all the world would know he was abandoning racing because of the death of Peter Collins.

Ferrari has not quit racing but Louise says she is still fond of him as Peter had been. "Ferrari is famous for giving up racing," she said wryly. "But somehow it never works out that way."

Portago and Hawthorn, both now dead, always spoke fondly of Ferrari also. "He does not go to races" Hawthorn told me once, "because he is afraid for us."

Portago once described dining with Ferrari, who suddenly said chidingly, sadly, "You have no loyalty. If I stopped building the fastest cars you would leave me in a minute." When Portago, who had never driven any other marque, protested his loyalty, Ferrari said: "Think about it a moment. You know I'm right." Later in the recorded interview issued posthumously by Riverside Records, Portago said, "I suddenly realized that he *was* right. . . . I would drive somebody else's cars if they went faster than his."

Collins, Portago and Hawthorn all believed Ferrari loved and admired them, and depended on them.

It would be unfair to blame Ferrari for spectators killed by his cars the half dozen or so times they have sailed into crowds. All three major disasters happened under bizarre circumstances. In Cuba there was a revolution, rebels were holding Fangio, sabotage of the race had been threatened, and all drivers were panicky; the driver who actually went into the crowd was a Cuban amateur, selected by Dictator Batista, not by Commendatore Ferrari. In the Mille Miglia there was no crowd control at all over a thousand miles of public road, and cars had been killing people for years. The Ferrari crash was merely the last and loudest. In Argentina, too, there was no crowd control; police holding back the mob had been withdrawn by Dictator Perón, who had cried: "My children, let them in."

What is within Ferrari's control is his choice of drivers and the pressure he puts on them to go faster and faster. Ferrari has hired old, safety-first drivers like Harry Schell (he'd been racing fourteen years when he was killed at Silverstone in 1960 while practicing) and Maurice Trintignant on occasion. But he obviously is more inclined to such daredevils as a Portago, a Castellotti or a Collins. Portago was killed in the Mille Miglia because he refused to be stopped by a broken front-wheel assembly, or even to wait while the tire, which was actually rubbing against the frame of the car, was changed. Castellotti was the type driver who would pass other cars on the verge in a shower of stones, grinning like a fiend. Stirling Moss called him "really one of the most daring drivers." When he entered his final curve, Castellotti was evidently waving at friends in the crowd. Collins was killed in a high-speed turn during the Grand Prix of Germany. It was late in the race and probably his brakes were gone. "Peter was a great one for pushing on when he had no brakes," said a teammate.

Musso was the last of the great Italians, and sometimes drove as if the honor of his country depended upon him either winning or going off the road trying. He almost always drove scared, beyond his ability. He was killed trying to follow a better driver (Hawthorn) into a turn he was not good enough to take at such a speed.

These dead daredevils were dedicated to speed, men under a compulsion to drive very fast. Naturally such men are most likely to win, and naturally they are most likely to be killed, too. All coaches look for the same trait in players: how much does the boy want to play?

Talented drivers who waver or retire because of a crash, business or marriage are, to the astute race manager, already dead. He makes no attempt to woo them back. Such a man can no longer be depended upon to drive fast enough.

Once Ferrari offered a tryout to Count von Trips, who promptly crashed the car at 200 kilometers an hour, completely destroying it. Trips, barely alive, bloody and battered, was sent back to Germany without a contract. Two weeks later, his right arm strapped to his side, nearly blacking out several times from the pain of his wounds, Trips won two races the same day in his own cars.

"Ferrari decided that if I wanted that badly to drive, I could drive for him," said Trips. "And he sent me a contract."

In contrast, and in fairness, it must also be remembered that Ferrari has employed, and still does, such fast but safe, quiet drivers as Phil Hill and Olivier Gendebien.

The Commendatore pressures his drivers in various ways. Last year he accused Collins of deliberately breaking the car at Le Mans, a race all drivers hate. Collins protested his innocence, but Ferrari told him there would be no car for him at Monza the following week. At Rheims a week

after that, Collins didn't know until the last minute whether he would have a car, and when he finally got one he drove so hard he spun off the course. He was still trying to redeem himself in Ferrari's eyes when he crashed at the Nürburgring.

According to many drivers, Ferrari enjoys inciting (and then watching) rivalries among them. He does it with calculated comments and/or the assignment of his cars. At races, drivers feel his pressure at all times, although he is not there. He is in constant contact with Tavoni, who is more an extension of the telephone line to Modena than a team manager.

The pressure of Ferrari is felt most of all in that there are always six contract drivers and, in Grand Prix racing, never more than four cars. This means that the regulars are always pushing to the limit to stay ahead of the reserves. Ferrari could end the competition if he named his Grand Prix team, and wrote the drivers' status into the contracts, as other marques always have done. But he chooses not to. So the struggle within the Ferrari team is often more interesting than the race itself. "I wouldn't want to be in the shoes of the boys," Harry Schell once said, "too much competition." Stirling Moss is in essential agreement: "Ferrari has too many drivers." One of the 1959 drivers, Cliff Allison, gave up a first-string job with Lotus to sign as a Ferrari reserve. "With Ferrari I will co-drive in the six sports-car races anyway," he explained. "As for the Grand Prix races (which is where the money is) I'll take my chances there." The inference: there would be an opening before long. There always was.

If any reasons can be ascribed for the rash of Ferrari fatalities, they are those outlined above, plus the fact that there are simply more Ferraris racing than any other marque. Essentially, Jaguar, Aston-Martin and Porsche race only in sports-car events, Vanwall, B.R.M. and Cooper only in Grands Prix. But Ferrari enters both with full teams. And only Ferrari goes on year after year.

To the Commendatore, numerical superiority is one way of hedging his bets. Another is to build such stamina into his cars that they will simply go on longer than anybody else's. For an Italian, Ferrari races with an almost Teutonic thoroughness. He prefers to overpower the opposition. He is not interested in a close race, narrowly won by one of his cars. A race like the final event of 1957 is much finer. Ferrari and Maserati were tied for the sports-car world championship, and now Ferrari won it: one, two, three, four.

Ferraris are so much stronger than other cars that they complete twice as many, or maybe five times as many laps in a season. So statistically it is only natural they can be expected to have more accidents. Ferrari has an Italian's love of beautiful things, and he alters the shape of his cars slightly, year after year, for purely aesthetic reasons. But, more importantly, they must finish the race. "If they are beautiful, but stop out on the circuit," says the Commendatore contemptuously, "people will say: 'What a pity, it was so beautiful.'" He could lose with honor, provided it did not happen too often, but he could never break down with honor.

Of all charges leveled against Ferrari, the two most ridiculous are that: 1) his cars go so fast they have passed beyond human ability to control; and 2) they are mechanically unsound.

All race cars, Ferraris included, go a good deal slower today than before the war, when the Hitler-sponsored Mercedes and Auto Unions were built two or three times larger, developed 600 horsepower, touched 210 miles an hour and killed drivers with astonishing regularity. Today's cars reach perhaps 175 on some circuits; they have beaten pre-war lap times because of superior brakes and suspension, not superior power, and they are certainly safer to drive. On many circuits, lap records have not even risen significantly. An Auto Union did 85.57 m.p.h. on the Nürburgring in 1937; twenty years later a Maserati won at 91.53. At Monte Carlo the lap record has been stuck at about sixty-eight m.p.h. for twenty-three years.

Race cars have always been driven on the ragged edge, or just beyond it, and, although the speed at which the ragged edge is encountered moves up or down with road conditions and engineering developments in the car, the fact of the ragged edge and of death lurking just beyond it does not change at all. Drivers have always moved as close as they could get and still get back alive; some moved too close and did not get back. Ferrari himself added nothing to this.

Men who had never driven anything faster than horses could not react fast enough in 1903 to keep from getting killed if something went wrong at fifty miles an hour. But man's tolerance for speed seems to improve as fast as his machines. Then as now race cars were driven until that speed was reached where the driver felt he was driving on glass; i.e. he could barely feel the road through the steering wheel. This is the limit of road adhesion, the ragged edge, the point at which cars have always been raced. On a given day a Ferrari driven at the ragged edge might be going a mile or two faster than other cars. This is not significant. If one is going to hit a tree, it makes very little difference whether one hits it at 125 or 130.

As for Ferraris being unsound mechanically, all drivers echo Stirling Moss who says: "Why do Ferraris win? Because they are the best car, that's why."

The central fact of Enzo Ferrari's life is certainly death. But not the death of drivers. It was the death in 1956 of his son, Alfredo (called Dino), of leukemia at the age of twenty-five. The boy had been bedridden part of every year from the age of sixteen. He kept asking his father why his body was so feeble when his mind was so alert, so eager to live. Ferrari had no answer. He had had much experience in death, but death had never been personal until now.

He had planned that the boy should be the greatest automotive engineer of all time, that his own name would be perpetuated by the greatness he had left behind in his son. This was his dream, all bound up in the son he worshiped and knew was going to die.

Ferrari has not accustomed himself to Dino's death. He keeps Dino's memory alive in every possible way, even ordering the boy's name embossed on the engine blocks of the cars.

Every day Ferrari visits Dino's tomb, locks himself inside and broods. Associates say he goes there when drivers are killed, too.

Ferrari's life has become his cars. He works twelve to fifteen hours a day, Sundays included. "A man has no need of entertainment, which only distracts him from his duty," he told me. "Better to concentrate on that duty. If a man has his duty, that is enough."

Ferrari is said to be wealthy, but all the money goes back into his cars. He lives with his wife and three dogs in a five-room apartment above the warehouse in Modena, and when he goes to the factory in Maranello he drives a Fiat. He keeps a blue Ferrari coupe, but uses it mainly for meeting clients. His two offices are starkly furnished. The only ornament in Maranello is a big, black-bordered picture of Dino. In Modena there is a smaller picture of Dino and, standing in a row on a shelf, six photos of the six contract drivers. The snapshots and the men are impermanent. Any errant breeze could blow one over, any minute error of judgment at 150 miles an hour.

It is evident that Ferrari lives only for the perfection of the racing automobile, the perfection of the breed. He is happiest when he is losing, faced by an immediate challenge, a problem to be got round. When it was suggested that there was nothing further for him to win he replied coldly: "There is always something to learn. One never stops learning. Particularly when one is losing. When one loses one knows what has to be done. When one wins one is never sure."

Why does he race? For glory, money, prestige?

"I race because it amuses me," he says. "Why else would a man dispute with race organizers, sponsors, drivers, the press? Why else would a man work twelve, fifteen hours a day? But if a man loves something enough, no sacrifice is too great."

It was not a fatal crash which caused Ferrari to quit going to races, but a driver with an unassailable lead in the 1936 Grand Prix de France, who ignored Ferrari's frantic signals to slow down, who went for the lap record instead, broke the engine and lost the race.

Now Ferrari tries to explain. "When a man has taken something, some material and, with his own two hands, transformed it into something else, he has made not a machine out of it, but a soul, a living, breathing soul. Well, then, he goes to a race and he hears this soul which he has created, hears it being mistreated, hears that it is not going right—" Ferrari places his hand over his heart and says, "It makes a man suffer, here. A man cannot bear such things. And so I do not go to races because I suffer too much there."

He is a tall, heavy man with iron-gray hair, a long nose, a thin, ascetic mouth and a limp handshake. His manner is austere.

One asks: "You mean you suffer too much for the car, not the driver?" and the answer comes: "The driver, too, of course."

The driver, Phil Hill, had been present for the interview. As we left the office, Hill said: "I never thought he would say such a thing in front of a driver. I guess we like to think he loves us because we are all so brave and drive so fast. But deep down I suppose all of us knew he cares more about his cars than he does about us."

6
FOOTBALL: THE OLD COLLEGE TRY

TO THE SPECTATOR NO SPORT HAS MORE SPECTACLE *than football. To the man on the field, no sport offers greater glory—or greater pain. He must be a man, for he spends much of his time literally on the field (with a number of other men on top of him). But when he breaks loose—ah! what can compare with that great moment? All life henceforward must of necessity run downhill, even the great personal moments, such as his marriage, the birth of his children, appointment to high office— do 100,000 screaming people attend these ceremonies with his name upon their lips? The great men and great moments clamor to be recorded. At one time Esquire polled 100 players and coaches of reputation and asked them to name the greatest game and play they ever saw and every answer was different! Here are stories from the more than quarter-century of Esquire. Here is the answer*

to the question "What moment is greater than the ball-carrier running the length of the field for a touchdown?" (The answer: "When a player runs the length of the field twice," or, "When two players run twice the length of the field," etc.) Here are Jim Thorpe, Red Grange, George Gipp—the man Rockne considered the greatest who ever fought for Notre Dame—and, of course, the Four Horsemen as observed firsthand by Grantland Rice. Here is a profile of Sammy Baugh, of whom it has been said that if there had been no such thing as the forward pass, he would have invented it. As with the chicken and the egg, it is difficult to tell which came first. Finally there is a description of the whole magnificent scene, a crisp, sunny Saturday in November, raccoon coats, pennants, pompoms and oh yes! the game supreme: Harvard vs. Yale. Pass the flask, here come the teams!

The Day Jim Thorpe Wrecked Army

by JIM THORPE

November 9, 1912, saw America's greatest athlete at his peak. The athlete, Jim Thorpe, who here called himself "Jim" as often as he called himself "I," told his story of the day he'll always remember—when he met Dwight Eisenhower and one of the best teams in Army history on a football field at West Point.

THERE WERE A LOT OF THRILLS FOR JIM in those days. Pop Warner, the coach back at Carlisle College, always said I could do more with a football than any man he had ever seen. But he also thought Jim was lazy, and he never knew how hard I was going to try. Maybe he was right. I played for fun. I always have, ever since I was a kid.

But I'll tell you one day when Jim was trying. We were at West Point back in 1912. We had won all our games that season except for a 0-0 tie with Washington and Jefferson. I felt badly after that game and went out. I almost missed the train back to Pennsylvania. Pop didn't like my going on the town. He said it would hurt the team; but we beat Syracuse the next Saturday, and then Pitt and Georgetown and Lehigh, and we were really keyed up for Army.

They were looking for us, too. They were the number-two team in the country, and they were out to stop me.

It was a rough game from the beginning. Big Powell, our fullback, got into a fight with an Army player and was thrown out of the game in the first quarter. Jim got mad then. We moved down close to their goal line and they gave me the ball. Three of the Army players hit me, one right after the other, and they were still hanging onto me when I dragged them across for a touchdown.

That slowed them up a little. We got the ball again. I threw some passes to our right halfback,

Arcasa, and we made another touchdown. Army was supposed to have a great defense that year, but they couldn't stop us. Their right halfback, Dwight Eisenhower, was hard to get away from, but mostly they just tried to bang you as you went through.

That third quarter was the most exciting one of my career. First their captain, Devore, was sent out for slugging. A few minutes later, Jim was out, too, on the ground and the left shoulder felt funny. I couldn't move for a minute. But I got back and those West Point people gave me a nice hand. That was when we opened up.

BIG JIM'S BIGGEST DAY by Gustav Rehberger
(Army's Defense Crumbled Under Thorpe's Smashing Runs as Carlisle Swamped the Cadets, 27 to 6.)

We lined up in kick formation on our own ten-yard line. I got the ball, started wide and cut back. Guys were diving at me and I was running as hard as I could with them bumping me and sliding off. All of a sudden, Jim was across. Arcasa was pounding me on the back and the crowd was on its feet, cheering; but one of our players was off-side. Well, we lined up once more and I did it again. Ninety-five yards this time. That was Jim's biggest thrill.

We finally beat them 27-6. Eisenhower made some good runs on that touchdown march of theirs. I got twenty-two of our points, and some pretty fair kicks. Some tackles, too. They made only four first downs all afternoon.

We lost a close game to Penn the next week and missed an undefeated season. I'd like to have had that one. It was my last year at school. But it didn't matter too much. The Army game is the one I'll always remember.

Red Grange: Houdini of the Gridiron

by PAUL GALLICO

HIS NAME WAS HAROLD GRANGE, HIS nickname "The Galloping Ghost," and he played for the University of Illinois during the lush years of the Great Golden Decade of Sports, 1924 and '25. He was a giant who stood out in an era of giants. His specialty was eluding capture.

Styles and tastes change in football. Now, the forward passer has become the hero because of the large slices of enemy territory that can be vanquished by the accuracy of his heaves. But there is still no thrill comparable to the one furnished by a fast, shifty, elusive runner who tucks that wind-jammed pig rind under his arm and swivel-hips his way through a broken field to climax his effort by crossing the goal line standing up.

The forward pass is a pretty precision play. It diddles the enemy in front of your eyes. It frustrates his heft, discombobulates his cerebration and unhinges his strategy. But there is nothing to thrill the human eye and heart like the sight of a runner, twisting, turning, evading, dodging the reaching talons of his foe, weaving his pattern of hairbreadth escape down the green, white-striped field, and leaving as debris in his wake the prone bodies of his rivals littering the field in futile heaps to mark the triumph of his passage.

For this is a mirror held up to life and symbolizes the daily hazards that surround us, our constant struggle to avoid the clutching fingers of defeat and wriggle through to victory.

In literature, the theater and moving pictures, the escape has a powerful hold upon the imagination of the average man. The story of dangers avoided and obstacles surmounted is one of which we never tire. The American game of football is such a story constantly enacted before our eyes. Its great protagonists are not easily forgotten.

And the greatest of these in modern memory was Red Grange because he was an expert in his peculiar art—carrying a football unscathed through eleven beefy and acrimonious parties all bent upon capturing him and slamming him to earth.

He was a flash in the pan or physical freak, an accident of sport. He was an artful dodger drilled and practiced in the techniques of avoiding tacklers, skilled in the employment of every artifice of mental and physical razzle-dazzle and bafflement.

He ran with a peculiar sliding motion and wonderfully timed weaving of the hips that always kept his body moving away from the point of impact. He flowed rather than ran, with variable speeds that functioned instinctively with direct relation to the problems facing him, now fast, now imperceptibly slower, then bursting forth brilliantly like a crescendo of music, always in a sweet antirhythm to the thundering phrases set up by the defense. He had likewise the co-ordination and ability to come to a full stop in midflight and change his course to start off at another tangent, destroying with one movement the rigid threats to his progress initiated by the enemy.

Grange engendered a new kind of hysteria in the football stadia, as time after time the reaching hands slid from his thighs, smothering arms bounced from his wriggling flanks and solid bodies hurled through the air at his darting form, missed their target by shocking margins and tumbled to earth in feckless and frustrated fury.

The stands would rise *en masse* to the rhythm of his running and the bodies of the spectators would move with his in a kind of a mad, mass dance of flight from seizure. A rising scream would be torn from their throats, a mounting crescendo of sound that rose pitch by pitch until the final magnificent climactic shout when the goal line was crossed, when it would subside into a long, trembling sigh of relief.

None of the 67,000 souls present will ever forget Grange's performance at Urbana, Illinois, on October 18, 1924, when Illinois defeated Michigan by the score of 39 to 14 and the Galloping Ghost scored five of Illinois' six touchdowns.

Four of these touchdowns came in the first period on runs of ninety-five yards, sixty-seven yards and two of fifty-six yards. The ninety-five-yard run occurred in the first fifteen seconds of play, for Grange picked up the kickoff on his own five-yard line and carried it through the entire Michigan team to score.

This first run itself was one of the greatest demonstrations of deception and elusiveness ever seen on a gridiron, for Grange crossed the field twice from sideline to sideline, ducking, slipping, shifting, evading and dodging before he broke into the clear.

It is this run that Rico Lebrun captured in his dynamic painting depicting one of the great moments of American sport. Disaster was always at Grange's heels for, unlike a run from scrimmage, the defending field was fluid. Tacklers who had missed him picked themselves up from the ground

and tried again; pockets of resistance formed themselves to trap him, walls of flesh grew in front of him to melt away, annihilated by his timing.

Naturally, Grange was not alone in his efforts. There is always the tendency, in singing the saga of such an individual, to neglect the contributions of his teammates. Ten other men were providing interference, diving at the legs of would-be tacklers, screening and protecting him.

But interference is in itself a hazard, for the leg of a fallen friend can trip you and bring about downfall as certainly as the effort of an enemy. But it was also a part of Grange's peculiar genius and fantastic athletic judgment that he could use those patterns of interference and not be trapped by them. He could size up a coming collision between his own interferer and a defender and swing away from it just enough to keep clear of reaching hands or a blocking pile of fallen beef. He would run behind friends as long as they were useful to him and cut away from them the moment they threatened to impede his progress.

We will see his like again, as long as the game is played and American boys play it. But that day has not come yet, and until another gridiron ghost appears to sway the stands with the magic of his rhythm and the sweet pattern of escape, it is pleasant to think back upon a master Houdini of the gridiron.

The Gipper Didn't Die

by AL STUMP

CLASSES CLOSED AT NOTRE DAME AS the word spread. Students knelt in the snow to pray outside the campus chapel. From early evening until three-thirty in the morning grieving South Bend townsfolk stood at the St. Joseph's Hospital gates. The next day, sports pages across the country bordered the story in black, and Knute Rockne, the tough-spirited Irish football coach, went into seclusion. "It's the first time I've seen him break," said an assistant. "Nobody can talk to him."

At the little mining town of Laurium, Michigan, mourners bucked eight-foot snowdrifts to follow a horse-drawn sled bearing the coffin to a cemetery on a hill overlooking Lake Superior. The state's leading citizens came to pay last respects. Fifteen years later, in 1935, a fifteen-foot monument to the fallen native son was dedicated in the memorial park named in his honor. Today a bronze plaque marks the spot:

"George Gipp, All-American, 1895-1920."

They've never forgotten the Gipper. He was one of the most dazzling, dramatic, idolized athletes of all time. His running, passing, kicking and generalship lifted an obscure Indiana university to fame. In thirty-two games the cleated fury scored fifty-eight touchdowns, riddling Army, Nebraska, Indiana, Purdue and Northwestern, and stunned thousands with his sixty-yard drop kicks. Fans didn't cheer when the Gipper left the game. They sat in silent awe.

"They felt any demonstration would be a kind of sacrilege," says Lawrence (Buck) Shaw, coach of the San Francisco Forty-Niners and a tackle on the unbeaten Gipp teams of 1919-'20. "It was eerie. I've never known another who got people that way."

Against Purdue in 1920 Gipp loafed through the first period without a long gain. A Boilermaker lineman made a sneering remark. On the first play of the second quarter Gipp fielded a punt with one hand, showed half a dozen tacklers a hip, pulled it away and bolted ninety-two yards for a touchdown. Minutes later, a trainer was sponging the unconscious Purdue forward. Gipp had knocked him kicking on another scoring gallop—this one for eighty yards.

In the 1919 Army game at West Point the burly Cadets piled up a 9-0 second-quarter lead before a glumly surprised crowd of 15,000, many of whom had traveled by special train from New York to see the Gipper. Then Gipp switched into his "wild horse" running style and carried twenty-two yards with three tacklers clinging to his pants. Another rush was good for fifteen. With the defense pulled in, he threw six straight passes, and completed every one of them, to a first down on Army's ten-yard line. As quarterback Joe Brandy barked signals, Gipp broke in with a sharp, "Pass me the ball!"

Rockne called it the fastest piece of thinking he ever saw. Gipp had caught a flash of the head linesman lifting his horn to signal the end of the first half—and had yelled at center Fred Larson to get a play legally in motion. As the horn sounded he took the ball and head down, shoulders heaving, bulled into Army's end zone. Notre Dame, 12-9 victor, returned to South Bend on a tide of publicity.

Once, against Nebraska, Gipp decided to give an unsung third-stringer the glory of a touchdown. Twice the boy was thrown for a loss; then Gipp told him, "Grab onto my belt—and don't let go."

A human tow truck, Gipp plunged from the ten-yard line and hauled the ball-carrier across. The boy didn't get his touchdown though—an alert field judge caught the trick and handed the Irish a fifteen-yard penalty.

Rockne won much of his reputation as a raconteur and humorist telling stories about Gipp on the banquet circuit. His favorite was about a 1919 game in which Gipp ran eighty yards but had the play called back on a penalty; broke away for sixty-eight yards but lost it on another whistle; ghosted seventy yards—and had the toot go again.

The Gipper came up to the referee and said quietly, "Let's get together on this to save time. From now on, give me one whistle to stop—and two to keep going."

Gipp was made for the sport. Six foot two, weighing 185 pounds, he had the build of a heavy-weight fighter, with sloping shoulders, a long, sinewy torso and immense thigh muscles. He could cover 100 yards in $10\frac{2}{5}$ seconds—in football pads. Combining brute force with tigerish speed and a cold, calculating approach to the game, he was the complete ballplayer. He was a defensive genius— in four years not one pass was completed in his ter-ritory. He perfected the trick of herding a runner toward the sidelines, then knocking him out of bounds with a diving shoulder block. A born show-man, he taunted rivals with drop-kicking demon-strations before the games.

"There was that time at Army that Gipp chal-lenged Cadet Red Reeder," recalls Ed (Slip) Madi-gan, another teammate. "They started at the twenty-yard line and backed up. At the forty, Reeder missed and dropped out. Gipp then called for four balls, booted two of them over one cross-bar, turned and slapped the others over the other goal—four perfect fifty-yard drop kicks!"

He was a great passer, but he loved best to run, and he ran when he could—and sometimes when he couldn't. Notre Dame brought a fifteen-game winning streak to the 1920 Indiana game and with only a few minutes left the Hoosiers led, 10-0. Gipp, on the bench with a dislocated shoulder, threw off his blanket. "I'm going in," he told Rockne.

"Not today," Rockne said.

Gipp stared at the fiery Norwegian, picked up his helmet and trotted out to the crowd's hysteri-cal roar. Rockne was a taskmaster, a martinet, a dictator; he could rule anybody else, but he couldn't handle Gipp.

Carrying tacklers on his back, hammering straight downfield, ignoring passes, Gipp went sixty yards in seven plays. On the final smash at

massed Indiana he tore his shoulder from its socket—but scored over the bodies of two groggy defenders.

Notre Dame won, 13-10.

Gipp was the leader of a cocky, fun-loving crew and a national celebrity, but nobody knew him well. He disliked personal publicity and rarely mixed socially with his mates. "An enigma that we never solved," wrote Father Charles O'Donnell, later president of the university. Gipp was a Con-gregational minister's son, and his upbringing had been Puritan, but he was too sophisticated for schoolboy pleasures. He spent his off-field time in gaming joints, and would bet $100 on the flip of a coin.

At Hullie and Mike's, a South Bend hangout, the Gipper ran racks in Kelly pool the way he sliced off-tackle. He paid his own way through Notre Dame on his card, billiards and dice win-nings. Players low on funds could always count on a loan from Gipp—in fact, he financed several boys through Notre Dame. Traveling professional sharks learned to avoid him like the cops; he could beat them with either the pool cue or the paste-boards.

He gambled on his football genius, too. Between the halves of Gipp's last Army game; with Notre Dame trailing 17-14, Rockne delivered one of his most impassioned locker-room speeches. When he was finished he looked around to note the effect. The Irish were fighting mad—all but Gipp, who was lounging against a door, bored.

"I don't suppose you have the slightest interest in this game," Rockne shot out.

"You're wrong there," Gipp said. "I've got five hundred bet on this game, Rock, and I don't in-tend to blow it."

It was Gipp's greatest game. He ran back a punt thirty yards, threw a forty-yard touchdown pass to Roger Kiley and kicked the extra point, then re-turned another punt fifty-five yards with eight sprawling Cadets in his wake. He gained 236 yards running and another ninety-six passing for a total of 332—more than the entire Army team. Notre Dame's 27-17 triumph "made" the young Rockne as a top-flight coach.

In high school Gipp had been a baseball star, a kid outfielder who got offers from both Chicago big-league clubs. He came to the Catholic university because he had friends there and because Notre Dame had a good baseball team. Rockne, then an ambitious chemistry professor and assistant coach to Jesse Harper, saw a rangy boy in street shoes kicking footballs fifty yards on the practice field behind Bronson Hall in the autumn of 1916. Rockne had to work on him to get him out for the freshman team. "He knew nothing of football," Rockne said later, "wasn't much interested in learning and let me know that he was doing it only as a favor."

Gipp first showed his Merriwell touch in the freshman game against Western State Normal. The score was tied in the final three minutes, and Gipp was ordered to punt. "What?" he yipped. "Settle for a tie?" Dropping back, he thumped a sixty-two-yard drop kick over the crossbar. It still stands as one of the longest in the collegiate record book.

Rockne then sent Gipp to masquerade as Army's All-American Elmer Oliphant in a practice game against the hard-jawed varsity. Crude as he was, Gipp tore eighty yards through the regulars. From then on he was the Gipper and the happy Rockne had a cross to bear.

Only special handling by Rockne, who became head coach in 1918, brought out the best in the indifferent, withdrawn Gipp. He was often in trouble with the Notre Dame faculty, and Rockne had to work on him to keep him in school. His academic major was law, but it didn't much interest him. In the spring of 1919 he was fired from college for missing too many classes. He asked for a special oral examination.

Rockne was the first to speak to Gipp when he emerged from the two-hour grilling. "How did it go, George?"

"Passed," Gipp said without emotion, and walked on.

It developed that he had surprised the professors with what he knew. He had a fine mind—when he wanted to use it—and he got a little help from fellow classmates. Father O'Donnell once told an after-dinner audience that in his class the student sitting on Gipp's right got 50 per cent of the lecture, the student on Gipp's left got 50 per cent—and between the two hero-worshipers George managed to get 100 per cent. But even the faculty was finally converted to the belief that the lean, silent ballplayer was as much a part of Notre Dame as the Golden Dome.

By Gipp's last season, the Notre Dame Athletic Association—once too poor to replace torn uniforms—had more game bids than it could fill, and the Irish were on their way as football's top box-office attraction. Of Gipp's last twenty games Notre Dame won nineteen, tied one, scored 506 points to 97 for the opposition.

With Gipp passing and running and kicking, the Irish took a 16-7 win over Nebraska, crushed Army, blanked Purdue, 28-0, and snatched a last-minute victory from Indiana. The shoulder injury kept Gipp benched for most of the Northwestern game, next-to-last on the schedule. But it was "Gipp Day" at South Bend and fans set up a steady roar: "Gipp! Gipp! Gipp!" Rockne reluctantly sent him in for a few plays.

Nobody knew that he had come from a sickbed to the stadium, and nobody could have guessed as he ran the team with his usual efficiency and threw a forty-five-yard touchdown pass. But when he left the game he looked haggard.

During a team banquet two weeks later, Buck Shaw saw Gipp leaving quietly before the final speeches. Shaw followed him to the Hotel Oliver lobby and asked, "What's wrong, George?"

"My throat," Gipp said as his hand went up to loosen his collar. "Feels sore."

Then it was only tonsillitis, but soon it was worse. For three weeks in the hospital Gipp battled steptococcic infection and pneumonia, while transfusions from his teammates prolonged his life. On December 14, 1920, he began to sink. Mrs. Matthew Gipp sat tearlessly at the bedside, as stoic as her son. A message came that Walter Camp had picked him as Notre Dame's first All-American. Rockne was bending over the bed when somebody blurted, "It must be tough for him to go."

Gipp heard. "What's tough about it?" he whispered. "I'm not afraid."

Then he made the famous request. "Some time when things are going wrong, when the breaks are beating the boys," he told Rockne, "tell them to go in and win one for the Gipper. I don't know where I'll be, but I'll know about it and I'll be happy."

The canny Knute used many tricks to fire a team—but this one only once. In 1928, strong Army had a weak Irish team on the run at the Polo Grounds. As the team got ready to leave the dressing room for the second half, Rockne gave them Gipp's message. The players wept openly. Notre Dame came out in an exalted mood—"a flivver that wrecked the caisson of Army," as West-brook Pegler put it. Fifty thousand watched wonderingly as Jack Chevigny plunged across for the first of two winning touchdowns, crying, "There's one for the Gipper!"

In a way they still win them for the Gipper, because Gipp is a bright light in Notre Dame's blazing background of victory. "He is still one of us, a very real part of our winning tradition," says Frank Leahy, coach of latter-day South Bend destroyers. "No—the Gipper didn't die."

The Four Horsemen by GRANTLAND RICE

ON AN OCTOBER AFTERNOON BACK IN 1923 I took my friend Brink Thorne, one of Yale's greatest football stars from the era of Frank Hinkey, across the bridge to see Army and Notre Dame meet in Brooklyn at Ebbets Field.

Brink and I had sideline passes where we could follow the play at close range up and down the field.

It was in this game that the name "the Four Horsemen" received its subconscious birth, to find life a year later. Brink and I were crouched along the sidelines around midfield when on a certain play Notre Dame's four flying backs came sweeping from the Rockne shift around Army's left end. The interference was headed by Harry Stuhldreher at quarter. Elmer Layden and Don Miller were part of the speedy compact attack with Jimmy Crowley carrying the ball. They had picked up twelve yards on the play before Crowley was finally forced out of bounds. But he was still moving at such high speed that he had to hurdle both Thorne and myself to keep from trampling us underfoot.

"We'd better move back," I said to Brink. "They are worse than a flock of wild horses on a stampede."

This thought was in my mind as I saw them swing into action against another strong Army team at the Polo Grounds a year later. I know I felt much safer up in the press box than I had felt along the sidelines in Brooklyn where the back of my neck was almost impaled on Crowley's flying cleats.

It was the start of the second period, with the score 0-0, Army dominating the earlier play, that Stuhldreher, Miller, Crowley and Layden came rushing out from the Notre Dame bench. There they were again—a backfield that ranged in weight from 155 to 163 pounds, an average displacement of 161 pounds, by many pounds the lightest in the starring ranks of football history.

What they lacked in mere poundage they more than made up for in speed, spirit, smartness and driving force.

They worked with a rhythm that was unbelievably beautiful to watch, whether or not football happens to be your favorite game. You might remember that in this game Army also had its share of stars, including Light Horse Harry Wilson, Wood, Garbisch, Farwick, Ellinger and several others who made up Coach John McEwan's able Cadet squad.

It was at the start of the second period, or just after the start, that the Four Horsemen earned their name. (And at the risk of explaining the obvious, perhaps I should add that the name derived from Vicente Blasco Ibáñez's *The Four Horsemen of the Apocalypse,* who, in turn, got *his* idea from the Revelation of St. John the Divine. The four horsemen were known as Famine, Pestilence, War and Death. These were the component ingredients of Notre Dame's famous backfield.)

After Wood's kick, Notre Dame had the ball on her twenty-yard line with Army goal eighty yards away.

It was here that the swift, striking stampede started. Crowley picked up fifteen yards on the first play. Layden and Miller added sixteen more. A pass from Stuhldreher to Crowley gathered twelve just before Don Miller's twenty-yard sprint carried him to Army's ten-yard line. Over cracked Layden for the first touchdown—eighty yards in just seven plays.

It should be noted here that "The Seven Mules" who made up Notre Dame's forward wall, headed by such stars as Adam Walsh and Rip Miller, deserved far greater credit than they received while playing brilliantly in the shadow of their famous backfield, a backfield that caught and held attention at every move through any game they played. These South Bend linemen, while not bulky in any way, were also smart, fast and alert, matching one of the best lines in the Army annals.

But when one had finished writing about "The Four Horsemen," there wasn't enough space left to give "The Seven Mules" the credit they deserved. Harry Stuhldreher, later head football coach at Wisconsin, was the team's directing general. Keen and alert, cool under heavy fire, he handled his fast attack superbly. Stuhldreher was also a hard-hitting blocker who rarely found trouble in meeting an opponent from thirty to fifty pounds heavier.

But, after all, Notre Dame's main asset was her backfield speed. In addition to Stuhldreher, Crowley, Miller and Layden were all exceptionally fast.

Crowley and Miller, the two halfbacks, started quickly, cut alertly, and picked up pace as they moved along.

It isn't often that you hear of a 162-pound fullback on a team called upon to meet the country's best. But that was Elmer Layden's weight. Layden was no fullback to hit the line like a bludgeon. He was more the rapier type that struck with dizzy swiftness and held his feet as well as any 200-pound fullback you might see in action. Layden had run the 100 in less than ten seconds, but it was his flash-lighting start that found even a half opening before it could ever close. Above all else he was the main point of danger against any hostile pass. Elmer, later football czar of the National Pro League, proved this against a powerful Stanford team in the Rose Bowl game of 1925. The star in this big Stanford squad was big, blond Ernie Nevers, one of the best of all time. He proved his place on the gridiron to such an extent that Pop Warner, the Stanford coach, placed him above Jim Thorpe as the all-time greatest.

Nevers, weighing 200 pounds, was the vital factor in the Stanford attack. But what both Pop Warner and Ernie Nevers overlooked was the speed and agility of Layden's forward pass defense.

No matter where Ernie Nevers threw the ball in that Rose Bowl tilt, there was Elmer Layden on the wing, under the ball and on his way for touchdown runs. Layden was a pass-intercepting centipede that sunny afternoon in Pasadena as he covered almost every square yard of the defensive field.

Notre Dame's Four Horsemen might not have been the best backfield that football has ever seen. They lacked the offensive power and crash of Rockne's 1930 squad that knew Carideo, Savoldi, Schwartz and Marty Brill. They may not have been as good as Notre Dame's 1943 outfit with Creighton Miller, a nephew of Don Miller's, Bob Kelly, Bertelli and several others—or the fast, powerful Army delegation of 1944 with Blanchard, Davis, Hall, Kenna and a few more. Not to overlook an old Carlisle avalanche that carried Thorpe, Calac and Guyon. But certainly, pound for pound, they stand alone. They had no need for any sheer power. If you consider such assets as speed, brains, heart, alertness and rhythm important, they had no equal.

After graduation Layden, Crowley and Stuhl-dreher all became successful coaches at Notre Dame, Fordham, Michigan State, Villanova, Wisconsin and Carnegie Tech, while Don Miller stuck to the law to find his place as a well-known judge in Cleveland.

In my roving day and time, looking back more than forty years, I have seen a thousand backfields, east and west, north and south, pass by in review. No member of the Four Horsemen could be named on an All-Time selection. But as a unit, as something to watch, they remain more vivid in memory than any of the others I have seen.

As some poet almost said—

"Of all the beautiful pictures that hang on memory's wall,
That one of the old Four Horsemen—it seemeth the top of all."

THE FOUR HORSEMEN by James Bingham

"Slingin' Sam," The Redskin Man

by VINCENT X. FLAHERTY

IN 1937, ON A MURKY JANUARY EVEning, George Preston Marshall, president of the Washington football Redskins, laundryman and cosmopolite of some renown, herded a group of cameramen and sports writers over to the old Washington Airport.

A lean greyhound of a football fellow with a bull whip for an arm was coming in, and his name was Sam (not Samuel) Adrian Baugh, late of Texas Christian University.

"Greater than Jim Thorpe; greater than Grange," Marshall was saying extravagantly. "The greatest football player of all time . . ."

Just then a great winged thing slid down out of the skies, leveled off and landed and, in another

minute, here she came, taxiing up to the gate of the airport. The great moment had arrived.

One passenger got out, yawned, stretched and descended the metal steps. Then came another, and another, and so on until fourteen or fifteen had passed in review. No Baugh. Marshall was wearing his chin for a bib.

Finally, after an unaccountably long pause, a towering young man in cowboy harnessings appeared in the oval opening, stooped low so as not to dislodge his enormous white hat, and stepped through the door. The high heel of his boot caught on the first step, but he righted himself and started scuffling down with no great show of assurance. He didn't look too well. His complexion was an unhappy kind of pale, pale green. But he managed to wring out a weak smile and proceed toward the group at the gate . . . boots, white hat, flowing silk handkerchief and all.

"Well, well," said Marshall, loping forward to extend the official welcome. "How was the trip?"

Baugh had no need to say anything. In fact, he didn't say anything. He underwent a facial manipulation wherein a large tumor shifted from one cheek to the other.

He spat: "Put-twang!" And it wasn't a clean shot at all; no finesse. It was easy to see he was a new hand at chewing. It was also easy to see he was a new hand at flying. The trip hadn't set too well.

Nevertheless, after Baugh shook hands all around, the delegation departed for the Occidental Restaurant on Pennsylvania Avenue. Baugh, with his stilted heels giving him a kind of forward list, rolled along like an old wagon on loose wheels as the reporters raked him with questions.

"Are you a cowboy?" one reporter asked.

"Nope!" said Baugh, and the group converged its gaze toward Marshall, who said nothing.

How did Baugh think he would do in professional football?

"I reckon I'll do all right," said Baugh.

Everything was "I reckon," which Baugh used in place of "I think," or "I suppose," or "I believe." Paradoxically enough, Baugh ate heartily that night.

But let's whoa down here and skip back a few days preceding Baugh's flight to the nation's capital. Marshall, having signed Baugh to a contract, was talking to his latest acquisition by long-distance telephone—Baugh being at home in Sweetwater, Texas.

As Marshall told it, the conversation ran like this:

Marshall: "Now Sam, be sure and go to a store and buy yourself a cowboy outfit. Get a big white hat, a pair of good boots, a cowboy shirt and all the trimmings."

Baugh: "But, Mr. Marshall, I've never worn those things in my life."

Marshall: "Never mind that. People up here are expecting to see a Texan when you get off the plane, and I want them to see a Texan. Understand?"

Baugh: "Okay, Mr. Marshall, and I'll mail you the bill."

Marshall, by the way, has heard the last line many times since.

Nevertheless, Baugh spread himself magnificently and carried out his masquerade to the letter. The tobacco-chewing can be chalked up to Baugh's ingenuity, for he is something of a showman himself.

But here's the pay-off: Baugh has been wearing cowboy togs ever since, he took to them that much. What's more, since brushed by the Marshall influence, he has become an expert horseman (he rode a little as a child) and good enough with the rope to appear in rodeos. Two days before he reported to the Redskins' training camp at San Diego Baugh appeared in a rodeo at Snyder Texas, where he roped and tied a calf in sixteen seconds. He was runner-up for first prize.

Moreover, Baugh's earnings bought him a 4000 acre ranch (Double Mountain Ranch) eighteen miles from Rotan, Texas, where he rides over an ample herd of white-faced cattle.

"We've got plenty of horses, hogs and chickens," Sammy tells you. "And we've got a swell farm—everything we need."

Baugh's actual earnings have never been published. Most guesses have been amiss one way or the other. It is safe to say he was the highest-paid performer in pro football during his career.

For the Western type of movie, Baugh is a natural. He is a lean, loose, home-on-the-range type with a cleanly chiseled face, scowling black eyes and a slow gliding gait. His six-feet-two-inch frame is accentuated by his cowboy boots; makes him look larger than his 182 pounds.

But Baugh seems almost too frail for football. Whenever he was tackled, every loyal Redskin fan looked on with apprehension lest a loud cracking sound herald the ruination of one of Sammy's painfully thin legs. But Sammy never got hurt. Ask him why, and he'll wink and tell you:

"I never let 'em get a good shot at me."

Baugh's apparent lack of ruggedness almost ended his football career before it really got under way. He was a good high-school player, starting out as an end at Temple High School in Temple, Texas. When his family moved to Sweetwater, Sammy, because of his passing ability, was switched to the backfield at Sweetwater High, where he was overshadowed by a youngster named Red Sheridan.

One afternoon before a game in Sheridan's senior year, the coach called the squad together in the dressing room.

"Boys," he said, "Francis Schmidt, the coach of Texas Christian, is here today to take a look at Red Sheridan. If Red goes good, he's going to get a scholarship—and, as we all know, Red deserves that scholarship.

"So," said the Sweetwater coach, "I want you boys to go out there today and make Red look good. I want you to block for him as you've never blocked before!"

With that, amid much elation, the Sweetwater players crowded around Sheridan, pledging their support.

To say that Red Sheridan had a bad time of it that afternoon is putting it charitably. Overanxious and nervous as he performed before the great Schmidt, Sheridan succeeded in doing everything wrong. He fumbled. His punts wobbled sloppily out of bounds after miserable flights of ten and fifteen yards.

So, at the close of the game, it called for some surprise and wonderment when Schmidt visited the Sweetwater dressing room. Upon entering, the Texas Christian coach strode to the rear of the room, past Sheridan, and straight to Sammy Baugh who was removing his jersey.

"Son," said Schmidt, "where in the world did you ever learn to throw a football like that?"

"Don't know," said Baugh. "I just throw 'em."

Baugh got the scholarship.

It wasn't a great while thereafter that Baugh became the star of Texas Christian's greatest teams. He passed Marquette into submission in the Cotton Bowl game of 1936 by a score of 16 to 6. And his punting was the paramount factor in T.C.U.'s Sugar Bowl victory over Louisiana State in 1937. The score was 3 to 2. Even so, Baugh failed to make any of the so-called "official" All-America teams.

So it was that Baugh was overlooked when the National Pro Football League held its annual draft meeting in New York. Baugh was passed up by every coach and owner except George Preston Marshall, who had heard of Baugh repeatedly and continuously from Amon Carter, the Fort Worth pub-lisher. When Baugh's name hit the draft list, bing! Marshall nailed him.

Baugh, at that time, was considered great shakes as a baseball player. The St. Louis Cardinals took him to their St. Petersburg training camp following his sensational freshman football season with the Redskins. Indeed, Frankie Frisch, then the manager of the Cardinals, all but succeeded in convincing the lean Texan his future was in baseball, not football.

Frisch might have succeeded had not Marshall hung on and talked louder, longer and lustier in favor of football.

With the Cardinals, Baugh launched himself in terrific style. He was a natural infielder; owned a great throwing arm and sure hands. He opened the training schedule in Florida by belting home runs over the far fences. It was a brief splash. Baugh suddenly collided with a siege of abject hitlessness, and the Cardinals shipped him to Columbus, and then Rochester. He quit cold when they tried to send him to Sacramento.

"I couldn't hit a change of pace with a bull fiddle," he now tells you. "When Mr. Marshall told me I had to choose between football and base-ball, I didn't have to think twice."

But what sport do you think Baugh prefers above all others—this tailor-made cowboy who was dropped out of the clouds upon Washington in that gray and murky January evening away back in 1937?

"You can take football and baseball," he'll tell you readily. "I'll take calf-roping. If I'm not doing the roping, there's nothing I love more than watching the top-notchers. . . . I can sit and watch them for hours. . . . That's the greatest sport!"

Throughout professional football, Baugh was known as one of the cleanest players in the game. He commanded the respect of all rival players and not once did an opposing man rough him unnecessarily. Why? Because Baugh, himself, always played the game that way.

Once, when a member of the Chicago Bears smashed into him and knocked him to the ground after the whistle had blown, the player, quite visibly embarrassed, helped Sammy to his feet, patted him on the back, cleared his throat and said:

"Sorry, Sammy—couldn't stop myself. But ain't this a helluva way to make a living?"

During his years of professional football, Baugh made an astonishing record. To start with, he introduced a new style of throwing which revolutionized the professional game.

Because of his superlative passing, most fans lose sight of the fact that Baugh was one of the greatest punters in the history of the pro game. He was also a master of the quick kick and it was not uncommon for him to boom them seventy-five yards from close formation.

"You, Charlie Malone," said Flaherty, speaking to his star end, "must run straight down and then buttonhook around in back of the defensive fullback.

"And you, Baugh," he said, turning to Baugh, "I want you to hit Malone right in the eye with that ball!"

"Just a minute, Coach," interrupted Baugh. "There's one thing I'd like to know."

"Yes," said Flaherty, patiently.

"Which eye?" asked Baugh.

Gridiron's Greatest Gallop

by TOM NORTON

WHAT WAS THE LONGEST RUN MADE IN a football game?

A quick leafing through the archives reveals a standard that will never be beaten—officially.

Yale's Wyllys Terry in the Wesleyan game, November 4, 1884, grabbed a pass from center while standing in punt formation, five yards behind his own goal line, ran the entire length of the then 110-yard gridiron, a distance of 115 yards in all.

Officially this lope of Terry's will always stand as tops because football's graybeards who promulgate the rules subsequently decreed that from then on no player would be credited in the records with a run greater than 100 yards, the present length of the field, no matter from where he started his gallop.

But remember, we started this discussion not with a query on the longest official run, but with the longest lope ever made in a football game.

Perhaps one of the most celebrated and best-known gallops is the zany credited to Snooks Dowd of Lehigh University, Bethlehem, Pennsylvania, against their traditional rivals, Lafayette College of Easton, in the final game of 1918.

The score was 10-0 in favor of Lehigh when, as the story goes, the play called for Dowd to circle the end. Snooks started a wide sweep, but a Lafayette tackle broke through the line, causing Dowd to circle back five yards and head for the opposite side line.

A charging rival end shifted the Lehigh runner's course backward another five yards, and when Dowd reached the side stripe, he reversed his field, starting in the opposite direction.

By this time, the entire Lafayette team had sifted through and, in evading tacklers, Snooks' sense of direction became confused and he headed toward his own goal.

Pursued by the entire remaining twenty-one players—his own men trying to haul him down, the Lafayetters intent on faking plunges to keep him going on his wrong-way run—Dowd crossed his own goal line and, just as he was about to down the ball, realized his error. He then ran back ten yards to his own end zone, shook his pursuers, circled the goal post and once more headed in the right direction.

On the way to the Promised Land, he picked up interference who safely convoyed him to pay dirt, and a 17-0 victory, after an exhausting 210-yard run.

But the *Globe*, of Bethlehem, Pennsylvania, deflates the story in this description of the action of the second half of the Lafayette-Lehigh annual of 1918:

"From the twenty-yard line Hoffman kicked to midfield. Dowd came racing toward the ball, picked it out of the air while on a dead run and started for the right side of the field. The Lafayette defense came sweeping down on him and it looked as though they would force him out of bounds, the fleet-footed runner being within a foot of crossing the side line. Stopping short, Dowd cut in toward the opposite side of the field, warding off what would-be tacklers did come near reaching him, and, after a sensational exhibition of broken field running, covered the distance of fifty yards to place the ball behind Lafayette's goal line."

So with our illusions shattered on a story that, for years, has been bandied about as solemn truth, let's delve into the musty past and see what gives.

The scene—the Texas A & M versus Louisiana State University game, at Baton Rouge, Louisiana.

The time—1907. Texas A & M quarterback, Vincent "Choc" Kelley moves back to his own forty-five yard line for what looks like a side-line play. But when Kelley receives the pigskin, he heads laterally for the opposite direction. By the time he reaches the boundary he's surrounded by L.S.U. men and reverses his field.

Across the gridiron he runs, almost in a straight line, barely evading the outstretched hands that clutch at him on the way. Choc reaches the side line from whence he made his start, but forward progress is again blocked and he wheels and heads across the field for the opposite side.

By now the gridiron around the forty-five yard stripe is a mass of surging players, the L.S.U. lads trying to haul down the elusive Kelley, the Texas boys trying mightily to prevent such an occurrence.

A plunging drive by a rival almost upsets Choc as he reaches the side stripe for the third time. A knot of L.S.U.-ers stop his forward direction and for the fourth time he crosses diagonally to his original starting point.

Kelley's blockers have gone to work now, and those rivals not grounded are chasing the fleet-footed Texan in complete exhaustion.

Choc sees a clearing and this time wheels straight ahead, scooting the remaining fifty-five yards to a TD and covering a total of 245 yards on the play.

And so Choc Kelley's run of 245 yards for Texas A & M against L.S.U. is the longest trek on a football field?

Wait a minute!

We're witnessing a contest by two semipro teams, one of which was the Ironwood Polar Bears of Ironwood, Michigan. They were playing a team from Minneapolis in 1939:

The Polar Bears' backfield man, Harry Newby, receives the hog hide on his own twenty-seven-yard stripe, around ten yards in from the right side line. Harry slants off tackle, bearing left toward the opposite side in an oblique direction, and gets as far as his thirty-nine-yard marker where a group of rival players force him to turn backward, in the direction of the far side line to his twenty-four-yard stripe.

From there, for a second time now, Newby starts forward, with a slanting run across the width of the battleground, and this time he gets as far as his forty-seven-yard line when he's compelled to retreat a second time over almost the identical space that he has just traveled, back to his sixteen-yard marker.

Once more he circles toward his left and the right side of the field and advances now to the twenty-five-yard line. There, for the third time, he is forced back toward his own goal line.

About eighteen yards in from the right side line and sixteen yards from the Polar Bears' own goal, he heads right again, and turning in a short arc

five yards from the edge of the field, heads for the rival goal.

By now the opposition's strength is so spent Harry has an apparently clear field and legs it down the gridiron, scampering along five yards in from the side line to his rival's ten.

At the ten-yard line, Newby cuts to his left and heads directly for his opponent's goal, where he completes what is probably the longest run—265 yards—in the history of football.

Undefeated and Undetected

by LLOYD MANN

As the autumn of 1941 punted and plunged its way through the sports columns, bewildered stockbroker Morris Newburger of Newburger, Loeb & Company, New York, pondered on how the exploits of such teams as Slippery Rock, for example, rated weekly coverage in the local press. Where were these obscure schools—and how many people were there in New York who cared what happened to their football teams?

The dilemma so tortured his imagination that one frosty Saturday evening he rose from his table at the Bird and Bottle at Garrison, New York, and telephoned the sports departments of the New York *Times* and the *Herald Tribune*. He would like to report, he reported, that Plainfield Teachers in New Jersey—an institution as authentic as the School of Hard Knocks—had just walloped the equally mythical Scott by a score of 12 to 0. Furthermore, Plainfield's offense had been sparked by a triple-threat Chinese quarterback named Johnny Chung, the "Celestial Comet," who had darted all over the field like a chickaree.

Unsuspecting and swamped with scores from all over the country, the papers swallowed the story, cleats and all, and printed it. It was a delight to Newburger to pick up the New York *Times* the next morning and skip airily from the war in Europe, to the account of Plainfield Teachers' smashing victory over Scott, complete with the line-ups which included Morris Newburger at right tackle for the Teachers and a smattering of his business partners and relatives in other key spots.

The newspaper accounts the next week were even better. Plainfield Teachers, inspired by Johnny Chung, bowled over Chesterton 24 to 0. Newburger was still at right tackle, fighting alongside his senior partner and his uncle. But aside from Johnny Chung—who, by the way, consumed a crock of rice between halves and came out for the kickoff like a wildcat—there were other interesting features of the Teachers' attack. Most unusual was coach Ralph "Hurry Up" Hoblitzel's new "W" formation in which the ends faced the backs and generally accounted for a fifth man in the backfield. It was sensational, so the papers commented, and opened great holes for lightning, snake-hipped Chung, the Celestial Comet. Herbert Allan of the New York *Post* warned that if Hoblitzel didn't watch out, Chiang Kai-shek would grab Chung for his own offensive. Within a week, Chung's name came up for more man-in-the-street comment than all the Chinese generals combined.

Succeeding weeks brought triumphs over such fantastic opposition as Winona, 27 to 3 (the only points ever scored against the Teachers); Randolph Tech, 35 to 0; Ingersoll, 13 to 0 (Chung scored on a forty-seven-yard run for the first tally and dragged five tacklers with him for the second); St. Joseph's, 6 to 0. There remained only games with Appalachian Tech and Harmony Teachers.

The *Times* as well as the *Tribune* listed Plainfield Teachers among the unbeaten, untied teams in the country. The Monday morning quarterbacks spent a great many happy hours comparing Chung's playing with that of his brothers in the better-publicized and larger Eastern colleges, and there was considerable speculation as to which of the pro teams would be lucky enough to sign him up.

By this time Newburger had fallen in love with his own creation and was going all out. His team had gained a reputation beyond his wildest expectations and he now had an accomplice in Philadelphia who fed the Philadelphia *Record* with stories of Plainfield Teachers and the Celestial Comet. In New York, Newburger installed a one-way telephone through which a character known as Jerry Croyden, the publicity agent for the Plainfield Teachers Athletic Association, fed juicy morsels to the press. Releases went out on the Athletic Association's new stationery, usually date-lined Newark, New Jersey, and bearing a telephone number that didn't work for incoming calls. On outgoing calls, the agent's voice resembled that of right-tackle Morris Newburger.

At this point Johnny Chung's meteoric career blew up in his face. The story was too good to keep within a small group. It passed from office to office, from luncheon table to luncheon table, and from club to club, and the weekly accounts of the Plainfield Teachers' games had an ever-growing and always eager group of readers who enjoyed the stories all the more because they happened to be in on the hoax. It was inevitable that somebody would blab to an editor of *Time* Magazine; and *Time* takes delight in exposing hoaxes. When Newburger got wind of the treachery, he rushed, headguard in hand, to *Time*'s offices. Please, he begged, let Plainfield Teachers finish her season unbeaten and head for the grand finale—the Blackboard Bowl championship. He'd give *Time* the advance scores right then if it wanted them.

But *Time* was adamant. Disconsolate, right-tackle Newburger shuffled back to the bench. But he fired one last release. It announced that so many of Teachers' stars, including Johnny Chung, had flunked their exams and become ineligible for athletics that heartbroken "Hurry Up" Hoblitzel had decided to cancel the remaining games with Appalachian Tech and Harmony Teachers.

Even trusting sports writers suspected that one. The *Tribune*'s ferret-minded Caswell Adams found the genuine Chamber of Commerce of New Jersey's genuine city of Plainfield ignorant of any such institution as Plainfield Teachers. Then, behind perfect blocking by the telephone company, he overtook Newburger in his office and brought him down viciously on top of his one-way telephone, his athletic association stationery and a bundle of releases on the Blackboard Bowl game. At the bottom of the heap lay the ephemeral Celestial Comet, never to rise again. At that very moment on the newsstands, *Time* Magazine was serving its scoop to an astounded and delighted public. The *Tribune* took time out to laugh, but the stately *Times* remained mum.

December 28, 1958: The Colts Win the Pro Football Championship Defeating the Giants in a Sudden-Death Overtime

The men at work were beef trusts.
Knots bulged behind their necks.
Their thighs seemed like the thighs of elephants.
Within the grotesque press of pads and helmets,
they surged and butted one another,
as mercenaries trained to an ordered rage,
and from their grossness this cool winter day
the beef trusts spun
almost a dance.

The Game Supreme

"Gentlemen, you are about to play football for Yale against Harvard. Never in your lives will you do anything so important."—T. A. D. Jones

NOW IN NOVEMBER THERE ARE THOSE, as there have been in all the other Novembers but nine since 1875, who will give exuberant expression to their approval of what a Yale football coach named "Tad" Jones told his squad on a long-vanished Saturday afternoon. This November, the moment of truth occurs on the nineteenth, and at Harvard Stadium, where, in the number of some 40,000 or more, at six dollars a seat, these people will gather in anything but solemn conclave to observe the seventy-seventh Harvard and Yale football game, or, as they so cozily refer to it, The Game. Their brevity is understandable. For this—come Army-Navy, come the Baltimore Colts versus the New York Giants; come the World Series, come Forest Hills; come, for that matter, all the Kentucky Derbies ever run—this, Harvard and Yale, remains, as it has for so many aristocratic autumns, the most rejuvenating and, at once, the most nostalgic; the most patrician yet the friendliest; the most ceremonious and, at the same time, the least ostentatious; the most vigorous and yet the most venerable; the best-bred as well as the most uninhibited; the sloppiest but nevertheless the most properly attired; and, by all odds, the most cheerful major sports event in the United States. What's more, it could hardly be more clannish, what with such tribal rites as accommodations for the weekend at the Ritz in Boston being handed down from generation to generation; such folkways as the buxom nude in the oil painting on the street floor of Locke-Ober's restaurant being draped with a mourning sash when Harvard loses at Cambridge; such liturgy (when The Game's at New Haven) as a legendary Harvard figure named Rinehart being paged incessantly in the lobby of the Taft ("Call for Mr. Rinehart!"), though everybody is aware that there will never, never be any response; and such pageantry as thousands upon thousands of grown men derisively waving white handkerchiefs at thousands of other grown men, different only in that *their* champion is being vanquished. And as if all this litany were not enough, there is a negative kind of tribal rite, too, for never yet, neither at the Stadium nor at the Yale Bowl, have the proceedings been profaned by the presence of a drum majorette—though, truth to tell, there *was* a time, albeit a long time ago—when Yale had a woman as co-coach.

By noon on the day of The Game, Harvard ("They have a college in Cambridge, about four miles from Boston," wrote Patrick McRoberts in 1775, "where divinity, mathematics, philosophy, and the Oriental languages are taught") and the Square beside which it stands (still a formidable fortress against the assaults of reconstruction, with the kiosk erect as ever, and Leavitt & Pierce's tobacco shop bereft only of the pool tables in the back room)—by noon on November the nineteenth these ageless streets will be teeming with people who have come from all over the East, and, in many instances, from the South and Midwest, for what, when you come right down to it, is nothing so much as it is a family reunion. Inside the undergraduate clubs (all but one of which—the august Porcellian—now admit women on the day of The Game) there will be drinks and fortifying food, while, outside, there will be lovely vintage cars, most of them taken from their garages just for this day of days.

Across the Charles River, on Soldier's Field, which encompasses the Stadium, there will be class-reunion luncheons in the indoor baseball cage or in tents hard by and, all about, there will be picnics, with huge Thermoses of Martinis and charcoal grills that send wisps of smoke up against the horizon. And then, very, very suddenly, there will be the sound of distant drums and of all the urgent anthems, all the flaring fight songs, that keep coming back, November after November, to remind Old Crimsons and Blues that they do indeed want victory today. And now, with the bands' brassy brayings, the air of suppressed excitement around the Square finds release and, almost as if it were a single person, the crowd begins gathering up its blankets and inching its way down Boylston Street, past the Harvard houses, past the boathouse, across Larz Anderson Bridge, past scullers on the river below, past the Boston skyline in the distance to the left, past hawkers with everything from favorite colors to (or so they say) fifty-yard-line seats, past the Business School, and, finally, through the gates of Soldier's Field, an interminable procession made a splash of color by the yellow of its chrysanthemums and the blue and crimson of its feathers and pennants.

So this, then, is part of The Game, too—as much a part of it as, say, the noble acts of running back a punt or throwing a forward pass or tackling a ball-carrier. And there is this about the spectators—their appearance: the men in venerable coonskins or casual camel's-hairs or handsome astrakhan-collared coats, in Inverness capes or parkas, in bowlers or fur trappers' caps or hatless; and most of them looking like something straight out of Abercrombie & Fitch. As for the women, especially the older ones, they rather remind one of people one's seen in *Vogue* or *Bazaar* or perhaps *Town & Country,* people pictured at field trials or hunt breakfasts or merely lounging beside some rustic fence. Which is not surprising, because one probably *did* see them in *Vogue* or *Harper's Bazaar* or *Town & Country.* They have that country look, but with a transcendent chic that, on safari, would tempt a white hunter to serve two masters. But though they are Hemingwayish women, their voices, like Daisy Buchanan's in *The Great Gatsby,* are "full of money." As for the girls, their cheeks flushed and their eyes moist from the sting of the cold air, they are, so overwhelmingly many of them, ineffably, heartbreakingly lovely, stabbing reminders that once upon other November afternoons these others, the older women, must have been exquisite too. Then, of course, there are the college boys, and, as James Barnes phrased it, "You can always tell a Harvard man, but you can't tell him much,"

which, as far as that goes, is not untrue of Yale either. And, naturally, there are little boys, too, so many of them being initiated, here and now, into the faith of their fathers. These, of course, are not *all* the people at The Game, but they are nevertheless the ones—the rich and the renowned, the highborn and the handsome, the chic and the charming, the young and the beautiful—who lend the special aura that exists at no other large sports event in this country.

And then, after one has crossed Soldier's Field and entered the Stadium, there is the pause at the foot of the stairs while one gazes up into the sea of faces and realizes, a little smugly, a little snobbishly, that these are one's people, one's own kind and, because classes are seated together, one's own generation. And this, the sense of security and of well-being, is an important part of The Game, too. After all, you went to Harvard (or Yale), didn't you? And that's the best, the very best, isn't it?

So all this is The Game—this, and the bright bunting, and the drone of planes silvery in the sunlight, and, of course, the cheers; the (straight out

Brekeke-kex, koax, koax . . .

of Aristophanes' *Frogs,* which is even more ancient than The Game itself) exploding like a tattoo from the Yale stands, and then in the impassioned exhortation from across the field:

Har . . . vard Har . . . vard
Har . . . vard
Rah Rah Rah Rah Rah Rah
Rah Rah
Fight Team Fight

which, as seems no more than appropriate for the occasion, is the oldest of all football cheers. And the songs, too, which are as fragrant and familiar as, somewhat more personal than, a Christmas carol:

Good night, poor Harvard
Harvard, Good night!
We've got your number,
You're high as—a kite;

and:

March, march on down the field
Fighting for Eli,
Break through the crimson line,
Their strength to defy;

which, once upon a vagabond time, used to be directed by a leader of the Yale band named Hubert

Prior Vallee and which afterward became his theme song when he was at the Heigh-Ho Club, where all the young beauties and their beaux used to go dancing after The Game at the Bowl. And:

Bingo, Bingo,
Bingo, Bingo, Bingo, that's the lingo.
Eli is bound to win. . . .

and:

Bull-dog! Bull-dog! Bow, wow, wow
Eli Yale,—
Bull-dog! Bull-dog! Bow, wow, wow
Our team can never fail . . .

both of which, for all one knows, may well be the two most enduring numbers ever written by a Yale graduate, class of 1913, named Cole Porter.

And then, from the other side of the Stadium:

With Crimson in triumph flashing
'Mid the strains of victory,
Poor Eli's hopes we are dashing
Into blue obscurity . . .

or:

Ten thousand men of Harvard want vict'ry today. . . .

It is there, this special magic, in the teams huddling, and in the hush as the massed bands play "The Star-Spangled Banner," and in the sight of the two teams lined up just before what an Old Crimson named Ben Beale calls "that pumping moment," the suffocating, more-than-merely-a-momentary moment when the whistle pierces the whole world and penetrates every part of our being, and, finally, it is there in a cyclone of a roar from some 40,000 throats as toe meets ball and sends it spiraling into the sanctified sky. So this, then, is it—for "Veritas" or "For God, for country, and for Yale."

"What" (asked the late Bill Cunningham, who was a Dartmouth man) "does Harvard versus Yale mean? . . . It's not a game; it's a rite. It's not a contest, but a sort of reaffirmation of faith. . . . It is the same thing that makes England revered among nations, the words of Confucius endeared of philosophers, the Ten Commandments still quoted in most modern courtrooms. In brief, it's age, tradition, consistent performance. . . . And when it's over, you'll see Harvard men and Yale men departing together, chaffing each other good-humoredly, but under it all and over it all, the very best of loyal friends. And that's perhaps the finest thing that Harvard versus Yale means. It's the one thing that all other colleges envy and that none of them has—a gallant, a worthy, a hell-roaring rival who, for it all, is a sincere, a loyal, a till-death-do-us-part friend.

"Harvard versus Yale?

"It's Harvard and Yale!"

This beautiful friendship began at Hamilton Park in New Haven on November 13, 1875, when a crowd of around 1700 (150 of whom were Harvard students) paid fifty cents apiece to watch fifteen representatives of each college engage in ninety minutes of a style of football that would seem hideously primitive by modern standards. Harvard won, four goals to nothing, under a scoring system whereby not touchdowns but only the goals resulting from them counted. Although Yale had such stars in the early years as Pa Corbin, Bum McLung and the two all-time All-Americans, Frank Hinkey and the fabled Pudge Heffelfinger, far and away the most influential figure on the New Haven football scene was Walter Camp of the class of 1880. He played first-string for six years and was twice captain despite the fact that he was so wee of stature that when the Harvard captain saw him for the first time, he complained, "You're not going to let that child play, are you?" whereupon the Yale leader stiffened and said, "Mind your words! He may be small, but he's all spirit and whipcord." After graduating, Camp, who was to become the architect of modern football and whose annual All-America selections were to be accepted as holy writ, spent some time coaching Yale. On days when he found himself unable to get away from his business, his wife would go to the field and relay his instructions to the captain. After practice, which she followed closely, she would inform her husband of her observations. Indeed, her contributions were so substantial (she participated in strategy discussions, originated plays and recommended players whom she felt had been overlooked) that Pa Corbin, the captain of the formidable 1888 team, recognized them by designating her co-coach.

There were stars at Harvard, too, among them Ben Dibblee, Bernie Trafford and Marshall Newell, but none of them—nor none of the Yale galaxy either—seems so remarkable in retrospect as William H. Lewis, the center for Harvard in 1892 and '93. After graduation from Amherst, where he captained the football team, Lewis, the son of slaves, attended Harvard Law School, which, in that era, permitted graduate students to participate in varsity athletics. Lewis' resilience was astonishing. Though knocked insensible four times against Yale in '93, he finished the game and was elected acting captain for the following week's encounter with Pennsylvania, thus becoming the first Negro ever to lead an Ivy League team—fifty-three years, in fact, before Levi Jackson was to be privileged to sit on the Yale Fence. In a warming and wonderful way, Lewis' recognition was a garland on the grave of Harvard president Edward Everett, who, some forty-five years earlier, had summarily stifled undergraduate objections to the college's accepting a Negro applicant. "If this boy passes the examinations," he decreed, "he will be admitted; and if the white students choose to withdraw, all the income of the college will be devoted to his education." Yale's indoctrination was to take somewhat longer. When, at a banquet given for both teams after The Game in 1892, the lineman against whom Lewis had played all afternoon discovered that he was expected to sit next to the Harvard center, he announced that he had no intention of eating with "any damn nigger," whereupon, with a muted and massive dignity, Lewis arose and moved down the table to a place beside a teammate. After finishing law school, Lewis, who was one of the first Negroes ever admitted to the American Bar Association and a defense attorney of exceptional skills, served as Harvard line coach for fifteen years.

Though he must have brooded over the regularity with which Yale won The Game during his playing and coaching days, Lewis was not to be without considerable cause for pride, for it was a lineman whom he had coached, Percy D. Haughton, '99, who, when he became head coach in 1908, proceeded to mold Harvard into a devastating football power. Of the twenty-eight games played between the two teams up to that point, Yale had won twenty, lost five and tied three. In contrast, during Haughton's tenure, which lasted through the 1916 season, when the series was interrupted by the war, Harvard won five, lost two, and tied two. His most impressive single achievement was prob-

ably the 41-0 victory over Yale in 1915, a game, by the way, in which Yale, having recovered a fumble, seemed on the way to a touchdown until a bad pass from center abruptly returned the ball to Harvard. Shaking with rage, Wilson, the Yale captain, confronted the hapless center. "You idiot!" he screamed. "Can't you remember the signals?" "I can't even keep track of the touchdowns," said the center.

Students of the more intricate points of football are disposed to rank Haughton as one of the three or four ablest coaches of all time. He converted a game that was largely a matter of brawn into one of speed, deception and imagination, doing so by a relentless insistence upon precision, an unremitting emphasis on fundamentals, and, perhaps most important, an utterly merciless taskmastership. When, for example, he was developing his hidden-ball plays, Haughton, who was never addressed as anything but "Sir" or "Mr. Haughton," even by such authentic All-Americans as Ned Mahan, Sam Felton, Tack Hardwick, Charlie Brickley and Stan Pennock, invited several players to his summer home on Block Island. He began by asking a group of children to try to discover which player had the ball after it had been snapped back from center. But instead of being pleased that there wasn't a single correct answer, he paced moodily back and forth. Finally, he summoned his Chesapeake retriever and for the next hour or so he watched happily as, on every pass from center, the dog would race in pursuit of everyone but the ball-carrier. Haughton's quest for perfection made him sparing in his praise and caustic in his criticism. At a dinner in the Taft Hotel after the opening of the Yale Bowl in 1914, the Harvard players, who had won 36-0, chuckled when he began his speech by remarking, "Well, boys, I said a lot of mean, cutting things to you this season, didn't I?" Then while they waited for the apology that seemed inevitable, he roared, "Well, God damn it, I meant every damn one of them!" Even such a paragon of a player as Tack Hardwick was not above reproach. "There, you All-American end!" he said one day, thrusting forward a photograph that showed Hardwick guilty of one of his rare lapses in judgment. "Here, take it. Stick it over your desk. Study it every hour. That'll show you how great

THE GAME SUPREME 157

you are!" Yet there was never any malice, only the everlasting drive for perfection. Years later, when Haughton was dead and a memorial to him had been erected outside Dillon Field House on Soldier's Field, Hardwick, whenever he approached it on his way into the Stadium on the day of a game, would slacken his pace, gaze up at the likeness and, his eyes brimming with tears, reverentially tip his bowler.

Haughton was gone by 1920, but the system he had installed at Harvard had resulted in the most powerful college team in the country. At any rate, on New Year's Day that year, Harvard, coached by Bob Fisher, defeated Oregon in the Rose Bowl. In view of that, it was little wonder that tickets for The Game that fall were in such demand ($100 a pair was the going price) that, on the morning of November 20, men refused to remove their coat jackets in New Haven barbershops lest their tickets be appropriated by some stranger. Harvard, besides a nucleus of eight men who played in the Rose Bowl, had two brilliant sophomores—a dazzling quarterback named Charlie Buell and a great halfback named George Owen, who later became, with the Boston Bruins, one of the first Americans ever to play in the National Hockey League. Harvard prevailed that afternoon, as, indeed, it was to continue to prevail until 1923, by which time Owen and Buell had departed.

There are those who maintain that Charlie Buell was the brainiest quarterback in Harvard annals, and, what's more, they can provide documentation. In 1921, for example, when a comparatively mediocre Harvard team met undefeated Yale, Buell lulled the Blues into a false sense of security by signaling for fair catches on all Mal Aldrich's prodigious punts during the first forty-minutes. Then, with a minute to go in the third quarter and with Harvard behind 3-0, Buell flabbergasted the defense by electing to run back an Aldrich kick. He went forty-five yards to Yale's eleven-yard line before being brought down. When the pile-up was unscrambled, he was lying at the bottom of it, inert. "Charlie, are you hurt?" Tom Thorp, the umpire, asked him. "Hell, no," said Buell, his eyes still closed, "but I'm damned disappointed." Then, as is customary under such circumstances, Thorp asked him what the score was.

"Yale three, Harvard nothing," said Buell, getting to his feet, "but it won't stay that way very long." Nor did it, for on the third play of the fourth quarter Owen plunged across for what turned out to be the winning touchdown. This was the game in which Aldrich, the Yale captain, decided to make good use of referee "Tiny" Maxwell, a genial behemoth of a man who stuttered when excited. Receiving the pass from center, Aldrich, instead of following his own blockers, shielded himself behind Maxwell's massive figure and ran thirty yards before a Harvard player managed to get between him and the referee. Maxwell grinned sheepishly as the Harvard team glared at him, but then, recovering his composure, he blew his whistle and raised his hand. "T-t-t-time out, boys," he said, "while I g-g-get my bl-bl-blue j-j-jersey."

Somehow, in 1921, this did not seem entirely inappropriate, for the nonsense of the twenties was as evident in The Game as it was in everything else that was festive. There was, for instance, the 1923 game at the Stadium, when Yale partisans created a new and presumably enduring American folkway by tearing down the goal posts. Then there was the case, peripheral though it be, of the Hollywood producer who used to have, at a staggering cost, a play-by-play account of The Game relayed to him by telephone and, simultaneously, amplified for the enlightenment of his guests, all of whom were somewhat awed by his old-school-tie devotion. It wasn't until he died and his obituaries appeared that people discovered that he had never progressed beyond the second year in high school. On the other hand, though, there were those millionaires, authentic Old Blues or Crimsons, who considered it unthinkable not to hire a private Pullman to transport their friends to The Game. And it goes almost without saying that when the locale was New Haven, no self-respecting Harvard was without *its* own Pullman. And then, of course, once in New Haven there were those crazy open trolleys that went down to the Bowl, spilling people all over the place. And as for what went on the nights before The Game in the speak-easies of Boston or New York, in Harvard Clubs across the country and in retreats like the Racquet Club—the wagers, the disputes, the memories of games past. And as for the wild things that went on in the twenties among the college boys and the sweet young things from Vassar and Bryn Mawr and the like, there was a song of the era that sort of captured the general idea. It was called "Was I?" and the refrain went something like this: "Was I drunk? Was he handsome? Did my ma give me hell?"

Tickets were at such a premium in those years that eventually Harvard, in an effort to thwart the scalpers, originated its so-called Black List, whereby ticket privileges would be denied any undergraduate or alumnus who could be proved guilty of having sold any of his allotment at a profit. Harvard also had its "personal use" clause, which compelled an applicant to agree in writing that he, personally, would occupy one of his two seats. And even then there weren't enough tickets to go around. One year, in fact, the Harvard and Yale Athletic Associations had to refund more than a quarter of a million dollars to applicants whom they could not accommodate.

But it was fun—such wonderful damn fun; like the year the *Lampoon,* the Harvard humor magazine, came out with this cartoon showing the entire Yale backfield sprinting horror-stricken from the field as some heckler yelled, "Skull & Bones," the idea being, of course, that any member of that sacrosanct secret society must leave the premises if an outsider so much as breathes the name of the lodge. But apparently there aren't any flies on Bones either, because, on the eve of The Game several years ago, four of its members kidnaped three *Lampoon* editors who had gone to New Haven to sell an issue carrying an article that purported to give the straight dope on all that Skull & Bones mumbo-jumbo. But that's The Game for you—anything for a laugh, like kidnaping Handsome Dan, Yale's bulldog mascot, or, in retaliation, sneaking into a Harvard Yard the night before The Game and applying several coats of blue paint to the statue of John Harvard outside University Hall. Nor have coaches necessarily been immune to the madness either. In 1952 at the Stadium, for example, with Yale ahead 40-0, its quarterback, instead of kicking the forty-first point, threw a pass over the goal line to number 99, a substitute who had dashed onto the field only a moment before. As it turned out, number 99, unlisted in the pro-

gram, was Charlie Yeager, Yale's 138-pound manager, whom coach Jordan Olivar had sent into The Game pretty much as a lark. Everything considered, however, the most merry-andrewish of mentors would seem to have been the late Herman Hickman, an amiable giant who was as skillful at quoting the classics as he had been at playing guard for Tennessee. As his squad was about to take the field for a practice session one Friday afternoon in the late fifties, he suddenly raised his hand for silence. The players were tense, waiting for the formula that might enable them to defeat Harvard. And then his voice began reverberating through the dressing room:

" 'Ye call me chief,' " he declaimed, " 'and ye do well to call me chief. If ye are men, follow me! Strike down your guard, gain the mountain passes, and there do bloody work as did your sires at old Thermopylae!' " His voice impassioned now, his features grim with determination. " 'Is Sparta dead? Is the old Grecian spirit frozen in your veins, that you do crouch and cower like a belabored hound beneath his master's last. O, comrades, warriors, Thracians! If we must fight, let us fight for ourselves. If we must slaughter, let us slaughter our oppressors! If we must die, let it be under the clear sky, by the bright waters, in noble, honorable battle!' "

Then, having concluded his rendition of *Spartacus to the Gladiators,* he snapped his fingers. "Whadya say, men," he growled. "Let's go, gang. Whadya say, let's go chew up those Harvards."

But always and forever, there is about The Game the haunting awareness of evanescence—the bittersweet remembrance of tea-dancing in the twenties, of walking back over the darkening bridge in the frosty dusks of other years, of all the radiant girls grown matronly. And always there is the rueful realization that though the playing fields of Harvard and Yale are ever verdant, always ageless, the players are not, and youth is replenished by youth, year after year, autumn unto autumn, so that what is varsity today is, inevitably, Old Blue or Old Crimson in autumns all too soon to come. So against the backdrop of bunting billowing in the breeze and against the counterpoint of cheers booming out from deep below the ribs and of smearing trombones and reedy woodwinds, always there is the memory of captains and kings departed, of men, middle-aged now or perhaps even dead and in the ground, who in the valor of other Novembers were strong and swift and as golden as ever golden boys can be—men like Memphis Bill Mallory, a battering ram of a back who was Yale's captain in 1923 and who ("For God, for country, and for Yale") perished in the service of his native land; like Raymond Pond, who, in a driving rain at the Stadium in 1923, scooped up a Harvard fumble, sloshed sixty-seven yards for a touchdown, thereby becoming "Ducky" forever after; like Albie Booth, who, though small, was "all spirit and whipcord" too, "the Mighty Atom" or "Little Boy Blue," who came out of Hillhouse High in New Haven, was the toast of the "townies," and died before his time; like Larry Kelley, "last man tapped for Bones" and, as such, the biggest man on campus—the shiftiest pass-catching end in the annals of New Haven, All-America and, in 1936, winner of the Heisman trophy in recognition of his being the very best football player in the whole United States that year; and like Clint Frank, Bones too, winner of the Heisman award in 1937, and, all in all, quite possibly the most bruising back of all the Blues since Ted Coy. And, for Harvard, men like Bill Ticknor, a star tackle, who, at the Harvard Stadium in 1929, enraged the "townies" by tackling Albie Booth none too gently around the neck; like Barry Wood, profes-

sor at the Johns Hopkins School of Medicine now, but in the days of his gilded youth, the most remarkable scholar-athlete in the university's history and an All-American quarterback who, though he ended his career on the seat of his pants, yards behind the line of scrimmage, against Booth's team, nevertheless won the hand of a girl who was once a member of the Vassar Daisy Chain; and like Endicott "Chub" Peabody, now an able Massachusetts politician, but, from 1939 through 1941, an All-American guard of such sinew and sagacity that head coach Dick Harlow, who recently lectured on, of all things, gardening, did not demur when Peabody broke precedent by refusing to stay with the rest of the squad at a hotel the night before the 1941 Yale game, insisting, quite sensibly, it would seem, that he wanted to sleep in his *own* bed.

And now in November, late in the afternoon of the nineteenth at Harvard Stadium, hard by the Charles River in Cambridge, Massachusetts, the Harvard stands will rise, and their voices will be wafted through the wintry dusk:

Fair Harvard! Thy sons to thy Jubilee throng,
And with blessings surrender thee o'er,
By these festival rites, from the age that is past
To the age that is waiting before. . . .

And The Game will have gone into the records— and into the memory as well.

7 BOBBY JONES' TYING PUTT IN THE '29 OPEN by Robert Fawcett (Winged Foot Golf Club, Mamaroneck, New York, June 29, 1929)

GOLF: THE SPORT OF PRESIDENTS

GOLF IS THE ONLY SPORT IN WHICH MAN COMPETES *strictly with himself. There are of course, terrain, wind, water and luck to contend with, but these opponents, as well as those human obstacles between the tee and the cup—the loving cup that is— are incidental. The other golfers have all these hazards in common too, including themselves. All in all it balances out and the best man always wins. It's best to have it explained by Tommy Armour, whose article here is the finest analysis to date of the struggle with the "yips." Then meet the great men:*

Walter Hagen (there are two pieces on him here). Bobby Jones (by the only man who saw him win all thirteen of his major titles), Ben Hogan (one of sport's great men at his greatest moment, when he proved his legs were as strong as his heart), Johnny Montague (a legend in his time whose feats had to be seen to be believed, reported by one who saw them), and a look at the new executive of professional golf, complete with ulcer: big Mike Souchak. Fore!

Tension: Golf's Greatest Hazard

by TOMMY ARMOUR

I ATTESTED MY CARD FOR THE FINAL round of the National Open Championship at North Shore. Although it was the most disappointing championship that I had ever played in, I didn't have the usual feeling of fatigue and despondency that accompanies the completion of a big tournament, because drama was in the offing.

Playing immediately behind me was Ralph Guldahl, who I knew needed a four to tie Johnny Goodman for the title. I got a seat on the edge off the green and waited the results of Guldahl's effort with great anxiety. Even though I was not playing the hole, I could easily put myself in Ralph's shoes. I knew the strain he was undergoing.

His drive was perfect, leaving him about 160 yards to the pin. All he had to do was put the ball on the green and get down in two putts for a tie, and the odds to beat Goodman in the play-off were definitely in his favor, because Goodman then wasn't nearly as good a player as he ultimately became. The excitement, of course, was terrific. Ralph is a very methodical player, taking plenty of time to make any stroke, which added to the tension.

He looked around very carefully and selected his club. Though we were 160 yards away, we could hear the click of the well-hit shot. We knew the shot was well struck, but it faded to the right, gradually, more and more each yard, and all the body English that the gallery could muster didn't prevent it from going in the bunker to the right of the green. That was bad. Ralph had to get down in two. The hole was approximately twenty-five feet from the edge of the bunker, and Ralph's recovery shot left him about six feet from the cup. This famous putt has gone down in history anywhere from one foot to three, but actually it was six feet.

With the right-to-left slope and the grain of the grass on the green running very strong, it made the putt practically impossible. To the uninitiated, it was merely a matter of a great golfer walking up and tapping the ball into the cup, but those of us who have been through these soul-breaking experiences knew differently. The hole then looks about the size of a thimble, the ball twice as big as usual. There were two ways for Guldahl to make the putt: trickle it with a very big borrow from right to left, or hit it firmly at the hole. The consensus of the experts around the green was that the latter was the correct method, and Ralph selected that one. He hit the ball firmly on the right edge of the cup, but the grain was too strong and the putt broke very fast, finishing below the hole.

A new champion had been crowned, and Guldahl retired in defeat, the target of all the ignorant and unenlightened.

A couple of months later I was sitting in the lounge of a celebrated club in Chicago playing cribbage with a multimillionaire. At the completion of the game he owed me exactly $375. When we sat down to lunch, the subject of conversation turned to the Open, and of course ultimately hit upon Guldahl's famous putt. The scorn with which my friend denounced what he called Ralph's "feeble effort" provoked me, and I upbraided him with a few caustic remarks, telling him that he didn't know what he was talking about. He had never taken part in competitive golf, barring the local club championship, and hadn't the slightest conception of the terrific strain championship golfers are under in a situation like Guldahl's. I decided to have a little gamble. . . .

I had practically stolen $375 from him, so I asked him if he'd like to make a six-foot putt for double or quits. He said he'd love it. So the remainder of the lunch hour was spent in my describing the difficulties of short putts under the conditions that they had to be made. I impressed upon him the fact that he had only *one* chance. He wanted to go right then and make the shot, but I said we had plenty of time. I carefully inquired of the manager if he had a tape measure. He had. I continued my tirade of the uninitiated's denunciation of feeble-minded golf pros playing critical shots; of criticism by people who I knew had no more intestinal fortitude than a jellyfish.

As we walked out on the golf course to start our round, I said, "This is the time—we'll putt it now."

We got out the tape measure and I asked what kind of putt he'd like—uphill, downhill, sidehill or just straight putt. He selected uphill. We got a new ball, carefully measured off the six feet and placed his ball on the spot.

As he was preparing to make the putt, I took great pains to advise him of the fact that he had only one chance. Mr. Millions looked over the putt from all conceivable angles, took his stance, stood over the ball for fully thirty seconds, then walked away. He wasn't ready. Once again he took his stance, and then made what reminded me of a spasm—the most violent jerk at the ball—and he didn't even come close to holing it. As a matter of fact, he was at least six inches short and six inches to the right. He immediately requested another try, but I reminded him that he had had his chance. "The putt you were making," I said, "meant absolutely nothing to you. You're a multimillionaire and the loss of $375 is of no importance to you. You gamble in thousands of dollars every day on the stock market, and even the loss of $100,-000 has never meant anything to you. You're famous for that. But the financial investment has nothing to do with the point I'm trying to illustrate to you. I want to show you that with nothing to gain or lose, you made one of the most ridiculous efforts at holing a six-foot putt that I ever saw. Guldahl, when he tried to hole a six-foot putt, was trying for the American championship. It meant money, and I happen to know that at that moment Ralph's entire bankroll wouldn't have kept you for one day. He needed desperately to win, and in spite of that strain he made a magnificent effort."

No doubt the public knows less about the inside intricacies of first-class golf than of any other sport.

It seems to be their particular delight to watch a famous golfer miss a shot and then hold him up to ridicule.

When I hear those remarks they really infuriate me. I remember an incident at Oakmont when Sam Parks won the championship. At the tenth hole on the last round he had a very delicate little chip shot of about fifteen yards. To the average golfer it looked simple enough. But what that average golfer didn't know was that the greens were lightning fast, and Parks would have been unable to control a pitch-and-run. He had to play a little backspin niblick shot, which is extremely difficult, and under the circumstances the difficulty was multiplied ten times. He started to play a pitch-and-run shot, then changed his mind—and the club. He started to play a backspin shot and changed his mind again—and the club. He went back to his original club and was just about to strike the ball when he stopped and went back to the niblick for the backspin shot.

As I watched him I heard a spectator at my side say in a loud, raucous voice, "Why doesn't he hit the damned thing?"

I was able to appreciate both Parks' state of mind and nervous tension, and the difficulty and importance of the shot. I couldn't keep my two-bits' worth out, so I remarked, "If you were to try to play it I don't think you'd even hit the ball."

He turned on me like all belligerent Monday morning critics and asked me what I knew about it. Or how did I know?

(Parks executed the shot perfectly and laid it a foot from the hole, getting a very, very much needed four.)

"Pal," I said, "I know all right."

Somebody in the gallery must have told him about me, because he came up later and very magnanimously said, "Friend, I guess you do know."

"Yes," I replied, "I know. And that shot was probably the finest short shot that will be played in this championship."

The fellow really wasn't to blame. It's just the fact that people don't understand. Golf is a game which is entirely different from any other sport, because the ball is at rest. You can take as long as you like to hit it—or practically as long as you like —and fellows who only watch the experts play can't understand why these little shots should be so difficult—because they are made to look so easy. They never stop to realize that one stroke thrown away, one little false movement, one moment's lack of concentration, one disconcerting move on the part of the gallery, is enough to ruin a man's entire score. The quiet adds to the tension. The game calls for perfect nerve and muscular control and complete co-ordination. Just think of the physical gyrations a man must go through to hit the golf shot! He's got a club with a small face. He's got to twist his anatomy into the most peculiar, fantastic positions and strike that ball on what amounts to a square quarter of an inch! And not only once—he has to do so time and time again, hole after hole and day after day.

It's impossible for the spectator to realize what a tournament player goes through. It isn't merely the three and a half hours the day of the match. His nerves start working about a week before. Eating becomes an effort. Sleep becomes more restive night by night. Day and night, unceasingly, his mind dwells on the forthcoming contest.

When the actual day arrives, he's probably in fine physical shape, but extremely nervous. Great tournament players like Bobby Jones find it practically impossible to eat during the tournament. Bobby, for that matter, has been known to regurgitate at least once a day. It's pure nerves. And Byron Nelson, one of the most nervous of all players, doesn't eat enough food during the tournament to compose one decent meal—and even at that he can't keep it in his stomach. The last time he played Ben Hogan for the play-off of the Masters' Tournament in Augusta, on three occasions he tried to keep down a cup of consommé—but he couldn't do it. Yet his was one of the most beautiful rounds of golf ever played.

It's like tightening up a spring to the breaking point. Watch the faces of these contestants after the completion of a big championship. There is no other sport in the world that is even comparable.

You've got to remember this: once the shot is gone, it's gone and nothing on God's earth can recall it. In first-class competitive golf it isn't a matter of hitting one, two or three shots well in succession; it's a matter of hitting dozens of shots

with exactly the proper clubs, exactly the precise flight, with all the different types of swings the experts use: left-to-right swings, right-to-left; low shots, high shots; and the ball must still be struck on that quarter of an inch with perfect timing and footwork. All you have to do is to relax mentally for one moment and you're gone. Not that you lose the stroke—that is inconsequential. But it may result in the loss of several strokes. It's a simple matter to turn a four into a seven by that one bad stroke, as all golfers know—simple even for the experts to do. The matter of making a bad shot which costs you one or two or three over par also has other effects. It upsets your equanimity. Your tempo is changed. It has very seldom happened that a man starts a championship with a seven and finishes with a fine round. He has immediately put himself behind not just one, but ten "eight balls." He's fighting everything, himself included. Every shot must be perfect now. Every swing must be beautifully timed. Every movement of his body must be perfectly balanced if he's going to win. What usually happens, of course, is that the strain of the initial seven, or whatever it may be, destroys his concentration. It's like being hit on the jaw—you can't get it out of your mind—you think of it between every step you take during the rest of the round. That accursed seven becomes as big as a colossus. Even though you do play the next two or three holes well, the dread of having another seven—of eliminating yourself entirely from the competition for which you've probably trained carefully for weeks—looms up constantly.

In other games you get another chance. In baseball you get three cracks at it; in tennis you lose only one point. But in golf the loss of one shot has been responsible for the loss of heart. Strain—that hackneyed word, incomprehensible to 99 per cent of human beings—the strain of competitive achievement. The desire for glory is something that I would not wish on my worst enemy, but the desire for conquest has made us all struggle to excel at our chosen endeavors. It goes through life in everything we do, and when it touches our recreation it prevails. The plea of the 100-shooter to do a ninety soon becomes the same plea for an eighty. Then he's in danger. It has ever been thus. As soon as he does eighty, he wants seventy, and when he gets in the seventies (a score very few accomplish) golf ceases to be recreation. It is then a mental and physical strain during his weekends, on his days or hours of supposed relaxation. It becomes hard, grinding work instead. He can't miss a shot! If he does, he is upset. A housewife peers with great concern at the face of her beloved returning from Saturday and Sunday golf sessions. If her beloved smiles when he enters, he's played well. If a look of fatigue and irritation is present, he probably did an eighty instead of a seventy-eight. Weekends of healthful exercise with congenial friends have given way to a contest of man vs. golf clubs, and the golf clubs usually win. That situation exists in practically every home in the country where a man shoots in the high seventies or low eighties. That poor individual imagines that he's going through the same tortures that the experts do. But he isn't. He hasn't even approached the strain they have to endure. By Monday at lunch he's forgotten all about Sunday and he's again looking forward to another battle next weekend. Not so the expert.

Several years ago, during a golf conversation with Robert T. Jones at Pinehurst, I told him that I had the "yips." Robert, who undoubtedly has one of the keenest minds in this country, had never heard of the "yips" and asked me what they were. "Well, Bobby," I said, "I'll describe them to the best of my ability.

"The 'yips' are a mental condition which attacks certain golfers when they endeavor to hole a short putt. You've lined up your three-footer, you step up to the ball with complete confidence in your ability to hole it. You're perfectly relaxed. But—just at the moment you start your backswing with the putter, your mind goes absolutely blank. You go blind, a shudder goes through your body as though you were being electrocuted. All muscular control disappears. The putter automatically strikes the ball, but only because you've made the stroke so many thousands of times. You return to consciousness to find that the ball is not in the hole. You raise your head to the high heavens, gradually recovering from the tremendous ordeal, and walk along to the next tee preparing yourself for the same shock that's going to happen to you on the next green."

Jones smiled. "God, that must be terrible!"

I assured him it was the most awful feeling in the world.

Time marched on. Peculiarly enough, the scene was again at Pinehurst. My phone rang.

"This is Bobby."

"Yes, Robert, what can I do for you?"

"I want to see you."

I went up to his room. He greeted me with, "Thomas, I've got the 'yips'!"

"You have?" I questioned. "Describe them to me."

Bobby made the most graphic dissertation on the effect of "yips" that I have ever had the pleasure of hearing.

A year passed. We were playing at Augusta in the Masters' Tournament. I saw the Immortal Jones in the locker room and asked,

"How are the 'yips,' Robert?"

"I got rid of them," he replied.

With a look of skepticism I said, "Impossible, Robert, impossible. I shall watch you today."

On the first green Mr. Jones very successfully "yipped" a putt of two feet. His jaws jumped like the muscles on the back of a cat. After two magnificent shots on the second hole, a par five, he putted within two feet again and made one more beautiful exhibition of a "yip" putt. On the third hole he put the ball eight feet from the hole in two. He putted it a foot and a half from the cup and he never even came close to holing it.

Robert is a man with the finest control of a very violent temper, and I had no wish to be visited by his wrath, but as I walked back when he was on his way to the fourth tee, I casually said, "Robert, you certainly have got rid of the 'yips'!" and I continued to walk straight toward the clubhouse.

"Yips" are a by-product of many years of competitive golf.

One of the most pathetic cases of the result of nervous strain in championship golf was Joe Kirkwood's exhibition at Troon—I think it was in 1923. I met him on the fourteenth tee, asked how he was doing, and he said very well. He told me his score: he had just completed the previous five holes in three apiece! I said, "Joe, you can kick the ball around and win!"

On the fourteenth Joe hit a fine shot, but just a yard short of carrying the bunker. As there were no dynamiters (or sand clubs), his explosion shot was forty feet from the hole, and he promptly three-putted. Though he was two over par on the hole, there was really no cause for concern because he had such a big lead, but he was obviously shaken. On the fifteenth hole he topped his drive, and his second and third shots.

Now it was obvious to the initiated that his nervous and physical control were practically shattered. He got down in six, another two over par. He hit the first four shots along the ground at the sixteenth, and finally holed out in seven. Another two over par. At the short seventeenth he hooked his ball to the left of the green, got on with his second and down in two, and finished the eighteenth

with a five. There was the real tragedy of the tournament. A man whose golf had been very fine up to that point, whose physical and mental coordination was nearly perfect, had suddenly collapsed and literally thrown the tournament out of the window.

To describe Kirkwood's feelings would, of course, be impossible. It was not a mere matter of Kirkwood becoming frightened or nervous. He's a big, rugged fellow, extremely strong and brave as a lion. His courage could never be questioned at any time. It was just that terrible strain that made him absolutely incapable of concentrated movement and thought.

That is tension.

The Great Emancipator by HERB GRAFFIS

IN THE VERY OLD DAYS PROFESSIONAL athletes were slaves.

Then the best break a pro got was to be permitted by holders of Roman arena ringside seats to nominate the lion to gnaw on his meat and framework.

Things softened up a bit for pros when practices of slugging each other with lead-ballasted cesti or plunging runt swords into gladiatorial vitals were introduced. The softening consisted of slightly delaying the inevitable finish of the athletes which was by sack to the glue works.

It took almost ten centuries before professional athletes advanced in status far enough to separate the names of the vanquished in any athletic contest from obituary notices; defeat and death were one and the same in the simple times prior to that flowering of civilization represented now by such developments as boxing and wrestling commissions.

Then it required almost another ten centuries before professional athletes were allowed to prowl on the loose, subject only to the commands of the sporting nobility that willed them to perform in contests of more brutality than skill.

It was not until the sparkling nineties that the professional athlete achieved some social standing and then merely as a museum piece for men only.

So the pros again were left out in the murky, hoppy limbo of transfer corner saloons, which was not much of an improvement over the bloody arenas of the Roman days.

Here we have, roughly, about 2000 years in professional athletics with the pros having gained for themselves during all this time only the right to keep living among the lower species.

Then Mr. Hagen arrived. In ten years after the time Hagen won his first national golf championship, at Midlothian Country Club in the southern *faubourgs* of Chicago in 1914, the condition of professional athletes improved more than during the 2000 years prior to the Hagen debut as an athletic notable. True, there were professional baseball players, for instance, who were accepted socially before Hagen registered in, but their social conquests were limited to acceptance by persons in trade. Polite society had not been polite to workingmen athletes.

Hagen changed all that. Well, maybe Hagen and conditions, but you can't blame a fellow for having been born at the right time and taking advantage of it.

Walter's playmate, the sage Tommy Armour, jests with Hagen by calling Walter "the Great Emancipator," but in a serious vein Armour stands solid on this verdict.

Hagen was Mister Hagen by his own introduction to his public long before he was Walter. He did not allow undue familiarity on the part of either peasantry or plutocracy while he was in his early twenties. Recall, that this was back in the days when American newspapers and magazines referred to professionals in golf stories by the raw address, Bill Mugg or Jock McGoof, and to the amateurs always with the respectful title of "Mister," a practice that now has vanished even in England and which disappeared mainly because of the Hagen influence.

It was at Midlothian, when Hagen came to win his first championship, that the old caste system classifying professionals as untouchables was first swept aside by the self-sufficient Dutch-Irish boy. The golf professionals had nails in the clubhouse basement on which to hang their coats. They could change to golf shoes either outside the clubhouse or in the basement. The golf officials and club members didn't care which, and the pros thought nothing of being neglected or scorned. Hagen had been a full-fledged professional golfer only three years but the Rochester ex-caddie paraded blithely into the Midlothian locker room, selected a vacant locker in a conspicuous and convenient spot and made himself at home with the members and amateur contestants. Then he went on the golf course, gave the Liberty Bell lusty yanks, the golf ball deft smacks, and won the championship.

Golf as the favored sport of the wealthy and influential gradually let down the barriers of twenty centuries that had prevented professionals from mingling with the select populace. After golf had succumbed because of the Hagen action, the sports of lesser social standing promptly approved the credentials of their professionals.

Pugilists married into society and cowpunchers became polo players; society and polo getting the long end of what pugilists and cowpunchers had been perfectly willing to have go as a draw decision. Tennis amateurs formally turned professional, college football players graduated into professional football instead of becoming cappers for security houses. Slavery days for the professional athletes were over. Hagen had fought the civil war for the pros single-handed. He cocktailed his way to victory at Shiloh, danced triumphant engagements at Lookout Mountain and Gettysburg and played well-bred bridge hands marching through Georgia. Time after time he outsnooted the shock-troops of society snobs. In the diplomatic phases of the war for pro freedom he never lost a skirmish. Even the Prince of Wales played along with Hagen and it helped the Prince socially, commercially and athletically.

The subtle and subconscious campaign Hagen conducted for professionals' release from bondage was unquestionably one of the most unusual in military history, for it was conducted on a financial basis that at times showed more red than all the blood that ever drained into the Marne. Hagen has made well over a million dollars with his golf clubs alone. The testimonial silver that rained on Hagen when the advertisers were going strong in this department of copy amounted to a soaking shower for two years, but with Walter's facility for putting legal tender into circulation he stood in this downpour and dried out almost instantly. Hagen's amazing contempt for money has one lovely aspect: when he is flush he pays off with great joy that people should be so delighted to put their hands on something that is merely an item for poor people to worry about; that's Walter's idea of money.

When he sailed for England in 1928 to win the third of his four British Open titles Walter could have floated his entire cash assets out to sea on a cigarette paper, but he traveled in style. At the dock as he sailed were so many evil-looking men with writs for Hagen in their mitts that it appeared as though the troops were sailing.

Engineering the departure was the companion and business manager of Hagen's golfing activities for many years, Robert Harlow. Hagen played the Grand Duke role for the team and Harlow was simply Comrade Harlow, a stalwart, epicurean ex-newspaperman who disclaims having been Hagen's "manager" because, he makes clear, no one could manage Hagen.

The Hagen-Harlow combination had put its hands on approximately $6000 for the English trip, including $1500 which was to be wagered in a seventy-two-hole match with Archie Compston. Harlow bought the transportation and pushed the $1500 wager ahead to England. The Grand Duke and Comrade Harlow reasoned that the $1500 would become $3000 immediately after the match with Compston was played. Therefore there would be no need of funds other than for tips en route. Having arrived at this logical conclusion, the patriots decided to spend American money with Americans and personally conduct their own farewells, each according to his manner. The Grand Duke held open house for three days, working twenty-hour shifts each of the days. Comrade Harlow, gypsy evangelist of the Great God Gut, spent his percentage of the commune's funds at excellent eating places.

Harlow parked early in his cell on the boat,

cramming his quarters with medicinal waters, indigestion tablets and philosophical volumes in which authors go to great lengths to prove that man is not born to waste in toil.

Leisurely concluding his packing for the journey, Hagen left his hotel suite with an allowance of less time for making the boat than the New York fire department would set for the run to the pier. With the Grand Duke was a Hagen associate in the golf-club and -ball business named Walter Ring. Ring's build is about that of Hagen and he rather resembles the Grand Duke in contented and well-fed features. While Hagen had been packing, Ring selected a gaudy suit of Hagen's, which had been given the Great Man by an enterprising tailor who recognized Hagen's standing as the ace male mannequin of the age. Hagen not only would give a fellow the shirt off his back, but coat, vest, trousers, shoes, hosiery and tie to complete the sartorial scheme. Thus it happened that Ring was to outward appearances another Hagen as the taxi jerked to a screaming stop at the wharf.

Ring recognized the enemy at the docks. He stepped out of the cab, hailed porters, who grunted the Hagen luggage aboard, and serenely accepted the papers shoved at him by the process servers as Hagen followed out of the cab after an interval and modestly edged aboard. As the boat swung out into the channel with Hagen safely aboard, Ring turned to the group of men who had presented him with papers.

"Now, gents, what can I do for you?" he asked.

"Stick around and kick in, I guess, Mr. Hagen," volunteered one of the serving men.

"But I'm not Hagen," explained Ring.

Whereupon Mr. Ring and the process servers adjourned to a tavern and at this comfortable distance from Mr. Hagen wished Mr. Hagen *bon voyage*.

That journey did not work out as planned. Compston dusted off Hagen, eighteen and seventeen—the worst defeat Hagen ever suffered. The $1500 blew then and the team was playing strictly from scratch. But Hagen, who had trained on champagne, Scotch and seltzer and sharpened his vision by staying up to see the English sunrises, hired a bodyguard to shanghai him into sleep at reasonable hours. Shortly after the defeat by Compston Hagen won the British Open with 292. His compatriot, Sarazen, was 294 and Compston was in third place with 295.

In exhibition matches played during a few weeks after his British Open title Hagen earned about $5000 but when he and Harlow steamed into New York Harbor, homecoming, Harlow craned his neck over the steamer rail looking for a welcoming pal who would get the champion out of hock. Fortunately, Eddie Conlin, a famous tennis official turned golf-ball sales manager, was on hand to see the circus come to town.

Harlow energetically beckoned Conlin aboard. Conlin dug down for bail; Hagen lavishly tipped the boat staff and the conquering hero landed. Hagen lives to live.

When Hagen is opulent he is perhaps the softest of all targets for touches. When he spent part of his winters in Hollywood he ran a relief station for impecunious actors and actresses, conducting the operation in a manner that aided without embarrassment. The mob scene would be put on in Hagen's suite around dinnertime, with Hagen signing tabs the size of the national debt. Then there would be some social bridge. When the Thespians won, Hagen paid off in cash. When Hagen won, the score was written on Hagen's cuff and vanished the next day when the hotel laundresses busted the suds with the Hagen shirts.

During those times when the Grand Duke's funds cannot be seen with the naked eye he considers the situation in a very logical manner—a manner worthy of wider adoption. He reasons: "My only troubles are money. I have no money. Therefore, I have no troubles. Q. E. D." Comrade Harlow would differ slightly with Hagen concerning that decision about no money—no worry, and arrange exhibition tours among the nobility and the mujiks. The rubles would roll in again and all would be at peace.

Hagen and Harlow joined forces in 1922 at Pinehurst. Hagen then had won the United States Open championships in 1914 and 1919. His first start in the British Open—that of 1920—had resulted disastrously; he didn't finish among the first fifty. His second attempt, in 1921, brought him in a seven-cornered tie for sixth place. In 1922 after he and Harlow had agreed to investi-

gate the commercial possibilities of exhibition golf Hagen won the British Open. He was the first American-born professional to win that title.

With Hagen, the lion-tamer, as the big attraction to ballyhoo, Harlow quit his job under Sheriff Bill McGeehan on the New York *Herald* sports staff, and the two set out on what was supposed to be a business but actually was the greatest money-making ten-year holiday any two fellows ever enjoyed. It is true that when they slipped the knot of their business tie in 1932 both of them were behind the eight ball, financially, but in view of what had happened in American finance, they called themselves lucky for not having wasted time saving.

The Grand Duke was not much of a drinker, contrary to the popular belief. He could play with one drink for an hour or more in the same deliberate manner he does everything else, but he will do his share right along with relays of the merrymakers and go for weeks without looking at a timepiece. That disregard for sleep is something that only one of his playing companions on exhibition tours ever was able to match. Hagen and Tommy Armour brightened the land one year with a tour that was long discussed where fellows got the good song ringing clear. They played astonishingly good golf, shattering course records at most of the places they played. After the afternoon pastiming for which they were paid, the real business began. Their suite always looked like night sessions of conventions were being held. Most of their sleeping they did in automobiles between country clubs.

At one city along the line of march a wealthy golf enthusiast put up $1500 in prize money in addition to the guarantee the club made for the exhibition. The $1500 was to be paid out as follows: $500 if either player broke the course record of seventy; $500 if either player scored seventy, and $500 if either player equaled the course's par of seventy-two.

Playing in a near-by city the day prior to this $1500 added-money performance, Hagen and Armour were given the eye by two striking young women. Be it said for the Grand Duke when in his prime and for Armour, when likewise, that no striking young women ever gave them the eye without being given eye for eyes.

While striding along between shots the Grand Duke talked over conditions with one of the dazzlers.

"You boys must get very lonely and homesick in the evenings," she remarked.

Hagen thought that it was a perfect opening but as a discreet stranger, let it go with a nod of agreement.

"Possibly some young women whose social standing is not very high importune you," the lovely young thing added.

Hagen guessed he knew what "importune" meant, so what could he do but say "yes"?

"Tonight is going to be different. My friend and I are going to call at the hotel for you and Mr. Armour and I am sure that we will pleasantly entertain you." When the Grand Duke heard that from the obviously high-class female native, he made haste to acquaint Armour with the happy tidings. Instead of lingering after the exhibition Hagen diligently passed around word that he and Armour were leaving town immediately and it was no use to expect them to be central figures in the usual evening frolic.

Promptly at eight that evening the telephone rang in the Hagen-Armour quarters. In patrician tones and accent one of the two lovelies announced they were waiting with a car by the hotel entrance. Walter and Tommy couldn't have made the lobby quicker if they had slid down a brass pole in a fire station.

Through the midsummer evening the quartet drove while spots of interest in the city were pointed out and polite persiflage exchanged. Night fell.

"Well, where are we going now?" asked Hagen of the charmer who was driving.

"Oh, we're going to take you boys where you'll really enjoy yourselves. We're going to the Wednesday evening lecture of the Exegesis Culture Society in the parsonage of the First M. E. Church."

"Oh no. We have to go back to the hotel," protested dazed Mr. Hagen.

"Yes. I don't feel well," said Armour weakly.

"Well, then we'll be late for the meeting," pouted one of the girls.

"No you won't," Hagen assured them. "We're getting out and walking. It will do Armour good to walk back himself."

So Walter and Tommy walked back to the hotel and were sound asleep by nine o'clock. After this indulgence in sane slumber they went out the next day after the $1500. Armour shot seventy-seven and Hagen a seventy-eight; absolutely the worst golf either of them had shot in two years.

This was one of the very few times when the Grand Duke went wrong seriously. He is far smarter than his casual manner indicates. Walter began changing his swing years ago when he realized that time was going to make his muscles stiffer and his bones more brittle so he would be unable to take the sweeping slash that distinguished the playing style of the younger Hagen. He is still good—very good.

Hagen Treatment

by WILSON HICKS

MAYBE AN ATHLETIC CHAMPION DOESN'T have to be a psychologist, but even a sports dullard will admit that there are many times when it helps.

The day old John L. kept staggering forward into the path of Jim Corbett's conversational fire as well as his left hooks, he was as much a victim of psychology as he was of the dancing master's boxing skill.

And Mr. Psychology was on the mound with Pete Alexander that afternoon when he had the late Tony Lazzeri frantic in search of soft curves that just about got to the plate.

There are even some horsemen who swear that Seabiscuit used psychology on War Admiral when he lapped himself on Sam Riddle's fast-breaking colt and broke his spirit by not letting him get his nose in front at any stage of the race!

Walter Hagen is, of course, a fabulously talented athlete, as well as a *bon vivant*, showman, philosopher and—psychologist. As a tournament golfer, the genial Haig was a man who maneuvered more than his sticks; he maneuvered opponents as well. But never was he so skillful at the latter task than on the afternoon at Cedar Crest Country Club in Dallas, Texas, when he did a job of psychological work on Joe Turnesa in the final match of the 1927 Professional Golfers' Association tournament.

The Haig had an international reputation as one of those athletic freaks, a golfer who never stopped enjoying the game, come sweaty palms or ulcers. He took tournament golf as he took everything else—in stride. While his competitors breathed heavily over three-foot putts and hovered dangerously near thrombosis on the fairways, the Haig sailed along, getting as much of a bang out of the game as he did out of living. He wasn't one to worry about losing. And he was cagey enough to sense that his opponents worried a great deal about it.

Said the Haig: "Take it easy—relax—laugh. As you travel down the road of life, there are times to be serious, but you've also got to have fun—and a smell of those flowers as you go along."

Haig was the defending P.G.A. champion in 1927 when he entered the tournament that was to give him his record four wins in a row. But he was badly off his game, a fact which was obvious as he teetered through an erratic start. He steadied down then, knocked off Tommy Armour and Al Espinosa in the quarter- and semifinals and moved up to meet twenty-six-year-old Turnesa for the title. Walter's golf was good now, but so was Turnesa's, and the genial master was taking no chances. For an extra weapon, he dug deeply into his reserve of psychology and prepared to give Joe what was known as the special Hagen treatment.

The match was scheduled for ten o'clock; the Haig arrived blithely at the first tee at ten-thirty while the officials fumed and Joe Turnesa fidgeted with false nonchalance. That was psychological step number one.

Turnesa's approach on the first hole was good, falling ten feet short of the cup. Lying a potential one stroke back, Walter surprised everyone and Turnesa especially by knocking the latter's ball out of the way and conceding the putt. Startled, Turnesa asked if Haig had gone crazy, conceding ten-footers in a P.G.A. final. Walter just grinned and said, "You'd have sunk it anyway, Joe. Besides I owe you something for keeping you waiting." That was psychological step number two.

Playing steady but not brilliant golf, Walter made the turn three strokes back (after conceding putts on the second and third holes to the amazed Turnesa) and had to turn it on in earnest in order to take the title and—incidentally—make his psychological scheme work.

Walter turned it on—genially and intensely. After thirty-four holes, he was only one down with two to play. Now it was time to administer step number three—which was to be the psychological *coup de grâce.*

Hagen and Turnesa were lying even on the thirty-fifth green, facing a piddling two-footer. Half-kidding, half-serious, Joe turned to Walter and asked him if he wanted to concede the putt again.

"I don't know," said Walter, taking his time, stooping to sight the lie, waggling his own putter thoughtfully. "This could be a tough one, Joe. Better shoot it," he advised.

Turnesa took his bead, nudged the ball—and missed. The gremlins had him for fair.

Still smiling and nonchalant, Walter muttered words of consolation and put his own putt away to square the match, with one last hole to go. But it was as good as over. His clubhead weighted under a whole caravan of gremlins, Turnesa bogied the thirty-sixth hole and Hagen took his expected par—and the championship.

Preparing for Competitive Golf

by BOBBY JONES

THE QUESTION HAS BEEN SO OFTEN PUT to me, "What do you consider of greatest importance in preparing for an important tournament?" Indeed, I had asked myself that question, in one form or another, through the many years I played competitive golf. For I knew that there must be some "best way" to bring my game to the proper pitch for some important event; but I had not found it easy to come upon the magic answer. I have, however, been able to reach the conclusion that the most important maxim to observe is "Don't play too much golf."

And I should like the word "play" to be understood here to include the worrying you do at night over those iron shots that will not go right, or the putts that won't go down.

The golf stroke requires to a high degree coordination of mind and muscle. But if your golfing muscles have been properly schooled and thoroughly drilled in what they have to do, you need fear nothing from them. It is the mind you must train. From the force of old habit your muscles will respond if the mind by conscious effort does not interfere.

To help me illustrate my point, ask yourself a few questions. Which sand trap are you more likely to go into, the one you don't see or the one you are afraid of? When are you more likely to hole a long putt—when you think you will, or when you know you won't? Don't you drive straighter when you are not consciously attempting to guide or steer the shot? You know the answer and the reason for all is that a conscious effort to control the stroke is usually attended with disastrous results.

It has always been my contention that the practice field is the proper and the only place where the player should attempt to mold or alter his method of hitting the ball. After the first tee is left behind, every faculty should be concentrated upon the result rather than upon the manner of execution. I think I can truthfully say that when I am playing my very best the direction of my conscious mind ceases when I step up to the ball and take my stance. I have then determined upon the club I should use, I have selected my objective.

There remains only to allow the muscles to go through the motions they have made numerous times before. Call it habit, or the control of the subconscious mind or what you will, I am firmly convinced that this other man will play the shot for you if you will only let him. Any nervousness, indecision or fear of consequences will interfere with his work and your shot will be ruined.

In the championship of 1925 at Oakmont, Watts Gunn, of Atlanta, afforded me, in addition to several uncomfortable moments, an excellent illustration of subconscious playing. Watts had come up for his first tournament of any great importance. He had qualified comfortably but not in brilliant style and had been drawn against Vincent Bradford in the first round. Watts having started badly, found himself three down going to the twelfth hole.

I have it from Watts himself just what had been troubling him and the remarkable way in which he pulled himself out of a seemingly hopeless maze of bad shots. Anxious to make a good showing, he had consciously attempted to steer every shot away from Oakmont's terrifying bunkers.

The not unusual result had been that he had been caught by a great many more than he had avoided. Playing his third shot at number twelve, Watts had again tried to control his shot, the ball lodging in a sand pit to the left of the green. And here Watts made the wisest decision of his golfing career.

He afterward said to me, "I was so disgusted with myself and so sick over my play that I was ready to give up. When I went down into that trap I made up my mind that I couldn't get any worse, so from there on I was just going to stand up and hit that ball for all I was worth and let it go where it would." He did. He came out of the trap, holed a long putt to win that hole, and then won the next fourteen holes in succession. He continued to play magnificent golf in his succeeding matches and became the outstanding player of the tournament.

This story is so well known that I have felt some hesitancy in repeating it. But it affords such an excellent illustration of my theory that I could not resist using it. What happened to Watts was that he simply eliminated from his mind all thought of what he was doing with the club.

He forgot about the bunkers, ditches and traps.

He saw only the flag and his ball. He knew what he wanted to do and did it. He told me himself that after that twelfth hole he never once gave a thought to his swing.

For my other illustration, I must be permitted to draw upon my personal experience. It was at Inwood, in 1923, in a play-off with Bobby Cruickshank for the National Open championship—an iron shot over the water to the last green which luckily brought up right and enabled me to win. It may sound foolish, but I have never been able to recall hitting that ball. I remember drawing the iron from the bag and that is all, until the ball hit the green. Now, I couldn't have been thinking of my stroke that time.

This has all been said in support of my statement that a person should not play too much golf before a tournament. Practice and play all you like when you have no important matches. Cultivate and drill into yourself the proper strokes. But don't wear out your disposition and your love of the game just before the test comes, when you want to play well.

If you have the tournament instinct and can stifle to a certain extent the efforts of your conscious mind to steer your ball, you will play the shots as you have always done and play them well. Whatever new ideas you may have gained in the past few weeks will be forgotten anyway, so you have only taken a chance of ruining your game. Just play enough to keep your hand in, and don't worry, would be my earnest advice.

Of course, it is a very difficult matter to alter one's habitual mental attitude toward the game. But I do believe that a great deal can be accomplished by perseverance in the determination to swing with only one object—to hit the ball straight for the pin. Forget the bunkers. You must go into some of them anyway.

My only excuse, of course, for writing this article lies in setting down something that will be of interest to those who read it. I realize that only a few of my readers have championship ambitions, or desire in any way to acquire great reputations as competitive players. But I can't help thinking that even to those casual golfers who play once a week or less, with never a thought of even a club competition, it must be interesting to see how the other fellows feel about things, and to see what difficulties they must encounter which the average player is never called upon to meet.

Innis Brown, I think, said that there was no strain in sport as great as the pressure of the last nine holes of an Open championship when the pace was hot and the field close. I could not be prepared to go that length, for I have never engaged seriously in any other sport, but I can say that there is nothing else like it in golf.

Golf is not exacting upon the physical powers of a man, but it is trying upon his nerves, and the nervous strain usually reacts in some way upon the physical body.

I remember standing beside my ball in the eighteenth fairway at Columbus, gazing toward the green, and wishing devoutly that my knees would stop knocking together long enough for me to hit the ball. Up until that shot I had been nervous, of course, but the tension had been all of the kind that fires the muscles with energy and fills the heart with determination. But when I reached the point when I had only to play an iron shot to a wide-open green and got down in two putts to win the championship, I suppose I got the "buck ague." I began to think how miserable would be a failure at that point. My attitude became entirely defensive where before it had been aggressive, and right now, I think it was only the merest accident that I got that shot onto the green.

I suppose everyone has experienced the feeling that I have tried to describe, but I have encountered another difficulty to which I think I may claim sole rights, and which I am unable to overcome. It has its inception, I suppose, in some mistake of diet, but it is nevertheless directly traceable to nervous disturbance.

During the five or six years preceding my retirement from tournament play, throughout the early morning of every day of competition I found myself continually on the verge of active nausea. It could not be that my breakfast caused it, for I was rarely able to eat anything at that meal, and it could not be, as Ty Cobb has found in his case, that the cream in coffee was to blame, for I gave up everything even remotely connected with milk or cream when engaged in competition.

Whatever was the cause it was most unpleasant

and it usually rendered me unable to button my shirt collar or to put on a necktie at least until late into the morning. When I played Evans at Minikahda I went tieless and with my collar open all morning because of it.

In playing competitive golf there is nothing so important as concentration upon the game. And, unfortunately, it isn't simply a matter of concentrating upon the shot while you are standing over the ball. Just as soon as one shot is played the player's mind becomes busy with the next and the only rest comes after the last putt is holed.

It would be a fine thing for any competitor if his well-wishing and well-meaning friends could appreciate the intensity of the strain of competition. Time after time you will see them, in their anxiety to lend moral support, do the thing that is the very worst they could do if they want their man to win—that is, speak to him while he is playing. A great many men have unjustly gained a reputation for gruffness and incivility when accosted on the course in the midst of play. Sometimes they fail to hear remarks addressed to them, and other times the tension under which they are playing may lead them to answer rather shortly.

I remember when I was playing Cruickshank in the play-off at Inwood, as we left the ninth green, someone grabbed my arm and began talking about some sort of an exhibition he wanted me to play the next day at some course or other. Now, the last thing I was thinking about or wanted to think about was what I was going to do the next day, and I was extremely grateful when Francis Ouimet, who was walking around with me, pounced upon the man and led him away. Of course, he meant the best in the world and had no idea but that he was doing the right thing.

At Merion in the finals of the tournament of 1924, I was so well protected that it was hard to escape the feeling that I was in the custody of the whole New York police force. Cyril Tolley and Bob Bristowe, both of the British Walker Cup team, most graciously volunteered to see me through the crowds that day, and throughout the entire match I walked along quite free and untrammeled, between Bristowe and Tolley, the former, by the way, of even more ample dimensions than Cyril. They were an immense help, too.

THE FIVE CARDINAL SINS—A Frightful Fivesome of Foolish Failures.
Drawings by Robert Osborn

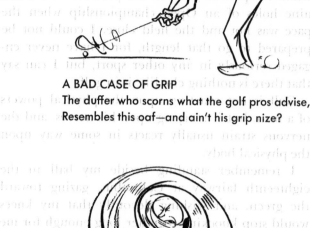

A BAD CASE OF GRIP
The duffer who scorns what the golf pros advise,
Resembles this oaf—and ain't his grip nize?

TEE IS FOR TENSION
He's a frightening sight as he misses his shots;
His teeth are on edge and his muscles in knots.

SUPERSONIC SWING
MacMayhem's swing has such terrible force
He misses the ball as a matter of golf course.

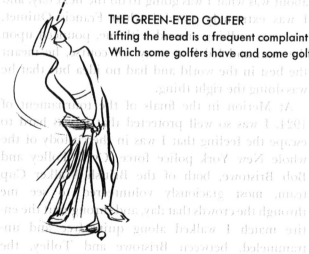

THE GREEN-EYED GOLFER
Lifting the head is a frequent complaint
Which some golfers have and some golfers ain't.

UNBALANCED BEHAVIOR
With unbalanced stance in addressing the ball
The address is unknown—if he hits it at all.

At St. Andrews one year, Sherwood Hurt of Atlanta accompanied me around the course on every round. The first day, I had signed so many autograph albums that Sherwood became fearful that I would get writer's cramp and lose my touch with "Calamity Jane"—which, in fact, had been my only salvation in the first round, except a lot of good luck. That night, as we were playing bridge in our rooms at the hotel, he suggested that I then and there do all my autographing for the rest of the tournament. So I wrote my name all over three or four sheets of foolscap, whereupon Sherwood cut them out and carefully stowed them away in his pocket. "Now," he said triumphantly, "I'll do your autographing for you." That was a great relief, too.

When I attended my first Open championship, I was struck particularly with Jock Hutchison. Jock had played magnificent golf in the qualifying rounds at Toledo, and was looked upon by everyone as the most likely candidate for the championship. Throughout three and a half rounds Jock looked to be the winner. Vardon, playing ahead, had been blown off his feet by a gale of wind and everything looked rosy for the St. Andrews boy.

I first saw Jock in that round as he approached the twelfth green. The twelfth at Toledo is a long three-shotter and Jock was on nicely in three. He ran his approach putt up about three feet past the hole, and as he walked forward to hole out, he caught sight of my head, craning over some conveniently low shoulder. "They won't drop today, Bobby," said he, and continued with some Scotch sallies which started the gallery twittering.

At that time Jock looked a certain winner but he slipped a few strokes in the closing holes and finished one stroke behind Ted Ray, who won. I thought then and have since that Jock Hutchison, if his Scotch blood had given him the proverbial Scotch dourness instead of a gay wit, would have been champion many times.

To a man with the temperament of Hutchison, or of Evans, distraction may be a relief. But to the other ninety-eight of the hundred, golf is an exacting game which requires every bit of attention we can give to it.

Prelude to the 1930 Grand Slam

by O. B. KEELER

THE DATE: SATURDAY, JUNE 29, 1929.

The place: Winged Foot Golf Club, Mamaroneck, New York.

The event: Open Golf Championship of the United States. Fourth and final round in progress.

The leader: Bobby Jones, closely pursued by Al Espinosa, Gene Sarazen, Densmore Shute and Tommy Armour, professionals, and another amateur, George Von Elm.

The background: Six successive years Jones had been National Champion of the United States,

either Open or Amateur. He had won eight national titles in the United States and Great Britain.

In prospect: The Grand Slam of 1930, when, as Mr. George Trevor phrased it, his record "was entrenched safely and forever, within the Impregnable Quadrilateral of Golf."

An opinion: I was with Jones at twenty-seven major championships in the United States and Great Britain. I am the only person who saw him win all thirteen of his national titles. And I'll always believe that the Grand Slam of 1930 stemmed from a single stroke played at Winged Foot in the U.S. Open the year before.

This is the story.

Through the seventh hole of the final round, Jones was spinning easily along with a widening margin of strokes over his nearest rivals—Al Espinosa, Gene Sarazen and Densmore Shute. Then at the dog-leg eighth he followed a great drive in the angle by holding up a long pitch too emphatically against a hard wind from the right. The ball was bunkered. He blasted out across the green into another bunker, and back again into the first hazard. He was barely out with his fifth and took two putts for a ghastly seven.

The jolt took some of the strain off, and he holed a fine birdie four at the ninth, and when he walked off the green of the long twelfth he had a clear lead of six strokes over Espinosa, who had blown himself to a dreadful eight at that hole.

Now see what can happen when the pressure comes off. Espinosa, convinced that it was all over, played the last six holes with an incredibly brilliant run of four fours and two threes, for a round of seventy-five and a total score of 294.

And now the pressure was on Jones. He lost a stroke at the 213-yard thirteenth, got his par four at the next, and then picked up another devastating seven after a sliced drive among the trees at the fifteenth. His lead was gone, now, for Espinosa was on the board—he couldn't lose any more strokes. And Jones needed four-four-four to win by a single stroke, and the sixteenth was a par five.

Pressure? After a great drive and iron, he was on the sixteenth green, twenty feet from the flag. Then his first putt was five feet short, and he missed the second.

And now it was four-four . . . to tie.

He got the first four. Then after a good drive he pulled his pitch for the home green, and the ball trickled down the steep bank of a deep bunker, stopping in the grass just short of the sand. And his wee pitch was soft. The ball lay twelve feet short of the hole. And it was that—or nothing.

Or worse than that. I'll always believe that the rest of Bob Jones' golfing career hung on that putt. If he missed, it would be the first time in the U.S. Open he had scored as high as eighty. He would have blown a lead of six strokes, and one more, in the last six holes. . . . Standing back of that home green, with a gallery of 10,000 closing round it, I knew in a sort of bewildering flash that if that putt stayed out, it would remain a spreading and fatal blot, never to be wiped from his record.

I was standing where I could see all right. But I couldn't watch it. Some way it seemed that the ball couldn't sink if I were looking at it. Bobby stood up to putt, and I looked at the ground, and the gallery subsided into a strange, breathing silence pressing into the ears; but it seemed that somewhere, a long way off, I could hear a bell ringing slowly.

Then the breathing stopped, and I heard the faint, thin click of the stroke, and the beginning of a kind of sigh in the gallery. The ball was on its way.

Only a dozen feet to go? How long it took! The sigh grew in volume—changed to a gasp!

Missed?

No!

The gasp changed to a stunning roar; the crash of a thunderbolt. . . . The ball had rolled, slowly and more slowly, across a sloping green as fast as ice, to the rim of the hole; had hesitated—stopped. And then—well, then it had dropped.

It was Al Watrous, Bob's fellow competitor, who described that putt to me a few minutes later in the locker room. It was twelve feet, said Al, and a slope in the lightning-fast green necessitated a "borrow" of about ten inches from the left of the line. Al said the range was so nicely gauged that if the hole had been a four-and-a-quarter-inch circle on the green, the ball would have stopped in the middle of it.

Next day, the rebound. Playing his best golf of the week, Bobby Jones won the thirty-six-hole play-off from Al Espinosa, weary and stale, by the widest margin in history.

But it all dangled on that putt, and (I'll always believe) the Grand Slam climax of 1930.

Ben Hogan's Great Comeback

by HERB GRAFFIS

NOBODY ELSE IN SPORTS HAS EVER EXperienced anything like Ben Hogan's circuit trial to determine if a sound golf swing and a short game of icy finesse would stand up after a long layoff with knitting bones, torn muscles and deadly peril to the circulatory system—result of an auto smashup. A long sentence? Just a short putt compared to Ben's comeback.

Hogan hauled up the curtain on his Revival Meeting in January 1950 with a 275-yard down-the-middle drive on Riviera Country Club's 513-yard first hole in the $15,000 Los Angeles Open. That's history. Following an opening round of seventy-three (two over par) he hammered out sixty-nine, sixty-nine, sixty-nine for a seventy-two-hole total of 280—likewise old copy, as was the eventual play-off with victorious Sam Snead. The big story was, remains and is that Hogan, inches away from a slab in a morgue eleven months before, was back, minus a wheel chair. Incidentally, his 280 total was but four strokes more than his own record 276 over the same Riviera course a year and a half earlier, in the summer of 1948, when he won the National Open.

Certainly, he threw away shots in the Los Angeles Open; he threw away a bushel more during the Bing Crosby $10,000 Invitation that followed immediately. At Pebble Beach, Hogan lapsed and limped painfully. Had he listened to his own dictates instead of his loyalty to pal Crosby, he would have rested for two weeks with his legs in the air, to restore some semblance of normal circulation, after the first tournament.

Dispatches from Pebble Beach were melodramatic. Here's a typical one:

"Sentimental favorite, Ben Hogan was far back among the professionals. Finishing in semidarkness, but followed by a huge gallery, came the tragic figure of the tournament. Still limping from the auto accident that nearly took his life, Hogan posted a three-round total of 223 . . . not good enough to cut for any of the money in terms of the top fifteen scores. Not that he needs it. He won this same tournament a year ago with an eight-under-par total of 208 and rounds of 70-68-70. On the same three courses this time, he posted scores of 77-74-72-223 where scores of 221 paid off.

". . . Cold, wind and mushy going combined with Hogan's fatigue to check the little ex-champion. Poor chips to the green cost him many strokes throughout the three-day play."

"I shouldn't have tried to make two tournaments in a row," Hogan himself ruefully remarked.

Hogan was at the top of the heap when a bus crashed into his car near Van Horn, Texas, February 2, 1949. He'd won thirteen of thirty tournaments he'd been in since January, 1948, had been the year's top money winner with $32,112, and had won the Vardon Trophy with an average of 69.30 shots for seventy-six rounds of stroke play against the sharpest dog-eat-dog nomads of the PGA circuit. To wrap it up in a blue ribbon, he'd won the PGA, National Open and Western Open in four weeks—something of a modern grand slam.

Then disaster!

After lying by the side of a highway for an hour, Hogan was taken more than a hundred miles into Hotel Dieu at El Paso. There I saw him, a few days after the wreck. Hospital authorities were discreetly noncommittal. The best one could get on Hogan was that he had a fighting chance. His lovely wife, Valerie, who suffered only minor injuries in the crash, was desperately prayerful; the look in her eyes lighted up that hospital room. Ben, bandaged so that he looked like a tackling dummy, smiled at her wanly.

"I'll make it," he said.

Ben had a shoulder bone cracked almost in two.

The round bone in his left ankle was split as though it had been chopped by an ax. There were numerous other internal ruptures. His legs and hips were badly hammered. Until a few days before he started in the Los Angeles Open his legs were bandaged from crotch to ankle. There, he played with bandages only from the knee down.

When Hogan crashed, he weighed less than 130 pounds, compared to his fighting weight of 137. Worn out from strenuous campaigning, he was headed home for a rest. Dried out, Ben didn't have much physical reserve.

He laughs now as he gives credit for the miracle of his recovery to the readiness of doctors to agree on technique more quickly than pro golfers do when studying a sidehill lie. Dr. Barker of Mayo Clinic at Rochester, Minnesota, and Dr. Ochsner of New Orleans were consulted when Hogan, after cheating death, went into a sudden relapse. Blood clots were thrusting toward his heart. Ochsner performed a ligation of the vena cava. (From the Sanskrit, that means tying off the particularly large blood vessel that carries venus blood to the heart. This means that other veins must take up the burden—a condition that can be dangerous.) Before that skilled cutting and repair job had healed, Hogan began training for his comeback.

Ben started working his legs months before his shoulder injuries had healed to a point where he was allowed to swing a club. After tentative roadwork in a hospital walking device that supported his weight, came that great day when he first was able to walk around the living room of his home at Fort Worth. In the same determined manner with which he'd gone at those hours of golf practice—a chore that's a little like digging ditches—he managed to go three laps of the room.

A few days later, he made five laps, then ten, and eventually worked himself up to forty-five circuits. Days passed drearily. He got so he could risk running around the room. He'd run until he was ready to drop.

"That was very hard work," he recalls, "because there didn't seem to be much point to it—just driving yourself. When you hit golf balls hour after hour, you can see where they're going . . . where they land. The improvement in my legs couldn't be seen or felt until weeks later."

Hogan's recovery was not entirely due to the normal desire to be physically sound. Countless letters, telegrams and phone calls touched off a responsibility he felt deeply. Not one to talk sentimentally, Ben said he *had* to come back. "So many folks were praying for me . . . and they let me know it!"

He had some bad setbacks in his convalescent routine. After his indoor running he paid a penalty of overexertion. The nights were not altogether hours of healing sleep. His wife would watch him tossing, holding his hands in front of him as though he were gripping a club, and waving a hand as if he were signaling the gallery to "get back on the left."

With a fine courage of her own, Valerie Hogan, from the day they were married in 1935, has been her husband's strongest, most consistent booster. And in those early days it had been rugged. During this stretch, Hogan tried invading the pro-tournament field and went broke. To restore meat to the table, he became a croupier at a gambling casino near Fort Worth. Today Hogan retains the inscrutable features, the ice-green eyes of a percentage-wise laborer in a wagering house.

When he finally hit the jackpot, in the North-South Open at Pinehurst, North Carolina, in 1940, Hogan didn't fool. Walking to the eighteenth tee in the final round, he could have taken an eight and still got home the winner! When Valerie, tagging at his heels, realized this, she broke down, crying joyously and quietly, and admonishing Ben, "Don't break a leg . . . don't break a leg!"

The day finally came when Hogan was able to get outside and walk a couple of blocks. Followed a ride out to Colonial Country Club at Fort Worth, where he walked three holes, and Ben knew that the return trip to competition was merely a question of time.

He practiced putting until his legs were weary. After walking nine holes one day at Colonial he decided to venture his first round of eighteen holes. That landed him back in bed for two days with a sick stomach. His doctor said he'd pushed himself too much.

Ben got over that relapse quickly. He'd discovered that he still had the old game in good enough shape to respond to polishing. That soul-soaring revelation confirmed what he'd believed the first day he was able to get up.

He played three or five holes a day, but prior to arriving at Los Angeles he had played only two complete rounds. Weighing 155, he looked fresher than the fidgety trouper who had quit the tournament grind after losing the Phoenix play-off to Jimmy Demaret late in January, 1949. As far as Hogan could ascertain, the excess weight wasn't an added burden. The only time he felt sharp physical discomfort during the Los Angeles tourney was the Monday morning after he'd played ten holes in a cold rain during that washed-out third round.

A couple of practice-round sixty-nines before the L. A. affair on Riviera's 7020-yard par-seventy-one course signified that Hogan was Hogan again, although there's a great difference between practice-round play and the pressure of tournament play. In one of those rounds, Hogan and Ed Furgol were playing against Jackie Burke and John Barnum for a ten-dollar Nassau. At the fourteenth, Hogan and Furgol were one down and Ben asked for a press bet for thirty dollars. The other boys, all of whom can belt the ball, had been outdriving Hogan. With a chance to convert a loss into a profit, Ben outdrove them all on the fifteenth, was inside them on the 145-yard sixteenth and outdrove them again on the 585-yard seventeenth and the eighteenth.

Furgol, collecting his half of the wager, said to Burke and Barnum, "It's later than you think."

Jimmy Thomson appraised Hogan's comeback as an exhibit of "a hell of a lot of will power." "Ben," remarked Jimmy, "is the sort of a fellow who would lie in bed unable to move, and keep thinking, 'I'll do it again.' And so he will. Remember Georgia Coleman, the diver, who was stricken by polio and made herself walk again by sheer, stubborn driving force of a real champion's mind? Hogan has that same magnificent temperament."

What change was there in Hogan's game during the eleven months' hiatus? Says Tony Penna, always a shrewd analyst of a swing, "There's more hand action than Hogan formerly showed when making full shots. That could be a subconscious compensation for damaged legs."

Lloyd Mangrum agreed with Penna, although Mangrum diagnosed the slight difference as resulting from Hogan's favoring his left side a bit and easing on the leg spring. "What happens in a good golf swing happens too fast to make coordination a conscious operation," said Mangrum. It's his observation that Hogan is naturally a little "wristier" than he himself or Sam Snead, and that the experts, scrutinizing Hogan's footwork, leg action, and hand action, simply became more aware of this fact.

Mangrum was convinced that Hogan's comeback success was based on the superior soundness of the swinger's technique as contrasted with the old-style hitting.

"One thing that'll help Ben," Mangrum said, "is knowing, after his long session of being laid up, that everything from then on was sure to be an improvement. The Army experience helped me. After I got out of that jeep smashup alive, I knew that everything from there in was for free. Some of the boys worry themselves sick about losing a tournament by a few shots, but I get well immediately by realizing I was lucky to have been able to play at all."

Before the Los Angeles play-off, Snead said, "It's still the same. The only things I fear in golf are lightning, a downhill putt and Hogan."

Jimmy Demaret, who has played more with Hogan than any other star, was jubilant. "It's amazing. When we were coming home from the Ryder Cup matches, a doctor on the *Queen Mary* had to give Ben some shots to ease his pain. The strain of being nonplaying captain of our squad hadn't been mild on a man of Ben's temperament. I thought his nerves were shot . . . perhaps for good. He's answered that!"

Just before that smashup, Hogan told me, "From here on I'm gonna spare myself a little instead of beating myself into the ground." In a sense, he was forced into that.

There were hours of putting and chipping on Hogan's routine, which would tire the legs, arms and hands—but not his competitive heart. That heart returned Hogan to the headlines.

Paul Bunyan–Golfer

by FRANK SCULLY

JAMES STEVENS, WHO WROTE PAUL Bunyan's biography, never met Bunyan, but I have met Johnny Montague. Don't ask me if Johnny Montague is his real name. Did anybody ever ask Stevens if Bunyan was the real name of the colossus of logrollers? And whether it was or not, what bearing would a matter of billing have on the plausibility of the old logger's Olympian feats? A Hercules of the hillbillies by any other name would smell as strong.

And whether Paul Bunyan did or didn't exist doesn't nick the fine polish off the fact that after months of pursuing him I finally cornered the Paul Bunyan of golf. I was as curious as anybody to find out if it was true that he made holes-in-one by teeing off one course and holing the drive on another course ten miles away. I wanted to see if he could stop dead a big wind which was bothering his putts by coughing right in its face.

Like others I had my doubts about those pitches of his out of sand traps on a downhill lie, pitches with so much "English" on them they spin back to within a few inches of the cup. Most golfers, champions included, are glad to get out of a trap any way they can, and none I ever met will try a trick shot when in trouble, and certainly not the most difficult trick shot in golf. None, that is, except this Man Mountain Montague.

Did anybody, I wanted to know, ever *see* him hit a bull's-eye on a rifle range at 400 yards, ten in a row, for a perfect sharpshooter's score? What was underneath these skyscrapers of legend, these sagas of a Samson shorn of his beard and reduced in his rage to playing society shinny to keep him in cocktail money?

For years I had heard these fantastic tales of Montague's prowess over California fields where once giant redwoods cracked in two when Paul Bunyan sneezed, fields now given over to the lavender game of Park Avenue shinny, or, as it's known in sissier circles, gashouse hockey. I had chased him through boulevard stops, only to get tickets while he zoomed on to one more incredible feat in an incredible game. But in the end I got my man.

I caught up with him one night in the mid-1930's at the Lakeside Golf Course, which is bounded on the east by Warner Bros. studios, and on the south by the Universal studios.

On one side of Man Mountain Montague as I entered the clubhouse was Ed Kennedy, 210-pound comic, famous from left to right for the "Kennedy burn," and once a pretty good heavyweight palooka in his own right. On the other side of him was Oliver Hardy, 285-pound comic of Hal Roach's pie penitentiary. Behind him was Grantland Rice, the good old romantic of the rose-tinted realm of sport. They were playing straight for the Popeye of golf.

Their handshakes were routine, done, especially the comics', in deadpan. You know, comics. Anything for a laugh.

Then came Montague. He shook hands as if I were a Capulet.

All golfers, duffers more than top-flight players, are horny-handed Elks on this handshake thing. That's not what I mean. This Montague, if his name *is* Montague, has calluses, but he's got muscles, too. When he handshakes you, you wince, and when you quit wincing, you cry out, and when you cry out, you collapse. Then the bodyguards walk away, figuring their work is done.

Montague is a killer. Bobby Jones attributed his own success to never minding what his opponent was doing but always playing against par. Montague, like Little, hounds his opponent from tee to tee—a Dempsey of golf.

He's not fat, but he looks fat in a sweatshirt. He isn't thin either. He's chunky. Not over five feet ten, he must weigh well over 200 pounds. His hair is black, his teeth are good, and he can smile now and then to prove it.

He wears what the fashion editors would call a

gray ensemble—consisting of a gray sweatshirt, gray trousers, and black and white sport shoes over gray socks. He drinks Scotch and soda, and if prodded with a pitchfork, he'll talk.

He doesn't deny all the supercolossal things others attribute to him on the golf course. He says if you have the physique and something more than the brain of a gnat, you can duplicate the things he does. He wasn't born with a silver putter in his mouth. In fact, he started playing golf late in life. All right, "nuts." I'm only telling you what he told me.

The nearest approach to such a player as Montague was the old-time trick-shot billiard expert. Charlie Peterson of St. Louis, for instance, could play any trick shot made and beat any man in the business, any man but a top money player like Hoppe. Hoppe learned three-cushion billiards from Peterson and then took the world's stiff shirt away, Peterson's included.

Montague is like that in golf. He lives and earns. If there's money involved, he'll play eagles and birdies wherever the stakes are biggest. I asked him why he didn't win a couple of Opens just to get his skill into the record. He said he wasn't interested enough to play in a tournament five days running.

No, he's hardly interested in records. On the Pebble Beach Course, world famous for its beauty and difficulty, Montague once reached the eighteenth green with two putts left for a sixty-six and a new course record. Instead of holing the ball, he reached down and picked it up and walked off. He wasn't interested in records anyway, was his only explanation.

His specialty is outsharking sharks when the game goes fishy. His many trick bets often bring up arguments when the pay-off comes. His most potent trouble-settlers are two enormous fists backed up by something better than 200 pounds of hard muscles.

"The bet was fair," he will say. "Now pay me, sire, or I'll break your goddamned neck."

He usually collects pronto.

He was approached on one occasion by one of those fishy-eyed guys who carry a deck of aces up their sleeve and a heart as weak as a pullet's under their vest.

"Where you've got it on us, Monty, is in your drive," he said.

"All right," says Johnny. "I'll play you a hole for a thousand bucks and swap balls after the drive."

The other man agreed. Montague, leading off with the driving, sent his ball over 300 yards down the fairway with a tremendous whack. The shark teed up and deliberately dubbed his drive for about ten or fifteen feet.

Montague took the shark's ball and got 320 yards on his brassie shot, but even so the shark come in one stroke under Monty.

"I don't like to get beat this way," said Johnny calmly. "What do you say to playing another hole for—2000 bucks under the same conditions? We'll change balls after the drive, same as this time. Maybe my luck will change."

"Okay," said the shark.

This time he was afraid to top his ball, so he made a fair drive about 150 yards.

When Montague came to bat, he very carefully teed his ball as if he were going to drive it 300 yards and give the guy this hole, too. Then he stepped up, got his position and drove his ball with the wind for about 375 yards—but it was in the opposite direction from the green they were playing for.

"Now pay me," he said to the shark. "Or I'll break you in two."

The shark paid off.

But he has a reputation for square shooting so long as his opponents keep on the level. He will play with anybody and bet any denominations on any points of the game. He doesn't mind playing with dubs even, and will give them their own handicap so long as it is at all reasonable. With Lakeside's par at seventy Montague gave Jack Oakie a handicap of sixty-five strokes and beat him twice.

Of tremendous strength, in actuality as well as legend, he is easily capable of hoisting an average man without bending his elbows. Lakeside once suspended him for heaving a fellow member over the bar in a little tiff.

One strong man of the films made the mistake of questioning Montague's physical prowess once. It was in the Lakeside locker room. As if it were much ado about nothing, Monty seized the film player, bundled him struggling into a locker and turned the key. No one had any desire to question his strength after that.

But when he came upon a man in Hollywood who was demonstrating his strength by jiggling the front end of a light car off of the ground, Montague ogled him scornfully and reached down and hoisted the front end of a Lincoln eight inches above the sod.

Even at Lakeside he remains a mystery man. As a mystery man he is accepted. No fellow member is interested in prying too closely into Monty's personal affairs. There are rumors, of course, plenty of them. He is commonly credited with having a hidden gold or silver mine in the desert as fabulously rich as Death Valley Scotty's. He drops out of sight from time to time and no one knows where he goes.

But Johnny knows among other things the character of a legend from its peasant birth till it becomes ennobled as enduring literature. Sprout an anecdote and leave the storytellers to make an epic of it. Keep quiet and let the poets do the work. Lindbergh flew the Atlantic, kept quiet and shunned publicity; he became the most famous flier in the world. And when Johnny Montague pulled off a few stunts that made the peasants gap, retired to his Scotch and soda and refused to be interviewed, he became folklore around the nineteenth hole.

There is no doubt that he is a tremendous golfer. Grantland Rice was in dead earnest when he said the national amateur championship tournament in golf would not be won by the best man because Johnny Montague wasn't playing in it. Mysterious Montague had no need of loving cups when he could have a library of legends woven around him. Paul Bunyan didn't go in for medals either. He waited until the peasants built a statue of him so big they had to use a pine log for his mustache.

So when Johnny took his eighteen-ounce driver and in five strokes drove a golf ball for a distance that varies in every account from a quarter of a mile to a whole mile (a member of Lakeside who says he saw Montague do it swears to me it was a

mile) the press thought it was news, and cameramen went out to mug him. When they snapped him, Montague politely asked for the negatives and tore them up and let it be known that he was not for publication. The gentlemen of the press went home with a better story. Here was a man of tremendous feats who for some reason shunned publicity. Mysterious Montague was born, and Paul Bunyan frowned with apprehension amongst the temples of Valhalla.

So in a short time tales that would stun a Spaniard's imagination were afloat about Silent Johnny, the golfer who wielded a colossal club like a fairy's wand and kicked in the faces of news cameramen when he was caught in the act of sending a small white pellet on a one way trip to the moon.

Even *Time* could only march on by catching this Goliath while dozing. The news weekly cackled when it got a couple of very bad snaps of the mysterious Monty by trick photography.

Bob Wallace hid in a clump of bushes at Lakeside, clicked Montague twice with the aid of a long-range lens, handed the films to his brother, stuck another film in the camera's magazine, clicked a few more shots and made enough noise doing it to attract Monty's attention, and then surrendered the stooge films when Monty came running over and demanded them, or else.

The pictures Wallace's brother got away with show a guy putting, and his white cap so completely blackens out his face that it could be a picture of anybody weighing 200 pounds. You have to know Montague to know they are pictures of him, whereas the real value of pictures is to help you recognize in the flesh somebody you know only from pictures.

Monty isn't adverse to giving out a few tales himself at times, when he feels like it. I asked him if the tale of his killing the bird with a golf ball was true. He said it was.

He was playing a foursome at the Fox Hills Country Club. At the tenth tee the party was forced to wait for players ahead to get out of range. Bored with the idling, Montague's roving eye spotted a row of birds on a telephone line 175 yards away.

"See those birds?" he said to the others. "Watch me pick off the one farthest to the right."

Teeing up an old ball he took his brassie and hit a full drive. The bird fell with his head snapped off as cleanly as if guillotined.

That's a sampler. Other more credible tales are no less remarkable.

There is, for instance, the time he made one of the queerest handicap wagers in link history with Bing Crosby. When the mighty Montague offered to take him on for good at twenty bucks a hole, using only a baseball bat, a shovel and a rake for

clubs, while the crooner used his regular full set, it looked like pennies from heaven for Bing.

Playing from the tenth tee at Lakeside Monty, as a drive, hit the ball with his bat fungo-fashion as a baseball player does. It landed in a trap about 300 yards away and to the left of the green. With a terrific heave of his shovel Monty got out of the trap and on the green. Then he sank the ball for a birdie three, using the rake as a billiard cue for his putter.

Crosby holed out in five, paid off, and went home.

Gray-Flannel World of the Golf Pro

by THOMAS B. MORGAN

CROWDS AT PROFESSIONAL GAMES REflect the personality of the sport almost as much as those who play it. Watch the crowd and you will see the nature of The Game in the fan's expressions and even in their sounds. Thus fight fans are mean and boxing is the meanest of sports. Baseball fans alternate between boredom and delirium. Football brings out the lions. And professional golf attracts the most sophisticated, cool, businesslike spectators in sports—which three adjectives can be applied to the players who participate in its gains.

When on the first tee in the first round of the Carling Open a couple of years ago, a tournament typical of the professional-golf circuit, Mike Souchak swung his driver into a ball and sent it flying 300 yards down the fairway at Cleveland's Seneca Golf Course, a crowd of about 500 typical golf fans whispered in unison: "Geeee-eez!" This sound was an almost reverential sigh of awe and appreciation which has come to be, universally, the golf fan's polite, hot-ice way of saying: "Olé!"

Only after Souchak had holed out for a birdie three did the gallery permit itself a conventional shout, a brief thawing spasm that seemed to shake up those older fans in Panama hats and plaid shirts who were not prepared for a sudden noise. The sound drifted away, replaced by the soft rattle of the wind in the trees, and the fans talked in hushed tones as they pursued Souchak and his playing partners, Doug Ford and Al Besselink, to the second tee.

Following Souchak in Cleveland on the four days of the week—Thursday, Friday, Saturday and Sunday—when, about forty-seven weeks a year, big-money golf tournaments are held, one could distinguish a few other characteristic golf sounds. One was the Fateful Groan, which followed any putt Souchak missed, and especially those that entered the cup, rolled around and came out the other side. Another was the Modified Geez, which became "Geeee-R Usalem!" when a stout Souchakian drive landed in the rough.

By and large, however, the golf fans were a

singularly restrained group. They were as sophisticated as the bullfight *aficionado* who knows his passes and his matadors, cool as the kibitzer at the poker game who himself plays for smaller stakes, and businesslike. The latter quality is virtually unique among golf fans because they actually *profit* from watching the game: since almost every fan is a player-of-sorts, he not only enjoys the contest but also learns from it. Golf is the one pro sport which is so easy for an amateur to play that the spectator is able to patronize it in his own self-interest. With 8,000,000 people playing golf nowadays, it is no wonder that the pro game is doing sensationally well. The average number of paying customers at golf tournaments throughout the year is more than 25,000.

The game has no "season": tournaments are scheduled so that fans at each stop along the "Tour" may see those seventy-five American and Canadian players who are the hard core which sustains the professional side of golf.

These seventy-five men, supplemented by a fluid group of about 250 who play an occasional tournament, roam the Southwest and the South on the "Winter Tour" until the ice melts up north. Then they crisscross the country in milder months wherever there is a purse. Their Tour reminds one a little of a floating crap game, except that nobody is chasing the pros; instead, tournament promoters are begging them to play and are putting up heavy loot to induce their co-operation.

Taken as a group, modern pro golfers aren't playing for fun; tournament golf is the work they do for a living in the prime of their lives. They sacrifice the fun of golf for concentration. They affiliate with country clubs, but usually they are never around to give golf lessons; they earn their club salary merely by lending their name to the club. They fly in planes and drive their own cars rather than ride trains in groups. Most of them are married; over half are accompanied on the Tour by wives and some even bring the kids, lugging them from motel to motel. There are so many good players among them that none can afford (for long) to live a roistering life that would take its toll in physical condition. The Tour grind is so relentless and the tension on the course so sharp, week after week after week, that the sheer

ability to survive, to endure, can be the difference between a profit-making year and a losing one. Dick Mayer, for example, had a bout with tranquilizers brought on by an excess of anxieties in 1956 which almost ruined his career. Fortunately, his wife joined him on the Tour, helped him get back into shape and was with him in 1957 when he won the U.S. Open—and a total of $100,000.

Eighty per cent of the top money winners on the Tour are college men. They have had lots of intercollegiate competition and it has not hurt them, either, that their college credits include the study of economics. They see golf as a career, which minimizes frivolity (with such exceptions as Tommy Bolt). In short, they make a total commitment to pro golf that may last well into middle age.

Consider Mike Souchak. He is a burly man (five feet eleven, 200 pounds) with a Slavic face, brown hair and a square jaw. He's in his mid-thirties and feels his best years in golf are ahead of him.

On the first day of the Carling Open, Mike was resplendent in a navy-blue polo shirt, sky-blue trousers and matching sky-blue glove. He was no Jimmy Demaret, who, according to Herbert Wind, had a wardrobe "consisting of nineteen sports jackets, fifty-five shirts, twenty jerseys, seventy-one pairs of slacks and forty-three variations in headgear," but Souchak did have a touch of the peacock. Never far from him was his caddy, seventeen-year-old Harold Olson of Cleveland, who liked to run his fingers through the mink fur of Mike's wood covers. On the side of Mike's bag, the name of MacGregor, the sporting-goods manufacturer for whom he works, was stitched in six-inch letters. Doug Ford had the name of his sponsor written on his bag with equal verve, but Al Besselink's was more modest. Behind or ahead of them were most of the top money winners of golf—Arnold Palmer, Art Wall, Gene Littler, Billy Casper, Marty Furgol, Bolt, Mayer, Rosburg, etc. . . . In four days, they would hit golf balls and walk 27,864 yards for a slice of the $25,000 prize money. The winner's share would be $3500 unless he had won the Carling Open before, in which case he would receive a $5000 bonus. The maximum Souchak could win was $3500.

For most of that first eighteen-hole round, Souchak and his playing partners played relaxed golf. Between shots, they talked about golf shirts and endorsement deals and money. They sounded like three admen having lunch at P. J. Clarke's. Of the three, Souchak was making the most money for the year, thus far. At the start of the Carling, he had already won almost $40,000 in prize money with five months left to play, if he chose to follow the Tour to the autumn's end. This included a $10,-000 bonus which had been given to him by a Calcutta pool gambler after his victory in the Tournament of Champions at Las Vegas. (The Calcutta is a form of auction-gambling on golf legal only in Nevada. Each player in the Tournament of Champions was "sold" to the highest bidder. The money was pooled, ten per cent was taken off for charity, and the balance redistributed proportionately according to the order of finish. When Mike won it, the pool was $380,000, of which his "owner" collected considerably more than $100,-000 on a less than $20,000 investment. As is customary, Mike received about ten per cent of the winning gambler's share.)

Furthermore, Mike had earned his salary, bonuses, and golfing equipment from MacGregor; plus $2000 from Grossinger's, an upstate-New York resort which claims him as a club pro; plus salary and bonuses from the Izod company, whose colorful shirts and trousers he sports on the fairway like a human billboard; plus bonuses and free golf shoes (he now has a contract with shoe-manufacturer Johnson Murphy); flat sums (minimum $1000) for posing in cigarette ads (Mike never smokes on the golf course); plus flat sums for appearances on three different TV golf shows; plus proceeds from an investment with Jimmy Demaret and Jackie Burke in an elegant Houston country club, The Champions; plus profits from distributing an electric golf cart in the South; plus income from a little real estate in his own town, Durham, North Carolina; plus, plus, plus.

At the edge of the fairway, the caddies talked a bit about money, too. Each knew the financial status of the man he was working for—in terms of caddy fees. The minimum fee posted was $5 per round. The word was that Souchak paid a minimum of $12.50 and as high as $25 per round if he won the big money. Realizing the possibilities for

himself, Harold Olson was one of the most intense observers of Souchak's game. He shook his head sadly whenever Mike missed a putt and could not repress a smile when Mike had a good hole.

Souchak and Ford played evenly at par, while Besselink was one over at the par-five sixth hole. Mike's drive sliced just enough to be troublesome. It perversely rolled into the crowd behind the fairway ropes. The fans formed a small pocket around it and waited for Mike. To further complicate the lie, a water hazard lay across the fairway near the green. Shooting before Mike, Ford and Besselink used their irons and placed their shots on the nearer, safer side of the water. Mike studied the situation like an artillery spotter. He squinted his eyes ("My most valuable piece of equipment") and decided to gamble on a wood shot. The ball would certainly go as far as the water, but there was a chance that it might drop in it.

"What club you going to use?" a fan asked, politely.

Faithful employee that he is, Mike answered: "I'm going to hit this ball with a MacGregor wood."

"I like a gambler," said the fan. "Taking chances is what wins."

Mike turned cold, set himself over the ball and blasted it with his brassie. The ball soared up and over the water, almost to the green.

"Geeee-eez!" the people sighed.

On the back nine, the pressure was turned up a notch. Mike was at par, but par never wins in pro golf, so he began looking for birdies.

"You build up to a Sunday of pressure," he said, "but a stroke saved on Thursday counts as much as a stroke saved on the last nine." It was a humbling thought.

Mike extended his putting ritual a few seconds longer on each hole. On the twelfth green, he took his time inspecting the path from ball to cup, picking up stray leaves and pieces of dirt. From a squatting position behind the ball, he sighted along the shaft of his putter to the hole. He cased it the other way: from hole to ball. Twenty yards away, a marshal seemed to sense the mounting urgency and scurried out of Mike's line of sight. Mike practiced swatting an invisible ball, stepped inches closer and prepared to putt the ball about twelve feet. In the hot silence, broken only by the bird sounds and the far-off clatter of a bulldozer, he putted. The ball stopped short.

"You can't win them all," he said, matter-of-factly.

On the fourteenth fairway, play was stalled by the threesome ahead, which was now taking its own sweet time with the putting. Mike said he was going to play two more tournaments and then go home for a while. He said he wanted to see his family because there were only three things in the world he cared about: his family, his religion (he's Catholic) and his golf game. He said he thought he'd like to do some duck hunting. Then he handed his two-iron to Harold Olson and, with his hands, described the way he likes to cook a duck:

"Let me tell you how I make it. You slice up six ducks, really thin, then you mix some bacon grease, some lemon and orange juice and whatever other fruit juices you have, and you marinate the slices of duck in this. Then you cook it nice over a charcoal fire like a steak. Tastes like filet mignon."

Mike got his birdie and finished the round at seventy, one under par. Ford had three birdies, including one based on a thirty-yard chip shot that found the cup. His score was sixty-eight. Besselink, playing with a sprained wrist, finished with seventy-four. They were to meet again in the morning for the second round.

Souchak drank a beer in the clubhouse and repaired to the practice green to sharpen his putting. Harold Olson fished out balls as Mike stroked them in the cup. After forty-five minutes, Mike quit.

"Maybe I'll be better tomorrow, Harold," he said, believing, as gold miners do, that tomorrow will be the day.

Mike changed his shoes in the locker room. He was tired and depressed, the way all athletes are in all locker rooms everywhere whenever they have not had a winning day. He was endlessly willing, however, to talk about golf. The way the pro game was going thrilled him.

"I have to make a thousand a week out of golf just to pay my bills," Mike said. "It costs me two-fifty to three hundred a week just to live on the road and that doesn't count my home expenses for the wife and kids. I've got no manager. Nobody pays me any expense money. I have to keep all the details up here," pointing to his head, "from investments to sending out the laundry. (That reminds me, I have to pick up the laundry.) Yet, I have to play well before anything else works. Can't blow it. All any of us have going for us is the ability to play. And there is no law that says you're going to win, ever."

Mike was right about that unromantical, sophisticated fact. The records kept by PGA bear him out. In 1958, only thirty pros won $11,500 or more in prize money.

Even as winners, some of them could not laugh and joke. Since it costs a man at least $8000 to stay on the Tour for six to eight months, prize money alone won't support even those in the top thirty, let alone those in the bottom forty-five. The best guess would be that from all sources of income only twenty pros make more than $25,000 gross a year. The rest get plenty of fresh air.

The curious thing about golf, though, is that the losers *look* as affluent as the winners. Souchak was driving a new, white, four-door Cadillac, which had been sold to him at cost in a publicity deal. But parked next to it at Seneca were three equally expensive models (two Cads and an Imperial) owned by pros you never heard of. There *are* some beginning pros who seem to be scrimping, who travel in trailers to save motel fees and who appear rumpled and wrinkled much of the time. For the most part, though, win or lose, the majority of pros are well dressed, their equipment is first-class, and they eat so well that the casual observer might be misled into thinking everyone in the game was kin of Croesus. This is not true; at least not yet.

The open secret is that many pros with no visible means of support are receiving money either from an individual or a syndicate back home. The practice of investing in the care and feeding of a young pro is now widespread. As the amount of money to be won on the Tour increases, it may become as popular as angeling plays on Broadway. The names of those who have tried the Tour and failed, losing the money of investors, are better forgotten. What inspires investors (besides the possibility of a tax write-off) is the famous killing that was made on Billy Casper, Jr. For two years Casper was sponsored by two businessmen from his home town, Chula Vista, California. In return for investing $24,000 at the rate of $1000 a month, which covered Casper's major expenses, the businessmen made a $30,000 profit while Casper himself netted $70,000. Even so, James Gaquin, field secretary of the Professional Golfers' Association and *the* authority on pro golf records, says: "Investing money in a pro is not a very good risk. Period." But the trouble—or the blessing—is that investors, too, have the gold miner's way of looking at life.

Some men have criticized the practice of sponsoring young pros. The main argument seems to be that the hungriest golfer is the best golfer, an argument that hardly holds water when you consider that the best golfers make the most money. Besides, golf isn't boring. It never was, although it is customary nowadays, especially when older golf writers get together, to bemoan the fact that the game lacks the character and "color" it once had. No doubt, the differences between the generations of pros are marked. One veteran professional, Al Ciuci (of Wingel Foot Country Club, Mamaroneck, New York), who helped raise Gene Sarazen from a caddy to a champion, recalls:

"The pros were different before the war because they were, most of them, just having fun. They rode trains together and stayed together in hotels and rooming houses. They had golf club jobs back home and saved money to go on the Tour as on a vacation. Most of them were single and had never been to college. Like Sarazen, they started out as caddies. They weren't really as hungry as today's pros because there wasn't that much money in it. Today, there's maybe $1,500,000 in prize money available, while between the wars $300,000 was a lot of money. A few big names made a lot and the rest had fun. Then at age thirty or so, they found a girl, got married and left the Tour. That's the way it was."

But such differences notwithstanding, golf has remained the same in one crucial aspect. From Hagen to Hogan to Mike Souchak, the best pro golfers have all been hardheaded, serious men when they settled down to play, no matter what the condition of their night life. Pro golfers through the years have shared a remarkable ability to preserve restraint, to keep their tempers, to play cool when the chips are down. Unlike other games, which call for a hell-for-leather slide, a wild run, a crushing right hand at the peak-moment of suspense, pro golf demands that a man contain himself just at the point when he would like to let out all the pressure in one violent act. Like the cool fans who rejoice in the sport, the cool pro is uniquely characteristic of golf. In this way, golf has not changed; the pros have merely had to wait until a large enough number of people were playing the amateur game in America so that they could be properly appreciated.

This is not to say that there are *no* high livers among the supported and self-supporting pro golfers of today, no hotbloods, no party boys. Some are, indeed, better at elbow-bending and girl-watching than at golf and some even do both well, but Mike Souchak, who typifies the pro golfer of our time, bends the elbow modestly, calls home almost nightly and gets his sleep. The farthest thing from his mind is horseplay which could be only a step from enforced retirement at Happydale Country Club or a future selling, rather than busting, golf balls.

Mike was the ninth child in a family of ten. His father was a hammer man in a steel mill in Berwick, Pennsylvania. A family friend gave him, at age five, a hickory-shaft brassie, and he decided forthwith, to become a great golfer. His brother John, whom he greatly admired, was the pro at the local country club. John encouraged him and Mike hardly considered any other career. Under his senior-class photograph in the Berwick High School yearbook it says that Mike Souchak wants to be a professional golfer. At Duke University in Durham, Mike was single-minded about several things: he had played four years of football (he was an all-Southern Conference left-end), four years of golf, and four years of boy friend to his wife-to-be: he married the girl in 1952 and never thought of living anywhere except Durham, which was Nancy Souchak's home town. He was hired that year as assistant pro at a country club in Philadelphia. In 1953, he wet his feet for two months on the Tour without success. He met though, an established pro (Jackie Burke) who helped him make a deal with MacGregor. "I felt like I had conquered the world when I made that contract with them," Mike recalls. The arrangement with the sporting-goods manufacturer was a basic step. It provided him with $750 cash and all of his equipment: clubs, bag (with advertising on it) and balls at the rate of three dozen per week. Then he became assistant to Claude Harmon, the pro at Winged Foot, in the summer of 1953. "Tommy Armour was a full-paying member of the club," Mike recalls. "He helped me a lot. I gave lessons and played with people like Gerald Shattuck who runs Schrafft's, and William J. McCormack. (Mr. McCormack was called 'Mr. Big' of the water front, but I think all that stuff they wrote about him was crap.) Those people saw to it that I could make ends meet." The next year, Mike went touring in earnest. Leamon Couch, a Durham furniture maker, financed him. "You want to play, you go ahead and play and don't worry about the money," Couch said. He had done the same for Tommy Bolt. In 1955, Mike's second on the Tour, he began in February at the Texas Open. His first round tied the existing PGA record for eighteen holes of competitive golf: sixty. On the second nine of that round, he shot twenty-seven! For seventy-two holes, he hit the ball only 257 times, which is still a record. The next week, back-to-back, Mike won the Houston Open. In two weeks, he became a big-time professional golfer. He played most of 1955 and won about $30,000 in prize money. He was the fourth leading money winner. "Leamon Couch, my sponsor, would never take a nickel," Mike says. "I had to *make* him take back even the money he had given me. He was making no investment. He did it for me simply because he wanted to." Mike went on to become eighth leading money winner in 1956. Then he grew careless and let his weight go up to the fat-boy division. He made money in 1957 and 1958, but won only one first prize—the St. Paul Open. He had been making a living but had not been doing the thing he had always said he wanted to do—"be the best golfer there is." Then he started dieting in January, 1959. No one had told him to lose weight. In pro golf there's no one to tell you much of anything. He had simply realized where he was wrong and had begun to cut down on what he

ate. "I lost twenty-five pounds in a few months," he says. "Look what it's done for my game."

With so much potential in golf for himself, a little thing like Mike's weight could have been decisive. What's more, it could have had a profound effect on pro golf itself because there aren't that many colorful, friendly, dandy Mike Souchaks around. The game depends upon a mere handful of superb athletes; without them there is no game.

Saturday in Cleveland, a clear blue sky and soft, dry winds brought more than 10,000 people to the third round of the Carling Open. Paired with Gene Littler and Jim Ferrier, Mike Souchak teed off eagerly in the afternoon. His eagerness was something one felt rather than saw; outwardly, he seemed placid and narrow-eyed as ever, but his walk was brisker and he was full of golfing homilies as he moved from hole to hole.

"Golf is the only game we have with room for the individual."

"In golf, you compete against no one but yourself and you don't have to share the satisfaction of winning with anyone."

"Anything you get in golf is due to your ability and only that."

Meanwhile, his game went (for him) to pieces.

On the fourth green, he missed a two-foot putt for a bogie. He went for his wedge in the trap to the left of the sixth and overshot the hole by twenty feet. He three-putted in spite of the most deliberate attention to the putting ritual. "You're on," he said sagely, "or you're not on." Mike went two over par and could not find the birdies. The sun was hot and he began using the towel more often. Then, to tighten the screws a little, Gene Littler began to get the range. Mike picked up a stroke on seventeen. He drove the green on eighteen, but two-putted for a mediocre seventy-two, one over par.

From the scorer's table, Mike went directly to the practice green, shunning the cold beer and chitchat in the clubhouse, and practiced putting for an hour. Even here, the balls wouldn't go down. Harold Olson, the caddy, was worried, tried not to show it, but the listless manner in which he returned the balls seemed a foreboding of doom.

"Tomorrow it may be better," Mike said, as he

quit working and turned now to join his comrades. "Tomorrow, Harold."

The clubhouse was filled with grim-visaged pros. Mike had a beer with Rosburg, Ford, and Wally Ulrich. There was enough felt-pressure in the room to drive a steam engine. The men talked, swearing at themselves and at their game. They talked about the weight of putters and the speed of greens. They talked about the goddam hazard on the sixth.

"See, this is a funny game," Mike said. "It changes from hour to hour and hole to hole. It's all mental. You can go out of your mind if you're not careful."

To deter that, Mike took himself to the movies that evening with Jim Gaquin. Back at the motel, he also watched the Late Show and did not fall asleep until it was over. It starred Victor McLaglen, whom Mike liked.

As the saying goes, "A tight match is good for business on Sunday." At least a dozen pros had a chance to win when the final round began. Mike was still only two strokes off the pace; others had had their troubles, too. About 15,000 fans showed up to watch the finish. Mike went around with a large gallery. Hole by hole, the common nerve of suspense was pulled tighter. They used the Fateful Groan when he drove an iron shot nearly 200 yards and yet missed the green by ten feet. The Modified Geez accompanied Mike into the rough.

At the eighteenth hole, the bleachers were full and shirt-white in the sun. It had happened that Dow Finsterwald, starting out three strokes behind, had come in three strokes under. His eight-under-par total of 276 for seventy-two holes made him suddenly the man to beat. Following him, Paul Harney, Gene Littler and Mike Souchak all had a chance to tie. Each man needed a birdie two on the final hole. The crowd was frozen in the heat. There could have been few places in the world where so many people were at that moment giving so much attention to something they deemed important and yet were not making a sound, not so much as rattling a candy wrapper. Neither Harney nor Littler were able to do better than par on the hole. Mike Souchak, however, drove the green

with a five-iron. The ball stopped forty feet from the cup. Its lie was back and above the hole on a faint slope. Mike began the ritual of the putt. He examined the turf, picked at imaginary obstacles and prowled about from ball to cup and back again. Even the wind stopped. Mike looked down the shaft of the putter and walked again along the grade to the hole in the ground. The difference between sinking and missing was the difference between $2050 and $3500 in prize money; plus bonuses from MacGregor, Izod, Grossinger's; plus; plus; plus.

Now Mike swung at an imaginary ball for practice and now he stroked the ball.

The Fateful Groan.

The ball had gone truly and well toward the $1450 hole and had fallen dead inches away. Harold Olson put Mike's ball in his pocket.

"Next week, Detroit!" someone shouted at Mike, referring to the Motor City Open at Meadowbrook Country Club.

Mike smiled and waved. He congratulated Finsterwald, who had won the $3500 plus the $5000 bonus for being a repeat winner. The fans stood around, obviously enjoying the close but well-mannered proximity to the players. Whatever Mike felt, he did not show, almost. He just wasn't happy, that's all. But he did say this:

"I want to be able to walk off the eighteenth green and not have anyone know how I feel. That would mean I've really got my emotions under

control. I want to reach that point. It would help me with my game."

The cool pro among the cool fans (more normally ebullient now that it was over) walked about for a while and then left Seneca in his white Cadillac.

Next day, Mike drove to Detroit alone. He found a motel and sent out his laundry and his suits. He tries to do that on Mondays or Tuesdays. He had a good meal in town that evening. Many pros have stomach trouble, but Mike does not; his appetite was fine. Tuesday, he attended to chores, wrote letters, called Nancy and went to Meadowbrook for a practice round. Wednesday he practiced again. Thursday was fair and Friday he equaled the course record with a brilliant sixty-three. Sunday he won it by seven strokes. His prize was $3500, plus, plus, plus.

Which is the way it sometimes is in golf: better tomorrow.

8
GOOD SPORTS ALL

To PARTISANS OF PARTICULAR COMPETITIVE CON-
tests not heretofore included this section is dedicated, a sort of expanded decathlon of events not
on the regular program, but nonetheless important,
not to be slighted, no indeed. There is not room
in these pages for all the great men and great moments, and it is to our sorrow that we have not
been able to print all of the selections from Esquire which might have been gathered under this
title. Squash, billiards and bowling fans, alas! Perhaps next time. But for the moment rejoice aficionados. Here are three great toreros described by
three fine writers: Carlos Arruza, by Barnaby Con-
rad; Joselito, by the American matador Sidney
Franklin; and Dominguín and Ordoñez, by Eric
Sevareid. Airplane enthusiasts: here is Jimmy Doolittle. His greatest moment was thirty seconds over
Tokyo, but who can forget his twenty-three minutes and 44.69 seconds over Cleveland? Mon Dieu!
Hockey fans we present to you a rare treat: the
story of Alfie Moore, an obscure goalie who had
only one great moment and was heard from no
more. That moment—in the Stanley Cup play-off!
Sorry, nothing for spelunkers, but a consolation
for skiers: a view from the top of the world by
James Hilton. Tallyho! old chaps from the hunt-
club set, but pride yourselves on Tommy Hitchcock, a great man in sport who died a hero in the
war. Love means something to us, though to tennis
fans it means nothing. We wouldn't let you down.
We give you Bill Tilden. Snorkelers and Scubas,
you'll have to come up for air. Here's Trudy Ederle
(the only lady in our book, too, and she earned it!).
Runners, on your marks! Get set, we have two for
you: the ordeal the athletes undergo before and
after they set the records, here recorded for the first
time, and a moving tribute to the first Negro to
win an Olympic medal—his great moment; when
Hitler fled—written by his classmate, Budd Schul-
berg. Avast! We have not marooned thee, good
sailor. Yonder sail on the horizon is the Resolute,
plying the waves off Sandy Hook for the America's
Cup. Last but not least (get out your hatpin), presenting Antonino the great, the world's most popu-

lar sports attraction . . . especially if you like wrestling. We understand you're supposed to boo. Now look, if we've left anyone out, don't gang up. We've chosen up a tag team and he's on our side.

At the sound of the bell (gun, whistle, flag or what have you) you're off. Good reading!

The Greatest Bullfight Ever

by BARNABY CONRAD

I HAD A PRETTY NICE BIG HOUSE IN Málaga and I was a friend of Carlos Arruza, the matador, so that's why the Town Council came to me. *"Mira, Señor Vice Consul,"* they said. "We are going to present a gorgeous diamond medal to the *torero* who gives the best performance at the bullfights during our annual fair. It is an exquisite thing, made especially in Madrid at a cost of 5000 *pesetas* and we should enjoy the honor of presenting it to your friend Arruza in your house."

"The honor will be mine," I said. "And I shall plan a party for that date. But how can you be sure Arruza will give the best show?"

"He cannot fail," they said. "First he is fighting both Friday and Sunday; if he is out of form or the bulls are bad on Friday, he will have another chance on Sunday. And secondly, Manolete, Arruza's only real competition, has been wounded and will not be able to fight."

"And thirdly," spoke up a member of the Council uneasily, "he *has* to be the best, for we already have his name engraved on the medal."

On Friday, Carlos arrived for the first fight and Málaga was agog, for he had become the most sensational thing in bullfighting. Most people defended the classic purity of Manolete's style, but for sheer brute courage this young Mexican was unchallenged.

Then, too, the *señoras* and *señoritas* weren't oblivious to that beautiful physique, and the unruly brown hair that topped his shy, handsome face. Arruza had donated the entire proceeds of his first fight of the season, $7000, to the mother of a bullfighter killed in the ring. After that he was the most popular matador in Spain.

This season Arruza was contracted for the staggering number of 140 fights in 180 days! This meant fighting in Madrid one day, Barcelona the next, going to Lisbon, Bilbao, Mallorca, in planes, cars, trains, snatching a meal and a bit of sleep when he could and every day leaving thousands of people thrilled by his skill and courage.

When I went to see him this afternoon before the fight his face was pale and drawn and I could see that the ninety fights he had already fought under his regime had aged him.

"Chiquillo," he said after we'd talked awhile and as he wiggled into the gold brocaded pants, "what's this about a medal?"

I explained.

"Caracoles!" exclaimed Carlos. "They have put my name on it already! But anything can happen in a bullfight! How can they know if I feel like fighting? Or what about the wind? Or what about the bulls, eh? That slight detail must be considered—the bulls."

At four o'clock they paraded into the brilliant sun and the band blared forth with the *paso doble, Carlos Arruza.* Carlos grinned nervously and threw his dress cape up to me.

His first bull was a bad one, but he did pretty well, and the *presidente* let him take a lap around the ring to receive the crowd's applause. The second bull was Estudiante's and he did a very good job, being conceded two ears from the dead animal as an evaluation of his bravery and skill. Morenito de Talavera felt the pressure of the two good fights that had gone before him, and surpassed by far his natural ability, cutting one ear and taking a lap around the ring.

Arruza, seemingly unconcerned by this competition as he waited for his second bull to come out, looked around, hugging his big red and yellow cape to him and smiling his little-boy smile at friends.

His bull skidded out of the *toril* and brought boos from the crowd because it was so small. But the boos switched to *"Olés"* when Arruza passed the bull closely three times, the lethal horns inches away from his knees. Few people objected when, after he had placed three beautifully executed *banderillas* and one sword thrust, the *presidente* granted him both ears and the tail for his brilliant fight. Women threw down roses to him and men threw cigars, hats, even overcoats. A few people booed, though, saying he didn't deserve the tail since the bull was so small.

However, the medal seemed cinched, especially after Estudiante and Morenito de Talavera were bad on the last two bulls, and I left the plaza jubilantly. The next day the program was Estudiante and Morenito again plus a little Mexican Indian named Cañitas. Nothing to fear, we thought, for the bulls were giants; we had seen what Estudiante and Morenito had to offer and who ever heard of Cañitas?

None of the three fighters was anything but discreet on his first bull. But then—the trumpet sounded for Cañitas' second, and out it came—a black and white monster weighing 750 kilos!

Cañitas went pale when he saw the creature rip part of the wooden barrier apart, but he set his Indian jaw and you could see him telling himself, "If I'm going to die I'll die in a blaze of glory." The bull ran around the empty ring twice looking for something to kill, and then Cañitas stepped out and dropped to his knees, letting it go by with a *whoosh,* as the great horns passed his head. A gasp of surprise went up from the crowd who had expected him to play the bull as safely as possible. Then when he passed the bull even closer, they set up a continuous roar. After numerous fancy passes with the cape, he placed three sets of *banderillas* with the arrogance of a gypsy, with the *muleta* he accomplished a *fuera* that bullfighters dream about, then drew back and dropped the bull with a sword thrust almost to the hilt. The crowd went wild and insisted upon his getting both ears, tails and a hoof, the most you can get. I left the plaza for the day, feeling a little sick.

The next day was Sunday, and the Town Council came to see me with long faces. "Now what do we do?" they asked reproachfully, as though it were my fault. "Order another medal," was all I could suggest.

Arruza arrived at six in the morning after hav-

ing fought in Cadiz the afternoon before and driving all night to Málaga. I went to the hotel to wake him at three, and the Idol of Spain was a mess; he looked green and staggered as he got up to go to bathe.

"I'm exhausted." The words tumbled out. "I've got a fever of 102, I can't go on like this every day. I never want to fight again. I'm going to go to bed for ten years when the season is over. How was the fight yesterday?" he continued wearily while putting on his frilled shirt. "I haven't seen the papers as yet."

"Cañitas turned in the best fight of the season," I said.

Carlos stopped tying his tie. "Are you joking?"

"No," I said. "He got inspired—fought as he's never fought before—cut ears, tail and a hoof." I cleared my throat. "But—uh—you'll come up to the house for the ceremony *anyway,* won't you?"

Arruza regarded me quietly and said: "I'll be there, *chiquillo.*"

I made the error of taking two women to the last fight. Carlos was first on the program, and when he got to his knees and let the bull pass by him four times so close that it removed part of his embroidered jacket, the girl on my right passed out; the other girl was just about to faint, too, but she was too busy reviving her friend. Carlos did every pass in the book plus two of his own invention, and the girls couldn't stand any more; they left just about the time he dropped the bull with one thrust. The crowd went wild, and the *presidente* signaled with his handkerchief for the *banderillero* to cut one ear, two ears, two ears and tail, two ears, tail and hoof, and Arruza circled the ring, triumphantly holding his prizes aloft.

It was a wonderful fight, but we all knew Cañitas had been just a bit more graceful, more daring, more suicidal the day before.

After Arruza came Parrita and Andaluz, both good bullfighters, but people were still limp from the first fight and didn't pay much attention to them. When Arruza came out and stood waiting for his second bull people applauded wildly, but we really didn't expect him to do anything more; it's rare when a bullfighter puts up a good performance on both bulls.

The bull was a monstrous creature, and Arruza

studied it from behind the fence for a few moments. Then he stepped out shaking into the ring and stood there swaying and putting his hand up to his feverish head and pressing his hot temples with his fingers, but as the bull drew near he collected himself, let the cape unfurl in front of the animal's nose and passed it by in a series of classic *verónicas* that drew great *"Olés!"* from the crowd. Then in a few moments they were yelling "No! No!" as he passed the bull in the graceful butterfly pass, letting it come so close each time it seemed he would be caught and spitted on one of the huge needlelike horns.

Came time for the *banderillas,* and Carlos placed the three pairs of barbed sticks superbly, running at an angle at the bull as it charged and sticking them in the withers with his arms high and finally spinning to one side to let the bull hurtle by. Then he begged permission from the *presidente* to risk his life in still another pair. It was granted and Carlos picked an impossible way to place them: with his back against the fence, he incited the bull, "Uh-huh, toro! Uh-huh-huh!" and stood there calmly watching it bear down on him. When the enraged animal was two feet away, Carlos raised his arms, dropped the *banderillas* in place, ducked to the side, the left horn grazing his chest as the bull crashed into the fence.

The trumpet blew for the death; with the scarlet rag and the curved sword in his hand, Carlos dedicated the bull, facing the crowd with exhausted, unseeing eyes. Then he went out for the last round.

His first pass with the *muleta* was the "Pass of the Dead One," so called because so many bullfighters have been killed doing it. Carlos called the bull from twenty feet away, and as it *whooshed* by he remained absolutely motionless and straight, letting the bull choose whether he was going to crash into the cloth or into his legs. Still motionless, he let the bull wheel and charge three times. Then Arruza decided to try a pass of his invention—the "Arrucina." The *muleta* is held behind the back so that only a tiny portion of the deceptive cloth shows, leaving the entire body open as a target for the bull.

When he put the *muleta* in back and people realized what he was going to do they screamed "No! No!" again, but the bull had already charged and somehow the horns missed Carlos by centimeters. But when he tried it again from the other side, the right horn went around Arruza's leg and the bull hurled him high into the air. He somehow spun around on the horn so that when his body slapped the ground he was stretched out under the bull, the length of his body between the animal's front legs, and his head between the wicked horns. People hid their eyes, yet before the needle points could find the inert form, Carlos had reached up and locked his arms around the bull's neck in an iron grip. The bewildered bull spun around and around. Finally he gave his neck a mighty snap, flung the man from him like a rag doll to the ground ten feet away, but before he could charge, Arruza's men were between them and had attracted the bull's attention. Arruza lurched drunkenly to his feet and stood there swaying, bruised and dazed, his uniform in ribbons, but miraculously not wounded. He picked up his sword and the rag.

"Fuera!" he yelled at his *banderilleros.* "Get out of the ring."

The amazed men retreated several feet behind him.

Arruza whirled on them and snarled: *"Fuera,* I said! Leave me alone with him!"

When they had all left the ring, the matador calmly turned to the bull, who was pawing the ground and studying him ten feet away; got to his knees and inched forward toward the animal. The bull shifted his feet and the crowd gasped, sure that he would charge. But he didn't; it was as though he were hypnotized and cowed by the enormous brute courage of this man-thing on its knees and Arruza kept coming, staring fixedly at the bull until he arrived in its very face.

Then, with the muzzle of the bull almost touching him, he leaned forward and rested his elbow on the bull's forehead!

He turned around and stared up at the crowd with the bull's nose against his back. We were afraid to scream for fear the noise would make the bull charge, but when he faced the bull again and, still on his knees, made it pass by four times, spinning in against the shoulder each time, a great roar burst from our throats. And then suddenly

Carlos rose to his feet, and hurling himself on top of the horns, he sank the sword in between the shoulders to the hilt, the bull reeling and its hulk crashing over backward to the sand.

Delirium took over the plaza, and the *presidente* waved his handkerchief for one ear, again for two ears, again for the tail, again for a hoof—*and still again for another hoof, for the first time in bullfighting's long history!*

So Arruza got the medal and we had the party, but our honored guest left early. He had to hurry to Valencia for a fight the following day.

There Was a Man: Joselito

by SIDNEY FRANKLIN

A BULLFIGHT FUNDAMENTALLY IS A drama of courage. And of all the exponents of the art, science and profession (it is literally all three) of bullfighting, Joselito in his way was unquestionably the most courageous.

His was a refined courage, not brute, raw bravery, but a cold, precise confidence that was born of a tremendous knowledge of bulls, perfect timing, showmanship and an exact sense of proportion and rhythm. Whenever and wherever he fought, he enthralled crowds with his masterly control. At the time of his tragic and spectacular death in the ring at Talavera de la Reina in Spain, he was at the zenith of his career, and his passing was marked by the deepest sorrow ever shown in a country that takes its mourning seriously.

They remembered, for example, how he would draw his handkerchief three-fourths out of his jacket pocket, then call the bull. "Huh, toro!" Nearly a ton of fury came charging at him. For a split second, man, animal and *muleta* were one. Then the bull was by, Joselito's handkerchief fluttering on the tip of his horn. In that maneuver the slightest misjudgment of the bull's speed and direction would have been fatal; or, had the bull failed to carry off the cloth, the matador would have lost face with his audience.

Joselito, like every good matador, was scrupulously true to the principles of honor and artistry that govern the sport. If he said he was going to do something, he did it, regardless of the risks involved or the extenuations that might arise after he had committed himself. He was able to foresee the behavior of the bulls better than any other matador before or since.

He would, for example, gesture to the crowd that he was going to make five successive passes with the *muleta* at a given spot in the ring. Calling for a chair, he would sit on that spot while his assistants maneuvered the bull toward him. With the animal in position he would shout, *"Fuera!"* (Clear the ring!) Alone and virtually defenseless he would then make the announced number of passes. He never got up after, say, three or four passes. That would have been a default on a promise. He made all five passes, no more, no less, to prove his amazing ability with animals. Usually the bull, by his early actions in the ring, will tell the men where and how to fight. Joselito, on the other hand, told the bull what to do.

Once in Málaga he found himself with a particularly cowardly bull. The animal kept hugging the barrier and refused to be attracted to the center of the ring. It looked like a poor fight. A lesser

matador would have performed his cape work around the perimeter of the ring, working between the animal and the center. Not José Gomez Ortega (Joselito's full name). In this case he got between the bull and the fence, the most dangerous place in the ring, and jiggled the cape. The bull charged and smashed into the fence with a sickening crash, missing the matador by less than inches. Again Joselito called him. Another splintering collision of bull and wood. This required cool, pure daring, but it taught the bull a lesson: stay away from the fence. Thereafter the bull went to the middle of the ring of his own accord and Gallito (another nickname) was able to proceed with the fight in style.

Another trick Joselito developed to perfection was to spread his handkerchief at a spot in the arena and announce to the crowd exactly how many and which *muleta* passes he would make in succession without moving from that spot. Then he would kneel on the handkerchief and fulfill his promise. The people in the stands watched in silence and awe, as though a noise or a cheer before the completion of the indicated passes might break the spell he apparently held over the bull. They knew that each consecutive pass compounded the danger to Joselito and that it required a stead-

ily mounting courage to bring the series to a climax. After the fifth flawless *pase de la firma* or *natural,* there was a sudden mass gasp followed by a burst of *"Olé!"* Joselito had done it again.

A full matador at the age of sixteen, in 1910, he grew in stature year by year. His career was brilliant in every respect. Each season he earned a fortune. He went through fight after fight without a mistake, without a disappointment. The public adored him. He was five feet ten inches tall, slim, lithe and graceful. He wore his dark hair brushed straight back from his forehead. Unlike many of the melancholy prima donnas of the profession, he was full of liveliness and good humor. Men admired and worshiped him. Women were hysterical about him.

As he went on disposing of bulls with seemingly effortless technique and consistency, there began about him a legend of invincibility. "The only way," they said, "a bull will ever get Gallito will be when he is home in bed asleep. The bull will have to come in quietly, detach its right horn and stab him with it before he wakes up."

There is no telling whether or not he had any illusions of his own indestructibility. He had been wounded before, but only very slightly. For a man who fought as many fights and worked as close to the animals as he did, this was like getting off without a scratch. He never showed fear, never spoke of it to those who were closest to him. It is quite possible that he considered himself invulnerable.

He continued to astonish all Spain with his feats in the ring. He would tie his ankles together and give a promised number of passes with the *muleta*. He would go through an entire *faena* (a varied series of connecting passes that combine to make a rounded-out performance) with his left hand alone, his right hand tucked behnd his back, as though one-armed. Frequently he would leave (or be carried triumphantly out of) the ring with great rents in his tight-fitting jacket or trousers where the driving horn of the bull sliced cloth but not skin.

One afternoon in Madrid he drew an animal that would not be distracted by anything. It was all the makings of a bad fight. Joselito ordered everyone from the ring and quieted the crowd. He slid out from behind a barrier until he caught the bull's eye, then disappeared and came out from behind another barrier, and so on around the ring until the bull was concentrating exclusively on him. When he finally picked up the cape and called the bull he drew a perfect charge. It was resource and cunning such as this that made Joselito the brightest light the bull ring has ever known.

On May 16, 1920, he consented to fight in Talavera de la Reina, a small town that ordinarily would not have been able to afford him. He wanted, however, to help out a friend who had arranged a fight for a very deserving charity. Joselito appearing on the card would assure a sellout.

The bulls turned out to be cowardly, yet vicious. Joselito came into the ring to meet his second bull, the fifth of the six scheduled for the *corrida*. The animal was named Bailador (the Dancer) and, as fighting bulls go, was neither big nor brave. It was the kind of animal the matador dispatched with ease usually. It was the 1431st bull of his professional career. The capework had been completed, the bull pic-ed, and the *banderillas* placed in his neck muscle.

Joselito stood in the ring about fifteen feet from the bull, preparing to work with the *muleta*. As he was spreading the cloth over the sword, the bull charged unexpectedly. Suddenly realizing where he was, Joselito tried to jerk himself into proper position. In doing so he slipped and began falling in the bull's path. This time the sharp tip of the horn caught the matador's jacket. He was picked up and tossed ten feet in the air. As the body came down, the bull made a jab at it while it was still in the air, seeming to miss. Actually, however the wicked point of the horn had slashed across the man's middle. Joselito fell face-down on the sand. The action was over in an instant.

While the crowd looked down in stunned silence, Joselito lifted his head. An assistant had drawn the bull away. Pressing his palms flat against the ground, Joselito started to get up. He lifted the upper part of his body and then he happened to look down at the ground. There, spread out on the sand, were his viscera. He fainted and was carried to the infirmary for treatment. He never recovered consciousness and died two days later.

The wound in itself was not mortal. The intestines were found to be intact. They were washed and sewn back inside the abdominal cavity. It is generally felt that when Joselito saw what had happened to him, he went out from surprise and shock, that his mind was simply unable to accept the fact that he, the unequaled matador, had at last been gored by a bull.

This being true, it can be said that Joselito died of a broken heart.

Art and the Bullfight

by REX SMITH

Etchings by John Groth

TAUROMACHIAN ART IS AS OLD AS RE-corded time. Ancient religions, mythology and history left the proof on archaeological tablets and pedestals and the painted walls in caves of Spanish stone. The centuries have brought many changes in man's preoccupation with this animal whose ancestor was feared and respected beyond all beasts; a symbol of gods in early civilizations because of its power and fertility. During the days of knighthood, the fighting of bulls in Spain became a ceremony of courage, strength and dexterity, practiced by noble mounted lancers. Toward the middle of the eighteenth century the *corrida* had blended into a public performance by professionals, mostly on foot. That was the beginning of the modern bullfight.

This kaleidoscope of color, symbolism and peril attracted artists to the sun-swept arenas. They found special emotion and inspiration in the ritual of the spectacle, and art developed along with popular acceptance. The pioneer was Antonio Carnicero, late in the eighteenth century. He produced a series of engravings on the *corrida* in 1790 that was to become a source for artists over many years.

Early in the nineteenth century came Goya with his Tauromaquia, a group of thirty-three etchings. The immortal of Aragon changed the course of tauromachian art. He produced lavishly in paintings, drawings and etchings that brought the bulls to heights of artistic importance.

Goya's influence has not ceased. Spaniards and foreigners followed him, with an eye to popular appeal, by blending his basic genius and uncom-promising power with the narrative facility of Carnicero into the "romantic era" of lithographs, engravings and drawings. There were Spaniards, such as Lameyer, Ferrant, Perea; Frenchmen, Adam, Doré; the German, Gail; the Englishman, Price. The most versatile of these was Doré.

After the turn of the twentieth century, talented artists began to receive wider public interest as their work appeared in more publications, as well as in galleries. They assumed an important role in the understanding and appreciation of the *fiesta brava*. The list is long; the ablest: Roberto Domingo.

Several distinguished painters, well known to the world, have contributed to the lengthening gallery: Sorolla, Zuloaga, Manet, Picasso and the American painter-writer Tom Lea.

Another artist must be awarded a place in the high tradition. John Groth, an American, has brought a new mastery to the *corrida*. Not since Goya has an artist etched the exotic ritual with such skill and dramatic power. Groth has created a panorama of the basic elements of the ceremony, from the dark avalanche of the bull's explosion into the arena, through the phases of horseman, cape, *banderillas, muleta* and sword, to the awesome solemnity of death. The eloquence of these etchings is endowed with somber beauty in dramatic tragedy, and merits garlands of prose or prosody, even the accolade of a gypsy's deep song.

Groth's etchings rank with the masterpieces of tauromachian art.

Etchings by John Groth

Mano a Mano

by ERIC SEVAREID

MÁLAGA, SPAIN: IN SEVILLE, WHERE modern bullfighting was born, an estimated 80 per cent of the male population has tried fighting the bulls at one time or another. This makes the crowd in the Seville arena the toughest to please in the whole country. In the whole country an estimated 80 per cent (my estimate) of American summer visitors have read Hemingway's *Death in the Afternoon*. This makes us equally authoritative. We are even more impressively expert than the Spanish experts because, I think, there are more expletives in English than in Spanish. We are especially positive in the post-mortems in the Hotel Miramar barroom after the Málaga fights and have been known to upset two waiters and one and a half trays of dry Martinis while demonstrating how the local boy, Manolo Segura, went over the right horn wrong, making his kill.

Now, in 1959, I have graduated from the *novillero* class as an observer and can hold my own in any bullfight café, because I have seen the worst fights of the season here and what was possibly the greatest fight of the twentieth century. At least when it was over, last Friday, and I got to the Miramar saloon, I put the question straight and true to Hemingway and he said, "It was the greatest bullfight I have ever seen in my *life!*" And Ernest has been going to bullfights for nearly forty years. Coming from the man who revolutionized writing by eliminating most of the adjectives, this is a considerable statement.

This has been my first season with the bulls and it has been a very smug one. It began in Mexico City last December, where I learned the basic requirements of *corrida* observing: luck and patience. Eight out of ten bullfights are bad, anywhere. I know Spaniards who have never managed to hit a good one in their lifetime. A good fight is a beautiful, exalting ballet of frail man versus wild beast. A bad fight is not only different in degree,

but in kind; it is a travesty, a sordid, cruel mockery. As someone else has remarked, the beauty is the sole justification and when that is absent the affair is a sickness.

The first four fights in that Mexico City *corrida* were horrid and my more sensitive or less patient colleagues, Mark Childs and Roscoe Drummond, fled the arena in a high dudgeon. (They rented it, with driver.) I stayed for the fifth bull, one so beautiful, so perfect in his ceaseless charges that even the *novillero* fighting him was perfect and the berserk crowd forced the judges to grant the bull pardon and turn him back to pasture for breeding purposes.

That was bullfight history and last Friday's affair was bullfight history, partly of course because it was the first completed two-man duel (three bulls apiece) of those celebrated brothers-in-law, Dominguín and Ordoñez. I guess they were fighting it out for the world championship, but I only guess. *Life* Magazine, which had reporters and cameramen all over the place, will probably be quite certain; they usually are. They have a way of enthroning and dethroning all champions, from atomic physicists to checker players, at the flip of a page.

According to the crowd, which gave him handful of ears and tails plus *two* hoofs, the twenty-seven-year-old Ordoñez won. I think he won, too, but I had just become acquainted with him the day before and I always vote for my friends. When I met him he was butting tennis balls with his head in a swimming pool and everybody knows you can't meet in more intimate circumstances than that.

I may as well go back to the beginning. My plane got to Málaga June 11, 1959, but I was not on it; I was delayed in Madrid. Ordoñez was on it, coming from a hospital recuperation period, and Hemingway met him at the airport. So I got here and went swimming for a few weeks, waiting for the August fiesta in Málaga when the *mano a mano* duel between Ordoñez and Dominguín would crown the week of bullfights. In the interval, I got all my news from Pepe, my hotel waiter, since every day around here is a saint's day and the newsstand is always closed.

"Big news," Pepe said one day as he served the salad. "Ordoñez was in the street crowd during the running of the bulls at Pamplona and he was the only man in the crowd to get gored. Hemingway is with him." I began to get nervous about that long-awaited *mano a mano* in Málaga.

Many days later Pepe put down the toothpick container and said, "News! Ordoñez and Dominguín were doing their first *mano a mano* at La Coruña and they never decided it because Dominguín got a bad goring." Later dispatches from Pepe established that the goring was in the thigh or in the groin or in the cheek. The Málaga city fathers began to get nervous about their festival and scalpers' prices for bullfight tickets began to drop.

"What do you think!" Pepe exclaimed a few days later as he uncorked the red wine, "Ordoñez was gored at Palma! A bad one! The radio says it is in the kidneys or in the shin or maybe in the abdomen." Hemingway flew up to Madrid to visit Ordoñez in the hospital.

Well, the Málaga fights started and most of them were terrible. But the Hemingways were there, and on the strength of the fact that Mary Hemingway was born in Minnesota and I was born in North Dakota, two states separated only by a narrow river, and in dry times not separated at all, we became acquainted. Mary is gentle at all times and Ernest is gentle when not passionate about something and I fell in love with both.

Ernest sat through the bad fights in the front row, resting his beard on the rail. Sometimes a fighter would dedicate a bull to him and teen-age Spanish girls would clamber over for his autograph and then ask others who the man was. Usually they thought he was a prophet or perhaps a patron saint of bullfighting who had made it while still alive. More worldly wise teen-agers knew, however, that no prophet or saint wore a long-visored baseball cap. Saints don't lose their temper, either, and the thing that makes Ernest really passionate

is a knowing remark from somebody about something he knows not. A matador friend of Ernest's missed his sword thrust on one bull and Kenneth Tynan, the junior Delphic Oracle of the New York and London theater critics, announced, "He was four inches off." The reaction from Hemingway was confused by some with the dying bellow of the bull. I think Ernest apologized later to Tynan. I wish he hadn't; I never heard of Tynan apologizing to a playwright for wrecking his play with a careless paragraph.

The date for the great Ordoñez-Dominguín duel was postponed a week. The tension built up. Consider the situation: Dominguín, thirty-three years old, had reigned supreme since he competed the great Manolete to the latter's death in 1947. Antonio Ordoñez, who married Dominguín's sister, was now threatening to dethrone Dominguín. All Spain has been familiar with the stories of the bitterness between the two. So deep was this feeling at one time that when Señora Ordoñez' father died, she did not attend the funeral with her brother. Both men knew what would be at stake in their Málaga meeting. Both would be facing this supreme test as their first fight after the unnerving experience of a bad goring. The genius of a Tex Rickard could not have promoted a better box-office situation.

The day before the great showdown I gladly—nay feverishly—accepted a luncheon invitation to the Bill Davis estate near Málaga where Ordoñez was recuperating with the Hemingways and assorted friends. I found Ernest by the pool, swinging a club back and forth—for exercise, I hoped. He was bellowing, but *sotto voce*, about the *Life* Magazine man who had come the previous day, spent two hours with Ordoñez without knowing who he was because Ordoñez was in street clothes. I thought I had to defend my professional brethren. I did not tell him about the time I spent an hour with Winchell at a Stork Club table while impatiently waiting for Winchell to arrive for a scheduled interview. But I did tell him about the dinner in London when Dorothy Thompson talked for three hours, then rose to say she had to get ready for an interview with Viscount Cranbourne (I think it was) in the morning. Viscount Cranbourne was the little man with the mustache who had been sitting beside Miss Thompson all evening and who had just departed to get his rest. Ernest whooped and narrowly escaped falling into the pool.

Now, I had read books about bullfighters and I expected to find Ordoñez in prayer and meditation somewhere, somber-eyed with the fear that precedes a great contest with the big bulls. Or I would find him nervously trying to reply to the jokes of well-meaning friends endeavoring to take his mind off the terrible, impending trial.

Ernest said, "That's Antonio, there." That was when the ageless *mystique* about bullfighters vanished from me. Antonio resembled a husky, happy Purdue halfback *after* a winning game. Antonio was receiving tennis balls pitched by an American from the other end of the pool by leaping sideways into the air, whacking the pellet with his head like a soccer player and then falling into the water. He never missed and he shouted with pure joy every time he came up for air. *Dominguín*, I thought, *you've had it.*

Antonio came and sat in a chair. The thigh wound was high up, close to the groin. It was a good eight inches long, a twisted, jagged red line because bulls jerk when the horn goes in. This wound had been four inches deep and I counted some twenty stitches. A small hole was still open, for suppuration, I suppose. By the book he should never be in that unsterilized pool, but "Papa" Hemingway plastered a bandage over the hole in the flesh and we went to lunch.

Antonio ate everything in sight; Antonio drummed the table and sang calypso songs. Only a totally nerveless man can sing so loudly knowing he's off-key and not give a solitary damn. Antonio grabbed a girl and danced a *pasodoble* around the table. Antonio grabbed a child's guitar and did a rock-'n'-roll solo around the table.

I looked across at Hemingway with glazed and disenchanted eyes. A slow, wide grin spread through the gray beard and Ernest said, "He's not very spooky, is he? Good God, the way we write about bullfighters!" That night I had a bad dream in which Dominguín was trying to get away from a lion, among the trees.

At six the next afternoon I could see Dominguín in my binoculars as the fighters waited with their entourages for the parade across the plaza to salute the *corrida* president. Dominguín was tall, slim, with a proud, sensitive, civilized face, and he was wetting his lips. For a moment I wanted him to win; competing for the crown against a man with no nerve ends comes under the heading of cruel and unusual punishment.

Dominguín was nervous on the first bull, a staccato charging beast that crowded him so closely he once had to retreat. The kill was not clean and Dominguín did not receive even one ear from the crowd. When Ordoñez took two ears on the next bull with the laziest-looking, most graceful capework and the most perfect kill I'd ever seen, I thought Dominguín's nerve must be broken for good. But he hadn't been Number One for ten years for nothing. He ended that round with both ears and the tail, and the tension increased.

I won't detail the rest of this bullfight; it is history. With the next bull, Ordoñez took the works —ear, tail and hoof. On the next, Dominguín took the works. On the sixth and last animal, Ordoñez again got ears, tail and hoof.

Three hoofs cut in one afternoon. It was paralyzing in its perfection. Neither man missed a sword thrust; all three of Ordoñez thrusts went to the hilt and no dagger was needed. It was the kind of bullfight *aficionados* all over the Spanish world dream about. It was the theory of bullfighting made manifest. In reality it is not supposed to happen—ever.

Luis Miguel Dominguín is the world's second-greatest bullfighter. He represents, in his slim, sensitive body, the standard theater of bullfighting —human against beast—and when he was lifted like a willow wand on the horns of the fifth bull for what seemed an eternity, classic Greek tragedy seemed to have reached its climax. For a time, to the amateur observer, the husky, sure-footed Ordoñez does not provide the same dramatic contrast. You feel for a moment that he meets the bull on its own terms. Then, as you see him float the big cape along the horns in unbelievably slow tempo; as you see him wind the animal around and around himself with the *muleta* in perfect cadence; as you see him launch himself with the sword upon the beast like a great panther—as your eyes assemble this pageanty, your mind accepts a truth Hemingway discovered long ago.

It is this, I think: that the difference between the great and the master in any sport is more than a difference of degree; it is a difference of kind. The great has learned to do it by thought and training and enormous dedication; the master just does it, from the beginning, and does it to perfection when his natural endowments have reached their full bloom. A great bullfighter like Dominguín is in command of the bull because he knows the bull. Ordóñez, the master, is in command of the bull because he is in command of himself. He knows himself. It is the difference between talent and genius, between what a great man can do for himself and the gods do for him with their touch.

This is why I feel utterly sure that no bullfighter will ever seriously challenge Ordóñez while he remains in his physical prime; and he will stay in his prime for years.

After the fight, I found Hemingway in the Miramar bar. "Well?" I said.

"Antonio is the greatest bullfighter alive," he said. "It is quite likely that he is the greatest who ever lived."

"Ernest," I said, "enlighten me. Didn't Antonio do a crossover to the far horn while patting his hip?"

"He did."

"Isn't that horribly dangerous?"

Hemingway looked at me as if astounded that I could even ask the question.

"Didn't he do a pendulum pass, front to back, while still moving his feet?"

"He did, my friend."

"Why and how, in God's name?"

"Because he has absolute certainty about his own reflexes."

I told Ernest I had to ask him one more question. When Ordóñez was trotting around the ring with his hands full of ears and tail and the hoof and had run over to Hemingway at the fence, what was it that Hemingway had said to him? Had he suggested what Ordóñez then did—escort Dominguín out with him for a triumphal circle of the arena together?"

"Hell, no," said Hemingway. "I suggested he throw the hoof to Hutch." Hutch was the young American who had played the tennis-soccer game in the pool with Ordóñez the day before.

"They've been throwing things at each other all week," said Ernest.

Jimmy Doolittle: American Eagle

by PAUL GALLICO

THE AFTERNOON OF SEPTEMBER 5, 1932, 50,000 race-wacky flying enthusiasts packed the stands at Cleveland's Municipal Airport for the Thompson Trophy Race, the climax of the National Air Races. As many more were distributed around the course to watch the fastest airmen in

America fight it out over the 100-mile course.

Popeyed, they watched a stubby little red-and-white, Wasp-powered Gee Bee racing monoplane buzz down the straightaway past the grandstands at five and sometimes six miles a minute.

It flew 100 feet off the ground at full throttle,

JIMMY DOOLITTLE'S "FLYING ENGINE" by Boris Artzybasheff (Winning the Thompson Trophy Race at Cleveland's Municipal Airport, September 5, 1932)

turned on its side at 300 miles an hour to round the pylons marking the closed course, to take the lead from the other seven racing ships fighting it out for the great speed trophy.

The people in the stands snapped their necks to keep the ship in vision as she flashed by, and many a one said: "What the hell's keeping her in the air?"

For she had the stubby wings of a kiwi, and a stumpy tail that was about no tail at all. The Bumble Bee, as she was called, was nothing but a flying engine, a powered bullet with vestigial wings. Without the beating of the superpowered Wasp motor, she had the gliding angle of a brick, and the flying stability of a flatiron.

What the hell *was* holding her up? What was keeping her out front in the desperate, nerve-shattering race? Well, there was a man inside her, a little, thirty-six-year-old semibald pilot who was flying half blinded, because his eyes were running with the tears of chronic hay fever that was not improved by the fumes of oil and gasoline.

He was flying a hot-shot airplane which might at any moment turn into a flaming coffin because, while he was warming his engine on the ground be-

fore taxiing to the line for the take-off, the ship caught fire from a flooded carburetor.

The pilot and a couple of mechanics had grabbed extinguishers and smothered the blaze. Then they examined the ship and decided that not much damage had been done and, anyway, there wasn't time to do anything about it. And so the pilot crawled in, closed the hood over his head, revved her up and entered the race.

Twenty-three minutes and forty-four point sixty-nine seconds later he set his flying bullet to the ground, having flown the hundred miles at full throttle, doing defeat to such racing giants as James Wedell, Jimmy Haizlip, Col. Roscoe Turner and Lee Gehlbach.

The stubby ship rolled to a stop, the crowd in the stands stood roaring and waving their handkerchiefs in the time-honored salute of the air races, the hood popped back and Major Jimmy Doolittle crawled out of the cockpit. He was wearing business pants and a plain white shirt with the sleeves rolled up, and open at the neck.

Into a microphone the winner of the Thompson trophy said: "Hello, everybody. It was just a lot of good, clean fun."

Then his two kids, Johnny, aged ten, and Jimmy, Jr., aged eleven, got through the crowd to him and grabbed his hand. He winked at them and grinned, knowing that to them he was the greatest flyer in the whole world.

Those were the days when we flew for sport, for the thrill of being the kingpins of speed, to win a medal or a trophy for the greater glory of the industry, when you staked your nerve and your life against the other fellow for the sheer hell of the competition.

That was one of the great moments in American sport of the Golden Days, when Jimmy took that big Trophy in his daffy red-and-white buzz-fly. The days of the payoff came twelve years later, with little Jimmy Doolittle, the flying fool, a three-star general in the Air Force, and American speed and savvy, guts and ships ruling the skies.

Somewhere in Germany there must be a man who remembers the day when he was selling German airplanes in South America and ran up against some competition from an American demonstrator

named Doolittle. The German challenged Doolittle to a dogfight, because the setup was perfect from the Master Race point of view. The American salesman had both his ankles in plaster casts from an accident, so how could he possibly accept the challenge, much less win?

And wherever flying men forgather, they tell the story of how little Jimmy had himself hoisted into the cockpit of his plane and took off, how he dog-fought that Kraut right out of the skies, scaring him gray. That Heinie had either to get out of the air or die, because Doolittle was willing to crash him and kill them both, and the German knew it.

After the superman left his plane on the field and ran screaming into the hangar, yelling that the crazy American was trying to murder him, Jimmy zoomed the field and cut the German's ship to ribbons with his tail skid.

A great American was playing his game for fun, so that someday he would better know how to play it for keeps.

Puck Drunk

by JOHN C. CARMICHAEL

THEY FOUND HIM SITTING IN A TORONTO pub, drinking ale with some friends. It was six P.M. and they said: "Come on, drink up. You gotta play tonight." He looked at them through swimming eyes and stammered: "But you said you didn't need me . . ." and they replied: "That was this afternoon. Now you have to play."

So they took him away to the arena, to lock him between a pair of hockey goal posts before a home-town crowd. They had no other choice.

The day, April 5th, 1938, hadn't promised any such ending, though Alfie Moore had always planned to be present when the Chicago Black Hawks and the Toronto Maple Leafs opened play

for the Stanley Cup, the symbol of the world hockey championship. Alfie Moore wasn't going to be on the ice. He was a minor-league goalie with Toronto's Pittsburgh farm team, and if he wanted to see the play-off he had to get himself a ticket. He strolled toward the box office that afternoon, and as he walked Fate crooked an invisible finger in his direction.

Mike Karakas, Chicago goalie, had suffered a broken big toe on his right foot the night before, and the Black Hawk physician couldn't patch it up. He tried aluminum splints and slit shoes, but Mike still couldn't put any weight on the foot. General Manager Bill Tobin and Coach Bill Stewart tried to contact their spare goalie, Paul Goodman, but his season had ended a month earlier and he wasn't to be found. They were stuck, and forced to go into conference with Connie Smythe, the volatile owner of the Toronto club.

Dave Kerr, the regular New York Ranger goalie, was in town, and willing. Could Chicago use him in this emergency? In a burst of good sportsmanship, Smythe agreed, but just as the sun set he changed his mind.

Tobin and Stewart rushed to Smythe's office for a showdown. They appealed to the president of the National Hockey League, who upheld the Toronto boss. Smythe, with a smile, suggested Moore, his own minor leaguer. There was no time to protest further, as Smythe knew—but where was Moore? "I saw him earlier at the Gardens," said Stewart. But he wasn't there or at home now. "You better find him," said Smythe.

They found him. They had to. Stewart, later a National League baseball umpire, remembers it clearly, as do Johnny Gottselig and Paul Thompson, twin stars of the Black Hawks in those days. They checked his friends and his haunts, and finally dug him up and hustled him into a cab.

In the Black Hawk dressing room, they eased Alfie under a cold shower, forced him to drink hot, black coffee. The other players dressed slowly, almost painfully. They had sneaked into the playoffs through the back door—had won only fourteen games all season—had wound up in the Cup fight smelling of arnica and flinching from tape and determined to go all out. Now they had to play the finals with a minor-league goalie who was—to put it mildly—out of condition.

The Black Hawks clumped up the stairs to face a crowd of 13,737 Maple Leaf fans. When the crowd caught sight of Moore, it let out a roar of laughter. Word had got around that Smythe had stuck a knife in Chicago's back. At the moment, "English Alfie" ("Arf-and-Arf," they called him) couldn't even turn back Chicago practice shots.

The whistle blew, the referee dropped the rubber puck in center ice. There was a clash of sticks between centers, and the game was on.

Apps, Drillon and Bob Davidson, Toronto's No. One forward line, swirled into action. Once, twice, three times they swung against the Chicago defense, their white-jerseyed, blue-trunked bodies caroming off the boards as Art Wiebe and Earl Seibert, Hawk defense men, broke up the drives at their own blue line. Then the Maple Leaf trio came in again, and this time there was no stopping it. Drillon sped to his right, cut in behind Wiebe and took a perfect pass from Davidson. His stick

Hockey Portfolio by JOHN CULLEN MURPHY

flashed. The puck went hurtling past Moore and Toronto led, 1-0.

The first shot on the Chicago net, in one minute and fifty-three seconds of play, was good. The Toronto bench beat a rataplan of applause, and the crowd sat back to cheer an easy conquest. Unhappy Alfie looked flushed and foolish.

But he brushed the cobwebs away and bent his back once more, and Moore the patsy became Moore the cornered fox. A new Toronto line came onto the ice, charged the Chicago goal and went home without a score. They rushed in again, and again Moore turned them back. He kicked away shots at either corner, picked the puck out of the air above his head, flung it off his chest and his knee pads. He did the splits with the abandon of a ballet dancer. He sprawled on his back and on his belly, smothering every attempt to beat him, until, up in the press box, a reporter said: "You can't tell me he sees all those. . . ."

Maybe he didn't. But at the end of the first period Toronto still had one goal, and the Black Hawks had tied the score.

Through twenty minutes of the second period, Moore kept the gates closed, and Chicago took a 2-1 lead. Black Hawk forwards kept backchecking the Maple Leaf wings to ease the pressure on Alfie, who shuttled the width of his cage, his body soaked with sweat. Only a few hours before he had been relaxing in a taproom over a friendly beer; now he was a great goalie in a great game.

Toronto never scored again. The Maple Leafs drilled forty-five shots at Alfie and forty-five times he stopped the puck, until the final whistle blew, and the green light flashed, and the Hawks had won, 3-1, and were swarming over little "Arf-and-Arf." But he fought them off, broke away, and skated to the Toronto railing, and flung his face before the angry features of Connie Smythe. ". . . And if I'd had one more beer," he jeered happily, "you wouldn't have got that goal . . . !"

In the dressing room, players said things to him that made his eyes smart and then General Manager Tobin spoke: "We didn't make any deal. You got money coming. How much?"

Moore thought $150 would be about right. Tobin handed him $300. He was taken to Chicago with the team, given a great welcome in the Stadium, and a watch as a souvenir.

But Alfie didn't play again. Smythe wouldn't let him. With Goodman and Karakas in the nets the Black Hawks rode roughshod over Toronto, three games to one, for the world championship. A year later Moore tried to come back in the big time with the New York Americans. He got licked twice, 4-0 and 2-0.

He never won another major-league game after his once-in-a-lifetime stand.

Challenge of Mt. Everest

by JAMES HILTON

A HUNDRED YEARS OR SO AGO AN EAGER clerk rushed into an office of the Indian Trigonometrical Survey to report that he had worked out (on paper) the highest point on the earth's surface . . . a peak over 29,000 feet above sea level. He seems to have been right (despite recurrent rumors of higher "mystery ranges" in Tibet)

and the peak was accordingly dedicated to the former boss of his department, Sir George Everest, whose name proved happily apt for a mountain.

For more than half a century nobody except Tibetans ever came within fifty miles of Everest. Then, during the early twenties, three English expeditions were launched: The first a reconnaissance; the second an assault on the mountain it-self that reached within 1700 feet of the summit but brought death to seven native porters in an avalanche; and the third, that of 1924, which ended in sublime and tragic mystery. The basic facts about Everest were already known by this time—that it was not technically unclimbable like some other Himalayan peaks, and that men could exist for a period of days and nights at very great altitudes. The procedure, therefore, was to pitch camps at various levels, from the highest of which the summit might be reached in a single superla-tive effort by one or other small groups tackling it in relays. Success would depend in the last resort on the imponderables of weather and human re-sistance, but if it came, it would be all over in the daylight of a day.

The third expedition set its sixth and highest camp at 26,800 feet. Norton and Somervell, who were to make the first "dash," slept in a small tent at this fantastic height, with the summit only 2300 feet above them. In the morning they made their try, reached just over 28,000 feet, but had to return because of unendurable coughing and dizziness.

Next came the turn of the two others, and these were the legendary ones. Mallory, classic climber of our time, was an English schoolmaster of thirty-eight; Irvine, an Oxford undergraduate not much more than half his age. They spent a night at the sixth camp, and on the morning of June 8 set out in the track of their predecessors and were never seen again except by one man.

This was Odell, the expedition's geologist. Standing on a crag lower than Camp 6, Odell hap-pened to be staring upwards when suddenly the clouds cleared and revealed the huge pyramid of the mountain with two human figures outlined against a far rock ridge. They were moving up-ward, step by step, about 700 feet below the final peak. He watched them climb for a few moments till the clouds recurred. Even Odell did not see them again.

And so there is the mystery. That the bodies of George Mallory and Andrew Irvine lie amid the snows of Everest is certain, but *when did mishap come to them?* Is it possible that they reached their goal and lost their lives on the descent? The only faint clue is a rusted ice ax found nine years later by climbers of a subsequent unsuccessful expedi-tion. This ax was found *lower* than the point at which Odell had seen the two—hence, it can be argued, they must have reached the top, since neither would be likely to continue an ascent with-out his ax.

But the question is no more exactly answerable than the general one so often asked—why do men attempt these things at all? To this every climber has his own reply. Mallory said he climbed moun-tains "because they are there"—and not in the spirit of ambition or conquest. "Have we con-quered an enemy? None but ourselves," he added. Perhaps it is not without significance that the great attempts on Everest took place just after World War I, when the mood of the world was touched with remorse and expiation. That a schoolmaster and a student from the West should find death amid the topmost pinnacles of the Himalayas linked them spiritually with the East—with countless Hindoo devotees to whom death deliberately sought on mountains had always seemed a fitting end and one for the poet's praise.

And generalizing more widely, there must be some primitive human urge that finds spiritual comfort in "up" rather than "down"; it cannot be mere chance that heaven and hell are so placed. Probably there are Freudian or Fraserian roots in this. Maybe among our ancestors of a million years ago it was the rule to hide in underground caves when wild animals threatened, but the rare fellow would climb the hills up to steep rocks or the snowline where animals could not follow.

Even to those who, like myself, have reached no higher than half the height of Everest and on peaks offering no special difficulty, there may have come the kind of occasional mountain experience easier to remember than to analyze—some mo-mentary clairvoyance that sets the mind swinging free like a compass needle—perhaps a product of physical exhaustion giving an effect of disembodi-ment. But they are special moments, no more to be counted on than divine visitations to the Saint. For the main, if I was asked why I make the modest ascents accessible to me, I would answer that they offer a maximum of striving with a minimum of competition. Mingling ardors and arduousness, mountain climbing is perhaps the most enchanting way of not keeping up with the Joneses.

EDITOR'S NOTE: *The great men finally came to the great mountain (not quite equaling the feat of Mohammed) and scaled it in a great moment. Sir Edmund Hillary (knighted by Queen Elizabeth for the accomplishment) of New Zealand and Tenzing Norkey, a Sherpa of Nepal, stood on its peak on May 29, 1953—the final assault team of the expedition by the Royal Geographic Society and the Alpine Club of London led by Colonel C. J. Hunt. As if to prove that Mallory's statement is still cogent, Ernest Schmidt and Jurg Maramet repeated the climb on May 23, 1956, and Adolph Reist and Hans Rudolph von Gunter did it again the next day, because, after all, it is still there.*

Tommy Hitchcock: Ten-Goal American

by PAUL GALLICO

THE LATE THOMAS HITCHCOCK WAS A titan who dominated the American scene during the Golden Decade of Sport, a glorious era of the giants of play.

He was to polo what Jack Dempsey was to the ring, Babe Ruth to baseball, Bill Tilden to tennis and Bob Jones to golf.

But he was more than an athlete and a sportsman. He was the prototype of the perfect American. He was at once a living person and a legend. He gave his life for his country and he left the legacy of his personality and his character and the imprint of his life upon the memories of millions of Americans.

There might be some who would hold that his was not a useful life, that it was devoted to the playing of a game indulged in only by the rich. Well, maybe so, but, brethren, he sure played that game. He played it to the hilt. He played it the way nobody ever had in the memory of man, and when he was finished, a lot of people knew about polo who had never heard of it before, and many more knew the name of Tommy Hitchcock. They knew him as a rough, tough, slashing rider and the hardest and longest hitter the game had ever known.

We are really an unsnobbish people. We don't hold it against a guy for being rich if he can play his game like a true champion and produce those thrills. Poor boy makes good is our favorite nursery story, but we lift our skimmers just as high and huzzah as loud for the man of wealth who is a champion.

Pre-Hitchcock polo was attended by polite gatherings of two or three thousand people who sat around the field and pattered well-mannered applause. Polo in the Golden Decade, with Hitch socking the ball a hundred yards and further at a clip, drew from thirty to 40,000 people, who got up on their hind legs and yelled until all of staid Meadow Brook at Westbury, L.I., trembled.

There have been famous names in American polo, but none that captured the imagination of rich and poor alike as that of Tommy Hitchcock, Jr. He stood five feet eleven inches in his riding boots, weighed a 190 pounds, turfside, and wasn't afraid of anything or anyone in the world, either on the polo field or anywhere else.

TOMMY HITCHCOCK: TEN-GOAL AMERICAN by Tony Palazzo

He was a hero right out of the storybooks. When he was seventeen years old he tried to get into the American Air Force and was chased away for being too young. So he enlisted in the famous Lafayette Escadrille, flew a Spad over France, shot down three Germans, won the *Croix de Guerre* with three palms and was himself shot down inside the German lines with a bullet through his thigh.

You would figure this would be enough for any seventeen-year-old in one war, but not Hitch. On his way to a German prison camp in Bavaria, his guard fell asleep. Tommy stole a map out of his pocket and then dove through the window of the moving train, game leg and all. He walked eighty miles to the Swiss border and then made his way back to France.

In 1921 he was a member of the U.S. International Polo Team that went to England and brought back the Westchester Cup held by England since 1914. Between 1921 and 1939 Hitchcock played against England for the United States five times and the United States was never once defeated in that time. Not only that but the English never managed to win a single game from us in that period.

His last appearance in International play was at Meadow Brook in 1939 at the age of forty-four. In the first game which the Americans won 11-7, Hitchcock scored four goals and figured in two assists. In the second and deciding game, Hitchcock again scored four goals, with two assists, leading the American attack.

But what remains in the memory of the spectators at Meadow Brook that fair June day in 1939 was the spectacle of a man approaching middle age, who had been playing polo for thirty years, still dominating the play with his vicious, unrelenting attack and tremendous hitting power.

As always, against the bright background of the robin's-egg blue stands, the green turf and the confetti-colored crowds banked around the field, one seemed to see only Hitchcock.

There were seven other players, the best of England and America, riding hard and fighting bitterly, but again and again a high "Oooooooh!", a cry of wonder, would go up from the stands as the big fellow with the No. 2 on his back would swing and hit, and the ball would streak down the field as though fired from a cannon.

When Hitchcock hit, there was something that communicated itself to the crowds in the stands.

He was the only man who ever made the thrill of polo vicarious. When he began one of his thundering rides down on the ball and wound himself up to let fly you could feel the crowd in the stands gathering itself up and tensing like a cocked gun. You could feel it in yourself, the gathering effort for the climax, breath held, muscles tightening.

Then WHAM! And the shout and the long sigh, as the ball made a streak across the velvet turf. You knew it had been hit. And so did the opposing players. With one drive Hitchcock could change the whole pattern of play, break up an attack and turn it to deadly offense.

Hitchcock was rated at ten goals, the highest handicap in polo, for a period of thirteen years, an unequaled record. He played on championship teams to win every honor that the game had to offer. But more, he democratized polo and broke down the barriers that had existed for many years. In 1930 he scandalized the polo clique by selecting a couple of cowpokes from Texas, Rube Williams

and Cecil Smith, to play on the International squad. All he asked of a man who wanted to play polo was that he play it high, wide, rough, tough and handsome.

So there were honors enough for this man, and fame, and the respect of the American people. But not for Hitch, when the war came. For if polo was his game, flying was his love. He once said, "Flying is the best sport in the world. People call duck hunting sport, because they get the thrill of shooting something down. It's not real sport unless the duck can shoot back at you. That's what flying is during war."

Death came to Tommy Hitchcock, Jr., at the age of forty-four. He was wearing the uniform of the United States Air Force with the rank of lieutenant colonel. He was killed in the crash of a fighting plane near Salisbury, where he commanded a P-51 Mustang Group.

He had received a commission in the Air Forces soon after Pearl Harbor and was assigned to England as an assistant military attaché for air. But that wouldn't do for Hitchcock. He had to be in there where he could ride and rough and hit.

He fought his way through to a combat command in spite of his age. His plea was, "You almost kept me out of one war because I was too young. Are you going to keep me out of this one because I'm too old?" He backed up his demands by learning to fly the hottest ship in the Army.

He went out the way he lived—a fighting American.

The Astonishing Mr. Tilden

by VINCENT RICHARDS

THE USUAL MORNING PRACTICE SESSION had been called off and the entire cast of the Tilden tennis troupe was assembled in Bill's room. The latest flood extra was being shouted in the street below. Bill was at the telephone, a map spread out on the floor at his feet.

No, there were no trains leaving Mobile. No, it was impossible for a plane to take off. "We'll have to drive, then," said Bill, grabbing the map. "And Baton Rouge looks like the only place to get over." He was at the phone again. Yes, you could get over at Baton Rouge. You had better hurry, though, because the river was coming up pretty fast. But we had a match to play in the afternoon at the Mobile Country Club and we played it, under leaden skies to a small crowd.

We were lucky enough to get over at Baton Rouge that night and we kept right on driving night and day, stopping only for meals, until we got to St. Louis a few hours before we were scheduled to play there. I was able to get a couple of hours' sleep but Tilden beat me badly that evening. You can't play decent tennis after driving 1700 miles that way. That is, you can't and I can't. Three of us had taken turns at the wheel of one car and Bill had driven the other car all of the way himself. Of course he hadn't done any sleep-

ing in St. Louis before the match. There had been business to attend to.

This guy was astounding. Not just because of his endurance and the way he could play tennis at forty-four but also because of the way he lived, the things he did and the amount of money he earned and spent. He was eternally busy, always on the go, every day from the time he got up until

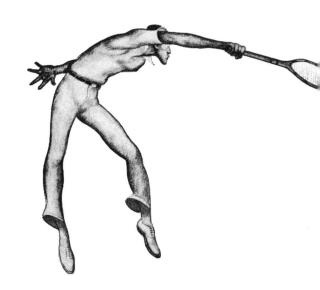

the last rubber was counted up and he had paid off. He was always broke but there always seemed to be more where the last came from. We were doubles partners when I was a kid. He amazed me then. I toured the country with him one winter and he amazed me more than ever.

When I first met Bill, in 1916, he was holding forth on the porch of the Merion Cricket Club in Philadelphia where I had gone to play a match as a member of a boys' team representing New York. In those days he was referred to generally as "one-round Tilden" because he was beaten in the opening round of almost every tournament. Yet even then he was attracting attention, on the court and on the porch. It was hard to put your finger on what it was about Tilden that always made him the center of attraction. It wasn't what the correspondence schools call personal magnetism, for even when he was kingpin at Forest Hills and Wimbledon he wouldn't have won a popularity contest. But in his early days it was, I think, his great enthusiasm for the game and his frequently expressed determination to be champion that made him interesting to people.

After my match he told me that he thought I had the making of a good player, and the following year, after beating me in a tournament, he said he was sure I could be one of the best players in the world if I wanted to and wound up by asking me to be his partner in the national doubles tournament next summer. We practiced together a good deal that spring and we won the national doubles championship at Boston in 1918.

Tournament tennis was an expensive pastime but Bill could afford it, and in style. His father, who had been active in Philadelphia politics, had died a few years before and Bill lived with two aunts who must have indulged him lavishly. He descended on Boston in a high-powered car, engaged a suite of rooms at the Copley Plaza and lived with a flourish that became the envy of other players. About this time he acquired his mania for bridge and began making contributions to the corps of experts who follow the tennis circuit. After a hard day's tennis he would spend the evening either at cards or driving his car over the countryside at breakneck speed or at both.

Our doubles championship was the first im-

DOMINIC

portant title Bill won. He was too wild that year to be a really fine player, and his brother Herbert, a better player than Bill in those days, used to nag him—as only a big brother can nag—to stop trying to knock the cover off the ball. But Bill played the way he wanted to. He had made up his mind that he was going to be national champion and he thought he knew the way to go about it. He was always practicing, always playing. He would go out in the morning and play eight or nine sets and then play a couple of tournament matches in the afternoon.

The following winter Bill absented himself from tournament tennis and went into intensive practice on the private court of Jed Jones in Providence. Jones was in the insurance business and Bill was working up leads for him. He was also writing regularly for the Philadelphia *Public Ledger* and getting together material for a book. But mostly he was playing tennis, practicing incessantly, and during the course of that winter he brought his game up to true championship level.

He emerged in the summer with a complete game; he had overcome his wildness, developed a strong backhand and improved his service tremendously.

The new stadium at Forest Hills was waiting for Bill Tilden. Only a champion of his color could have filled the stands, for tournament tennis was not so popular then as it is now.

Tilden drew not only the regular tennis fans but also people who simply wanted to see Big Bill. He gave them a show no tennis player had done before. Next to being tennis champion of the world the ambition fondest to Tilden's heart was to be a great man of the theater, but his several attempts on the stage had resulted only in damaging his pocketbook. Now, as champion, he had an outlet for his histrionics.

Most tennis players who perform with one eye on the gallery not only lose but make asses of themselves. That is because they don't know how to do it and they go too far, but with Bill it was different.

Ever since there have been linesmen I suppose tennis players have glared at them when they didn't agree with their decisions but it remained for Tilden to elevate the procedure to an art. He transfixed the blundering official; he craned his neck at him, and sometimes he would merely smile and that hurt most of all. The whole gallery loved it.

The crowd rarely agreed with Bill but they were always expressive and he could excite them at will. Even when playing a dub in the first round he gave the audience something for its money and, incidentally, made the dub feel good. If it was possible to do so, he usually permitted his early-round opponent to take a long lead in each set and then he would put on the pressure and come from behind. The gallery loved that, too.

During tournaments where the players do not live at the club, special rates are always available to them at some first-class hotel in town, but Bill never patronized the designated hotel. He has never been a snob by any means but he has always, to a certain extent, held himself apart from the contingent. His scale of living was higher than that of most players and of course he was more demanding. At the death of his brother he inherited a small fortune from his father's estate, but money doesn't stay with Bill for long and the time came when his aunts were broke and he was dependent on his writing for most of his income. He had a yearly contract with the *Ledger* syndicate for $12,000 a year and at the same time I had one with another syndicate that was good for $8000. It was by doing this writing that Bill and I were able to play tennis the year round—to be first-class tennis bums. But the United States Lawn Tennis Association suddenly decided that an amateur should

not report on tournaments in which he was competing, and although we argued our case before the officials time after time, the rule was passed. I think that rule was the beginning of big-time professional tennis.

The Tilden exchequer was in bad shape when Bill decided to turn professional, but I believe the fact that the French had beaten us in the Davis Cup and Lacoste and Cochet were on the top of the heap had a great deal to do with his decision. Bill was no longer head man and he insisted on being the main attraction.

Within six months after leaving the amateur ranks Tilden had netted $100,000 by making movies and playing matches under the banner of Jack Curley. This money that is made right after an amateur turns professional is the cream, and what he makes afterward comes hard in comparison. That first money is a good thing to hang on to.

But Bill didn't keep his long. Tilden Tennis Tours, Incorporated, an organization he formed to subsidize players and take them on a world-wide tour, consumed it and Bill was broke again. His friends wondered what was going to happen to Bill now.

Well, Bill went right on playing tennis, writing articles, playing bridge, racing around the country in fast cars and living in the style to which he was accustomed. He organized a group of players small enough to handle himself, and when things went sour here he took ship to Europe, recouped his fortunes, paid off his debts and came back for another crack at American barnstorming.

When Tilden toured he was happiest. It was his troupe. He was the star and the impresario. He was the boss and he was also the temperamental leading man. Rehearsal was at ten sharp and bring two rackets.

His entourage one winter consisted of three tennis players (assorted), one secretary (who took the part of straight-man), one ball-boy and one truck driver. One of the tennis players was on a flat salary of $200 a week and transportation; the other two took a percentage of the net. The secretary got $150 a week and transportation, the ball-boy $50 a week and expenses, and the truck driver $35 a week and expenses. Add to this $75 a week for truck expenses and another $100 for gas and garage for the two passenger cars and you have a fair idea of the fixed expenses of the tour. And this was in the mid-thirties.

Bill maintained no checking account and the percentage hands were paid off after every match in cash. The other help received cash once a week. And Tilden always paid off. After a couple of lean takes the help was inclined to be a bit jumpy but Bill never worried and he soothed the boys with a prediction that the crowd would be good in the next town. It usually was.

One winter, after several days of lean picking, we played in Miami to a good crowd and Bill's own profit amounted to $1800. Sums of this magnitude presented a problem to Bill when no immediate disbursements were necessary and on this occasion discussion took place between Tilden and his secretary over the handling of funds. Neither of them wanted to carry $1800 around in his pocket; in fact it developed, when the suggestion was made that they split it, that neither wanted to carry half that much around in his pocket. Tilden, of course, supplied the solution: they would get traveler's checks. A couple of days later when there was the matter of a hotel bill in St. Petersburg, Tilden called upon his secretary to produce the traveler's checks that had been entrusted to him. The secretary reminded Mr. Tilden that Mr. Tilden had taken the checks unto his own care. Well, that had been three days ago and the hotel bill was paid out of the gate receipts from the St. Petersburg match that afternoon.

Where did the money go? Almost all of it went for things you and I wouldn't spend important money on. All the time he was away a suite at the Algonquin Hotel in New York was under lease to

Bill. In his absence it was occupied by his friends and protégés who signed checks for food for themselves and for their friends. Tilden's own hotel bills were staggering. An hour after checking in he usually ran up telephone charges of fifty to a hundred dollars, calling up people in New York, California—sometimes Europe. He sent telegrams and cables by the ream. He lost regularly at an evening's bridge. He doesn't drink today, and he never has. He wears the same suit of clothes for a year. He spends his money on the thousand and one things that comprise his life—a life of constant activity in avenues most of us don't consider important.

TILDEN VS. LACOSTE by Fletcher Martin (1927 U.S. Championship Matches at West Side Tennis Club, Forest Hills, Long Island, New York)

Conquest of the English Channel

by PAUL GALLICO

ON AUGUST 6, 1926, THERE TOOK PLACE the greatest recorded athletic feat by a woman in the history of the world. Gertrude Ederle, the nineteen-year-old daughter of an Amsterdam Avenue, New York, German-American butcher, swam the English Channel from Cape Gris-Nez, France, to Kingsdown, England, in fourteen hours and thirty-one minutes.

Bonfires had been lighted all along the English coast to guide the gallant American through the last hours of her struggle against wind, storm, rain and cold and darkness. The leaping flames lit up the scene when, at 9:40 at night, she walked up onto the beach to receive her first ovation.

In the light of the cataclysms that overwhelmed us in the later years when, among other places, that stormy English Channel provided a grave for so many brave men, the swimming of that body of water fades into memory as a peculiar and unimportant bit of exhibitionism.

But, actually, it was not, for those were the lush days of peacetimes, the pause between two wars, and Trudy Ederle was the demonstration of those times that courage, training, will power and indomitable spirit comprise the secret weapon against seemingly unconquerable obstacles.

Nature has always challenged human beings. Conquest of that twenty-mile strip of treacherous tides and roaring currents has lured swimmers for the past ninety years, and who knows what attempts were made that remain unrecorded? Five persons had swum the English Channel before Gertrude Ederle. But they were all men. No woman had ever accomplished it. Several had tried and failed. As early as one week before Trudy succeeded, another American girl, Clare Belle Barrett of New Rochelle, New York, had failed by two miles. And Gertrude Ederle herself had twice failed the previous year. It did appear as though there was one feat of skill and endurance in which women could not approach men.

It is a curious thing that on August 6, the very day of Trudy's triumph, the London *Daily News*, editorializing on the question of women athletes in general, declared: "Even the most uncompromising champion of the rights and capacities of women must admit that in contests of physical skill, speed and endurance, they must forever remain the weaker sex."

The gent who wrote those words probably spent the next twenty-four hours eating them without cream or sugar, because Miss Ederle not only conquered the Channel, but her time was two hours and twenty-three minutes faster than the fastest man who had achieved the crossing before her, one Charles Toth of Boston, Massachusetts.

It was a big show, a great show. We had time in those days to stop and applaud a duel between woman and nature. Trudy was an American girl, sweet, gentle, unaffected. As a member of the famous Women's Swimming Association of New York, cradle of water champions, she had attracted attention by breaking the men's record for the classic twenty-one-mile swim from the Battery in New York to Sandy Hook. No woman had ever completed the trip before. She covered the course in seven hours, eleven minutes, thirty seconds. When she raised her sights to the English Channel, and particularly after she had tried and failed, the whole nation paused to follow her attempt and wish her well.

The New York *Daily News* backed her financially, win or lose, in 1926, and she moved to Cape Gris-Nez, France, and trained there under William Burgess, an Englishman who had conquered the Channel in 1911, after having previously failed *eighteen times*.

The Channel from Cape Gris-Nez to Dover is

only twenty miles wide. Tides and currents add from ten to twenty miles to the passage for a swimmer. Henry Sullivan, an American from Lowell, Massachusetts, who accomplished the feat in 1923, swam forty-five miles to get from one side to the other. The swimmer must be prepared to fight against the numbing discouragement that comes with battling forward one yard and losing five.

Anyone who has crossed the Channel in a boat knows it for the roughest, dirtiest, choppiest body of water in the world. It is never quiet. Wind and current and tides wage a never-ending duel and the surface of the sea is crisscrossed with nasty little waves that batter and buffet a swimmer, rolling and shaking, lifting and dropping and dizzying. The first time Trudy tried it the previous year, she had to quit because she got *seasick* while swimming.

On the morning of August 6, Trudy attired herself in black silk trunks, a narrow brassiere of navy-blue silk bearing the emblem of the Women's Swimming Association and a tiny silk American flag. She wore a red bathing cap and goggles of one curved piece of yellow glass. After she entered the water, she removed the brassiere.

Her body was first greased with olive oil. Over this was smeared a coating of lanoline and finally a thick, heavy mixture of vaseline and lard. She entered the water at 7:09 A.M.

A tug flying French and American bunting accompanied her. Aboard the tug were her father and sister Margaret, her trainer, Burgess, and newspapermen and photographers.

The story of the crossing is a classic of grit and stamina and guts. Trudy Ederle went through hell. Frozen, exhausted, battered, sickened, she never once complained, and she never for a moment thought of giving up. She had to fight not only the sea and the elements of wind, rain and cold, but the contents of the sea, dangerous red jellyfish with long, stinging tentacles.

At one point, after she had been in the water for eleven hours, the sea was raging so furiously and buffeting her so badly that trainer Burgess advised that the attempt be given up lest she be injured. The English coast was three miles away. Pop Ederle called to her to ask her whether she wanted to quit.

And out of the hissing spume of the stormy sea came her classic reply that was to ring around the world: "What for?"

And then, all of a sudden it was over and she was walking out onto the English beach in the glare of the bonfires and the roaring welcome of the people gathered there, while the wireless crackled and cables began to hum with the story of her achievement.

She went back aboard the tug by rowboat and sailed a few miles down the coast from Kingsdown to Dover, where she had been expected and a welcome awaited her. That welcome was held up for three hours, while a customs official quizzed the most famous girl in the whole world and was on the point of refusing to let her land because she lacked a passport to enter the United Kingdom.

Secret Agonies of the Olympics

by MARSHALL SMITH

THE EMOTIONAL EXCESSES GENERATED at an Olympic Games range from trickles of chauvinistic tears to outbursts of psychopathic convulsions. They afflict both the onlookers and the athletes.

When the band strikes up for the opening ceremony and the athletes begin to parade, led by the Greeks, there is gentle snuffling in the stands. Handkerchiefs dab at the first tears as Abyssinia and Afghanistan pass in review, and by the time the last of eighty-seven participating nations is in its place on the field there isn't a dry eye in the house.

This is customary at Olympic openings. I speak from experience. Mind you, I'm not the maudlin type. I cry only at *East Lynne* and some weddings. But I found myself knuckling away a salty tear at the opening of the 1948 Games in London. Four years later at Helsinki I blubbered again. At Melbourne in 1956 I didn't fight it. I surrendered without a struggle and became a participating member of a massive human sprinkler system.

For this reason I was apprehensive about Rome, where the games would be contested among the ruins on ground once trod by charioteers and gladiators. What particularly worried me was the athletes. They cry harder than anybody.

This is not generally known. It came as a shock, but my source was so unimpeachable that I had to believe. My informant was a particularly observant high-hurdler at Melbourne. "It's like Niagara down on the field," he reported. "The guy next to me was shedding tears as big as lollipops, and it was like that all the way down the line."

The athletes can't afford this luxury. As the deadline approaches for them to perform heroic deeds, they are taken by another and more devastating seizure. Their eyes roll and take on a glassy look. They aren't able to see or hear. They utter

sounds like a hyena cackling. Their muscles jump and twitch. They are afflicted with headaches and nausea.

Like a person feeling a fit coming on, they recognize the symptoms. Each athlete has experienced them many times before, and rather than recoil from the ordeal they welcome it. It is a prerequisite to outstanding physical performance.

The athletes don't like to talk about it, and since no outsiders are permitted in Olympic dressing rooms—not even the press—their seizures are never recorded when the whys and hows of Olympic prowess are put down for posterity. They remain as much of a deep, dark secret as the fact that great-great-grandfather made the family fortune as a slave trader.

I blundered onto this before the 1948 Games in London quite by accident. A threesome of Olympians had let down their hair and were discussing their symptoms. The conversation went something like this:

"When do you usually throw up?" asked the first Olympian, a lean quarter-miler from Southern California.

"About a half hour before I run," answered the second Olympian, a crew-cut half-miler. Then he added, "How about yourself?"

"I'd say sooner," replied the first Olympian. "At least an hour."

The third Olympian in the group was the holder of the world's record for the 100-yard dash, and he couldn't wait to get in his two cents' worth. He volunteered the information that he never threw up until after the race was over. "I'm funny that way," he said. "After the race I just keep on running around the corner of the stadium and let her go. It's as regular as clockwork."

If they had revealed that they boiled themselves in oil to ward off the cold on chilly mornings, I

could not have been more aghast. "But why throw up at all?" I blurted out.

The dash-man clammed up. The lean quarter-miler viewed me disdainfully. Obviously I didn't belong to the club. It was just as obvious that perhaps they shouldn't discuss such delicate matters in front of the uninitiated. I was about to go away when the crew-cut half-miler took pity on me.

"If you don't throw up," he explained, "you don't belong on the Olympic team. It's as simple as that. See!"

But I didn't see, and he saw that I didn't. So he took a deep breath and continued. "Now, take me. I start stoking up the night before a race. I got a full head of steam by morning. Then I flip my cookies and I'm ready. My feet don't even touch the ground for the first 200 yards of the race. I'm floating on air and not using any energy. Now, how's a guy who don't throw up and has to work while I'm floating going to compete?"

This made sense, but I still didn't understand why. I resolved to investigate this phenomenon further. I would observe it under actual conditions. It meant gaining access to the Olympic dressing room, but this proved an easy matter. I simply told the uniformed attendant guarding the door that I was a friend of one of the contestants and had an urgent message from his family. He not only let me in, but bowed as he opened the door.

I was amazed. A series of dungeonlike caverns extended before me and I got the feeling that I had entered a forbidden realm of souls. The walls were sweating and the sodden atmosphere was pervaded with the smell of fear. Athletes were lying or sitting on the damp floor, some with towels covering their faces. Those without towels reminded me of unfortunates I had seen in psychopathic wards. They stared fixedly as if in a trance.

Now and then one of them would rise and toddle resignedly off to another cell. Nobody talked, but I heard the sound of retching in the distance, interspersed with an occasional shrill laugh. In the midst of the flower of U.S. manhood I was surrounded by the living dead.

An hour later, out in the sunshine on the arena floor, the transformation was remarkable. The living dead were animated. All their anguished immobility erupted into superlative action—although I never did see an Olympian with his feet not touching the ground for the first 200 yards.

The details of this phenomenon, when seen through the eyes of a medical man, seem as natural as apple pie and ice cream. I know because I consulted one. I learned that the human body can tap unsuspected sources of strength in emergencies (i.e., when the victim is exposed to either anger or fear).

In this case the athletes were exposed to fear. What were they afraid of? "How the devil should I know?" replied my expert. "Could be anything. Of losing. Of being in a strange land. Of what the folks back home would say if they flopped. It doesn't take much."

The biological process that generates this extra horsepower is triggered by the adrenals. "Remarkable little glands," sighed my tutor. When they get the mad signal or the scared signal they squirt their magic juices into the blood stream and all hell breaks loose.

Blood is drained from the central part of the body—that is, in the vicinity of the belly button. It is forced into the arms, legs and brain, where strengthening corpuscles bombard the tissues. Under this stimulus a wife who is angry at her husband for staying out late can hit with the strength of ten when he finally gets home. A man who is being chased by a tiger suddenly discovers that he can run like a gazelle.

But there is a catch. If this extra energy is not used quickly, it can backfire—and this is what brings on "athlete's sickness." The midsection, drained of its warming supply of blood, turns cold and the organs are affected. The stomach develops "butterflies" and its owner is afflicted with nausea. The kidneys falter, hence the continual nuisance of the "bladder call."

Another abnormal situation is created in the extremities. The muscles, full to overflowing with emergency power, begin to quiver and quake. Static electricity builds up in the nerve ends, mainly in the wrists and ankles, causing them to stiffen.

As I was absorbing this cram course on the strange behavior of humans under stress, the reference to stiff wrists rang a bell. It explained suddenly why tournament golfers are afflicted with the "yips," an attack of nerves which makes the wrists so unpliable that they can't get the putter back so that they can stroke the ball.

My tutor pointed out that roughly nine people out of ten would suffer total collapse if subjected to the kind of ordeal Olympic athletes undergo. But Olympians, those stout fellows, learn to live with their "symptoms." Instead of recoiling from fear and its ravages, they hang out the welcome sign and turn it to their advantage.

Out of their fear comes the strength to achieve fantastic deeds.

Equipped with this knowledge I was able to talk sympathetically with Olympians and not be surprised by anything they said. No two had a set of symptoms exactly alike. At the peak of his adrenal build-up Jim Lea, a quarter-miler, would break out with a skin rash.

Thane Baker, a sprinter from Kansas, could almost set his watch by the muscle spasms in his back. When the painful contractions set in, it was one hour to race time.

The 400-meter hurdlers who performed for the United States in 1956 suffered side by side in the locker room. Eddie Southern had the sensation of being without legs. Josh Culbreath felt so weak he had to be helped up off the rubbing table. Glenn Davis (no kin to Army's football hero) got St. Vitus dance. "Look at 'em go," he said, watching his arms and legs quiver and twitch. But when the gun went off Davis sped to a new Olympic record for the 400-meter hurdles.

The great shot-putter Parry O'Brien had his own private formula for tapping the adrenal reservoir. Because he felt no fear, he induced anger by artificial means. His program of "planned hatred" began three days before the event. He forced it to rise until he was ripe for bursting—and then it all exploded in one monumental heave.

Sometimes it seems that Olympic track stars are more in need of psychiatrists than coaches. Jack Davis of Southern California, the high-hurdler, actually consulted one before beginning final training for the Melbourne games and should have kept him around for the astonishing letdown afterward. I stopped by his room at Olympic Village the morning after he lost a heartbreaking photo finish for a gold medal, and one of his roommates cautioned, "Better leave him alone. He just took some sleeping pills. Hasn't slept a wink all night." But at 11 A.M., when I looked in, he was propped up in his bunk, eyes wide open.

"I know it's over and there's nothing I can do about it," Davis said, "but I can't make my stomach believe it." He related how his father had called that morning to offer condolences from half-way around the world and he hadn't been able to utter a word—not even "hello" or "good-by." He just stood there tongue-tied, listening to his dad jiggle for the operator.

It was normal for an Olympian to have need for a "decompression chamber" immediately after competing. Most of them couldn't get off their adrenal jag for hours. Glenn Davis of the 400-meter hurdles went right back into his dance after the race and didn't stop shaking until he had had a steak and gone to a movie.

But no Olympic athlete ever needed a psychiatrist any more than sprinter Mel Patton during the 1948 Games in London. I know because I ended up substituting for one. He was my boy—the "world's fastest human" and the man nobody could equal for muzzle-velocity off the blocks. I had said all this in a magazine article just before the Games. If he flopped, I flopped along with him. I would never again be able to pose as an expert. This is what gave me my proprietary interest. And did he flop!

The "world's fastest human" finished so far back in the 100-meter dash that some observers thought he was in the next race. If the truth be known, this is what prompted me to invade the sacred soil of the Olympic dressing room. My boy had one more chance to redeem himself—in the 200-meter race—and after getting past the guard I searched among the bodies on the damp floor. I found the one I was seeking in the farthest nook of the innermost cavern.

My boy was lying on his back. His arms were folded. His legs were crossed. He was staring fixedly at a spot on the ceiling.

"Hello, Mel," I said pleasantly.

He kept staring at the spot on the ceiling.

"What's the matter?" I asked, after a moment. "Don't you know me?"

His head turned ever so slightly and he muttered, "Yes, I know you."

"What happened in the hundred?"

"Nothing," he croaked, still staring at the ceiling.

"What do you mean, nothing?" I went on. "Something must have happened. A poor start? Maybe somebody bumped you?"

"Nope," he said.

"Well, why did you finish so far back?"

For the first time since I arrived in the dungeon-like cavern his eyes turned from the ceiling to me. "I guess I tied up, that's all," he whispered hoarsely.

Suddenly, I recalled that the athlete before me had to be protected against "athlete's sickness" or it would reduce him to almost total ineptness. Back home in Los Angeles his wife performed this vital chore. She kept him so occupied that he never had time to worry, or even think, about an upcoming race.

Her set routine included inviting several couples over to the house the night before for a nonstop session of penny ante and singing. The husbands had instructions to keep Patton on his feet opening beer for them. Whenever he got a free moment the wives had him on his feet dancing, until finally he fell into bed exhausted and slept.

Next morning he was kept busy at the barbecue pit. More guests had arrived and nobody let him forget his obligations as host. He cooked, served and cleaned up. At noon Mrs. Patton would hand him a grip containing his spikes and running togs and say, "Good luck." But at this moment she was thousands of miles away in California, and if I ever saw a man disintegrating before my eyes, it was the one I was staring at.

His reputation was at stake—to say nothing of mine. Nobody spoke for ten minutes. Finally I said, "Are you all through over here after this race?"

"Nope," he answered. "Got the relay tomorrow."

"But then you're through?"

He nodded.

"That's great!" I exclaimed. "I'm going over to Paris the day after tomorrow, and you're going with me."

"Can't," he croaked, his eyes back on the ceiling.

"Why not?"

"No money."

"Forget it," I said hastily. "I'm loaded. I'll wangle it on the expense account. The plane fare doesn't amount to anything and we can share a hotel room. We'll have the wildest weekend on record. You ought to be about ready to break training."

My boy sat up. For the first time he looked at me without that glassy stare in his eye. He said, "No fooling. You think you can?"

"Leave it to me. We'll hit the Folies-Bergères. There's Montmartre, too, and dames doing dances with nothing on. We'll take in the works."

The co-holder of the world's record for one hundred yards (9.3 seconds) got up off the floor. He sat on the bench next to me. He was suddenly lit up like a schoolmarm looking at a travel poster. "This is going to be great," he said, and for the next twenty-six minutes we firmed up our plans. Then somebody stuck his head in and said in an official voice, "Contestants for the 200-meter finals report to the starting line."

My boy stood up and squared his shoulders. He was still talking excitedly as he reached for his towel and starting blocks. Then he walked out of the dungeon like a man who knew where he was going.

I got to my seat just in time to see a streak zoom off the blocks. Patton of the U.S.A. had a comfortable lead when he went into his "float," the runner's equivalent of overdrive, and was turning around to see where in the world the others were as he broke the tape.

It was a rewarding experience. Ever since then I have been telling everybody who will listen how I won my Olympic gold medal in London. Oh, yes, the time—it was 21.1 seconds.

May 6, 1954 Roger Bannister's Four-Minute Mile

Cold wind slanted across the track at Oxford
and the little group who stood there watching
shivered and wondered why they had come.

The runner, open-mouthed, thin-legged, knew only pace and goal,
spending his strength so that at the finish, at one mile,
there would be no more.
In his equation, perfection and unconsciousness were one.

When they carried him off,
after the first four-minute mile,
after one timeless barrier to body and to spirit lay shattered,
after the equation was resolved,
the runner slumped in their arms
Christlike.

Cornelius Johnson, U.S.A.

by BUDD SCHULBERG

THE CLOSEST I'VE EVER COME TO ATH-letic fame was to go out for track the same day as Cornelius Johnson. It was at L. A. High. In the locker room I happened to undress next to a tall, skinny, black-skinned boy—about fifteen years old, who was in my journalism class—a funny-looking kid with a boyishly grave face.

"What you going out for, Johnson?" I asked.

"High jump. You?"

"Six sixty," I said. "Class B." I noticed his thin legs, his undeveloped chest. "I suppose you're try-ing for the B's, too."

"Guess I'll try for the varsity," he said.

I finished a mile of jog-a-lap-walk-a-lap just as the high-jump tryouts were starting. I think they started at 5′3″. I watched a couple of kids mess it up, several more make it with effort or efficiency, and our star, Hal Baranov, ease himself over with six inches to spare. Then it was Johnson's turn. I will always remember that first jump. He didn't even bother to run toward the bar—just walked up to it and lifted himself over. Those of us who happened to be watching swore he had cleared it by a foot.

The bar was raised to 5′6″ and Johnson cleared that on his first try. At 5′9″, all he needed was an extra step or two and he was over with at least six inches between him and the bar. Quite a few of the trackmen were gathering around now, and everybody was asking everybody else who he was. "Name's Johnson," I said, already beginning to take vicarious bows. "Cornelius Johnson. He's in my journalism class."

At 5′11″, Hal Baranov made a real high-school try. He had been consistent at that height, but this was the opening day of the season and maybe the appearance of an unexpected rival was disconcert-ing. Anyway, he dove over the bar but brushed it off on his way down when it seemed as if he were clear.

Johnson took three or four slow and easy steps and floated over the bar.

Baranov made 5′11″ on his next try but went out at 6′. Johnson cleared that effortlessly and then went on to take 6′1″ and 6′2″ as if he had been winning meets for years. When the bar was raised to 6′3″, a respectable height for good college jump-ers, our coach stepped in. "All right," he said, "that'll be enough for today. Take a light jog around the track, Johnson."

From that moment, Johnson was a big man around L.A. Every Friday all spring he was up there in first place. He and I had adjoining lock-ers; and, since I was a man of influence on the *Blue and White Daily,* I'd go over some of Corny's copy for him before he turned it in. He was a good deal more eloquent sailing over that bar. He was a high jumper. Essentially a high jumper. Perhaps that was his trouble.

But it didn't seem like trouble then. In his fresh-man and sophomore years at L.A., he kept on per-fecting his technique; and a 6′6⅝″ in his junior year gave him a tie-for-first in the National AAU.

In reflected glory and the heat of summer, I sat in the Los Angeles Olympic Stadium in '32 watch-ing the high-school kid with the big U.S.A. on his chest in there with the world's best. And watching the familiar grace, as, along with three others, he finally cleared the winning height of 6′6″, I kept telling everyone: "Just think, only a year ago, Corny and I went out for track the same day. And we had adjoining lockers!"

After Johnson finished high school, I followed his career in the papers: 6′6″, 6′7″, 6′8″, 6′8⅝″— a new AAU record—and, finally, qualifying for the 1936 Olympic team with 6′9¾″, a new world record.

That 1936 Olympics in Berlin was the one in which our colored boys kicked up the cinders and the sawdust in the faces of the Supermen. Will sports followers ever forget what they did there—Owens with his three great wins, Williams and Metcalfe and Lu Valle and Robinson and Pollard and Edwards and Albritton and my boy, too, with a new Olympic record of 6'8".

By winning that Olympic championship, Corny put Adolf Hitler on the spot. Hitler, as the head of the state hosting the Games, was to receive and congratulate each victor. It had been rumored he would not extend this courtesy to Negro athletes. First Negro to win a victory was Corny. All eyes turned to Der Führer's box. As John Kieran described it, "There was a sudden hustle and bustle down there. Herr Hitler was leaving the stadium in haste. The official explanation was that it was very late in the day and it looked like rain. Down on the field, crowned with the Olympic wreath of victory, the black-skinned Corny Johnson saw the hurried departure—and grinned."

That was the peak performance of Corny's career. He kept on jumping for another season or two, but the pattern seemed to be reversing itself now. It was 6'7", 6'6", 6'5"—in the National Championships two years after the Olympics, he could place no higher than 6'6". Then his name dropped out of the papers.

I remember wondering, in '39 and '40, what he could be doing. He couldn't have been much over twenty-five years old. The only thing I was sure of was that he couldn't be earning his living as a journalist.

Then, one morning soon after the war's end, I had my answer. It wasn't the headlines he used to get—just a box on the sports page: Cornelius Johnson, former Olympic champion and world-record holder, more recently an able-bodied seaman in the Merchant Marine, had been the victim of a virus infection and had been taken off his ship in San Francisco harbor and rushed to a hospital, where he had died upon arrival.

I thought of the first time I saw him jump; of the marvelous way he used to float over those record-breaking heights; of my pride as we walked down the high-school corridors together; of his kid face down there in the big-time of the '32 Olympics. And I thought that if an artist could only manage us all for a while, Corny would have soared over that final Olympic height and plunged to a glorious death in the sawdust, as thousands cheered, while the band played our national anthem and the Stars and Stripes went up over Hitler's Berlin.

Fates don't write 'em that way often. Just the same, I wish they could have given us a better send-off for Corny than that pointless exit from the merchant ship.

A thing like this can bother you for a long time.

The Victory of the *Resolute*

by GRANTLAND RICE

IT WAS JULY 21, 1920, AND IT SEEMED to be a sure thing that Sir Thomas Lipton, after trying for some twenty-one years, was on the verge of taking the America's Cup back to Great Britain. For Sir Thomas Lipton's *Shamrock IV* had won the first two Cup races off Sandy Hook and he needed only one more victory to take the famous mug back home.

This was a contest between skippers as well as between boats. The skipper of *Shamrock IV* was William P. Burton, Great Britain's best. The skipper of America's defender, the *Resolute,* was

Charles Francis Adams of Boston. And on that July day, forty-one years ago, it looked as if Skipper Burton and Skipper Adams practically submerged.

I recall covering those 1920 races with Ring Lardner and Bill McGeehan. Our entire and combined knowledge of yacht racing could be packed into a cockleshell. Since we had been at sea for two days before, our unpatriotic hope was that Skipper Burton and *Shamrock IV* would clean up the series promptly and so permit us to leave the sea and find dry land again.

This seemed to be a sure thing on that July day forty-one years ago. For *Shamrock IV* had won a hollow victory in a light wind in the first race, the *Resolute* being disabled by the parting of her throat halyard just a quarter of a mile before the windward mark. It was no contest—except for Lardner, McGeehan and myself after two bad thundersqualls arrived. We looked whiter than the canvas spread on the two yachts.

In the second completed race on July 20, Skipper Burton and *Shamrock IV* again defeated Skipper Adams and the *Resolute* in a close finish by the margin of two minutes and twenty-six seconds.

Everyone now conceded victory to Lipton. But it wasn't to be that way. For not quite everyone had given up—merely everyone except Skipper Adams and his crew. The third race was the closest and most exciting ever sailed for the Cup. It added a great new chapter to the history of sports and a memorable footnote to the study of that scientific phenomenon known as American guts.

The *Resolute* won on time allowance, as the actual time of the two boats was exactly the same to a second. This was the first of the races sailed in a true breeze. *Shamrock IV,* of course, was still heavily favored with the series at two to one. But there was a sudden upsurge of nationwide interest in this great contest when the *Resolute* won the fourth race by a margin of two minutes.

Now it was all different on July 27. The two boats were all even at two and two. National pride, among millions who had never seen a yacht, came to the front. Here was the dawn of a new age. Radio was flashing its messages for the first time in

any big event. There were airplanes flying against the sky. A dirigible fell into the sea with seven or eight occupants, who escaped safely. Phototelegraphy of the race was cabled to London. And there was no longer a confident smile on Sir Thomas Lipton's usually friendly and placid features.

On the morning set for the fifth race, there was a fresh sou'wester blowing and both boats came out to the lighthouse under shortened canvas. Then the *Shamrock* lost her chance by agreeing to a postponement to July 27.

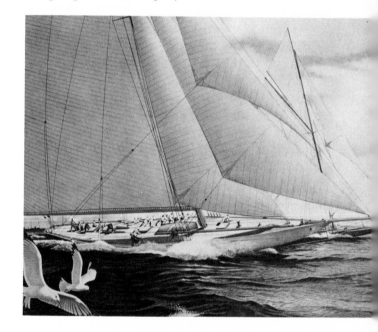

On that date an even more intense excitement prevailed. There were thousands packed and waiting in Times Square to hear the final result. There were inquiries from the red clay hills of Georgia and the sand deserts of the Far West—regions that had never seen a canoe, much less a yacht. It was now the United States against Great Britain.

A light wind was blowing on the day of the final race in which the *Resolute* scored an easy victory to win and hold the Cup by three straight victories. This was the closest call the famous piece of silverware ever had since it came to the United States in 1851.

In addition to squalls, falling dirigibles, radio, phototelegraphy, the great comeback and many other excitements, there were also bitter arguments over the postponement of the fifth race. This action called forth a storm of criticism by yachtsmen in general, who classed the Cup boats as afraid to sail in a sturdy breeze with a bit of a sea running. Nevertheless, it was good judgment on the part of the *Resolute,* almost sure to win in light or moderate winds but not so sure in heavier weather over heavier seas.

All in all, here was the most interesting and exciting race for the America's Cup ever sailed since a boat called the *America* brought the trophy home from England in 1851. The victory of the *Resolute* and Skipper Charles Francis Adams was one of the most notable uphill, or upwave, contests in the entire history of sport.

The saying up to that time had been "England rules the waves." But not the waves that lap our shore when there's a challenge to be met and a race to be won.

EDITOR'S NOTE: *The race around the Isle of Wight began in 1851 for the London Exhibition and was named "the America's Cup" because it was won by the U.S. entry called* America. *It has been sailed eighteen times since then with victory each time for the U.S., the last in 1958 by the yacht* Columbia. *This article is about one of the most famous of the great challenges by the man who instituted the race and never won it, Sir Thomas Lipton.*

Antonino the Great   by ROBERT O'BRIEN

SOMETIMES ON MONDAY NIGHTS IN THE winter Madison Square Garden sold out very fast and early and thousands of Puerto Ricans were left out in Eighth Avenue, shivering in the icy wind in their light cotton clothes and filled with misery because they could not see their idol, Antonino Rocca, wrestle.

One Monday in 1959 it was a different matter. Many Manhattan wrestling fans had other things to do on such an evening, and the Puerto Ricans swarmed into the arena and took nearly all the 18,000 seats, from the ringside all the way back and up out of sight into the reaches of the upper galleries.

When the two peroxide-blonds in spangled blue capes entered the ring for the main match, a storm of boos and catcalls filled the Garden vastness. The wrestlers wore their hair bobbed. Their skin was milk-white. They looked out of condition.

They ankled around the ring, swaying their hips and making the crowd howl.

Rocca and his tag-team partner, Miguel Perez, moved swiftly down the aisle. They bounded cleanly to the ring. The crowd greeted them with an exultant shout.

Rocca wore dark trunks and a red cardigan sweater. He was barefoot. Perez wore white trunks, white shoes and a white sweater. Rocca is a man in his thirties. His head is too large and his legs too short for his body. He carries his head lowered, and thrust forward. His hair is dark and cropped short. He has a mashed right ear and a large curving nose and a big chin. Perez is younger. He is tall and rangy, built like a stroke oarsman.

Antonino and Miguel watched quietly while the blond heavyweights strutted about preposterously like ham actors playing Nero.

The announcer, first in English, then in Spanish, awarded Rocca and Perez two glittering gold-plated trophies—*Ring* Magazine's award to the tag team which did the most for wrestling in 1958. In a tag-team match, there are two wrestlers to a side. They take turns at action in the ring.

Rocca and Perez handed the trophies over the ropes and peeled off their sweaters. Rocca danced lightly up and down. The announcer began the introductions. One of the blonds leaned out over the ropes, jeering someone in the crowd. Rocca lunged at him and smashed him in the face three times with the heel of his right fist.

The crowd screamed. Rocca's head, arms, legs and torso, so mismated in repose, suddenly blended into fluid, beautifully balanced components, moving with great, controlled, animal grace. He leaped high into the air, crossed the ring in a sequence of bouncing handsprings, then tore back and forth bellowing, waving his arms and whipping the crowd to a frenzy of excitement.

The bell clanged for order. The match began.

Perez absorbed a punishing series of monkey flips, sling shots, body slams, arm locks, flying mares, forearm chops and eye gouges. He reeled groggily around the ring. The crowd roared. Then, amazingly, he recovered. He hit the blond in the face with one forearm smash after another. The blond fell to his knees and begged for mercy.

The match was two out of three falls, and Rocca and Perez won the first fall in nine minutes. Perez was pinned and lost the second fall after twelve minutes. The end came fourteen minutes later in a wild melee that began when one of the blonds connected with a forearm chop to Rocca's head. Rocca staggered to a corner and reached for the ropes. Again the elbow crashed to his skull. Rocca slipped helplessly to the middle rope. His head wobbled. Another brutal smash pounded him to the canvas. The crowd was frantic. They slammed their chairs against the floor and stamped their feet. Suddenly Rocca came to life. He vaulted to the blond's shoulders and perched there like a giant gargoyle. He anchored himself with his heels under the blond's arms and brought his fist down on the blond's head. "Kill him, Rocca!" the crowd yelled. "Kill him, Antonino!"

Rocca sprang to the canvas. Leaping up, he shot his bare feet against his opponent's chest. The blond wrestler sprawled to the mat. They got to their feet. Rocca kicked out again, and again, and again. At each kick a triumphant shout burst from the crowd. The last time his opponent fell back, Rocca pounced on him and pinned his back to the canvas. The referee slapped the mat three times. Rocca and Perez had won again.

In the pandemonium a fight started in the crowd near the ringside. A dozen patrolmen converged on it. Rocca, with his red sweater on, stepped to the microphone and held up his arms. "Hey! *Amigos—aqui!—Momento!* Show the people that you are gentlemen!"

The Garden organ began "The Star-Spangled Banner." The blond wrestlers disappeared. Rocca and Perez stood in the ring with the announcer, singing the national anthem. The shouting died down. The crowd stood at attention. When the music stopped, the people streamed to the exits and out into the soft night air.

Their eyes were shining. Their faces were happy. Whether it had been real or not didn't matter. It had been a wonderful show. It had been a wonderful evening.

Antonino Rocca, without a doubt, is the greatest single sports attraction in the world today. He has broken attendance records in almost every major indoor coliseum and sports arena from Buenos Aires to Montreal, from Boston, Massachusetts, to Lima, Peru. In 1958 he wrestled eleven times in Madison Square Garden; seven of the matches were sellouts. Aggregate attendance totaled more than 200,000. Gate receipts soared over the $500,000 mark.

Run-of-the-mill wrestlers working New York Metropolitan area rings may earn between $10,000 and $25,000 a year. Ten or twelve—including half a dozen peroxided "queens of the mat"—may earn as much as $75,000 or $80,000 a year. Rocca pulls down $180,000 to $200,000 a year, and has averaged more than $150,000 annually ever since he arrived in this country ten years ago.

Rocca's working schedule would tax the stamina of an Armed Forces astronaut. He wrestles an average of three nights a week, month in, month out. To meet these engagements he travels more than 100,000 miles a year by air, and thousands of additional miles by train and car. During a booking spell close to home in New York he may appear one night in the Garden, the next night in a make-shift ring on the stage of a Harlem movie theater, and the next at an American Legion arena in Tea-neck, New Jersey. More often, he is hopping from one end of the country to the other. He has wrestled on Saturday night in Burbank, California, on Monday night at Madison Square Garden, on Tuesday night at Olympic Auditorium, Los Angeles, and two nights later at Knights of Columbus Hall, Bridgeport, Connecticut.

Professional wrestling today is a combination grappling match, side show, tumbling exhibition, Pier Nine brawl and medieval morality play. The best matches are fundamentally conflicts between hero and villain—good and evil.

In the interest of "showmanship," a galaxy of freaks has gathered on the wrestling scene: midgets, professional fat men, marceled males whose minions spray the ring with cologne before a match, bearded Turks, mat-chested Tarzans from the jungles of Hoboken, narcissistic weight-lifters who strike poses and ripple their muscles at housewives who, hair in pin-curls, sit quivering in the ringside seats.

King of this carnival crew is Rocca. As the recognized champion of the downtrodden, the oppressed and the kicked-around, Rocca, to millions of Americans, is a shining-hero image. He is the Siegfried of the slums, the hope of the hopeless, the Beowulf of the misbegotten.

To people like the New York Puerto Ricans—his most fanatic supporters—he is even more. Although he is not Latin American by birth, he came to America from Argentina. He speaks the language of Latin Americans. He eats their *arroz con pollo*, their *paella*, their *asopato*. He dances their *cuecas* and *pasodobles*, and sings the sad songs of the pampas. He has done what in their biggest dreams they dream of doing. With no resources other than his bare hands he has pitted himself against New York, and from its teeming, indifferent life he has wrested "the best"—money, cars, women, clothes, luxury, prestige. They glory in him and in his strength, and in the feeling that, with all he has won, he remains their big brother, a simple hero with a simple heart.

So they stream down out of their tenements and

cold-water flats on San Juan Hill and lower Harlem whenever he wrestles at the Garden. "Rocca," they say, "makes us forget our troubles. He makes us laugh. He gives us hope. He is one of us. And he never loses."

Rocca, from infancy, has been something of a prodigy. He was born in Treviso, Italy, on April 13, 1926. The hospital staff could hardly believe their scales: he weighed one ounce over eighteen pounds. To make things more awesome, he was followed into the world, moments later, by a twin sister weighing nine pounds.

Antonino was the sixth child. Not counting the infant twin, who died of pneumonia at the age of three months, there were seven children, one younger than Antonino. Six are still living. Far from falling back to normalcy, Antonino took off on a growth curve that became the talk of Treviso. At the age of six months, when the average child weighs twelve or fourteen pounds, he weighed twenty-eight. When he was eight years old, he weighed 140. Even so, his mother dusted him off occasionally. "On nights when I refused to go to bed," he recalled, "she grabbed me, picked me up, stuck me under her arm and carried me upstairs."

His mother, I remarked, must have been an Amazon such as is seldom seen today outside the Russian women's Olympic track and field squad. "No," Rocca replied, "she was not large. But she had a very beautiful, well-balanced body."

Two elements are very important to Rocca. If they are right, everything else will be right. One is this attribute of his mother's: balance. Rocca believes that you must be in balance. The key to winning in wrestling, for instance, is balance: you must keep yours, and deprive your opponent of his. This kinetic awareness figures in everything Rocca does, whether it is making coffee, walking, shaking the maracas or driving a car. He told me he soloed a plane after only twenty-four minutes of instruction. "A matter of balance," he said. "You can do anything in this life if you have balance."

The other element is "quality," meaning an intangible worth, or "class," or style, or heart. The supreme test with Rocca is whether or not a thing or a person has "quality." If it is there, he accepts everything that goes along with it, good or bad. If it is missing, he is not interested. He will say of a wrestler who has fallen out of condition, "That fellow now is no good. He has let himself go. He no longer has quality."

Rocca sketched the picture of a poor but proud and closely knit family living in the fertile flat country to the north of Venice. The father, Antonio, had been a fencing master, and an artillery officer with the Third Italian Army in World War I. At the war's end he turned to farming.

In the early 1930's Antonino's two older brothers migrated to Argentina and got work with a construction company in the big commercial city and seaport of Rosario. A few years later, Antonino joined them.

Rocca went to high school in Rosario, and then to the university. He wanted to be an electrical engineer. He studied hard for three years. But in the line of professional duty, he never so much as replaced a blown-out fuse.

Rocca was, body and soul, an athlete. He was 228 pounds of nothing but bone and muscle. He could high-jump well over six feet and heave the shot more than fifty-five feet. He was limber and tough, and fast on his feet as a pampas pony. An international troupe of more than fifty professional wrestlers—the best of five continents—blew into Buenos Aires to compete for the world heavyweight championship. As captain of his Rugby team and Argentina's outstanding amateur athlete, Rocca headed the list of local talent invited to compete.

Rocca hung back. He'd never even seen a professional wrestling match. He was happy playing Rugby and working for his degree. But as he watched the wrestlers, something clicked inside. "The man-to-man fight, the real shock, the real clash—I never got them in team play. I knew they were what I wanted. These big men crashing to the mat—everybody yelling and screaming—I wanted to jump into the ring with them."

Rocca's first opponent was Kola Kwariani, a 218-pound Georgian giant from Tbilisi who, in the world meet, was wrestling for the United States and who became Rocca's trainer and co-manager.

Kwariani, a ponderous bear of a man, towered well over six feet. His gleaming bald head was as big and round as a basketball and set almost neckless upon a pair of bullish shoulders. He was light-

ning fast. In twenty-one years of professional wrestling against the world's heaviest and toughest wrestlers, he had lost only four matches.

"The first three or four minutes, he threw me all over the ring," Rocca said. "But at seven minutes I blew my top out. All at once I knew what to do. I gave him the knees in the face, the elbows in the eyes, and I put him down and made him quit."

Kwariani, red in the face and breathing hard, climbed out of the ring and went over to Count Karol Nowina, the great Polish wrestling technician and protégé of the famous Stanislaus Zbyszko. Kwariani gasped two words: "Beat him." After two minutes in the ring with Rocca, Nowina quit. By the time the world championship matches were over, Rocca had defeated the best and was the idol of Argentina.

Also, he was completely and thoroughly ringstruck. When Kwariani asked him to turn pro, he said good-by forever to the classrooms and Rugby fields of Rosario, went south to Buenos Aires, sold out Luna Park for twenty-six weeks in a row, then took off on a sensationally successful tour of every town and city south of Panama. Kwariani went with him.

The older man, even in the sometimes zombie world of wrestling, was a picturesque figure. He spoke twelve languages fluently, had once operated a Left Bank restaurant in Paris, was a world authority on Sudanese cooking and had won a rating as an international chess master. His eyes, small for his heavy features, twinkled with quizzical good humor. His voice was as thick as long-brewed borscht, and when a subject moved him, what he said about it came out like a painting of Giotto's, full of guttural power and originality; sometimes his images glittered barbarically, like a Byzantine mosaic. Between Kwariani and Rocca there developed the complicated relationship that exists between the old pro, full of lore and craft and love, and the raw but gifted protégé whom he is grooming for the heights.

Several years passed in barnstorming. Rocca grew tougher, stronger, more seasoned. Joe "Toots" Mondt, the American wrestling impresario, on tour with Primo Carnera, watched Rocca wrestle in Rio de Janeiro. The Argentinian was obviously ready for the States. Mondt and Kwariani worked out the co-managership deal which remains in effect today. Two months later, Rocca stepped off a plane at Idlewild.

"My first appearance was in Ridgewood Grove, Brooklyn, in 1949," Rocca said. "It was like an atomic explosion." He's been hearing the roar of the crowd ever since.

In Kwariani's judgment, Rocca is a universal man. "Rocca could be a great engineer, a great composer, a great poet. The only thing he could not be is a great boxer. He is too strong. He would break his hands, like Carpentier."

We were sitting in Kwariani's small bedroom in his apartment in a West Forties hotel. There were three telephones on a coffee table; he said he had been on them for hours. (In addition to co-managing Rocca, Kwariani is a matchmaker.) It was three in the afternoon and he was still not dressed. He sat on the edge of his unmade bed in his underwear, with his gold-rimmed spectacles on, looking like a Slavic Buddha. The apartment was being redecorated. Books were piled everywhere. A dozen or more unframed paintings sat on the floor, faces to the wall. An unframed oil of Kwariani's lovely, dark-haired wife, Sidonia, perched on the air conditioner.

Kwariani told me how it had gone in that first match with Rocca, in Buenos Aires. "I wanted to show this young man something," he said. "I wanted him to respect me, like he would a master. For three or four minutes, I beat him. I was tying him in knots. Then he started to move. He was suddenly like a reptile in my arms. He was suddenly made of elastic steel, all arms, all legs. I have a twenty-two-and-a-half-inch neck, but I was choking. All I had learned in twenty-one years of wrestling, he learned in three minutes. I gave up.

"I was red from exertion. Rocca was not even pink. He was breathing easily, like a spring colt after a frolic in the meadow, and his face was aglow. At that moment he was a man who had found himself. He was released from the leash. He wanted to go—and go again. Then I wanted Nowina to punish him. But Rocca enjoyed beating him and he, too, gave up."

Rocca, he said, has the ideal structure for wrestling. He is not overdeveloped in the chest. Most of

his weight is from the waist down, in the legs. He is built like a monkey. "Once," Kwariani said, "I went to the zoo to study the animals. A monkey was collecting tickets at a restaurant. He moved with the same dynamics as Rocca."

Kwariani said that Rocca's blood is as swift as a mountain river. His normal pulse is sixty-two, some ten beats slower a minute than that of the average adult male; never, even during a hard match, does it rise above sixty-eight. His blood pressure, most of the time, stays down around 118. After a match it may go as high as 136.

"Rocca never wastes energy. He concentrates it for when it is needed. He saves his heart, his nerves, his ligaments and bones. He can relax at any time. If I tell him to sleep for two hours, he will sleep for two hours."

Sex plays an important part in Rocca's training regimen. "Many athletes practice self-restraint and denial," Kwariani said. "I, as a trainer, do not believe in this. Making love is the highest form of gymnastics. It is discharge of energy in the complete, natural way. In this activity, too, Rocca is a superman. Once, in South America, before a big match, Rocca asked for a girl, because making love is the best way to relax. So we found him a willing girl, and after eight and a half hours I went to call him for the match, and they were still making love. They had never stopped."

Rocca created his own holds, his own wrestling style. "Every hold I showed to him," Kwariani said, "he had no heart for. Some holds are axioms. Even those he does not like to use. Once he said, 'Kola, allow me to demonstrate my own technique.' He gave me a drop kick in the chest and fractured my sternum. He had wrestling shoes on, and that is why he never wears them in the ring today. He does not like to break the bones of others."

It was necessary to hold Rocca back. If he defeated all his opponents in seven minutes, no one would pay to see him. One day Kwariani watched his wife's cat, Pushkin, playing with a mouse.

"Pushkin gave me an idea. I told Rocca to give up the body scissors and the other big holds unless the other man is his equal. At all other times, he must be Pushkin with the mouse. When the mouse ceased to be dynamic, Pushkin picked him up and brought him to me—a trophy. That is what

I told Rocca to do. Be the cat, and when his man has ceased to be dynamic, beat him quickly and give him to the crowd."

Kwariani struck off into chess. Rocca was like the great American grand master, Paul Morphy. "Rocca has so much brilliance that, like Morphy, he can win in the middle game. So I teach him to start weak, like Emanual Lasker or Alekhine, and encourage his opponent to overconfidence. Then, when he senses that the crowd wants him to win, he sets up his combination, and wins."

Kwariani remembers that Rocca came from the country of a once-great republic. "Venice was a seafaring city, a crossroads, with many traders and adventurers. Rocca must have German and Slavic blood mixed in him. His eyes are bluish-green, but sometimes they have an orange tint. That is a trace of the Slavic."

If he had none of these talents and this background, Kwariani said, Rocca would be a champion anyway, because he was born in April. "April-borns have no fear. Their heartbeat is slower, so their heart is always ready to serve. The greatest wrestlers—Gamma, Londos, Lewis, Ivan Maximovich Poddubni—were April-borns. I was born in January. Like all January-borns, I am a reasoning, calculating man. But April-borns are the brave in heart. They are the champions."

Fifteen blocks from Kwariani's hotel, close to the stretch of tenements known as Hell's Kitchen, stands a modern, ten-story brick apartment house. It has a sidewalk marquee and a doorman in powder blue on duty at all times. Rocca's apartment is on the top floor.

Rocca lives in three rooms: a tiny kitchenette; a small, conventionally furnished bedroom with a double bed and a closet crammed with shoes, topcoats, jackets and suits, most of which are Ivy League enough to have come from Brooks Brothers; and a long, narrow living room with windows at one end, overlooking West Fifty-seventh Street. It is furnished in new French Provincial.

Here and there are touches of pure Rocca: the small Puerto Rican flag sticking out of an alabaster vase on the French Provincial coffee table; the humidor brimming with Garcia y Vega cigars in their glass tubes; the sideboard that opens up into a hi-fi radio-phonograph; the 400-day gilt clock atop the sideboard, beside a silk-shaded lamp with crystal pendants, and a gray-and-yellow stuffed rabbit; wrestling trophies, gold-plated, with fluted columns, cups and tiny laurel-crowned figures; the oil painting of Lake Como, ornately framed, over the sofa; the breakfront filled with glassware, automatic coffee-makers, and three books: the Bible, the *Complete Works of Oscar Wilde* in Spanish and *The Kefauver Story.*

I visited his apartment several times, and accompanied him from there to some of his matches, and then to the small Latin-American restaurant off Broadway where he goes after the wrestling. It was always a trip to another region—a region of incongruities, of spangles, sawdust and the sound of calliopes, and people who, for all I knew, made their living by being shot from a cannon. I could never quite believe that it was real.

One evening I walked in to find Rocca in gray track pants, red shirt and Japanese sandals, talking loudly with a small, worried-looking man in a dark suit and a pencil-thin mustache. Rocca introduced him as his friend George Unger. On the floor, spilling out of their packages and excelsior, were three automatic coffee-makers, a singing teakettle, a milkglass hurricane lamp, a clock, a picnic jug, a bottle of Scotch and an electric sander.

Rocca slapped me on the back. "My friend George has store on Forty-seventh Street. He has more bigness than anybody. He give me these things to give to poor Puerto Ricans, which I will do tomorrow. He has given me three thousand dollars' worth of toys for the kids of Argentina, and twenty watches, in Braille, for blind people in Argentina, who otherwise could not tell what time it was. George Unger, boy—a real American."

The night before a big match, Rocca deadens the bell on his telephone and sleeps until noon. He makes his own breakfast on fruit, cereal, toast and coffee. Once, when I arrived in time for coffee, he ate seven slices of white toast lavishly spread with a fine, bitter, English marmalade. After dressing, he descends to the lobby, gives the doorman a dollar bill (every day he gives the day and night doorman a dollar each) and goes for a stroll. He is well known in the neighborhood and talks with everyone. He is always giving things away—cigars to old men, dimes or quarters to street urchins, postcard pictures of himself to teen-agers. "When I give things to people," he says, "I give away my tensions."

Rocca never observes a strict schedule. This comes from Kwariani, whom he calls "the Philosopher." The concept is that no man, even an athlete in training, should be rigid, or fanatic—about anything; it is important to remain relaxed, fluid. "No man," Rocca says, "should be a dictator. Most of all, he should not be a dictator over himself."

So anywhere between 2:30 and 4 o'clock Rocca has his big meal of the day—meat, vegetables, fresh fruit—which he usually eats in a Greek restaurant down the street from his apartment house. Kwariani believes that sugar puts a wrestler in an aggressive mood: about 6 o'clock Rocca swallows several blockbuster vitamin pills made according to his own formula, and tops them off with a tall glass of concentrated grape juice, or orange juice mixed with honey. Then he relaxes in a sweat suit, listening to music, until it's time to leave for the matches. He sits alertly forward on the edge of his chair, smokes a cigar and looks around happily.

A flag waves from a housetop pole across the street. "Goddam, boy—look at that beautiful flag. It gives me an injection of happiness. Everything is beautiful. Even that chimney, blowing smoke into the sky, has poetry." He puffs his cigar. "Goddam, boy—what a country this is. She has got everything. People go to Switzerland to see the Alps; Rocky Mountains is better. People go to South America for vacation; Key Largo is better. Why don't they stay home? I will tell you." He taps his head. "No brains."

Rocca likes people. He takes a lively interest in them and in their troubles. He is always ready with an observation, a bit of philosophy, to weave a friend's anecdote into the larger fabric of life.

One evening before a tag-team match against the Graham Brothers in the Garden, a friend named Alejandro was at the apartment, and a crippled youth of eighteen or nineteen, named Carlos.

Alejandro was a slender man in his late thirties, a Spanish film producer whose movies had won several prizes.

Carlos, a blue-eyed Argentinean in a cardigan sweater, sat in a French Provincial chair with his left leg in a steel brace. Both arms and hands were withered. He had been a cripple from birth and had come to the United States for corrective surgery. He had already undergone seven operations. He spoke English hesitantly but clearly, and smoked one of Rocca's Garcia y Vegas. You could see that he was happy with the cigar, but it kept going out and he kept relighting it, with difficulty, with a cigarette lighter and his twisted hands.

Rocca sat listening to Alejandro, who was recounting the marital troubles of a friend.

"It is the end," Alejandro said. "He cannot stand her any longer. Before they were married, she was telling him all the time how handsome he was, and what brilliance he had, what intelligence. Then they are married. Overnight, he becomes a stupid pig. Now he is afraid of her. He takes her her meals to eat in the bed. She speaks, and he trembles. He is miserable. It cannot go on."

Rocca leaned forward, elbows on knees. His estranged wife and their six-year-old daughter live in South America.

"Very sad," he said. "But—" he sighed in resignation—"is typical. A woman can destroy you. Is worse than gun. Gun is clean. One shot—boom!— that is all, that's the end, let's go. But a woman hounds you twenty-four hours a day. She drags out the death of the heart. She keeps tearing at it—"

Alejandro looked unhappy. Even Carlos' young face lost its smile.

Rocca suddenly slapped his thighs and leaped up. "Let me make some coffee. I am a great technician at coffee." He went to the kitchenette. We heard running water, and Rocca singing "Amapola."

"All fighters," Alejandro said, "are a little of brutes." He stood up, hunched his shoulders and swung his arms like an ape. "All fighters but Antonino. He is the only delicate fighter. I cannot tell you how much he is this way." He held out his open hand, to signify giving. "Antonino is like a priest. He goes in the middle of the night to help people in trouble. If someone needs him, he is there. Yet he is like a child. Everybody likes Antonino—"

Carlos nodded eagerly. "He is strong for me— you understand? When I see him in the ring, I become Rocca. He gives me the feeling that I am living in the ring with him. I am big and strong. I am a conqueror. My legs are jumping with him."

Rocca came in with the strong, aromatic, all-Colombian coffee and, while he was pouring it, said: "My friend—what is the secret of happiness? It is to get up in the morning with a smile. To get up with responsibility, with the desire to do something worthwhile."

One evening, Rocca said, he came home from Denver. It was late, close to midnight. He was tired from the flight, and was booked the next night at St. Nick's. Before he could switch the bell off, the phone rang. Kola. An old man, an Italian in the Bronx, wanted to see Rocca. "I am tired," Rocca said. "I must sleep."

"You must go," Kola said.

The old man's son came and picked Rocca up in a car. Rocca slept all the way to the Bronx. The old man was in bed. His wife had died of cancer two weeks before this, and he didn't want to live, and was refusing to eat. Two of the old man's sons took Rocca to the bedroom. "Father," one said, "we have brought Rocca, as we promised."

The old man would not believe it was Rocca. Rocca stood there dazed. What could he do? Without any plan, he said to the sons, "Leave us alone." When they had gone he went to the bedside. "Old man," he said, "life is beautiful. You are going to live."

"I am going to die," the old man said. "My strength is gone."

Rocca pulled off his coat, then his shirt, then his undershirt, and sat on a chair next to the bed, stripped to the waist. He held out his hard muscular arm that was like the arm of a Roman gladiator. He said forcefully, "Touch this arm. It is the arm of Rocca."

The old man put a trembling hand on Rocca's forearm and gripped it. "Put your hand on my chest," Rocca said. "Feel the heart of Rocca beating." The old man did so. "Can you hear what it says, old man? It says, 'Live! Live! Be a man!'"

The old man started to cry. "I want to, but I am too weak." Rocca took the old man's hands between his own big hands. He tried to will his vitality and strength to flow into the old man. The

tears streamed down the old man's cheeks. Rocca himself began to cry.

The old man fell forward into Rocca's arms. "I will live!" he sobbed. "If you want me to, I will live!"

An hour later, when Rocca left, the old man was sitting up in bed, laughing and crying with his sons, and he is alive to this day.

"We live in the big hand of God," Rocca said. "When he drops us, we must go. But until then, we must have joy of living."

One Friday evening there were matches in Paterson, New Jersey. Rocca and I went to the garage in the basement. Rocca carried his Abercrombie & Fitch kit bag, containing his dark wrestling trunks and red sweater and towels. We got into his black Chrysler Imperial, and Rocca headed up the West Side Highway to the George Washington Bridge. He drove fast and with tenderness for the powerful sensitive car. He got a *malagueña* on the car radio.

The toll collector at the Jersey end of the bridge grinned. "Hi, Rocca." Rocca headed off on Highway 4 and I asked him what he was trying to do in the ring. He switched off the radio.

"You put a guy in a position to smile," he said, "and that is greatness. In the ring I try to transmit the desire to smile. My friend, some people find happiness in church, some in horses, some in rum or tequila, some with their wives and kids, and some in wrestling matches where they can yell and shout and call the referee a bum, and forget their troubles. I try to give them the dream that they are living with me in the ring, and winning at all times. I want everyone to have a young face with a big smile."

The fans, after a match, are always waiting. I remembered one night at a theater far uptown in Spanish Harlem. It seemed like a long time after the last match before Rocca appeared from backstage. Three people met him halfway up the aisle of the almost deserted theater: a woman in her thirties with a little girl of four or five, and a plain girl in her twenties in a threadbare coat and no hat.

The woman pushed the little girl forward. "This is my daughter, Mr. Rocca," she said in English. "She is little, but she is your good friend." Rocca squatted and spoke to the child. She stuck her finger in her mouth and rolled her eyes bashfully at her mother. Rocca chucked her under the chin. "What a little princess," he said.

As he stood up, the girl in the coat clutched his wrist. Her eyes were shining, and as she looked up at him something—some swift flame of hope and pride and fervor—came alight and alive in the aisle of the drab theater. "*Gana,* Rocca!" she choked. "*Gana!*" She turned and hastened up the aisle after the mother and child.

"What did she say?" I asked him. "What does '*gana*' mean?"

"It means, 'Win, Rocca! Win! Conquer!' "

At St. Nick's, I had seen young Puerto-Rican brides of less than a week thrust at Rocca pictures of themselves in bridal gowns and ask him to autograph the picture in ink across the front, "To Lupe, from Antonino Rocca," "To Eva, from Antonino Rocca—" Groups of teen-age boys, most of them neat, clean and well behaved, crowded around with glossy prints of Rocca in wrestling poses that they had bought at Harlem cigar stores or stationery shops.

While driving downtown, I asked him how long he was going to keep on wrestling.

"My friend," he replied, "I am a great improviser. I follow the curve of the situation. If your blood circulation is good and your reflexes are good, you can win matches. Perhaps I will wrestle five, ten more years. Who knows? We live in the big hand of God."

We left the West Side Highway and drifted off south into the West Forties and drew up in front of the Rancho Grande. It is a small Latin-American bar and restaurant with photographs of Cuban and Puerto-Rican baseball players and boxers on the walls. A dozen customers sat at the bar and in the booths, and all heads turned toward Rocca. There was good-natured banter in Spanish. Patsy, the manager, led us to a booth near the tiny orchestra platform.

"People know me here. It is like home," Rocca said.

He ordered Champion Steak *à la* Rocca and a big salad and a bottle of a dry Cuban beer called Cristal.

Rocca smiled. "This is the life, no, my friend?" he said, and lighted a cigar. He waved to the musicians. They flashed their teeth and played more loudly. Rocca laughed.

"Music elevates me. Arturo Toscanini was my friend. He said, 'When you wrestle, you give me something like a symphony.' Wrestling is to me like a symphony. I feel music inside of me when I wrestle."

The musicians began playing a quick, lively, rippling selection. Rocca put down his cigar and rose, smiling, chest out. "This is Gaucho music. I play the maracas and forget everything."

He went to the bandstand and picked up the drummer's maracas and shook them, expertly adding their dry, shifting rhythm to the music. A young Puerto Rican and his girl friend joined Rocca at the bandstand, tapping out the beat with spoons against the sides of empty Coke bottles. The people at the bar looked on. They were getting in Rocca's mood. Some of them began singing the Spanish words.

Rocca threw his big head back and laughed. "Play!" he shouted to the musicians. "Play, *amigos!*"

Hank Luisetti: Basketball Wizard

by WARD LAMBERT

ONCE EVERY GENERATION SPORT PRO-
duces individuals whose names will live as long as
the world reads sports pages and thrills to the sight
of a perfect athlete performing as only he can.

Baseball labored and bred its Babe Ruth, football its Red Grange, golf its Jones, tennis its Tilden, swimming its Weissmuller, boxing its Dempsey—and when they had passed along, those same
sports came up with Joe DiMaggio, Sammy Baugh,
Byron Nelson, Don Budge, Bill Smith and Joe
Louis.

The basketball wizard of this generation was a
long, lanky San Francisco Italian named Angelo
Luisetti, and called Hank. He was the answer to a
coach's dream. He could do almost incomparable
things with a basketball, but—and this is important
in life as well as basketball—he was a superb team
player.

In the heat of one of his peak games at Stanford,
while the crowd went wild with his uncanny shooting, he called time out. His teammates had been
tossing every shot to him.

"Listen, fellows," he barked, "this isn't basketball. You're 'feeding' me too much. Come on now,
let's use our heads and play the game the way it
ought to be played!"

Another time, in a game on the Pacific Coast, he
missed six shots in a row—shots that brought a gasp
from the crowd because they were so heartbreakingly close. Hank rushed over to the bench where
his coach, John Bunn, was sitting.

"Take me out, I'm terrible," he begged. Bunn
took him out, rested him a few minutes and sent
him back into the fray. Hank scored ten points to
help lead his team to victory.

Six-foot three, big-handed, loping Hank Luisetti
did much to break down the sectional barriers of
basketball and give the great game the nation-wide

scope it deserves. He and his Stanford team helped
spread the gospel of the game from Pacific to Atlantic, sometimes blazing new trails and always
performing in a way that made the game's fans—
and basketball has more fans and more players
than any other American sport—remember him
and want him, or players like him, to come back.

In painting a game of the period, James Bingham chose the night of December 30, 1936, in Madison Square Garden. Then Hank Luisetti led Stanford to victory over Long Island University in a
game which broke a three-year winning streak for
L.I.U. Bingham captured with all the vitality of a
motion-picture camera that intense moment when
Luisetti easily outleaped his opposing guard and
with one of his confident, one-handed shots tossed
the ball into the basket to turn the tide in favor
of Stanford. Looking at the canvas, you can feel
the expectant hush of the crowd during that dramatic moment and hear the excited roar which
followed the triumphant play.

Madison Square Garden was packed with nearly
20,000 spectators, a tribute not only to Luisetti
and the other fine players on the floor but also to
a young former sports writer named Ned Irish who
gambled and gave basketball this rich and deserved
fame.

Luisetti scored fifteen points that night to beat
L.I.U. 45-31, and when John Bunn took him out
of the game with thirty seconds left to play, the
huge place shook with cheers, and any doubts
which the basketball fathers had that the game
was a big league sport were dissolved.

Could Dr. Naismith, who invented the game of
basketball in 1891, possibly have foreseen his group
game develop into the highly skilled five-man team
game which was played that night, and which is
being duplicated now in huge arenas and great

college field houses and school gyms all over the land?

His mind probably would have gone back to the seamy early career of basketball . . . back to games played in storerooms, courts with three posts down the middle, courts that were caged in, courts with three walls, low ceilings which made only close-in shots possible, plaster falling from the ceilings, widely different sectional rules, fist fights and medieval dressing-room facilities.

If you are surprised when I say that more people see basketball and more boys and girls play it than any other game, remember that there are thousands of high-school teams alone, playing an average of twenty games a season. Frank Menke, the sports historian, has estimated that close to 80,000,000 persons see basketball played each season.

Basketball has become the national game for the American boy. It reaches almost everybody through the grade-school and high-school teams. Many of us think of the great game of baseball as the national pastime for the boy, but figures tell a different story. There have been factors that have made this come true. As a boy, I played baseball every day during the summer. There were kid teams in each end of every town. Now we have the automobile that takes the boy to rivers, lakes and other places of amusement. Golf gives the boy a chance to caddy and earn money during the summer months. You no longer see a baseball game on every common, but there is hardly a school in America that does not have its gym for basketball.

The game appeals to spectators because it is played on a floor where everyone can see everything that takes place. The finer points of technique, of offense and defense may not be well understood by the average spectator, but he can see the individual defensive and offensive efforts of the players, good or bad. The game is fast, the continuity of action is sustained. The rapid changes of possession of the ball, and the fluctuations of the score itself, give a constant thrill to the partisan spectator.

Great players like Luisetti have the poise and grace of outstanding ballet dancers. The game is one that requires balance, co-ordination, speedy reactions. It tempts every normal young boy because it does not require great physical strength, but mental stability and courage. The player must be in superb physical shape to have the endurance the game demands. It also demands unselfish co-operation; it provides valuable training, mental and physical.

Luisetti typified all these attributes a thousand-fold. His coach said of him, when Luisetti passed on from Stanford, "He was the perfect combination of everything needed for a top athlete. He was unselfish, co-operative, teachable. He had quick reactions, co-ordination, endurance, competitive and team spirit and right living habits." I might add that he could hit that basket.

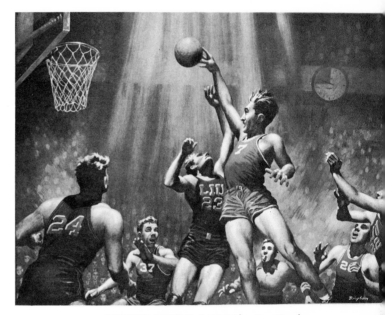

LUISETTI SCORES AGAIN by Jim Bingham

Chuck Hyatt, the former Pittsburgh star who later coached Luisetti when the player became a member of the Phillips 66 amateur club, had this to say: "I've seen most of them . . . I mean Beckman, Holman, Dehnert, Banks and the others who were gifted for this game. But this kid is the last word. He was born for this game. I've never seen him make a mistake. He's just one of those guys who come along once in a blue moon with just the right combination of speed, reflexes, good hands, good eyes and, above all, class."

We coaches thank the mothers and fathers of the nation, who, after all, starts the boys right, and dream of the day when we have five Luisettis on one team.

We have certain coaching techniques, drills and suggestions by which we hope to improve the skill of the boys we get. But we cannot tell a boy *when* to jump or start on a pass. The *when* is that intangible thing the great player has and we coaches try to find. It is born in them early.

Luisetti scored 1596 points during his career at Stanford. He led his team to three championships.

Stanford had never won a Pacific Coast Conference title before Luisetti enrolled. Not only did he set individual records for scoring but ran up new marks in departments that cannot be reduced to cold statistics—departments that might be classed under the general heading of "the team is bigger than the individual."

The Gentle Sport of Judo

by ROGER PURDON

WEDNESDAY NIGHT AT SIGWARD'S—THE Stillman's Gym of judo: In the sketch opposite (top), two men face each other in the first or grasping position for a throw. Below them (right), a circle throw is in progress and (at left) an ankle sweep has just been completed. At bottom, two men practice the forward stop fall and forward roll.

Judo clubs are active now in almost all large cities and very popular on the West Coast. Some headquarter in YMCA's, others in local gyms; usually they have Japanese coaches. A good judoist can sweep you up and crash you flat so ferociously the walls tremble. If you're a judoist yourself, you

arise as cheerfully as the magician's assistant who has just been sawed in two; if you're not, heaven help you. Some resourceful Chinese monks invented judo as a way to "gentle" robbers through the momentum of their own attack, and developed an art of falling so they could practice it without wiping out their Order. Today it is one of our fastest-growing sports and, unlike the jujitsu of Marine jungle warfare, it is "played" with a series of throws as formal as a ballet and as engagingly polite and cleanly scored as a fencing match—and twice as useful. Now, as 1500 years ago, wise guys don't want to tangle with a judoist a second time.

Kouchi Gari: when right foot leads

Fend off knives with the arm bar

Newaza: thrown but still kicking

Airplane: not real judo; just fun

Ukemi: fall arms out and chin in

Ukemi: take fall shock in arm, leg

9
"SPORTS: HAIL OR FAREWELL?"

THOUGH TEN YEARS HAVE PASSED SINCE THE RE-doubtable Red Smith posed the question for Es-quire, *the answer is still up in the air. But this much is certain—in the intervening years sports fans have thrilled to many great men and great mo-ments, and there is no reason to suspect that they* will not continue to do so. But even if sports were to suddenly and inexplicably decline and vanish (like poetic drama, say) from the American scene, the great men and great moments of sports would continue to live in the stories and pictures of them such as are preserved in this collection.

Sports: Hail or Farewell?

by RED SMITH

THE FIRST HALF OF THE TWENTIETH century witnessed the biggest boom in sports since Zeus pinned Kronos, two falls out of three, Graeco-Roman rules, in a wrestling match for possession of the earth (the last honest wrestling match on record).

The second half of the century began with basketball players dumping games for profits, baseball dumping Happy Chandler, football dumping the Purity Code and the courts dumping the Jockey Club.

It set thoughtful people to wondering what would happen next. Had American sports grown too big for their britches? Would the most enthusiastically sports-conscious people in the world, grown disillusioned and cynical, eventually turn their backs upon the games and seek their amusement in Canasta and sex?

The answer is that nothing is going to happen which hasn't happened many times before. There will be scandals and investigations, abuses and reforms, and sports will continue to grow as America grows—in travail and turmoil and contentiousness and inexhaustible vigor.

It is the nature of editors to believe that whatever happens today is happening for the first time. They read of a basketball team putting a game in the sack and they sweat with apprehension over the future of all sports, not realizing that bribery is at least the second-oldest of human undertakings. They forget that centuries before the first Olympiad in 776 B.C., the fix was in on a horse race on the plains of Olympia.

John Kieran and Arthur Daley, in *The Story of the Olympic Games,* tell of a king named Oenomaus whose daughter, Hippodamia, was luscious and lovable and royal and also rich. Recognizing these qualities as attractive to the young male, her old man set up ground rules as follows: to qualify as a son-in-law, a swain must wheedle the little pigeon into a chariot and get her across the county line ahead of her sire.

Oenomaus had the fastest horses in the land; he raced and overhauled thirteen ambitious suitors, whom he then skewered with his spear. This provided the fun-loving king with healthful exercise and kept Hippodamia at home to help with the dusting. Along came a sharp operator named Pelops who bribed the king's charioteer to tamper with the royal surrey. When their race turned into the homestretch, the monarch's chariot cast a wheel and the king went through the windshield, breaking his regal neck.

It is an open secret in fist-fighting circles that a whole covey of opponents went into the water, as the saying goes, for the Emperor Nero when he was an Olympic competitor. Tales of police shaking down bookmakers create no stir in informed quarters, where it is known that Mr. Sherlock Holmes, the most celebrated of law-enforcement officers, personally fixed and made killings on at least two horse races. There is ample evidence that Frank Merriwell, that paragon of amateur sportsmanship, was not above throwing an occasional ball game or boat race as a Yale undergraduate.

In short, jobs have been brought off as long as men and animals have engaged in organized competition. There are *no* grounds for fear that present-day skulduggery will discourage the slickers.

Then what has happened recently to alarm the worrywarts?

Well, the men who own major-league baseball unfrocked their high priest, Albert B. Chandler, without divulging their reasons to the public.

Chandler was unseated by a minority of his employers—seven out of sixteen—but it was a determined minority that voted "No, no and no," on the three occasions when a motion was before the house to continue the Commissioner in his $65,-000-a-year job.

Meanwhile baseball is going on, prosperous and popular and exciting. New Stan Musials and Joe DiMaggios will come along to capture public imagination. Nothing short of total war will loosen the game's grip upon the people.

A toothache can be beneficial, if not enjoyable, because it sends the sufferer to the dentist for repairs that would otherwise be neglected. In the same sense, the basketball scandal of a recent winter may have been the best thing to happen to the game since Dr. James Naismith first perverted peach baskets to unnatural uses.

Unless one is prepared to believe that all cops and college presidents are infallible, it must be true that basketball players were throwing games before anybody got caught at it. Disclosure of the extent to which Cadillacs and steam yachts had displaced Alma Mater in the affections of her sons called attention to a spreading evil and the necessity of remedial action.

Growth, not decay, led to corruption in basketball. When the game grew out of the cramped college gyms and moved into public arenas like New York's Madison Square Garden, it became a major sport drawing crowds of 15,000 instead of 1500. When colleges began to make money with a game they had been supporting out of the athletic department's pocket, emphasis shifted from character-building to the development of successful—and therefore profitable—teams.

When a coach must win to hold his job, he goes out and recruits the most talented athletes he can find, not necessarily the most righteous ones. And nothing blunts the vigilance of bursar and dean like an entry on the credit side of the ledger.

Expanding public interest in basketball led to public betting on games. The more popular the sport, the bigger medium of gambling it becomes, as baseball, football, boxing and horse racing have shown. And wherever there is gambling, there will be efforts to reduce the financial risks created by honest competition.

It requires something like the New York City scandals to bring about an awareness of these conditions and place responsibility where it belongs —with the educators and coaches. The shock must have made them realize that winning games and making money is the least part of their job, that guiding boys in the principles of decency is more important than teaching the fundamentals of the zone defense.

There is a feeling that a hall full of Broadway sharpshooters provides less than an ideal background for undergraduate sports, and this created an hysterical demand to take college games out of places like the Garden—as if an operative with larcenous leanings would be less larcenous on the west side of town than on the east. Surprisingly, an all-star group of players visiting New York at the height of this clamor remarked that the fans in the Garden were the fairest and most mannerly that they encountered anywhere.

"You should hear some of the crowds we play before in campus gyms in the West," one of them said.

Honesty in basketball isn't a question of geography, and a public that has learned to bet on the sport won't cease betting if the box-office address is changed. A boy who can be "talked to" by fixers can be talked to in a telephone booth, and he can throw the game in a cathedral.

If the game has merit it will survive and grow up and prosper, as all other sports have survived scandals of their own. There has been cheating in every known game, including solitaire, yet the manufacture of playing cards goes on.

Something of the same spirit that made basketball vulnerable has been making itself felt in college football. Cynical commercialism is a spreading peril on the gridiron; except that it is more difficult to fix a football game than a basketball match, there is no guarantee that the most popular of campus entertainments is safe from the influences that fouled up basketball.

Wherever boys are paid to attend college and play football—and some of them are—they are outrageously underpaid. When they realize this and resent it, they become ripe for plucking by the fixers. It can happen here. It may happen.

Fearing exactly such developments, the National Collegiate Athletic Association drafted its famous

Chastity Code a few seasons ago, setting it up as a sort of Fair Employment Practices Act establishing ceiling prices on cleated livestock. It was a monumental bust. It put college authorities on their mettle, challenging their ingenuity in evading the rules. The only schools put on trial for violating the Code were those that discovered they couldn't abide by the letter of the law and declined to lie about what they were doing.

There is a conviction in responsible campus circles that the antidote for overcommercialized football must be furnished by individual college presidents, not by any set of national rules. Colleges committed to the amateur spirit need schedule only those with similar views, and if one endeavors to cheat, the remedy is to quit playing with him.

The more ambitious ones will expand as their financial ability permits until a scandal, a major war or economic recession calls a halt. Football already has been suspended at a number of colleges.

A court ruling depriving the Jockey Club of the licensing power in horse racing tossed control of the sport into the laps of the several state racing commissions. This will not help improve the breed.

The Jockey Club is a league of hidebound traditionalists, but the rules of racing as they laid them down have constituted a bible of the turf for many years. Their stuffed shirts were an inflexible barrier against thievery, and a horseman would take great care to remain on the alkaline side of the Jockey Club, because to have his license lifted by this organization was a black mark against him even in the states where the jurisdiction of the Jockey Club did not extend.

Now the state commissions are the ruling bodies, exclusively. They'll hold the fort as long as they are composed of men as reputable as those now in office in New York, for example. But there is reason to fear the day when racing commissions will become political creatures like so many boxing commissions.

By the nature of their job, boxing commissioners owe their first allegiance to the party machine through which they were appointed and their second to the major promoters whose shows furnish the revenue and the jobs for all the judges, referees, deputies, inspectors, timekeepers and such who hold their positions as political patronage.

It makes for bad administration of boxing, as it would make for bad administration of horse racing. Yet somehow the fight game manages to stay alive, and now and then it achieves a peak with a great fight. Even poor commissioners don't matter much when there are good fighters, and there are at least a few good ones around today.

Some years ago there was a Broadway play called *The Fabulous Invalid*. It concerned the American theater, whose demise is perennially foreseen, but which somehow manages to get along year after year. American sports are much the same, just as fabulous and considerably more muscular.

Index

Set in Linotype Baskerville
Format by Séamus Byrne
Manufactured by American Book–Stratford Press
Published by HARPER & BROTHERS, *New York*